The Philosophical Discourse
of Modernity

Studies in Contemporary German Social Thought

Thomas McCarthy, General Editor

The Philosophical Discourse
of Modernity

Twelve Lectures

Jürgen Habermas

translated by
Frederick Lawrence

The MIT Press Cambridge, Massachusetts

This book was typeset by DEKR Corporation and was printed and bound by Halliday Lithograph in the United States of America.

Library of Congress Cataloging-in-Publication Data

Habermas, Jürgen.
  The philosophical discourse of modernity.

(Studies in contemporary German social thought)
  Translation of: Der philosophische Diskurs der
Moderne.
  Bibliography: p.
  Includes index.
  1. Philosophy, Modern—20th century. 2. Philosophy,
Modern—19th century. 3. Civilization, Modern—Philosophy. I. Title. II. Series.
B3258.H323P5513   1987   190   87-12397
ISBN 0-262-08163-6

Contents

Introduction
Thomas McCarthy

"In the philosophical discourse of modernity," writes Habermas, "we are still contemporaries of the Young Hegelians." Distancing themselves from Hegel's attempt to replace the subject-centered reason of the Enlightenment with Absolute Knowledge, Marx and the other Left Hegelians already announced the "desublimation of the spirit" and a consequent "disempowering of philosophy." Since that time, these tendencies have continued apace. The overwhelming "impurity" of reason, its unavoidable entanglement in history and tradition, society and power, practice and interest, body and desire, has prompted, among others, Nietzsche's heroic proclamation of the end of philosophy, Wittgenstein's therapeutic farewell, and Heidegger's dramatic overcoming. The current end-of-philosophy debates are largely echoes of and variations upon themes developed in these earlier rounds. For French poststructuralism, which serves as the point of departure for these lectures, it is above all Nietzsche and Heidegger who furnish the inspiration and set the agenda. Habermas is concerned here to respond to the challenge posed by the radical critique of reason in contemporary French thought by reexamining "the philosophical discourse of modernity" from which it issues. His strategy is to return to those historical "crossroads" at which Hegel and the Young Hegelians, Nietzsche, and Heidegger made the fateful decisions that led to this outcome; his aim is to identify and clearly mark out a road indicated but not taken: the *determinate* negation of subject-centered reason by reason understood as *communicative* action.

That strategy and aim define the focus and compass of the lectures. They deal with modernity as a theme of *philosophical,* not aesthetic, discourse. There are, however, some significant overlappings, for the aesthetic critique of modernity has played a crucial role in the philosophical critique — from Schiller and Romanticism to Nietzsche and poststructuralism. In particular, the realm of radical experience — of experience set free from the constraints of morality and utility, religion and science — opened up by avant-garde art has figured prominently in more recent attacks on the egocentric, domineering, objectifying, and repressing "sovereign rational subject." From Nietzsche to Bataille, it has seemed to provide access to the outlawed "other" of reason, which typically furnishes, if often only implicitly, the criteria for that critique. Habermas also discusses earlier accounts of art's potential to reconcile the fragmented moments of reason, as well as Nietzsche's and Heidegger's variations on the theme of an aesthetically renewed mythology (Dionysus as the absent god who is coming).

But the enhanced significance of the aesthetic is only one facet of the philosophical discourse of modernity, which turns centrally on the critique of subjectivistic rationalism. The strong conceptions of reason and of the autonomous rational subject developed from Descartes to Kant have, despite the constant pounding given them in the last one hundred and fifty years, continued to exercise a broad and deep — often subterranean — influence. The conception of "man" they define is, according to the radical critics of enlightenment, at the core of Western humanism, which accounts in their view for its long complicity with terror. In proclaiming the end of philosophy — whether in the name of negative dialectics or genealogy, the destruction of metaphysics or deconstruction — they are in fact targeting the self-assertive and self-aggrandizing notion of reason that underlies Western "logocentrism." The critique of subject-centered reason is thus a prologue to the critique of a bankrupt culture.

To the necessity that characterizes reason in the Cartesian-Kantian view, the radical critics typically oppose the contingency and conventionality of the rules, criteria, and products of what counts as rational speech and action at any given time and place; to its universality, they oppose an irreducible plurality of incommensurable lifeworlds and forms of life, the irremediably "local" character of all truth, argument, and validity; to the apriori, the empirical; to certainty, fallibility; to unity, heterogeneity; to homogeneity, the fragmentary; to self-evident givenness ("presence"), universal mediation by differential systems of signs (Saussure); to the unconditioned, a rejection of ultimate foundations in any form. Interwoven with this critique of reason is a critique of the sovereign rational subject — atomistic and autonomous, disengaged and disembodied, potentially and ideally self-transparent. It is no longer possible, the critics argue, to overlook the influence of the unconscious on the conscious, the role of the preconceptual and nonconceptual in the conceptual, the presence of the irrational — the economy of desire, the will to power — at the very core of the rational. Nor is it possible to ignore the intrinsically social character of "structures of consciousness," the historical and cultural variability of categories of thought and principles of action, their interdependence with the changing forms of social and material reproduction. And it is equally evident that "mind" will be misconceived if it is opposed to "body," as will theory if it is opposed to practice: Subjects of knowledge are embodied and practically engaged with the world, and the products of their thought bear ineradicable traces of their purposes and projects, passions and interests. In short, the epistemological and moral subject has been definitively decentered and the conception of reason linked to it irrevocably desublimated. Subjectivity and intentionality are not prior to, but a function of, forms of life and systems of language; they do not "constitute" the world but are themselves elements of a linguistically disclosed world.

Another important strand in the radical critique of reason can be traced back to Nietzsche's emphasis on the rhetorical and aesthetic dimensions of language. Thus, a number of critics seek to undercut philosophy's traditional self-delimitation from rhetoric and poetics as reflected in the standard oppositions between logos and mythos, logic and rhetoric, literal and figurative, concept and metaphor, argument and narrative, and the like. Pursuing Nietzsche's idea that philosophical texts are rhetorical constructs, they take aim at philosophy's self-understanding of its discourse in purely logical, literal — that is to say, nonrhetorical — terms. They argue that this is achieved only at the cost of ignoring or suppressing the rhetorical strategies and elements of metaphor and other figurative devices that are nevertheless always at work in its discourse. And they seek actively to dispel the illusion of pure reason by applying modes of literary analysis to philosophical texts, exploiting the tensions between reason and rhetoric within them so as to undermine their logocentric self-understanding.

In reconstructing the philosophical discourse of modernity, Habermas addresses himself to all these themes; he readily agrees with Foucault that reason is a "thing of this world." But for him this does not obviate the distinctions between truth and falsity, right and wrong; nor does it make them simply equivalent to what is de facto acceptable at a given time and place. The undeniable "immanence" of the standards we use to draw these distinctions — their embeddedness in concrete languages, cultures, practices — should not blind us to the equally undeniable "transcendence" of the claims they represent — their openness to critique and revision and their internal relation to intersubjective recognition brought about by the "force" of reasons. The ideas of reason, truth, justice *also* serve as ideals with reference to which we can criticize the traditions we inherit; though never divorced from social practices of justification, they can never be reduced to any given set of such practices. The challenge, then, is to rethink the idea of reason in line with our essential finitude — that is, with the historical, social, embodied, practical, desirous, assertive nature of the knowing and acting subject — and to recast accordingly our received humanistic ideals.

The key to Habermas's approach is his rejection of the "paradigm of consciousness" and its associated "philosophy of the subject" in favor of the through-and-through intersubjectivist paradigm of "communicative action." This is what he sees as the road open but not taken at the crucial junctures in the philosophical discourse of modernity. At one such juncture, Hegel chose instead to overtrump the subjectivism of modern philosophy with a notion of Absolute Knowledge, itself fash-

ioned after the model of self-consciousness. Feeling the need
to grasp "reason" in more modest terms, the Left and Right
Hegelians also chose paths still marked by the philosophy of
the subject — with, as Habermas shows, consequences that
continue to reverberate in contemporary praxis philosophy, on
the one hand, and in recent vintages of neoconservatism, on
the other. While it is his intention in these lectures to resume
and renew the "counterdiscourse" that, as a critique of subjectivism and its consequences, has accompanied modernity from
the start, his immediate focus is on the "counter-Enlightenment" path hewn by Nietzsche — or, rather, on the two paths
that lead out of Nietzsche into the present, one running
through Heidegger to Derrida, the other through Bataille to
Foucault.

At the heart of Habermas's disagreement with Heidegger
and his followers is the putative "ontological difference" between Being and beings, between world-view structures and
what appears within these worlds. In Habermas's view, this
distinction is deployed so as to uproot propositional truth and
devalue discursive, argumentative thought. After hypostatizing
the world-disclosive aspect of language and disconnecting it
from innerworldly learning processes, Heidegger leaves us
with a kind of linguistic historicism, outfitted with the quasi-
religious trappings of a "truth-occurrence," a "destining of
Being," to which we can only submit in an attitude of "expectant indeterminacy." Habermas argues that this construal
misses the dialectical interdependence between a historically
shaped understanding of the world and the experience and
practice possible within its horizon. Innerworldly practice is
indeed informed by general, pregiven structures of world-
understanding; but these structures are in turn affected and
changed by the cumulative results of experiencing and acting
within the world. Social practice submits the background
knowledge of the lifeworld to an "ongoing test" across the
entire spectrum of validity claims. Meaning cannot be separated from validity; and it is precisely the orientation of actors
to validity claims that makes learning processes possible —
learning processes that may well cast doubt on the adequacy
of the world views informing social practice. Because Heideg-

ger ignores this reciprocal connection between propositional truth and truth-as-disclosure and reduces the former to the latter, his "overcoming of metaphysics" amounts in the end to a "temporalized superfoundationalism."

This has broader implications for the Heideggerian reading of modernity. The "palpable distortions" of a one-sidedly rationalized world get enciphered into an "impalpable *Seinsgeschick* administered by philosophers." This cuts off the possibility of deciphering the pathologies of modern life in social-theoretical terms and frees their critique from the rigors of concrete historical analysis. "Essential thinking" consigns questions that can be decided by empirical investigation or theoretical construction — by any form of argumentative or discursive thought — to the devalued realm of the ontic and leaves us instead with the "empty, formulaic avowal of some indeterminate authority."

In a long excursus on the literary-theoretical reception of Derrida in the United States, Habermas deploys the same views of language and practice to resist the leveling of the genre distinction between philosophy and literature and the reversal of the traditional primacy of logic over rhetoric with which it is linked. Once the impossibility of a Platonic conception of logos is acknowledged and the omnipresence of the rhetorical dimensions of language is recognized, the argument goes, philosophical discourse can no longer be (mis)conceived as logical rather than literary, literal rather than figurative — in short, it can no longer be conceived as philosophical in any emphatic sense of the term. The strategies of rhetorical analysis, which is concerned with the qualities and effects of texts in general, extend to the would-be independent realm of philosophical texts as well. As Habermas reconstructs it, the heart of this argument is whether or not it is possible to draw a viable distinction between everyday speech (as it functions within contexts of communicative action) and poetic discourse. If not, then the aestheticizing of language proposed by Derrida carries, with the consequence that any given discourse can properly be analyzed by rhetorical-literary means. Habermas defends a position that, while not denying the omnipresence and ineradicability of rhetorical and poetic elements in everyday discourse, insists on distinguishing those contexts in which the poetic function predominates, and thus structurally determines discourse, from those in which it plays a subordinate and supplementary role. We are dealing here with a continuum, no doubt. Toward one end of the spectrum, we find the ordinary communicative uses of language in which illocutionary force serves to coordinate the actions of different participants: normal speech as part of everyday social practice. Toward the other end, we find those uses in which the fictional, narrative, metaphorical elements that pervade ordinary language take on a life of their own; illocutionary force is "bracketed" and language is disengaged from everyday practical routines. In the communicative practice of everyday life, language functions as a medium for dealing with problems that arise within the world. It is thus subject to an ongoing test and tied to processes of learning. In poetic discourse, by contrast, the everyday pressure to decide and to act is lifted, and the way is free for displaying the world-disclosive power of innovative language. In Derrida and his followers, Habermas argues, language's capacity to solve problems disappears behind its world-creating capacity. Thus, they fail to recognize the unique status of specialized discourses differentiated out from communicative action to deal with specific types of problems and validity claims: science and technology, law and morality, economics and political science, and so forth. In these discourses, as in the philosophy that mediates between them and the everyday world, the invariably present rhetorical elements of speech are "bridled," "enlisted for special purposes of problem solving," and "subordinated to distinct forms of argumentation."

Along the other main path leading from Nietzsche to the contemporary critique of reason, the key points at issue are somewhat different. The critique of metaphysics is not given pride of place in this more "anarchist" strain; there is no "mysticism of Being" conjured up here. The target is still subject-centered reason and the domination of nature, society, and the self that it promotes. But the guiding thread is now Nietzsche's theory of power, and the fundamental premise is that modern reason is nothing more than a perverted and disguised will to power. The aim of critique is, then, to strip away the veil of reason and to reveal naked the power it serves. In Bataille, this takes the form of an invocation and investigation of "the other of reason" — of what is expelled and excluded from the world of the useful, calculable, and manipulable. In Foucault, it takes the form of a genealogical unmasking that reveals the essential intrication of knowledge with power. Habermas devotes two lectures to Foucault, and readers might justifiably conclude that in his dialogue with French poststructuralism, Foucault is the preferred partner. More than any other of the radical critics of reason, Foucault opens up a field of investigation for social research; there is in his work no "mystification" of social pathologies into the "destinings" of this or that primordial force. Like Horkheimer and Adorno, he is sensitive to the power claims lurking in theoretical and practical reason; and also like them, he attaches to the concept of power both a transcendental-historical and a social-theoretical significance.

Genealogy is, on the one hand, a kind of transcendental historiography. Its aim, as Foucault once put it, is to construct a "history of the objectification of objectivities," a "nominalist critique," by way of historical analysis, of the fundamental ideas in terms of which we constitute ourselves as subjects and objects of knowledge. It treats any such constitution as a historical event, constructing an indefinite number of internal *and* external relations of intelligibility around it. The "theoretical-political" point of this "analytic decomposition," Foucault tells us, is to "show that things weren't as necessary as all that," to replace the unitary, necessary, and invariant with the multiple, contingent, and arbitrary. In particular, Foucault wants to break the hold on our minds of the modern "sciences of man," behind whose facade of universality and objectivity is concealed the ever-spreading operation of modern techniques of domination and of the self. This points to the second aspect of genealogy: It serves also as a historically oriented, more or less functionalist, critical sociology of knowledge, aimed in particular at types of knowledge that, incorporated into therapies and social technologies, serve as the main conduits for the normalizing and disciplinary effects of "truth."

Habermas's disagreements with Foucault certainly do not amount to a blanket rejection of this critical perspective on power-knowledge configurations. It is the "totalization" of critique that he objects to, the transformation of the critique of reason by reason — which from Kant to Marx had taken on the sociohistorical form of a critique of ideology — into a critique of reason tout court in the name of a "rhetorically affirmed other of reason." On his view, the real problem is too little rather than too much enlightenment, a deficiency rather than an excess of reason. And he supports this view with a double-edged critique of Foucault's "totalization," one edge applying to the transcendental-historiographic aspect of genealogy, the other to its social-theoretical aspect. Briefly, he argues that Foucault cannot escape the "performative contradiction" involved in using the tools of reason to criticize reason; this has the serious consequence of landing his genealogical investigations in a situation embarrassingly similar to that of the "sciences of man" he so tellingly criticized. The ideas of meaning, validity, and value that were to be eliminated by genealogical critique come back to haunt it in the spectral forms of "presentism," "relativism," and "cryptonormativism." On the other hand, the social-theoretical reading of modernity inspired by the theory of power turns out to be simply an inversion of the standard humanist reading it is meant to replace. It is, argues Habermas, no less one-sided: The essentially ambiguous phenomena of modern culture and society are "flattened down" onto the plane of power. Thus, for example, the internal development of law and morality, which on his view bears effects of emancipation as well as of domination, disappears from Foucault's account of their normalizing functions. It is precisely the ambiguity of rationalization processes that has to be captured, the undeniable achievements as well as the palpable distortions; and this calls for a reconstructed dialectic of enlightenment rather than a totalized critique of it.

As I mentioned at the outset, Habermas's strategy is to return to the counterdiscourse of modernity — neglected by Nietzsche and his followers — in which the principle of a self-sufficient, self-assertive subjectivity was exposed to telling criticism and a "counterreckoning" of the cost of modernity was drawn up.

Examining the main crossroads in this counterdiscourse, he points to indications of a path opened but not pursued: the construal of reason in terms of a noncoercive intersubjectivity of mutual understanding and reciprocal recognition. Returning to the first major crossroad, he uses this notion to reconstruct Hegel's idea of ethical life and to argue that the other of reason invoked by the post-Nietzscheans is not adequately rendered in their "model of exclusion"; it is better seen as a divided and destroyed ethical totality. Habermas follows Hegel also in viewing reason as a healing power of unification and reconciliation; however, it is not the Absolute that he has in mind, but the unforced intersubjectivity of rational agreement. At the second major crossroad, he follows Marx's indication that philosophy must become practical, that its rational content has to be mobilized in practice. This yields a counterposition to the post-Nietzschean privileging of "the extraordinary" — limit experiences of aesthetic, mystical, or archaic provenance. If situated reason is viewed as social interaction, the potential of reason has to be realized in the communicative practice of ordinary, everyday life. The social practice Habermas has in mind cannot, however, be identified with Marx's conception of labor; in his view, productive activity is too specific and too restricted a notion to serve as a paradigm of rational practice. Furthermore, it harbors an idealist residue — labor as constitutive of a world in alienated form that has to be reappropriated — that needs to be overcome if we are to get definitively beyond the paradigm of subjectivity. The solution he opposes to the simple elimination of the subject is a kind of "determinate negation": If communicative action is our paradigm, the decentered subject remains as a participant in social interaction mediated by language. On this account, there is an internal relation of communicative practice to reason, for language use is oriented to validity claims, and validity claims can in the end be redeemed only through intersubjective recognition brought about by the unforced force of reason. The internal relation of meaning to validity means that communication is not only always "immanent" — that is, situated, conditioned — but also always "transcendent" — that is, geared to validity claims that are meant to hold beyond any local context and thus can be

indefinitely criticized, defended, revised: "Validity claims have
a Janus face. As claims, they transcend any local context; at
the same time, they have to be raised here and now and be de
facto recognized . . . . The transcendent moment of *universal*
validity bursts every provinciality asunder; the obligatory moment of accepted validity claims renders them carriers of a
context-bound everyday practice. . . . a moment of *unconditionality*
is built into *factual* processes of mutual understanding — the
validity laid claim to is distinguished from the social currency
of a de facto established practice and yet serves it as the foundation of an existing consensus." This orientation of communicative action to validity claims admitting of argument and
counterargument is precisely what makes possible the learning
processes that lead to transformations of our world views and
thus of the very conditions and standards of rationality.

In sum, then, Habermas agrees with the radical critics of
enlightenment that the paradigm of consciousness is exhausted. Like them, he views reason as inescapably situated, as
concretized in history, society, body, and language. Unlike
them, however, he holds that the defects of the Enlightenment
can only be made good by further enlightenment. The totalized
critique of reason undercuts the capacity of reason to be critical. It refuses to acknowledge that modernization bears developments as well as distortions of reason. Among the former,
he mentions the "unthawing" and "reflective refraction" of
cultural traditions, the universalization of norms and generalization of values, and the growing individuation of personal
identities — all prerequisites for that effectively democratic
organization of society through which alone reason can, in the
end, become practical.

Preface

"Modernity — an Unfinished Project" was the title of a speech I gave in September 1980 upon accepting the Adorno Prize.[1] This theme, disputed and multifaceted as it is, never lost its hold on me. Its philosophical aspects have moved even more starkly into public consciousness in the wake of the reception of French neostructuralism — as has the key term "postmodernity," in connection with a publication by Jean-François Lyotard.[2] The challenge from the neostructuralist critique of reason defines the perspective from which I seek to reconstruct here, step by step, the philosophical discourse of modernity. Since the late eighteenth century modernity has been elevated to a *philosophical* theme in this discourse. The philosophical discourse of modernity touches upon and overlaps with the aesthetic discourse in manifold ways. Nevertheless, I have had to limit the theme; these lectures do not treat modernism in art and literature.[3]

After my return to the University of Frankfurt, I held lecture courses on this subject in the summer semester of 1983 and the winter semester of 1983–1984. Added afterwards, and so fictitious in this sense, are the fifth lecture, which adopts an already published text,[4] as well as the last lecture, only recently worked out. I delivered the first four lectures at the Collège de France in Paris in March 1983. I used other portions for the Messenger Lectures at Cornell University in September 1984. I also dealt with the most important theses in seminars at Boston College. I have received more inspirations from the lively discussions I was able to hold with colleagues and students on these occasions than could be acknowledged retrospectively in notes.

Supplements to the philosophical discourse of modernity, with a political accent, are contained in a volume of *edition suhrkamp* being published simultaneously.[5]

I

Modernity's Consciousness of Time and Its Need for Self-Reassurance

I

In his famous introduction to the collection of his studies on the sociology of religion, Max Weber takes up the "problem of universal history" to which his scholarly life was dedicated, namely, the question why, outside Europe, "the scientific, the artistic, the political, or the economic development . . . did not enter upon that path of rationalization which is peculiar to the Occident?"[1] For Weber, the intrinsic (that is, not merely contingent) relationship between modernity and what he called "Occidental rationalism" was still self-evident.[2] He described as "rational" the process of disenchantment which led in Europe to a disintegration of religious world views that issued in a secular culture. With the modern empirical sciences, autonomous arts, and theories of morality and law grounded on principles, cultural spheres of value took shape which made possible learning processes in accord with the respective inner logics of theoretical, aesthetic, and moral-practical problems.

What Weber depicted was not only the secularization of Western *culture*, but also and especially the development of modern *societies* from the viewpoint of rationalization. The new structures of society were marked by the differentiation of the two functionally intermeshing systems that had taken shape around the organizational cores of the capitalist enterprise and the bureaucratic state apparatus. Weber understood this process as the institutionalization of purposive-rational economic and administrative action. To the degree that everyday life was affected by this cultural and societal rationalization, traditional forms of life — which in the early modern period were differentiated primarily according to one's trade — were dissolved. The modernization of the lifeworld is not determined only by structures of purposive rationality. Emile Durkheim and George Herbert Mead saw rationalized lifeworlds as characterized by the reflective treatment of traditions that have lost their quasinatural status; by the universalization of norms of action and the generalization of values, which set communicative action free from narrowly restricted contexts and enlarge the field of options; and finally, by patterns of socialization that are oriented to the formation of abstract ego-identities and force the individuation of the growing child. This is, in broad strokes, how the classical social theorists drew the picture of modernity.

Today Max Weber's theme appears in another light; this is as much the result of the labors of those who invoke him as of the work of his critics. "Modernization" was introduced as a technical term only in the 1950s. It is the mark of a theoretical approach that takes up Weber's problem but elaborates it with the tools of social-scientific functionalism. The concept of modernization refers to a bundle of processes that are cumulative and mutually reinforcing: to the formation of capital and the mobilization of resources; to the development of the forces of production and the increase in the productivity of labor; to the establishment of centralized political power and the formation of national identities; to the proliferation of rights of political participation, of urban forms of life, and of formal schooling; to the secularization of values and norms; and so on. The theory of modernization performs two abstractions on Weber's concept of "modernity." It dissociates "modernity" from its modern European origins and stylizes it into a spatio-temporally neutral model for processes of social development in general. Furthermore, it breaks the internal connections between modernity and the historical context of Western rationalism, so that processes of modernization can no longer be conceived of as rationalization, as the historical objectification of rational structures. James Coleman sees in this the advantage that a concept of modernization generalized in terms of a theory of evolution is no longer burdened with the idea of a completion of modernity, that is to say, of a goal state after which "postmodern" developments would have to set in.[3]

Indeed it is precisely modernization research that has contributed to the currency of the expression "postmodern" even among social scientists. For in view of an evolutionarily autonomous, self-promoting modernization, social-scientific observers can all the more easily take leave of the conceptual horizon of Western rationalism in which modernity arose. But as soon as the internal links between the concept of modernity and the self-understanding of modernity gained within the horizon of Western reason have been dissolved, we can relativize the, as it were, automatically continuing processes of modernization from the distantiated standpoint of a postmodern observer. Arnold Gehlen brought this down to the formula: The premises of the Enlightenment are dead; only their consequences continue on. From this perspective, a self-sufficiently advancing modernization of society has separated itself from the impulses of a cultural modernity that has seemingly become obsolete in the meantime; it only carries out the functional laws of economy and state, technology and science, which are supposed to have amalgamated into a system that cannot be influenced. The relentless acceleration of social processes appears as the reverse side of a culture that is exhausted and has passed into a crystalline state. Gehlen calls modern culture "crystallized" because "the possibilities implanted in it have all been developed in their basic elements. Even the counterpossibilities and antitheses have been uncovered and assimilated, so that henceforth changes in the premises have become increasingly unlikely. . . . If you have this impression, you will perceive crystallization . . . even in a realm as astonishingly dynamic and full of variety as that of modern painting."[4] Because "the history of ideas has concluded," Gehlen can observe with a sigh of relief that "we have arrived at *posthistoire*." With Gottfried Benn he imparts the advice: "Count up your supplies." This *neoconservative* leave-taking from modernity is directed, then, not to the unchecked dynamism of societal modernization but to the husk of a cultural self-understanding of modernity that appears to have been overtaken.[5]

In a completely different political form, namely an anarchist one, the idea of postmodernity appears among theoreticians who do not see that any uncoupling of modernity and rationality has set in. They, too, advertise the end of the Enlightenment; they, too, move beyond the horizon of the tradition of reason in which European modernity once understood itself; and they plant their feet in *posthistoire*. But unlike the neoconservative, the anarchist farewell to modernity is meant for society and culture in the same degree. As that continent of basic concepts bearing Weber's Occidental rationalism sinks down, reason makes known its true identity — it becomes unmasked as the subordinating and at the same time itself subjugated subjectivity, as the will to instrumental mastery. The subversive force of this critique, which pulls away the veil of reason from before the sheer will to power, is at the same time supposed to shake the iron cage in which the spirit of modernity has been objectified in societal form. From this point of view, the modernization of society cannot survive the end of the cultural modernity from which it arose. It cannot hold its own against the "primordial" anarchism under whose sign postmodernity marches.

However distinct these two readings of the theory of postmodernity are, both reject the basic conceptual horizon within which the self-understanding of European modernity has been formed. Both theories of postmodernity pretend to have gone beyond this horizon, to have left it behind as the horizon of a past epoch. Hegel was the first philosopher to develop a clear concept of modernity. We have to go back to him if we want to understand the internal relationship between modernity and rationality, which, until Max Weber, remained self-evident and which today is being called into question. We have to get clear on the Hegelian concept of modernity to be able to judge whether the claim of those who base their analyses on other premises is legitimate. At any rate, we cannot dismiss a priori the suspicion that postmodern thought merely claims a transcendent status, while it remains in fact dependent on presuppositions of the modern self-understanding that were brought to light by Hegel. We cannot exclude from the outset the possibility that neoconservatism and aesthetically inspired anarchism, in the name of a farewell to modernity, are merely trying to revolt against it once again. It could be that they are merely cloaking their complicity with the venerable tradition of counter-Enlightenment in the garb of post-Enlightenment.

II

Hegel used the concept of modernity first of all in historical contexts, as an epochal concept: The "new age" is the "modern age." This corresponded to contemporary usage in English and French: "modern times" or *temps modernes* denoted around 1800 the three centuries just preceding. The discovery of the "new world," the Renaissance, and the Reformation — these three monumental events around the year 1500 constituted the epochal threshold between modern times and the middle ages. In his *Lectures on the Philosophy of History*, Hegel used these expressions to classify the German Christian world that had issued from Roman and Greek antiquity. The division still usual today (e.g., for the designation of chairs in history departments) into the Modern Period, the Middle Ages, and Antiquity (or modern, medieval, and ancient history) could take shape only after the expression "new" or "modern" age ("new" or "modern" world) lost its merely chronological meaning and took on the oppositional significance of an emphatically "new" age. Whereas in the Christian West the "new world" had meant the still-to-come age of the world of the future, which was to dawn only on the last day — and it still retains this meaning in Schelling's *Philosophy of the Ages of the World* — the secular concept of modernity expresses the conviction that the future has already begun: It is the epoch that lives for the future, that opens itself up to the novelty of the future. In this way, the caesura defined by the new beginning has been shifted into the past, precisely to the start of modern times. Only in the course of the eighteenth century did the epochal threshold around 1500 become conceptualized as this beginning. To test this, Reinhart Koselleck uses the question of when *nostrum aevum*, our own age, was renamed *nova aetas*, the new age.[6]

Koselleck shows how the historical consciousness that expressed itself in the concept of the "modern age" or the "new age" constituted a historical-philosophical perspective: One's own standpoint was to be brought to reflective awareness within the horizon of history as a whole. Even the collective singular *Geschichte* [history], which Hegel already uses in a way that is taken for granted, was a coinage of the eighteenth century: "The 'new age' lent the whole of the past a world-historical quality. . . . Diagnosis of the new age and analysis of the past ages corresponded to each other."[7] The new experience of an advancing and accelerating of historical events corresponds to this, as does the insight into the chronological simultaneity of historically nonsynchronous developments.[8] At this time the image of history as a uniform process that generates problems is formed, and time becomes experienced as a scarce resource for the mastery of problems that arise — that is, as the pressure of time. The *Zeitgeist*, or spirit of the age, one of the new words that inspired Hegel, characterizes the present as a transition that is consumed in the consciousness of a speeding up and in the expectation of the differentness of the future. As Hegel puts it in the preface to the *Phenomenology of Mind*:

It is surely not difficult to see that our time is a birth and transition to a new period. The Spirit has broken with what was hitherto the world of its existence and imagination and is about to submerge all this in the past; it is at work giving itself a new form. . . . [F]rivolity as well as the boredom that open up in the establishment and the indeterminate apprehension of something unknown are harbingers of a forthcoming change. This gradual crumbling . . . is interrupted by the break of day, that like lightning, all at once reveals the edifice of the new world.[9]

Because the new, the modern world is distinguished from the old by the fact that it opens itself to the future, the epochal new beginning is rendered constant with each moment that gives birth to the new. Thus, it is characteristic of the historical consciousness of modernity to set off "the most recent [*neuesten*] period" from the modern [*neu*] age: Within the horizon of the modern age, the present enjoys a prominent position as contemporary history. Even Hegel understands "our age" as "the most recent period." He dates the beginning of the present from the break that the Enlightenment and the French Revolution signified for the more thoughtful contemporaries at the close of the eighteenth and the start of the nineteenth century. With this "glorious sunrise" we come, as the old Hegel still thought, "to the last stage in History, our world, our own time."[10] A present that understands itself from the horizon of the modern age as the actuality of the most recent period has to recapitulate the break brought about with the past as a *continuous renewal*.

The dynamic concepts that either emerged together with the expression "modern age" or "new age" in the eighteenth century or acquired then a new meaning that remains valid down to our day are adapted to this — words such as revolution, progress, emancipation, development, crisis, and *Zeitgeist*.[11] These expressions also became key terms for Hegelian philosophy. They cast conceptual-historical light on the problem posed for the modern historical consciousness of Western culture that had developed in connection with the oppositional concept of a "new age": Modernity can and will no longer borrow the criteria by which it takes its orientation from the models supplied by another epoch; *it has to create its normativity out of itself*. Modernity sees itself cast back upon itself without any possibility of escape. This explains the sensitiveness of its self-understanding, the dynamism of the attempt, carried forward incessantly down to our time, to "pin itself down." Just a few years ago, Hans Blumenberg felt himself obliged to defend with a grand historical display the legitimacy or the *proper right* of modernity against constructions that tried to make a case for its cultural debt to the testators of Christianity and antiquity. "It is not self-evident that an epoch poses itself the problem of its historical legitimacy; just as little is it self-evident that it understands itself as an epoch at all. For modernity, the problem is latent in the claim of accomplishing, and of being able to accomplish, a radical break, and in the incongruity of this claim with the reality of history, which is never capable of starting anew from the ground up."[12] Blumenberg adduces as evidence a statement by the young Hegel: "Apart from some earlier attempts, it has been reserved in the main for our epoch to vindicate, at least in theory, the human ownership of treasures formerly squandered on heaven; but what age will have the strength to validate this right in practice and make itself their possessor?"[13]

The problem of grounding modernity out of itself first comes to consciousness in the realm of aesthetic criticism. This becomes clear when one traces the history of the concept "modern."[14] The process of detachment from the models of ancient art was set going in the early eighteenth century by the famous *querelle des anciens et des modernes*.[15] The party of the moderns rebelled against the self-understanding of French classicism by assimilating the aesthetic concept of perfection to that of progress as it was suggested by modern natural science. The "moderns," using historical-critical arguments, called into question the meaning of imitating the ancient models; in opposition to the norms of an apparently timeless and absolute beauty, they elaborated the criteria of a relative or time-conditioned beauty and thus articulated the self-understanding of the French Enlightenment as an epochal new beginning. Although the substantive *modernitas*, along with the pair of adjectival opposites, *antiqui/moderni*, had already been used since late antiquity in a chronological sense, in the European languages of the modern age the adjective "modern" only came to be used in a substantive form in the middle of the nineteenth century, once again at first in the realm of the fine arts. This explains why *Moderne* and *Modernität*, *modernité* and *modernity* have until our own day a core aesthetic meaning fashioned by the self-understanding of avant-garde art.[16]

For Baudelaire, the aesthetic experience of modernity fuses with the historical. In the fundamental experience of aesthetic modernity, the problem of self-grounding becomes acute, because here the horizon of temporal experience contracts to the decentered subjectivity that splits away from the conventions of everyday life. For this reason, he assigns to the modern work of art a strange place at the intersection of the axes of the actual and the eternal: "Modernity is the transient, the fleeting, the contingent; it is one-half of art, the other being the eternal and immovable."[17] A self-consuming actuality, which forfeits the *extension* of a transition period, of a most recent period constituted at the center of the new age (and lasting several decades), becomes the reference point of modernity. The actual present can no longer gain its self-consciousness from opposition to an epoch rejected and surpassed, to a shape of the past. Actuality can be constituted only as the point where time and eternity intersect. In this way, modernity is rescued, not from its infirmity surely, but from triviality; in Baudelaire's understanding, it is so disposed that the transitory moment will find confirmation as the authentic past of a future present.[18] It proves its worth as that which one day will be classic: "Classic" is henceforth the "flash" at the dawning of a new world — which will of course have no duration, for its collapse is already sealed with its appearance. This understanding of time, radicalized yet again in surrealism, grounds the kinship of *modernity* with *mode* (or *fashion*).

Baudelaire picks up on the outcome of the famous debate between the ancients and the moderns, but he shifts the weight between the absolutely beautiful and the relatively beautiful in a characteristic manner: "Beauty is made up, on the one hand, of an element that is eternal and invariable . . . and, on the other, of a relative, circumstantial element, which we may like to call . . . contemporaneity, fashion, morality, passion. Without this second element, which is like the amusing, teasing, appetite-whetting coating of the divine cake, the first element would be indigestible, tasteless, unadapted, and inappropriate to human nature."[19] Baudelaire the art critic emphasizes an aspect of modern painting: "the ephemeral, the fleeting forms of beauty in the life of our day, the characteristic traits of what, with our reader's permission, we have called 'modernity.'"[20] He puts the word "modernity" in quotation marks; he is conscious of his novel, terminologically peculiar use of the term. On this account, the authentic work is radically bound to the moment of its emergence; precisely because it consumes itself in actuality, it can bring the steady flow of trivialities to a standstill, break through normality, and satisfy for a moment the immortal longing for beauty — a moment in which the eternal comes into fleeting contact with the actual.

Eternal beauty shows itself only in the guise of the costume of the times. (Benjamin later adopted this feature under the rubric of the dialectical image.) The modern work of art is

marked by a union of the real or true with the ephemeral.
This character of the present is also at the basis of the kinship
of art with fashion, with the new, with the optics of the idler,
the genius, and the child, who, lacking the antistimulant of
conventionally inculcated modes of perception, are delivered
up defenceless to the attacks of beauty, to the transcendent
stimuli hidden in the most ordinary matters. The role of the
dandy, then, consists in turning this type of passively experienced extraordinariness to the offensive, in demonstrating the
extraordinary by provocative means.[21] The dandy combines
the indolent and the fashionable with the pleasure of causing
surprise in others while never showing any himself. He is the
expert on the fleeting pleasure of the moment, out of which
the novel wells up: "He is looking for that indefinable something we may be allowed to call 'modernity,' for want of a
better term to express the idea in question. The aim for him
is to extract from fashion the poetry that resides in its historical
envelope, to distill the eternal from the transitory."[22]

Walter Benjamin took up this motif in order to find a solution to the paradoxical task of obtaining standards of its own
for the contingency of a modernity that had become simply
transitory. Whereas Baudelaire had contented himself with the
idea that the constellation of time and eternity comes to pass
in the authentic work of art, Benjamin wanted to translate this
basic aesthetic experience back into a historical relationship.
He fashioned for this purpose the concept of a "now-time"
[*Jetztzeit*], which is shot through with fragments of messianic or
completed time; and in doing so he made use of the "imitation"
motif, which having become merely skin deep, so to speak, was
now to be ferreted out in the appearances of fashion.

The French Revolution viewed itself as Rome reincarnate. It evoked
ancient Rome the way fashion evokes costumes of the past. Fashion
has a flair for the topical, no matter where it stirs in the thickets of
long ago; it is a tiger's leap into the past. . . . The same leap in the
open air of history is the dialectical one, which is how Marx understood the revolution.[23]

Benjamin is not only rebelling against the *borrowed* normativity of an understanding of history taken from the imitation

of models; he is struggling just as much against two conceptions which, on the basis of the modern understanding of history, intercept and neutralize the provocation of the new and of the entirely unexpected: on the one hand, the idea of a homogeneous and empty time that is filled in by "the stubborn belief in progress" of evolutionism and the philosophy of history; on the other hand, the neutralization of all standards fostered by historicism when it imprisons history in the museum and "tell[s] the sequence of events like the beads of a rosary."[24] The model here is Robespierre who, in citing ancient Rome, provided himself with a *corresponding* past charged with "now-time" in order to burst the inert continuum of history. Just as he attempts to bring the sluggish flow of history to a stop, as if by a surrealistically produced shock, so must a modernity that has been evaporated into what is actual at any given time [*Aktualität*], as soon as it attains the authenticity of a now-time, constantly take its normativity from mirror images of pasts whose services are *enlisted* for this purpose. They are no longer perceived from the outset as exemplary pasts. We should look rather to Baudelaire's model of the creator of fashion to appreciate the creativity that sets the act of clear-sightedly detecting such correspondences in contrast with the aesthetic ideal of imitating classical models.

Excursus on Benjamin's Theses on the Philosophy of History

The consciousness of time expressed in Benjamin's "Theses on the Philosophy of History" is not easy to classify. A singular mixture of surrealist experiences and motifs from Jewish mysticism enter unmistakably into his notion of "now-time." This idea — that the authentic moment of an innovative present interrupts the continuum of history and breaks away from its homogeneous flow — is fed from both sources. The profane illumination caused by shock, like the mystical union with the appearance of the Messiah, forces a cessation, a crystallization, of the momentary event. Benjamin is not concerned only with an emphatic renewal of the consciousness for which "every second of time [is] the strait gate through which the Messiah

might enter" (Thesis XVIII). He twists the radical future-ori-
entedness that is characteristic of modern times in general so
far back around the axis of the now-time that it gets transposed
into a yet more radical orientation toward the past. The anticipation of what is new in the future is realized only through
remembering [*Eingedenken*] a past that has been suppressed.
Benjamin understands the sign of such a messianic cessation
of events as "a revolutionary chance in the fight for the oppressed past" (Thesis XVII).

In the framework of his investigations into conceptual history, Reinhart Koselleck has characterized modern time-consciousness, among other ways, in terms of the increasing
difference between the "space of experience" and the "horizon
of expectation": "My thesis is that in modern times the difference between experience and expectation has increasingly expanded; more precisely, that modernity is first understood as
a new age from the time that expectations have distanced
themselves evermore from all previous experience."[25] Modernity's specific orientation toward the future is shaped precisely
to the extent that societal modernization tears apart the old
European experiential space of the peasant's and craftsman's
lifeworlds, mobilizes it, and devalues it into directives guiding
expectations. These traditional experiences of previous generations are then replaced by the kind of experience of progress that lends to our horizon of expectation (till then anchored
fixedly in the past) a "historically new quality, constantly subject
to being overlaid with utopian conceptions."[26]

Yet Koselleck overlooks the fact that the notion of progress
served not only to render eschatological hopes profane and
open up the horizon of expectation in a utopian fashion, but
also to close off the future as a *source* of disruption with the
aid of teleological constructions of history. Benjamin's polemic
against the social-evolutionary leveling off of the historical materialist conception of history is aimed at just such a degener-
ation of modernity's consciousness of time open toward the
future. Wherever progress becomes a historical norm, the quality of novelty and the emphasis upon predictable beginnings
are eliminated from the present's relationship to the future.
In Benjamin's view, historicism is merely a functional equiva-

lent for the philosophy of history in this regard. The historian who practices empathy and comprehends everything assembles a mass of facts, which means that he places the objectified course of history into an ideal simultaneity in order to fill up "empty and homogeneous time." He thereby strips the present's relationship to the future of any relevance for understanding the past: "A historical materialist cannot do without the notion of a present which is not a transition, but in which time stands still and has come to a stop. For this notion defines the present in which he himself is writing history. Historicism gives the 'eternal' image of the past; historical materialism supplies a unique experience with the past" (Thesis XVI).

We shall see that to the degree that it has been articulated in literary documents, modern time-consciousness has repeatedly slackened and that its vitality has had to be constantly renewed by radical historical thinking: from the Young Hegelians via Nietzsche and Yorck von Warthenburg right down to Heidegger. The same impulse inspires Benjamin's "Theses"; they serve to renew modern time-consciousness. However, Benjamin was still not satisfied with the variations of historical thinking considered radical up to his time. Radical historical thinking can be characterized by the idea of effective history [*Wirkungsgeschichte*]. Nietzsche called it critical history. The Marx of the *Eighteenth Brumaire* practiced this type of historical thinking; the Heidegger of *Being and Time* ontologized it. Even in the congealed structure of the "existentiale of historicality," one thing remains clear: The horizon open to the future, which is determined by expectations in the present, guides our access to the past. Inasmuch as we appropriate past experiences with an orientation to the future, the authentic present is preserved as the locus of continuing tradition and of innovation at once; the one is not possible without the other, and both merge into the objectivity proper to a context of effective history.

Now there are different ways of reading this idea of effective history, according to the degree of continuity or discontinuity to be secured or brought about. One can have conservative (Gadamer), conservative-revolutionary (Freyer), and revolutionary (Korsch) interpretations. Always, however, the future-oriented gaze is directed from the present into a past that is connected as *prehistory* with our present, as by the chain of a continual destiny. Two moments are constitutive for this consciousness: on the one hand, the effective-historical bond of a continuous happening of tradition in which even the revolutionary deed is embedded; on the other, the dominance of the horizon of expectation over a potential of historical experiences to be appropriated.

Benjamin does not explicitly come to terms with this effective-historical consciousness. But it is clear from his text that he distrusts *both*: both the treasure of transmitted cultural goods that are supposed to pass into the possession of the present, and the asymmetric relationship between the appropriating activities of a present oriented to the future and the objects of the past that are made one's own. Hence Benjamin proposes *a drastic reversal* of horizon of expectation and space of experience. To all past epochs he ascribes a horizon of unfulfilled expectations, and to the future-oriented present he assigns the task of experiencing a corresponding past through remembering, in such a way that we can fulfill its expectations with our weak messianic power. In accordance with this reversal, two ideas can be interwoven: the conviction that the continuity of the context of tradition can be established by barbarism as well as by culture,[27] and the idea that each respective present generation bears the responsibility not only for the fate of future generations but also for the innocently suffered fate of past generations. This need for redemption on the part of past epochs who have directed their expectations to us is reminiscent of the figure familiar in both Jewish and Protestant mysticism of man's respnsibility for the fate of a God who, in the act of creation, relinquished his omnipotence in favor of human freedom, putting us on an equal footing with himself.

But such imputations from intellectual history do not explain very much. What Benjamin has in mind is the supremely profane insight that ethical universalism also has to take seriously the injustice that has already happened and that is seemingly irreversible; that there exists a solidarity of those born later with those who have preceded them, with all those whose bodily or personal integrity has been violated at the hands of other human beings; and that this solidarity can only be engendered and made effective by remembering. Here the liberating power of memory is supposed not to foster a dissolution of the power of the past over the present, as it was from Hegel down to Freud, but to contribute to the dissolution of a guilt on the part of the present with respect to the past: "For every image of the past that is not recognized by the present as one of its own concerns threatens to disappear irretrievably" (Thesis V).

In the context of this first lecture, this excursus is meant to show how Benjamin interweaves motifs of completely diverse provenance in order to radicalize yet again the effective-historical consciousness. The disengagement of the horizon of expectation from the handed-down potentials for experience is, as Koselleck shows, what first makes possible the opposition of a new age living in its own right to those past epochs from which modernity dissociated itself. Thus, the constellation of the present in relation to the past and future has undergone a specific change. On the one hand, under the pressure of urgent problems from the future, a present that is challenged to historically responsible activity gains ascendancy over a past that is to be appropriated for its own interests; on the other hand, a purely transitory present sees itself brought to account before the future for its interventions and omissions. Because Benjamin *extends* this future-oriented responsibility to past epochs, the constellation shifts once again: The tension-laden relationship to basically open alternatives in the future now touches directly the relationship to a past mobilized in turn by expectations. The pressure of the future is multiplied by that of the past (and unfulfilled) future. But at the same time, the secret narcissism of effective-historical consciousness is corrected by this rotation of the axis. It is no longer only future generations, but past generations as well, that have a claim on the weak messianic power of the present. The anamnestic redemption of an injustice, which cannot of course be undone but can at least be virtually reconciled through remembering, ties up the present with the communicative context of a universal historical solidarity. This anamnesis constitutes the decentering counterpoise to the dangerous concentration of responsibility that modern time-consciousness, oriented exclusively toward the future, has laid on the shoulders of a problematic present that has, as it were, been tied in knots.[28]

III

Hegel was the first to raise to the level of a philosophical problem the process of detaching modernity from the suggestion of norms lying outside of itself in the past. Certainly, in the course of a critique of tradition that integrated the experiences of the Reformation and the Renaissance and reacted to the beginnings of modern natural science, modern philosophy from late scholasticism until Kant had already expressed the self-understanding of modernity. But only at the end of the eighteenth century did the problem of modernity's *self-reassurance* [*Selbstvergewisserung*] come to a head in such a way that Hegel could grasp this question *as* a philosophical problem, and indeed as *the fundamental problem* of his own philosophy. The anxiety caused by the fact that a modernity without models had to stabilize itself on the basis of the very diremptions [or divisions: *Entzweiungen*] it had wrought is seen by Hegel as "the source of the need for philosophy."[29] As modernity awakens to consciousness of itself, a need for self-reassurance arises, which Hegel understands as a need for philosophy. He sees philosophy confronted with the task of grasping *its own* time — and for him that means the modern age — in thought. Hegel is convinced that he cannot possibly obtain philosophy's concept of itself independently of the philosophical concept of modernity.

Hegel sees the modern age as marked universally by a structure of self-relation that he calls subjectivity: "The principle of the modern world is freedom of subjectivity, the principle that all the essential factors present in the intellectual whole are now coming into their right in the course of their development."[30] When Hegel delineates the physiognomy of the new age (or of the modern world), he elucidates "subjectivity" by means of "freedom" and "reflection": "The greatness of our time rests in the fact that freedom, the peculiar possession of mind whereby it is at home with itself in itself, is recognized."[31]

In this context, the term "subjectivity" carries primarily four connotations: (a) *individualism*: in the modern world, singularity particularized without limit can make good its pretensions;[32] (b) *the right to criticism*: the principle of the modern world requires that what anyone is to recognize shall reveal itself to him as something entitled to recognition;[33] (c) *autonomy of action*: our responsibility for what we do is a characteristic of modern times;[34] (d) finally, *idealistic philosophy* itself: Hegel considers it the work of modern times that philosophy grasps the self-conscious (or self-knowing) Idea.[35]

The key historical events in establishing the principle of subjectivity are the Reformation, the Enlightenment, and the French Revolution. With Luther, religious faith became reflective; the world of the divine was changed in the solitude of subjectivity into something posited by ourselves.[36] Against faith in the authority of preaching and tradition, Protestantism asserted the authority of the subject relying upon his own insight: The host was simply dough, the relics of the saints mere bones.[37] Then, too, the Declaration of the Rights of Man and the Napoleonic Code validated the principle of freedom of will against historically preexisting law as the substantive basis of the state: "Right and [social] morality came to be looked upon as having their foundation in the actually present will of man, whereas formerly it was referred only to the command of God enjoined *ab extra*, written in the Old and New Testament, or appearing in the form of particular right . . . in old parchments, as *privilegia*, or in international compacts."[38]

Furthermore, the principle of subjectivity determines the forms of modern culture. This holds true first of all for objectifying science, which disenchants nature at the same time that it liberates the knowing subject: "Thus, all miracles were disallowed: for nature is a now system of known and recognized laws; man is at home in it, and only that remains standing in which he is at home; he is free through the acquaintance he has gained with nature."[39] The *moral concepts* of modern times follow from the recognition of the subjective freedom of individuals. On the one hand, they are founded upon the right of individuals to perceive what they are supposed to do as valid; and on the other hand, they are founded on the demand that each person may pursue the ends of his particular welfare only in harmony with the welfare of everyone else. The subjective will gains autonomy under universal laws; but "only in the will as subjective can freedom or the implicit principle of the will be actual."[40] *Modern art* reveals its essence in Romanticism; and absolute inwardness determines the form and content of Romantic art. The divine irony coneptualized by Friedrich Schlegel mirrors the self-experience of a decentered self "for which all bonds are broken, and which only will endure to live in the bliss of self-enjoyment."[41] Expressive self-realization becomes the principle of art appearing as a form of life: "But according to the principle before us, I live as artist when all my action and utterance . . . is for me only on the level of mere *semblance*, and assumes a shape which is wholly in my power."[42] Reality attains the status of artistic expression only through the subjective refraction of the sensitive soul — it is "a mere appearance due to the I."[43]

In modernity, therefore, religious life, state, and society as well as science, morality, and art are transformed into just so many embodiments of the principle of subjectivity.[44] Its structure is grasped as such in philosophy, namely, as abstract subjectivity in Descartes's "*cogito ergo sum*" and in the form of absolute self-consciousness in Kant. It is the structure of a self-relating, knowing subject, which bends back upon itself as object, in order to grasp itself as in a mirror image — literally in a "speculative" way. Kant carried out this approach of the philosophy of reflection in his three "Critiques"; he installed reason in the supreme seat of judgment before which anything that made a claim to validity had to be justified.

Along with an analysis of the foundations of knowledge, *The Critique of Pure Reason* also takes on the task of a critique of the misuse of our cognitive faculties, which are designed to deal with appearances. In the place of the substantialist notion of reason of the metaphysical tradition, Kant puts the concept of a reason that divides up into its moments, the unity of which now has only a formal character. He separates the faculties of practical reason and of judgment from that of theoretical knowledge, and he places each of them on its own foundation. In thus grounding the possibility of objective knowledge, moral insight, and aesthetic evaluation, critical reason not only assures itself of its own subjective capacity, not only makes perspicuous the architectonic of reason, but also takes over the role of a supreme judge, even in relation to culture. As Emil Lask will later put it, philosophy delimits from one another the cultural spheres of value — science and technology, law and morality, art and art criticism — under exclusively formal viewpoints, and it legitimates them within these limits.[45]

By the end of the eighteenth century, science, morality, and art were even institutionally differentiated as realms of activity in which questions of truth, of justice, and of taste were autonomously elaborated, that is, each under its own specific aspect of validity. And these *spheres of knowing* were separated off from the spheres of belief, on the one hand, and from those of both legally organized and everyday life, on the other. Here we recognize precisely those spheres that Hegel later conceives of as expressions of the principle of subjectivity. Because transcendental reflection — in which the same principle of subjectivity appears without any covering, so to speak — assumed a judicial competence in relation to those spheres, Hegel sees the essence of the modern world gathered into its focal point in Kantian philosophy.

IV

Expressing the modern world in an edifice of thought means of course only reflecting the essential features of the age as in a mirror — which is not the same as conceiving [*begreifen*] it. From a retrospective point of view, Hegel can understand Kant's philosophy as the standard (or authoritative) self-interpretation of modernity; he thinks he sees what *also* remains unconceptualized in this most highly reflective expression of the age: Kant does not perceive as diremptions the differentiations within reason, the formal divisions within culture, and in general the fissures among all those spheres. Hence he ignores the need for unification that emerges with the separations evoked by the principle of subjectivity. Such a need is forced on philosophy as soon as modernity conceives itself historically, in other words, as soon as it becomes conscious of the dissolution of the exemplary past, and of the necessity of creating all that is normative out of itself, as a historical problem. Then, that is to say, the question arises as to whether the principle of subjectivity and the structure of self-consciousness residing in it suffice as the source of normative orientations — whether they suffice not only for "providing foundations" for science, morality, and art in general but also for stabilizing a historical formation that has been set loose from all historical obligations. The question now is whether one can obtain from subjectivity and self-consciousness criteria that are taken from the modern world and are at the same time fit for orienting oneself within it — and this also means fit for the critique of a modernity that is at variance with itself. How can an intrinsic ideal form be constructed from the spirit of modernity, one that neither just imitates the historical forms of modernity nor is imposed upon them from the outside?

If the question is posed in this way, subjectivity proves to be a *one-sided* principle. It does possess, to be sure, an unexampled power to bring about the formation [*Bildung*] of subjective freedom and reflection and to undermine religion, which heretofore had appeared as an absolutely unifying force. But the principle of subjectivity is not powerful enough to regenerate the unifying power of religion in the medium of reason. The Enlightenment's proud culture of reflection has divided itself off from religion "and . . . established it *alongside* itself or itself *alongside* it."[46] The demotion of religion leads to a split between faith and knowledge which the Enlightenment cannot overcome by its own power. For this reason, the latter appears in the *Phenomenology of Mind* under the title of a world of spirit in self-estrangement.[47] "The further the culture advances and the more manifold becomes the development of the expressions of life within which the diremption can entwine itself, the greater becomes the power of diremption . . . and the more meaningless and alien to the whole of culture become the strivings of life (once sublimated in religion) to again give birth to itself in harmony."[48]

This statement is taken from a polemic against Reinhold, the so-called *Differenzschrift* of 1801, in which Hegel conceives the sundered harmony of life as the practical challenge to, and the need for, philosophy.[49] That the consciousness of time has stepped out of the totality, that the spirit has estranged itself, is for Hegel an axiomatic presupposition of contemporary philosophizing. He treats the concept of the absolute (which was taken over from Schelling to begin with) as a further presupposition under which alone philosophy can resume its business. With it, philosophy can make sure of its goal from the outset — the goal of exhibiting reason as the power of unification. Reason indeed is supposed to overcome the state of diremption into which the principle of subjectivity has plunged both reason itself and "the entire system of living conditions." With his own critique, which is directed immediately at the philosophical systems of Kant and Fichte, Hegel wants at the same time to engage the self-understanding of modernity that is expressed in them. By criticizing the philosophical oppositions — nature and spirit, sensibility and understanding, understanding and reason, theoretical and practical reason, judgment and imagination, I and non-I, finite and infinite, knowledge and faith — he wants to respond to the crisis of the diremption of life itself. Otherwise philosophical critique could not hold out the prospect of satisfying the need by which it is objectively called forth. The critique of subjective idealism is at the same time a critique of modernity; only in this way can the latter secure its concept and thereby assure its own stability. In carrying out this project, critique can and should make use of no instrument *other* than that reflection which it encounters as the purest expression of the principle of modern times.[50] If modernity is to ground itself, Hegel has to develop the critical concept of modernity through a dialectic residing in the principle of the Enlightenment itself.

We shall see how Hegel carries out this program and, in doing so, becomes ensnared in the following dilemma: Once he has carried through the dialectic of the Enlightenment, the very impulse toward a critique of the present age, which first set the whole project in motion, is exhausted. We shall have to show first of all what lies hidden in that "vestibule of philosophy" in which Hegel accommodates "the presupposition of the absolute." The motives for a philosophy of unification can be traced back to crisis experiences of the young Hegel. They stand behind the conviction that reason must be brought forward as the reconciling power against the positive elements of an age torn asunder. The mythopoetic version of a reconciliation of modernity which Hegel first shared with Hölderlin and Schelling still remained tied to models from the past — from primitive Christianity and from ancient times. Only in the course of the Jena period, with his own concept of absolute knowledge, does Hegel secure a position that allows him to go beyond the products of the Enlightenment — Romantic art, rational religion, and bourgeois society — without being oriented to alien models. With this concept of the absolute, Hegel regresses back behind the intuitions of his youthful period. He conceives the overcoming of subjectivity within the boundaries of a philosophy of the subject. In the end, this gives rise to a dilemma: Hegel has ultimately to deny to the self-understanding of modernity the possibility of a critique of modernity. The critique of a subjectivity puffed up into an absolute power ironically turns into a reproach of the philosopher against the limitation of subjects who have not yet understood either him or the course of history.

II

Hegel's Concept of Modernity

I

In 1802, when Hegel dealt with the systems of Kant, Jacobi, and Fichte from the standpoint of the antithesis between faith and knowledge, his aim was to burst the philosophy of subjectivity from within; nevertheless he did not proceed in a rigorously immanent fashion. He was tacitly relying on a diagnosis of the Age of Enlightenment; this alone entitled him to presuppose the absolute — that is, to pose reason (in a way different from the philosophy of reflection) as the *power of unification*:

Civilization has raised this latest era [!] so far above the ancient antithesis of . . . philosophy and positive religion, that this opposition of faith and knowledge has . . . now been transferred into the field of philosophy itself . . . . The question arises, however, whether victorious Reason has not suffered the same fate that the barbarous nations in their victorious strength have usually suffered at the hands of civilized nations that weakly succumbed to them. As rulers the barbarians may have held the upper hand outwardly, but they surrendered to the defeated spiritually. Enlightened Reason won a glorious victory over what it believed, in its limited conception of religion, to be faith as opposed to Reason. Yet seen in this clear light the victory comes to no more than this: the positive element with which Reason busied itself to do battle, is no longer religion, and victorious Reason is no longer Reason.[1]

Hegel was convinced that the age of the Enlightenment culminating in Kant and Fichte had erected merely an idol in reason. It had falsely put understanding [*Verstand*] or reflection in place of reason [*Vernunft*] and thus elevated something finite to the status of an absolute. The infinite element of the philosophy of reflection was in truth merely posited by the understanding, a rational element that exhausts itself in the negation of the finite: "In that the understanding fixes it, it posits [the infinite] as absolutely opposed to the finite: and reflection, which had elevated itself to Reason in that it sublated the finite, has again degraded itself to the understanding in fixing the activity of reason in opposition. Moreover, it now makes the pretension of being rational even in this relapse."[2] However, as the unqualified talk about "relapse" shows, Hegel surreptitiously slips in here what he is attempting to demonstrate: He ought first to *demonstrate*, and not simply to *presuppose*, that a kind of reason which is more than an absolutized understanding *can* convincingly reunify the antitheses that reason *has to* unfold discursively. What encourage Hegel to presuppose an absolute power of unification, therefore, are not so much arguments as biographical experiences — namely, those crisis experiences of contemporary history that he gathered and worked through in Tübingen, Bern, and Frankfurt and then brought along with him to Jena.

As we know, Hegel and his young contemporaries in the Tübingen seminary were partisans of the freedom movements of their day. They lived immediately in the tensions of the religious Enlightenment and engaged in debate especially with the brand of Protestant Orthodoxy represented by the theologian Gottlieb Christian Storr. Philosophically, they took their bearings from the Kantian view of morality and religion; politically, from the ideas set loose by the French Revolution. In this context, the strictly regimented order of life in the seminary also set them off: "The theology of Storr, the rule of the seminary, and the constitution of the government that lent its protection to both of the former, seemed to be worth a revolution to most [of the seminarians]."[3] Within the framework of the theological studies that Hegel and Schelling were pursuing at the time, this rebellious impulse took the restrained form of a reformative proclivity for primitive Christianity. The intention they attributed to Jesus — "introducing morality into the religious life of his people"[4] — was made their own. Thus, they turned against both the party of the Enlightenment and that of Orthodoxy. Both sides made use of the historical-critical tools of biblical exegesis, though they pursued contrary goals — that is, either to justify the religion of reason, as it had been called since Lessing, or to defend strict Lutheran doctrines against it. Orthodoxy had gone on the defensive and had to make use of the critical methods of its opponents.[5]

Hegel's position stands at odds with both these fronts. With Kant, he treats religion as "the power to act upon and to establish the rights which reason has bestowed."[6] But the idea of God can only attain such power when religion penetrates the spirit and morals of a *people*, when it is present in the institutions of the state and in the practices of the society, when it makes the modes of thought and the motivations of people sensitive to the commands of practical reason and imprints them upon their minds. Religion can give practical efficacy to reason only as an element of *public life*. Hegel takes his inspiration from Rousseau when he sets up three requirements for genuine popular religion [*Volksreligion*]: "Their doctrines must be grounded on universal reason. Imagination, heart, sensibility must not go away empty. They must be so constituted that the public actions of the government are joined to all needs of life."[7] Unmistakable, too, are the resonances with the cult of reason from the days of the French Revoluton. This vision explains the twofold line of attack in the theological writings of the young Hegel: against Orthodoxy and against the religion of reason. They both appeared to be complementary and one-sided products of a dynamism of the Enlightenment that ultimately strove to get beyond the confines of the Enlightenment.

As it seemed to the young Hegel, a *positivity of ethical life* was the signature of the age. Hegel applied the term "positive" to religions that are based on authority alone and that do not incorporate the value of human beings into their morality.[8] "Positive" applies to prescriptions according to which the faithful are supposed to be able to earn God's benevolence through works instead of moral action; to the hope for compensation in the beyond; to the divorce of a doctrine in the hands of a few from the life and possession of all; to the detachment of priestly knowledge from the fetishized belief of the masses, as well as to the detour that supposedly leads to morality only by way of the authority and miraculous deeds of one person; to the assurances and threats aimed at the sheer legality of action; finally, and above all, the separation of private religion from public life is "positive."

If all this is characteristic of the positive faith defended by the Orthodox party, the philosophical party ought to have an easy game of it. The latter insists on the principle that religion has nothing positive about it at all but is authorized by universal human reason in such a way that "each and every person understands and feels its bindingness, if they become clearly aware of it."[9] But Hegel contends against the enlighteners that the pure religion of reason is no less an abstraction than the fetishized beliefs, for it is incapable of interesting the heart and of having an influence upon feelings and needs. It, too, comes down to a private religion because it is cut off from the institutions of public life and arouses no enthusiasm. Only if the religion of reason were to present itself in public in cele-brations and cults, only if it connected up with myths and addressed the heart and the imagination, could it, as religiously mediated morality, "be woven into the entire fabric of state."[10] The reason in religion gains an objective shape only under the conditions of political freedom — "the popular religion which engenders and nourishes great convictions goes hand in hand with freedom."[11]

For these reasons, the Enlightenment is only the obverse side of Orthodoxy. Just as the latter adheres to the positivity of doctrine, so the former does to the objectivity of rational com-mands; both employ the same means of biblical criticism; both solidify the condition of diremption and are equally incapable of shaping religion into the ethical totality of an entire nation and of inspiring a life of political freedom. The religion of reason proceeds, like the positive religion, from something antithetical — "from something that we are not and that we ought to be."[12]

Hegel also criticizes the same sort of diremption in connec-tion with the political conditions and governmental institutions of his day — especially in connection with the rule of the city government of Bern over Waadtland, the constitution of the magistracy of Württemberg, and the constitution of the German Empire.[13] Just as the living spirit of primitive Christianity had vanished from the religion (become positive) of contemporary Orthodoxy, so too in the political sphere "these laws have lost their former life and so [too] the vitality of the present day has not known how to concentrate itself in laws."[14] Juridical and political forms rigidified into positivity turned into an alien force. In these years around 1800, Hegel made a case for the verdict that both — religion and state — had degenerated into sheer mechanisms, into a clockwork, into a machine.[15]

These, then, are the motives stemming from contemporary history that moved Hegel to project reason, in an a priori fashion, as a force that not only differentiates and breaks apart the system of life-conditions, but also reunites them again. In the conflict between Orthodoxy and Enlightenment, the principle of subjectivity engenders positivity, which, however, calls forth the objective need for its own overcoming. Before Hegel can carry out this dialectic of enlightenment, he at least has to demonstrate how the elimination of the positivity is to be explained from the same principle that is responsible for it.

II

In his early writings, Hegel operates with the reconciling power of a reason that cannot be derived without any discontinuity from subjectivity.

He always emphasizes the authoritarian side of self-consciousness when he has in mind the division brought about by reflection. The modern manifestations of the "positive" unmask the principle of subjectivity as one of domination. So it is that the positivity of contemporary religion — which is provoked by the Enlightenment at the same time as it is strengthened by it — and the positivism of morality in general represent the "need of the times" — and "in need, either man is made an object and is oppressed or else must make nature an object and oppress it."[16] This repressive character of reason is universally grounded in the structure of self-relationship, that is, in the relationship of a subject that makes itself an object. To be sure, Christianity had already rid itself of some of the positivity of the Jewish faith; Protestantism had already rid itself of some of the positivity of the Catholic faith. But even in the Kantian philosophy of morality and religion, an element of positivity turns up again — this time as the enlightened element of reason itself. In this connection, Hegel sees the difference between the "wild Moguls," who are subject to blind authority, and the children of modernity, who only obey their duty, not in the difference between slavery and freedom, but only in the fact

that the former has his lord outside himself, while the latter carried his lord inside himself, yet at the same time is his own slave: For the particular — impulses, inclinations, pathological love, sensuous experience, or whatever else it is called — the universal is necessarily and always something alien and objective. There remains a residuum of indestructible positivity which finally shocks us because the content which the universal demand of duty acquires, a specific duty, contains the contradiction of being restricted and universal at the same time and makes the most stubborn claims for its onesidedness.[17]

In the same essay on the "Spirit of Christianity and Its Fate," Hegel works out the concept of a reconciling reason, which does eradicate positivity in more than a pro forma way. Just how this reason makes itself felt by subjects as a power of unification, he explains, for example, in connection with the model of punishment experienced as fate.[18] Hegel now calls a social condition in which all members receive their due and satisfy their needs without injuring the interests of others, "ethical" [sittlich] in contrast to "moral" [moralisch]. A criminal who disturbs such ethical relationships by encroaching upon and oppressing the life of another experiences the power of the life alienated by his deed as a hostile fate. He must perceive as the historical necessity of fate what is actually only the reactive force of a life that has been suppressed and separated off. This force causes the one at fault to suffer until he recognizes in the annihilation of the life of the other the lack in his own self, and in the act of repudiating another's life the estrangement from himself. In this causality of fate the ruptured bond of the ethical totality is brought to consciousness. This dirempted totality can become reconciled only when there arises from the experience of the negativity of divided life a longing for the life that has been lost — and when this experience forces those involved to recognize the denial of their own nature in the split-off existence of the other. Then both parties see through their hardened positions in relation to one another as the result of detachment, of abstraction from their common life-context — and in this context they recognize the basis of their existence.

Hegel, therefore, contrasts the abstract laws of morality with the totally different lawfulness of a concrete context of guilt that comes about through the division of a *presupposed* ethical totality. But these proceedings of a just fate cannot be derived from the principle of subjectivity by way of the concept of an autonomous will, as can the laws of practical reason. The dynamism of fate results instead from the disruption of the conditions of symmetry and of the reciprocal dependencies of an intersubjectively constituted life-context, where one part isolates itself and hence also alienates all other parts from itself and their common life. This act of tearing loose from an intersubjectively shared lifeworld is what first *generates* a subject-object relationship. It is introduced as an alien element, or at least subsequently, into relationships that by nature follow the structure of mutual understanding among subjects — and not the logic of an objectification by a subject. Even the "positive element" thereby takes on a different significance. The absolutizing elevation of something conditioned to the status of the unconditional is traced back no longer to an *overblown* subjectivity that overextends its claims, but rather to an *alienated* subjectivity that has broken with the common life. And the repression that results from this goes back to the disturbance of an intersubjective equilibrium, instead of to the subjugation of a subject transformed into an object.

Hegel cannot obtain the aspect of reconciliation — that is, the reestablishment of the disintegrated totality — from self-consciousness or the reflective relationship of the knowing subject to itself. By having recourse to the intersubjectivity of relationships based on mutual understanding, he fails to achieve the goal essential to the self-grounding of modernity: thinking the positive element in such a way that it can be overcome by the same principle from which it proceeds — precisely by subjectivity.

This outcome is not so astonishing when one considers that the young Hegel elucidated the conditions of life that had congealed to positivity by evoking the correspondence of his own present day to the decadent era of Hellenism. He mirrored his own present in an epoch characterized by the breakdown of classical models. For the fateful reconciliation of modernity in its state of disintegration, he thus presupposed an ethical totality that did not grow from the soil of modernity but was *borrowed* from the idealized past of the primitive Christian communal religiosity and the Greek polis.

Against the authoritarian embodiments of a subject-centered reason, Hegel summons the unifying power of an intersubjectivity that appears under the titles of "love" and "life." The place of the reflective relationship between subject and object is taken by a (in the broadest sense) communicative mediation of subjects. The living spirit is the medium that founds a communality of the sort that one subject can know itself to be one with another subject while still remaining itself. The isolation of subjects then sets in motion the dynamism of a disrupted communication whose inherent telos is the reestablishment of the ethical relationship. This way of construing things might have given impetus to a communication-theoretic retrieval and transformation of the reflective concept of reason developed in the philosophy of the subject. Hegel did not take this path,[19] because up to this point he had developed the idea of an ethical totality along the guidelines of a popular religion in which communicative reason assumed the idealized form of historical communities, such as the primitive Christian community and the Greek polis. *As* popular religion, it is bound up with the ideal features of these classical epochs, not only by way of illustration but *indissolubly*.

The modern age, however, had attained its self-consciousness by way of a reflection that prohibited any systematic recourse to such exemplary pasts. As was to be gleaned from the conflict between Jacobi and Kant and from Fichte's reaction thereto, the opposition of faith and knowledge was displaced into philosophy itself. Hegel starts off his essay on the issue with just this consideration. It forces him to part with the idea that positive religion and reason could be reconciled by way of a reformative renewal of the spirit of primitive Christianity. During the same period, Hegel became familiar with political economy. Here, too, he had to see that the capitalist form of economic commerce had produced a modern society which, under the traditional name of "civil society," represented a completely novel reality, incomparable with the classical forms of the *societas civilis* or the polis. Despite certain continuities with the tradition of Roman Law, Hegel could not appeal to the social condition of the declining Roman Empire for a comparison with the commerce under civil law proper to modern "civil society." Hence, the foil against which the late Roman Empire was first perceived as an instance of decline — that is, the vaunted political freedom of the Athenian city-state — also lost its character as a model for the modern age. In short, the ethical quality of the polis and of primitive Christianity, however powerfully interpreted, could no longer supply the criterion for what was to be demanded of a modernity divided within itself.

This may be the reason why Hegel did not pursue any further the traces of communicative reason that are clearly to be found in his early writings; and why, in his Jena period, he developed a concept of the absolute that allowed him to break away from the Christian-ancient models, while remaining within the bounds of a philosophy of the subject — at the cost, to be sure, of a different dilemma.

III

Before I sketch the philosophical solution for the self-grounding of modernity that Hegel offered, it would make sense to glance backwards at the oldest *Systemprogramm*, which was passed down in his handwriting and which conveys the common conviction of the friends gathered in Frankfurt — Hölderlin, Schelling, and Hegel[20] — for here an additional element is brought into play: art as a power of reconciliation indicative of the future. The religion of reason is supposed to deliver itself up to *art* in order to be shaped into popular religion. The

monotheism of reason and of the heart is supposed to join
itself to the polytheism of the imagination and to fashion a
mythology in the service of ideas: "Before we make the ideas
aesthetical, i.e. mythological, they have no interest for the *people*; and on the other hand, before mythology is rational, the
philosopher must be ashamed of it."[21] The ethical totality,
which suppresses no power and makes possible the equal development of every power, will be inspired by a religion
founded poetically. The sensibility of this mythopoetry can
then take hold of both the people at large and the philosopher,
to the same extent.[22]

This program recalls Schiller's *Ideas Concerning the Aesthetic
Education of Humankind* of 1794;[23] it guided Schelling during
the elaboration of his *System of Transcendental Idealism* of 1800;
and it occupied Hölderlin's thought until the end.[24] However,
Hegel begins to doubt the aesthetic utopia almost immediately.
In the *Differenzschrift* of 1801 he no longer gives it any chance
whatsoever, because in the formation of the self-estranged
spirit, "the deeper, serious reference of living art" could no
longer get consideration.[25] In Jena the poetry of early Romanticism was springing up right before Hegel's eyes, as it were.
He recognized immediately that romantic art was congenial to
the spirit of the age — in its subjectivism, the spirit of modernity was expressed. But as a poetry of diremption it was
hardly called to be the "schoolmistress of mankind"; it did not
lead to the sort of religion of art by which Hegel, together with
Hölderlin and Schelling, had sworn in Frankfurt. Philosophy
could not subordinate itself to it. Rather, philosophy had to
understand itself as the place where reason, as the absolute
power of unification, entered upon the scene. And since this
had assumed the form of a philosophy of reflection in Kant
and Fichte, Hegel, following in the footsteps of Schelling to
begin with, had to try to develop a notion of reason starting
from the philosophy of reflection, that is, from the relation of
the subject to itself — a notion with which he might work
through his experience of crisis and carry out his critique of a
divided modernity.

The point of the intuitions from the days of his youth that
Hegel wanted to conceptualize was that in the modern world

emancipation became transformed into unfreedom because the unshackling power of reflection had become autonomous and now achieved unification only through the violence of a subjugating subjectivity. The modern world suffered from false identities because in day-to-day life as well as in philosophy it posited as absolute something that was conditioned. The *dogmatism* of Kantian philosophy matched the *positivity* of faith and of political institutions, and a bifurcated ethical life in general. It absolutized the self-consciousness of intelligent human beings, which gave to the manifold of a world falling apart "objective coherence and support, substantiality, multiplicity, even actuality and possibility — an objective determinacy that men look to and project."[26] And what holds true for the unity of the subjective and the objective in knowledge, holds equally true for the identity of the finite and the infinite, of the individual and the universal, of freedom and necessity in religion, state, and morality; all these are false identities — "the unification is a violent one; the one subsumes the other *under* itself . . . [T]he identity which should be absolute is incomplete."[27]

The demand for an unforced identity, the need for a unification other than the merely positive one fixed in relations of force, was for Hegel, as we have seen, confirmed by vivid experiences of crisis. If the true identity is in turn supposed to be developed from the approach of the philosophy of reflection, reason does have to be thought of as the relation-to-itself of a subject, but now as a reflection that does not merely impose itself upon another as the absolute power of subjectivity; rather, it finds its existence and movement in nothing else but resisting all absolutizing, that is, in doing away again with every positive element that it brings forth. In place of the abstract antithesis of finite and infinite, therefore, Hegel puts the absolute self-relation of a subject that attains self-consciousness from its own substance and has its unity within itself as the difference between the finite and the infinite. As against Hölderlin and Schelling, this absolute subject should not precede the world process either as being or as intellectual intuition; rather, it constitutes itself only in the process of the relating of finite and infinite to one another and, hence, in the consuming activity of coming-to-itself. The absolute comes to be neither as substance nor as subject; it is apprehended only as the mediating process of a relation-to-self that produces itself free from conditions.[28] This figure of thought, peculiar to Hegel, uses the means of the philosophy of the subject for the purpose of overcoming a subject-centered reason. By means of it, the mature Hegel can convict modernity of its offences without having recourse to anything other than the principle of subjectivity immanent within it. His aesthetics provides a suggestive example of this.

The Frankfurt friends were not alone in setting their hopes on the reconciling power of art. For just as before in France, so now in Germany the problem of the self-grounding of modernity came to consciousness in the battle concerning the normative status of classical art. H. R. Jauss has shown[29] how Friedrich Schlegel and Friedrich Schiller (in their works "On the Study of Greek Philosophy" (1797) and "On Naive and Sentimental Poetry" (1796)) brought into currency the problematic of the French *querelle*, elaborated the special character of modern poetry, and took a position on the dilemma that arose out of the need to bring the normativity of ancient art (recognized by classicists) into harmony with the superiority of modernity. The two authors describe the differences in style in a similar manner — as an opposition between natural and artificial cultivation, between the naive and the sentimental. They oppose modern art as an act of freedom and of reflection to the classical imitation of nature. Schlegel enlarges the boundaries of the beautiful even to the extent of referring to an aesthetics of the ugly that makes room for the piquant and the adventurous, the striking and the novel, the shocking and the loathsome. But whereas Schlegel hesitates to part unambiguously with the classical ideal of art, Schiller produces a ranking of antiquity and modernity on the basis of a philosophy of history. The perfection of naive poetry has indeed become unattainable for the reflective poet of modernity; but instead of this, modern art *strives for* the ideal of a mediated unity with nature — and this is to be "infinitely preferred" to the goal that ancient art *reached* through the beauty of imitated nature.

Schiller had conceptualized the reflective art of Romanticism even before it came into being. Hegel had it right before his eyes when he integrated Schiller's interpretation of modern art through the philosophy of history into his concept of the absolute spirit.[30] In art in general the spirit is said to catch sight of itself as the simultaneous occurrence of self-externalization and return-to-self. Art is the sensuous form in which the absolute is grasped *intuitively*, whereas religion and philosophy afford higher forms in which the absolute already *represents* [*vorstellt*] and *conceives* [*begreift*] itself. Art therefore discovers an inner limit in the sensible character of its medium and finally points beyond the boundaries of its mode of presentation to the absolute. There is an "after" of art.[31] From this perspective, Hegel can displace that ideal of art which, according to Schiller, modern art can only strive for but not attain, into a sphere beyond art where it can be realized as Idea; but then he has to interpret the art of his day as a stage at which, with the romantic form of art, art itself disintegrates.

In this manner, the aesthetic conflict between the ancients and the moderns finds an elegant resolution: Romanticism is the "completion" [*Vollendung*] of art — both in the sense of a subjectivistic disintegration of art into reflection and in the sense of a reflective penetration of a form of presentation of the absolute still tied down to the symbolic. Thus, the question mockingly posed again and again since Hegel — "whether [therefore] such productions in general are still to be called works of art"[32] — can be answered with an intentional ambivalence. As a matter of fact, modern art is decadent, but precisely on this account it has also advanced along the path toward absolute knowledge, whereas classical art maintains its normativity and yet has quite rightly been superseded: "The classical art form has attained the pinnacle of what illustration by art could achieve;"[33] nevertheless, the reflection on the limitation of the sphere of art as such — a limitation that emerged so visibly in the disintegrative tendencies of Romanticism — lacks the naiveté of the classical form.

Hegel takes his leave of the Christian religion in accord with the same model. The parallels between the disintegrative tendencies of art and of religion are clear. Religion reached its absolute inwardness in Protestantism; finally, in the epoch of the Enlightenment, it divided itself off from worldly consciousness: "It no longer gives our age any concern that it knows nothing of God; on the contrary, it is regarded as a mark of the highest intelligence to hold that such knowledge is not even possible."[34] Just as in art, so also in religion, reflection has broken in; substantive faith has collapsed either into indifference or into hypocritical sentimentality. Philosophy salvages the *content* of faith from this atheism by destroying the religious *form*. Philosophy has no content other than religion, but inasmuch as it transforms this content into conceptual knowledge, "nothing is [any longer] justified by faith."[35]

If we pause now for a moment and look back at the course of our thought, it seems that Hegel has reached his goal with this concept of an absolute that overpowers every absolutization and retains as unconditional only the infinite processing of the relation-to-self that swallows up everything finite within itself. Hegel can conceive modernity in terms of its own principle. And in doing this, he establishes philosophy as the power of unification that overcomes all the positivities that have issued from reflection itself — and thereby heals the modern manifestations of disintegration. But this sleek impression is deceiving.

If, that is to say, one compares what Hegel had in mind earlier in his idea of a popular religion with what is left over after the sublation of art into religion and of faith into philosophy, one understands the resignation that comes over Hegel at the end of his philosophy of religion. What philosophical reason is capable of accomplishing is at best a *partial* reconciliation, without the external universality of the kind of public religion that was supposed to make the people rational and philosophy sensible. Instead, the people find themselves abandoned more than ever by their now philosophical priests: "In this respect, philosophy is an isolated sanctuary," as he puts it at this point, "and its ministers form an isolated order of priests, [who] are untroubled by how it goes with the world. However the temporal, empirical present may find its way out of its estrangement, however it may form itself is to be left to it and is not an immediate practical affair and concern of philosophy."[36]

The dialectic of enlightenment, once it had attained its goal, had exhausted the impulse toward a critique of the age that originally set it in motion. This negative result can be seen even more clearly in the construction of the "sublation" of civil society in the state.

IV

In the Aristotelian tradition, the old European concept of politics as a sphere encompassing state and society was carried on without interruption into the nineteenth century. On this view, the economy of "the entire household," a subsistence economy based on agrarian and handicraft production and expanded through local markets, forms the foundation for a comprehensive political order. Social stratification and differential participation in (or exclusion from) political power go hand in hand — the constitution of political authority integrates the society as a whole. This conceptual framework no longer fits modern societies, in which the commodity exchange (organized under civil law) of the capitalist economy has detached itself from the order of political rule. Through the media of exchange value and power, two systems of action that are functionally complementary have been differentiated out. The social system has been separated from the political, a depoliticized economic society has been separated from a bureaucratized state. This development has put too great a strain upon the classical doctrine of politics. Since the end of the eighteenth century, it has split apart into a social theory grounded in political economy on the one hand and a theory of the state inspired by modern natural right on the other.

Hegel stands in the middle of this scientific development. He is the first to bring to expression a conceptual framework that is even terminologically adequate to modern society, in that he separates the political sphere of the state from "civil society." He integrates, as it were, the opposition between modernity and antiquity found in the theory of art into the theory of society. "In civil society each member is his own end, everything else is nothing to him. But except in contact with others he cannot attain the whole compass of his ends, and therefore these others are means to the end of the particular member. A particular end, however, assumes the form of universality through this relation to other people, and it is attained in the simultaneous attainment of the welfare of others."[37] Hegel describes market commerce as an ethically neutralized realm for the strategic pursuit of private, "selfish" interests, whereby this realm grounds a "system of complete interdependence." Under this description, civil society has to appear as an "ethical life split into its extremes and lost," as "an ally of destruction."[38] On the other hand, civil society, "the creation of the modern world,"[39] finds its legitimation in the emancipation of the individual to formal freedom: Unfettering the arbitrariness of needs and of labor is a necessary moment along the way "in order *to educate* subjectivity in its particularity."[40]

Although the term "civil society" comes up only in the late Hegel, in the *Philosophy of Right*, Hegel had already worked out this new concept in his Jena period. In the essay "On the Scientific Mode of Treating Natural Right" (1802), he takes up the topic of political economy in order to analyze "the system of universal and reciprocal depedendency in relation to physical needs and to the labor and the accumulation for these" as a "system of property and right."[41] Already here he confronts the problem of how civil society can be conceived not just as a *sphere of the disintegration* of the substantively ethical dimension, but at the same time, in its negativity, as a *necessary moment within the ethical dimension*. Hegel begins with the fact that the ancient ideal of the state cannot be restored under the conditions of modern, depoliticized society. On the other hand, he steadfastly maintains the idea of the kind of ethical totality that he first dealt with under the name of popular religion. He thus has to mediate the ethical ideal of the ancients, in the respect in which it is superior to the individualism of the modern age, with the realities of social modernity. With the differentiation between state and society — which Hegel in essence already anticipated at that time — he takes his leave of restorative political philosophy as well as of rational natural right. Whereas the former does not get beyond ideas of the substantively ethical dimension, and conceives of the state as an enlarged family relationship, individualistic natural right does not even raise itself up to the idea of the ethical and identifies the emergency state and rational state with the private-law relationships proper to civil society. The peculiar character of the modern state first comes into view, however, when the principle of civil society is conceived as a principle of marketlike — and that means *nonstatelike* — association. For "the principle of modern states has prodigious strength and depth because it allows the principle of subjectivity to progress to its culmination in the extreme of self-subsistent personal particularity, and yet at the same time brings it back to the substantive unity and so maintains this unity in the principle of subjectivity itself."[42]

This formulation depicts the problem of the mediation of state and society; but it also makes clear enough the tendentious solution Hegel suggests. In itself it is not evident that the sphere of the ethical — which is comprised of family, society, the formation of political will, and the governmental apparatus, taken altogether — should *concentrate* itself, that is, come into its own, only *in the state* (or, strictly speaking, in the regime and in its monarchical pinnacle). To begin with, Hegel can do no more than make plausible both that and why antagonisms erupt in the system of needs and of labor, antagonisms that cannot be taken care of by the self-regulation of civil society alone. This he explains in quite an up-to-date way, in terms of "a great mass of humanity sinking below the standard of a certain level of subsistence . . . , which brings along with it the greater facility with which disproportionate wealth is concentrated in a few hands once again."[43] From this there results the functional necessity for an antagonistic society to be embedded within a sphere of the ethical. This universal — which is, to begin with, merely *demanded* — has the twofold form of an ethical absolute that includes society within itself as one of its moments and a "positive universal" that is distinguished from society in order to head off its tendencies toward self-destruction and at the same time to preserve the results of emancipation. Hegel thinks of this positive element as the state; he solves the problem of mediation by the sublation of society in the constitutional monarchy.

This solution is cogent, however, only under the presupposition of an absolute that is conceived on the model of the

relation-to-self of a knowing subject.[44] Already in the Jena
Realphilosophie the figure of self-consciousness moved Hegel to
think of the ethical whole as "the unity of individuality and
universality."[45] For a subject that is related to itself in knowing
itself encounters itself both as a *universal* subject, which stands
over against the world as the totality of possible objects, and at
the same time as an *individual* I, which appears in this world
as a particular entity. If the absolute is then thought of as
infinite subjectivity that is eternally giving birth to objectivity
in order to raise itself out of its ashes into the glory of absolute
knowledge,[46] then the moments of the universal and the individual can be thought of as unified only in the framework of
monological self-knowledge: In the concrete universal, the subject as universal maintains a primacy over the subject as individual. For the sphere of the ethical, the outcome of this logic
is the primacy of the *higher-level subjectivity of the state* over the
subjective freedom of the individual. Dieter Henrich has called
this the "emphatic institutionalism" of the Hegelian philosophy
of right: "The individual will, which Hegel calls subjective, is
totally bound to the institutional order and only justified at all
to the extent that the institutions are one with it."[47]

A different model for the mediation of the universal and
the individual is provided by the *higher-level intersubjectivity of
an uncoerced formation of will* within a communication community existing under constraints toward cooperation: In the universality of an uncoerced consensus arrived at among free and
equal persons, individuals retain a court of appeal that can be
called upon even against particular forms of institutional con-
cretization of the common will. As we have seen, in Hegel's
youthful writings the option of explicating the ethical totality
as a communicative reason embodied in intersubjective life-
contexts was still open. Along this line, a democratic self-organization of society could have taken the place of the monarchical apparatus of state. By way of contrast, the logic of a
subject conceiving itself makes the institutionalism of a strong
state necessary.

But when the "state" of the *Philosophy of Right* gets elevated
to the "reality of the substantive will, to something rational in
and for itself," this has the consequence (already perceived as

provocative by Hegel's contemporaries) that political movements that press beyond the boundaries drawn by philosophy offend against reason itself. Just as the philosophy of religion dismisses in the end the unsatisfied religious needs of the people,[48] so too the philosophy of state withdraws from an unsatisfied political reality. The demand for democratic self-determination — announced so energetically in the July Revolution in Paris and registered so carefully in the Electoral Reform Bill of the English Parliament — evokes an even shriller "note of discord" in the ears of Hegel. This time Hegel is so disturbed by the discrepancy between reason and the historical present that in his writing "On the English Reform Bill," he frankly sides with the Restoration.

V

Hegel had hardly conceptualized the diremption of modernity before the unrest and movement of modernity was ready to explode this concept. The reason for this is that he could carry out his critique of subjectivity only within the framework of the philosophy of the subject. Where the power of division is supposed to be at work only so that the absolute can demonstrate itself as the power of unification, there are no longer any "false" positivities, but only divisions that can *also* claim a relative right. An "emphatic" institutionalism guided Hegel's pen when, in the preface to the *Philosophy of Right*, he declared the real to be rational. Certainly, in the previous lectures from the winter semester of 1819/20, we find the weaker formulation: "What is rational *becomes* real, and what is real *becomes* rational."[49] But even this statement only opens up space for a *pre*decided, *pre*judged present.

Let us recall the problem with which we started. An unprecedented modernity, open to the future, anxious for novelty, can only fashion its criteria out of itself. The only source of normativity that presents itself is the principle of subjectivity from which the very time-consciousness of modernity arose. The philosophy of reflection, which issues from the basic fact of self-consciousness, conceptualizes this principle. Naturally, the negative aspect of a self-sufficient subjectivity that is posited absolutely is also disclosed to the faculty of reflection applied to itself. Hence, the rationality of the understanding, which modernity knows as its possession and recognizes as its only source of obligation, has to be expanded into reason, following in the tracks of the dialectic of enlightenment. But as absolute knowledge, reason assumes a form so overwhelming that it not only solves the initial problem of a self-reassurance of modernity, but solves it *too well*. The question about the genuine self-understanding of modernity gets lost in reason's ironic laughter. For reason has now taken over the place of fate and knows that every event of essential significance has *already* been decided. Thus, Hegel's philosophy satisfies the need of modernity for self-grounding only at the cost of devaluing present-day reality and blunting critique. In the end, philosophy removes all importance from its own present age, destroys interest in it, and deprives it of the calling to self-critical renewal. The problems of the age lose the rank of being provocations because philosophy, perched at the height of its time, has taken away its significance.

In 1802 Hegel introduced the *Critical Journal of Philosophy* with an essay "On the Essence of Philosophical Criticism." In it he distinguishes two kinds of criticism. One is directed against the false positivities of the age; it understands itself as a maieutic of repressed life that pushes out of rigid forms: "If critique does not allow the work and the deed to be valid as the figure of the idea, still it will not deny the quest; thereby the properly scientific interest [!] in stripping away the husk which keeps the inner striving from seeing the light of day."[50] In this we recognize without difficulty the critique practiced by the young Hegel on the positive forces of religion and of the state. Hegel directs *another kind of critique* against the subjective idealism of Kant and Fichte. Of them it is true to say "that the idea of philosophy has been more clearly recognized, but that subjectivity has striven to guard itself against philosophy to the degree that it becomes necessary to save itself."[51] Here it is a question of discovering and laying bare a limited subjectivity which closes itself off to a better insight that has long since been objectively accessible. The Hegel of the *Philosophy of Right* regards critique as justified only in this second version.

Philosophy cannot instruct the world about how it ought to be; only reality as it is is reflected in its concepts. It is no longer aimed critically against reality, but against obscure abstractions shoved between subjective consciousness and an objective reason. After the spirit "executed a sudden jerk" in modernity, after it also found a way out of the aporias of modernity and not only entered into reality but became objective in it, Hegel sees philosophy absolved of the task of confronting with its concept the decadent existence of social and political life. This *blunting of critique* corresponds to a *devaluation of actuality*, from which the servants of philosophy turn away. Modernity as brought to its concept permits a stoic retreat from it.

Hegel is not the first philosopher to belong to the modern age, but he is the first for whom modernity became a problem. In his theory the constellation among modernity, time-consciousness, and rationality becomes visible for the first time. Hegel himself explodes this constellation, because a rationality puffed up into the absolute spirit neutralizes the conditions under which modernity attained a consciousness of itself. Thus, Hegel did not settle the problem of modernity's self-reassurance. As a consequence, in the period after Hegel, only those who grasp reason in a more modest fashion have any options at all in dealing with this problem.

Using a reduced concept of reason, the Young Hegelians hold fast to Hegel's project; they want to conceive and to criticize a modernity divided within itself by way of a *different* dialectic of enlightenment. And they are only one of several parties. The other two parties involved in the debate over the correct understanding of modernity attempt to dissolve the internal connections between modernity, time-consciousness, and rationality; by the same token, they cannot escape the conceptual constraints of this constellation. The party of Neo-conservatives stemming from right Hegelianism yields uncritically to the rampaging dynamism of social modernity, inasmuch as it trivializes the modern consciousness of time and prunes reason back into understanding and rationality back into purposive rationality. Aside from a scientistically independent science, cultural modernity loses any normative character for it. The party of Young Conservatives stemming from

Nietzsche outdoes the dialectical critique of the age, inasmuch as it radicalizes the modern consciousness of time and unmasks reason as absolute purposive rationality, as a form of depersonalized exercise of power. At the same time, it owes to the aesthetically independent avant-garde those unacknowledged norms before which neither cultural nor social modernity can stand up.

Excursus on Schiller's "Letters on the Aesthetic Education of Man"

Schiller's "Letters," which were published in 1795 in *Horen*, and on which he had labored since the summer of 1793, constitute the first programmatic work toward an aesthetic critique of modernity. It anticipates the Frankfurt vision of the Tübingen friends [Schelling, Hegel, and Hölderlin] inasmuch as it carries out its analysis of a modernity divided within itself using the concepts of Kant's philosophy and sketches out an aesthetic utopia that attributes to art a virtually social-revolutionary role. Art is supposed to become effective in place of religion as the unifying power, because it is understood to be a "form of communication" that enters into the intersubjective relationships between people. Schiller conceives of art as a communicative reason that will be realized in the "aesthetic state" of the future.

In the second letter Schiller asks himself the question whether it is not unreasonable to let beauty take precedence over freedom, "when the affairs of the moral world provide an interest that is so much keener, and the spirit of philosophic enquiry is, through the circumstances of time, so vigorously challenged to concern itself with the most perfect of all works of art, the building up of true political freedom?"[1]

The formulation of the question already suggests the answer: art itself is the medium for the education [*Bildung*] of the human race to true political freedom. This self-formative process is related not to the individual but to the collective life-context of the people as a whole: *"Totality* of character must therefore be found in a people that is capable and worthy of exchanging the State of need for the State of freedom" (p. 34). If art is to be able to fulfill its historic task of reconciling a modernity at variance with itself, it must not merely impinge on individuals, but rather transform the forms of life that individuals share. Hence, Schiller stresses the communicative, community-building and solidarity-giving force of art, which is to say, its *public character*. The point of his analysis of the present is that in the modern conditions of life, particular forces could be differentiated and developed only at the cost of the fragmentation of the totality.

Once again the competition of the new with the old affords the starting point for a critical self-reflection on the part of modernity. Even Greek poetry and art "split up human nature and scattered its magnified elements abroad among the glorious assembly of the gods, but not by tearing it in pieces, rather by combining it in varying ways; for the whole of humanity was never lacking in any single god. How completely different it is with us moderns! With us too the image of the race is scattered on an amplified scale among individuals — but in a fragmentary way, not in different combinations, so that you have to go the rounds from individual to individual in order to gather the totality of the human race" (p. 38). Schiller criticizes bourgeois society as a "system of egoism." His choice of words reminds us of the early Marx. The mechanism of an ingenious clockwork furnishes the model for both the reified economic process, which cuts off labor from enjoyment, means from ends, and effort from reward (p. 40), and also the increasingly autonomous apparatus of state, which alienates its citizens, "classifying" them as objects of administration, "subsumed under laws they receive coldly." In the same breath in which he criticizes alienated labor and bureaucracy, Schiller turns against an intellectualized and overspecialized science, removed from everyday problems:

While the speculative spirit strove after imperishable possessions in the realm of ideas, it had to become a stranger in the material world, and relinquish matter for the sake of form. The business spirit, confirmed in a monotonous cycle of objects, and inside these still further restricted by formulas, was forced to see the freedom of the whole snatched from under its eyes, and at the same time to become impoverished in its own sphere. . . . Hence, the abstract thinker very often has a *cold* heart, since he analyzes the impressions that really affect the soul only as a whole; the man of business has very often a narrow heart, because his imagination, confined within the monotonous circle of his profession, cannot expand to unfamiliar modes of representation. (pp. 42–43)

To be sure, Schiller regards these phenomena of alienation only as the unavoidable byproducts of advances that the race could not have achieved in any other way. Schiller shares the confidence of the critical philosophy of history; he makes use of teleological figures of thought without even the qualifications laid down in [Kant's] transcendental philosophy: "Only by individual powers in Man becoming isolated and arrogating to themselves an exclusive right of legislation, do they come into conflict with the truth of things and compel popular opinion, which ordinarily rests with indolent satisfaction upon outward appearance, to penetrate the depth of objects" (p. 43). Just as the business spirit becomes autonomous within the sphere of society, so too does the speculative spirit in the realm of the mind. Two contrary modes of legislation are formed in society and in philosophy. And this abstract opposition between sense and understanding, between the material impulse and the formal impulse, exposes enlightened subjects to a twofold compulsion: the physical compulsion of nature and the moral compulsion of freedom, both of which become all the more intensely felt the more uninhibitedly subjects seek to master nature (outer nature as well as their own inner natures). As a result, the spontaneous and dynamic state, and the rational and ethical state, are alien to one another; they converge only in the effect of suppressing common sense — for "the dynamic state can only make society possible, by curbing Nature through Nature; the ethical State can only make it [morally] necessary, by subjecting the individual to the general will" (pp. 137–138).

For this reason, the realization of reason presents itself to Schiller as the *resurrection of a disintegrated common sense*; it can emerge from neither nature nor freedom alone, but solely from a formative process that has to strip away the contingency of external nature from the physical character of nature, and the freedom of the will from the moral character of freedom, in order to put an end to the conflict between the two modes of legislation (pp. 30–31). The medium for this formative process is art, for it arouses a "middle disposition, in which our nature is constrained neither physically nor morally and yet is active both ways" (p. 99). Whereas modernity becomes ever more deeply entangled, as reason advances, in the conflict between the unleashed system of needs and the abstract principles of morality, art can "confer on" this dichotomized totality a "social character" because it shares in both legislations: "In the middle of the awful realm of powers, and of the sacred realm of laws, the aesthetic creative impulse is building unawares a third joyous realm of play and of appearance, in which it releases man from all the shackles of circumstance and frees him from everything that may be called constraint, whether physical or moral" (pp. 137–138).

With this aesthetic utopia, which remained a point of orientation for Hegel and Marx, as well as for the Hegelian Marxist tradition down to Lukács and Marcuse,[2] Schiller conceived of art as the genuine embodiment of a communicative reason. Of course, Kant's *Critique of Judgment* also provided an entry for a speculative Idealism that could not rest content with the Kantian differentiations between understanding and sense, freedom and necessity, mind and nature, because it perceived in precisely these distinctions the expression of dichotomies inherent in modern life-conditions. But the mediating power of reflective judgment served Schelling and Hegel as the bridge to an intellectual intuition that was to assure itself of absolute identity. Schiller was more modest. He held on to the restricted significance of aesthetic judgment in order to make use of it for a philosophy of history. He thereby tacitly mixed the Kantian with the traditional concept of judgment, which in the Aristotelian tradition (down to Hannah Arendt[3]) never completely lost its connection with the political concept of common sense. So he could conceive of art as primarily a form of communication and assign to it the task of bringing about "harmony in society": "All other forms of communication divide society, because they relate exclusively either to the private sensibility or to the private skillfulness of its individual members, that is, to what distinguishes between one man and another; only the communication of the Beautiful unites society, because it relates to what is common to them all" (p. 138).

Schiller then specifies the ideal form of intersubjectivity in relation to the foils of isolation and mass existence, the two opposite deformations of intersubjectivity. People who hide themselves like troglodytes in caves are robbed in their privatized mode of living of relationships to society as something objective outside themselves; while people who move about nomadically in great hordes miss in their externalized existence the possibility of finding themselves. Schiller finds the right balance between these equally identity-threatening extremes of alienation and fusion in a romantic picture: The aesthetically reconciled society would have to form a structure of communication "where [each] dwells quietly in his own hut, communing with himself and, as soon as he issues from it, with the whole race" (p. 124).

Schiller's aesthetic utopia is, however, not aimed at an aestheticization of living conditions, but at revolutionizing the conditions of mutual understanding. Over against the dissolution of art into life — which the Surrealists later programmatically called for, and the Dadaists and their descendants tried provocatively to achieve — Schiller clings to the autonomy of the pure appearance. Indeed, he expects of the joy in aesthetic appearance a "total revolution" of "the whole mode of perception." But the appearance remains a purely aesthetic one only as long as it forgoes all support from reality. Herbert Marcuse later specified the relationship between art and revolution in a manner similar to Schiller. Since society is reproduced not just in the consciousness of people, but also in their senses, the emancipation of consciousness must be rooted in the emancipation of the senses — "the repressive familiarity with the world of given objects" must "be dissolved." Still, art should not achieve the surrealist imperative; it should not pass over desublimatedly into life: "An end to art is imaginable only if people are no longer capable of distinguishing between true and false, good and evil, beautiful and ugly. That would be the state of complete barbarism at the high point of civilization."[4] The late Marcuse repeats Schiller's warning against an unmediated aestheticization of life: Aesthetic appearance develops reconciling force only as appearance — "only so long as he conscientiously abstains, in theory, from affirming the existence of it, and renounces all attempts, in practice, to bestow existence by means of it" (p. 128).

Behind this warning is concealed already in Schiller the idea of the independent logics of the value spheres of science, morality, and art, an idea that would later be worked out energetically by Emil Lask and Max Weber. These spheres are, as it were, "freed"; they "rejoice in an absolute immunity from human lawlessness [Willkür]. The political legislator can enclose their territory, but he cannot govern within it" (p. 51). If, without any regard for the intrinsic meaning of the cultural sphere, one were to break open the vessels of aesthetic appearance, the contents would have to melt away — there could be no liberating effect from desublimated sense and destructured form. For Schiller an aestheticization of the lifeworld is legitimate only in the sense that art operates as a catalyst, as a form of communication, as a medium within which separated moments are rejoined into an uncoerced totality. The social character of the beautiful and of taste are to be confirmed solely by the fact that art "leads" everything dissociated in modernity — the system of unleashed needs, the bureaucratized state, the abstractions of rational morality and science for experts — "out under the open sky of common sense" (p. 139).

III

Three Perspectives: Left Hegelians, Right Hegelians, and Nietzsche

I

Hegel inaugurated the discourse of modernity. He introduced the theme — the self-critical reassurance of modernity. He established the rules within which the theme can be varied — the dialectic of enlightenment. By elevating contemporary history to the rank of philosophy, he put the eternal in touch with the transitory, the atemporal with what is actually going on. He thereby transformed the character of philosophy in a way that was hitherto unheard of. He intended anything but a break with the philosophical tradition; this only came to consciousness with the next generation.

In 1841 Arnold Ruge wrote in the *Deutsche Jahrbücher*:

In the earliest stage of its historical development, Hegelian philosophy already manifests a character essentially different from *all* previous systems. This philosophy, which was the first to proclaim that philosophy is nothing else than the thought [*Gedanke*] of its age, is also the first to recognize itself as this thought of its age. What earlier philosophies were unconsciously and only abstractly, it is consciously and concretely. Hence, it could well be said of the former that they were only thoughts and remained so; but the latter, the Hegelian, portrays itself as the thought which cannot remain such but . . . has to become deed. In this sense, Hegelian philosophy is the philosophy of revolution, and the last of all philosophies in general. (p. 594)

The discourse of modernity, which we are still conducting down to our own day, is also marked by the consciousness that philosophy is over, no matter whether this is perceived as a productive challenge or only as a provocation. Marx wanted to overcome philosophy in order to realize it. During the same period, Moses Hess published a book bearing the title *The Last Philosophers*. Bruno Bauer spoke about the "catastrophe of metaphysics" and was convinced "that philosophical literature can be regarded as forever closed and finished." To be sure, the destruction or overcoming of metaphysics by Nietzsche and Heidegger meant something other than the sublation [*Aufhebung*] of metaphysics, and the farewell to philosophy by Wittgenstein and Adorno meant something other than the realization of philosophy. And yet these attitudes point back to the break with tradition (Karl Löwith) that occurred when the spirit of the age gained ascendancy over philosophy, when the modern consciousness of time exploded *the form* of philosophical thought.

Kant had already contrasted a "worldly concept" of philosophy with the "academic concept" of philosophy as the system of rational knowledge. He had related the "worldly concept" to what is "necessarily of interest" to everyone. But Hegel was the first to merge a worldly concept of philosophy incorporating a diagnosis of the times together with its academic concept. One might also recognize the change in the general situation of philosophy in the way that the paths of academic and worldly philosophy go their separate ways after Hegel's death. Academic philosophy, established as a specialty, is developed alongside a worldly philosophical literature whose place can no longer be clearly defined in institutional terms. From now on, academic philosophy has to contend with dismissed privatdozents, journalists, and private literary men like Feuerbach, Ruge, Marx, Bauer, and Kierkegaard — as well as with a Nietzsche, who gave up his Basel professorship. Inside the university, it cedes the task of a theoretical self-understanding of modernity to the political and social scientists as well as to ethnology. Moreover, names like Darwin and Freud and trends like positivism, historicism, and pragmatism testify to the fact that in the nineteenth century physics, biology, psychology, and the historical sciences set loose motifs that for the first time influenced the consciousness of the age without the mediation of philosophy.[1]

This situation only changed in the twenties of our own century. Heidegger brought the discourse of modernity into a genuinely philosophical movement of thought once again — surely the title *Being and Time* signals *this*, too. Something similar holds true of the Hegelian Marxists — Lukács, Horkheimer, Adorno — who, with the help of Max Weber, translated *Capital* back into a theory of reification and reestablished the interrupted connection between economics and philosophy. Philosophy also acquired competency for a diagnosis of the times by way of the critique of science that leads from the late Husserl via Bachelard to Foucault. But is *this* still the same philosophy that here, as with Hegel, overcomes its differentiation into academic and worldly concepts? No matter what name it appears under now — whether as fundamental ontology, as critique, as negative dialectics, deconstruction, or genealogy — these pseudonyms are by no means disguises under which the traditional form of philosophy lies hidden; the drapery of philosophical concepts more likely serves as the cloak for a scantily concealed end of philosophy.

Today the situation of consciousness still remains the one brought about by the Young Hegelians when they distanced themselves from Hegel and philosophy in general. And the triumphant gestures of mutually surpassing one another, in which we gladly overlook the fact that we remain contemporaries of the Young Hegelians, have also been in currency since then. Hegel inaugurated the discourse of modernity; the Young Hegelians permanently established it, that is, they freed the idea of a critique nourished on the spirit of modernity from the burden of the Hegelian concept of reason.

We have seen how Hegel, with his emphatic concept of reality as the unity of essence and existence, shoved aside just that element which had to matter most to the modern consciousness — the transitory aspect of the moment, pregnant with meaning, in which the problems of an onrushing future are tangled in knots. The old Hegel omitted precisely the actuality of contemporary history, out of which the need for philosophy was supposed to arise, from the construction of the essential or rational course of events — it became the "accidental," "transient," "insignificant," "fleeting," "stunted" existence of a "bad infinity." Against this concept of a rational reality that is raised up above the facticity, contingency, and actuality of sudden events and oncoming developments, the Young Hegelians (in the wake of Schelling's late philosophy and of Immanuel Hermann Fichte's late Idealism) make a plea for the *importance of existence*. Feuerbach insists on the *sensuous existence* of internal and external nature: Sensitivity and passion testify to the presence of one's own body and to the resistance of the material world. Kierkegaard adheres tenaciously to the *historical existence* of the individual: The authenticity of his existence is confirmed in the concreteness and irreplaceability of an absolutely inward, irrevocable decision of infinite interest. Finally, Marx insists on the *material being* of the economic foundations of our common life: The productive activity and cooperation of socialized individuals are the medium for the historical process of the self-generation of the species. Feuerbach, Kierkegaard, and Marx thus protest against the false mediations, carried out in the realm of mere thought, between subjective and objective nature, between subjective and objective spirit, between objective spirit and absolute knowledge. They insist on the *desublimation* of a spirit that merely draws the real oppositions emerging at a given time into the suction of an absolute relation-to-self, so as to de-actualize them, to transpose them into the mode of the shadowy self-transparency of a remembered past — and to strip them of all seriousness.

At the same time, the Young Hegelians adhere steadfastly to the basic figure of Hegelian thought. They pilfer from the Hegelian *Encyclopedia* the now available wealth of structures in order to make Hegel's gains in differentiation fruitful for radically historical thinking. This thinking lends absolute relevance to the most relative element, that is, the historical moment, without surrendering to the relativism of a scepticism soon to be revived in historicist terms. Karl Löwith, who has described the formation of the new discourse with a certain love-hate,[2] thinks the Young Hegelians deliver themselves over to historical thinking in an *unphilosophical* way: "To want to be oriented by history while standing in its midst would be like wanting to hold on to the waves during a shipwreck."[3] Of course, one has to read this critical characterization correctly: Certainly the

Young Hegelians wanted to get their present-open-to-the-future out from under the dictates of a reason that always knows better; they wanted to win back history as a dimension that makes elbow room for critique in order to respond to the crisis. But they could only hope to gain orientation in action if they did not sacrifice contemporary history to historicism and if they left modernity with a distinctive tie to rationality.[4]

The *other* features of this discourse can also be explained on the premise that suprasubjective and mutually intermeshing processes of learning and unlearning are interwoven in the course of historical events — in addition to radically historical thought, such features as the critique of subject-centered reason, the exposed position of intellectuals, and the responsibility for historical continuity or discontinuity.

II

The parties that have contended about the correct self-understanding of modernity since the days of the Young Hegelians all agree on one point: that a far-reaching process of self-illusion was connected with the learning processes conceptualized in the eighteenth century as "enlightenment." Agreement also exists about the fact that the authoritarian traits of a narrow-minded enlightenment are embedded in the principle of self-consciousness or of subjectivity. That is to say, the self-relating subjectivity purchases self-consciousness only at the price of objectivating internal and external nature. Because the subject has to relate itself constantly to objects both internally and externally in its knowing and acting, it renders itself at once opaque and dependent in the very acts that are supposed to secure self-knowledge and autonomy. This limitation, built into the structure of the relation-to-self, remains unconscious in the process of becoming conscious. From this springs the tendency toward self-glorification and illusionment, that is, toward absolutizing a given level of reflection and emancipation.

In the discourse of modernity, the accusers raise an objection that has not substantially changed from Hegel and Marx down to Nietzsche and Heidegger, from Bataille and Lacan to Foucault and Derrida. The accusation is aimed against a reason grounded in the principle of subjectivity. And it states that this reason denounces and undermines all unconcealed forms of suppression and exploitation, of degradation and alienation, only to set up in their place the unassailable domination of rationality. Because this regime of a subjectivity puffed up into a false absolute transforms the means of consciousness-raising and emancipation into just so many instruments of objectification and control, it fashions for itself an uncanny immunity in the form of a thoroughly concealed domination. The opacity of the iron cage of a reason that has become positive disappears as if in the glittering brightness of a completely transparent crystal palace. All parties are united on this point: *These* glassy facades have to shatter. They are, to be sure, distinguished by the strategies they elect for overcoming the positivism of reason.

Left Hegelian critique, turned toward the practical and aroused for revolution, aimed at mobilizing the historically accumulated potential of reason (awaiting release) against its mutilation, against the one-sided rationalization of the bourgeois world. The *Right Hegelians* followed Hegel in the conviction that the substance of state and religion would compensate for the restlessness of bourgeois society, as soon as the subjectivity of the revolutionary consciousness that incited restlessness yielded to objective insight into the rationality of the status quo. Since the absolutely posited rationality of the understanding [*Verstand*] was summed up in the fanaticism of socialistic ideas, the metacritical insight of the philosophers had now to be established against these false critics. Finally, *Nietzsche* wanted to unmask the dramaturgy of the entire stage-piece in which both — revolutionary hope and the reaction to it — enter on the scene. He removed the dialectical thorn from the critique of a reason centered in the subject and shriveled into purposive rationality; and he related to reason as a whole the way the Young Hegelians did to its sublimations: Reason is *nothing else* than power, than the will to power, which it so radiantly conceals.

The same battle lines are formed with respect to the role of intellectuals, who owe their exposed position to modernity's tie with reason. Like detectives on the trail of reason in history, the philosophers of modernity seek the blind spot where the unconscious nests in consciousness, where forgetting slips into memory, where regression is disguised as progress, and unlearning as a learning process. United in their goal of enlightening the Enlightenment about its narrow-mindedness, these three parties are indeed different in their evaluations of what intellectuals actually do. The *critical critics* see themselves in the role of an avant-garde that ventures out into the unknown terrain of the future and promotes the process of enlightenment. At times they appear as outriders of aesthetic modernism, at other times as political leaders influencing the consciousness of the masses, or in the shape of scattered and isolated individuals who leave behind their messages like letters in a bottle (Horkheimer and Adorno, for example, were thinking this way when they entrusted their *Dialectic of Enlightenment* to a small emigré publisher at the end of the war). In contrast, the *metacritics* see in others, whoever they may be in any given instance, the intellectuals who are the source of the danger of a new priestly domination. Intellectuals undermine the authority of strong institutions and simple traditions; and so they disturb the business of compensation which an uneasy modernity has to settle with itself, which a rationalized society has to conclude with the restraining forces of state and religion. The theory of the "New Class," which neoconservatives today advance against the subversive advocates of a supposedly hostile culture, derives more from the logic of our discourse than from the facts of restratification in the postindustrial occupational system that are brought forth as proof. Finally, those who place themselves in the *tradition of the critique of reason practiced by Nietzsche* criticize no less vehemently the betrayal by the intellectuals, that is, the crimes that avant-gardes, with their good consciences formed by the philosophy of history, have perpetrated in the name of universal human reason. But they do not except themselves from this distantiation; the projective element of the self-hatred of intellectuals is absent here. (So, for instance, I take the incisive observations of Foucault not as a denunciation but as a self-critical rejection of exaggerated claims.[5])

A third characteristic marks the discourse of modernity: Because history is experienced as a crisis-ridden process, the present as a sudden critical branching, and the future as the pressure of unsolved problems, there arises an existentially sharpened consciousness of the danger of *missed decisions* and *neglected* interventions. There arises a perspective from which the present state of affairs sees itself called to account as the past of a future present. There arises the suggestion of a responsibility for the connection of one situation to the next, for the continuation of a process that has shed its naturelike spontaneity and refuses to hold out the promise of any taken-for-granted continuity. It is not only the *philosophers of the deed*, for whom Moses Hess claimed the title of the "party of movement," who were gripped by this nervous tension. It also gripped the "party of inertia" that pressed for sobriety, the party of those who, in the face of a virtually automatic modernization, shifted the burden of proof for any planned intervention to the revolutionaries and movers, the reformers and changers.[6] Of course, the attitudes of these parties toward continuity varied. The broad spectrum reached from Kautsky and the protagonists of the Second International, who saw in the unfolding of the forces of production a guarantee for the evolutionary transition from bourgeois society to socialism, to Karl Korsch, Walter Benjamin, and the Ultraleftists, who could only imagine the revolution as a leap out of the eternally recurring barbarism of prehistory, as an exploding of the continuity of all history. This attitude, inspired by the surrealist consciousness of time, has something in common with the *anarchism* of those who, following Nietzsche, oppose the universal nexus of power and delusion by appealing to ecstatic sovereignty or forgotten Being, to bodily reflexes, local resistance, and the involuntary revolts of a deprived subjective nature.

Briefly, the Young Hegelians took over from Hegel the theme of the self-reassurance of modernity; they set the rules of the controversy with the critique of an excessively subject-centered reason, with the disputes about the exposed position of the intellectuals and the responsibility for the correct measure of revolution and historical continuity. Through their partisanship for philosophy's becoming practical, they provoked two opponents, who abided by the rules of the game and the themes. These opponents did not step outside the discourse in order to make way for the authority of models from the past; the old conservative recourse to religious or metaphysical truth no longer counted — everything that was "old European" was devalued. To the *party of movement* there responded a *party of inertia*, who wanted to retain only the dynamism of bourgeois society. They transformed the tendency to preserve into a neoconservative assent to a mobilization that was occurring anyway. With *Nietzsche and the neoromantics*, a third discourse partner entered the competition. This partner wanted to pull the rug out from under the radicals and the neoconservatives alike. This party struck the subjective genitive from the phrase "critique of reason" by taking critique out of the hands of reason, which the other two parties wanted to hold on to. Thus one outdoes the other.

It might occur to us now to distance ourselves from this discourse as a whole, to declare this nineteenth-century production obsolete. There is no lack of such attempts *on our part* to outdo the game of mutually outdoing. They are easily recognizable by a prefix, by the neologisms formed with the prefix "post." Even on methodological grounds I do not believe that we can distantiate Occidental rationalism, under the hard gaze of a fictive ethnology of the present, into an object of neutral contemplation and simply leap out of the discourse of modernity. So I would like to follow a more trivial path, taking up the ordinary perspective of a participant who is recalling the course of the argument in its rough features for the sake of searching out in each of the three positions their inherent difficulties. This path will not lead us out of the discourse of modernity, but it will perhaps allow its theme to be understood better. In order to do this, I shall have to put up with some drastic oversimplifications. Starting from Marx's critique of Hegel, I want to trace how the transformation of the concept of reflection ends up in the concept of production, how the replacement of "self-consciousness" by "labor" ends up in an aporia within Western Marxism. The metacritique of the Right Hegelians insists with good reason that the degree of system differentiation attained by modern societies cannot simply be turned back. From this tradition there proceeds a neoconservatism that, however, gets into difficulties when it is supposed to explain how the costs and instabilities of an automatic process of modernization can be weighed and balanced.

III The Continuation of the Hegelian Project in the Philosophy of Praxis

We know from many documents just how the first railroads revolutionized the contemporary experience of space and time. The railway did not create the modern consciousness of time; but in the course of the nineteenth century, it literally became the vehicle by which modern time-consciousness gripped the masses. The locomotive became the popular symbol of the dizzying mobilization of all life-conditions that was interpreted as progress. It was no longer only intellectual elites who experienced the release of the lifeworld from boundaries fixed by tradition; in the *Communist Manifesto* Marx could already appeal to everyday experience when he traced "the uninterrupted disturbance of all social conditions, everlasting uncertainty and agitation" back to the "revolution in the modes of production and exchange":

All fixed, fast-frozen relations, with their train of ancient and venerable prejudices and opinions, are swept away, all new-formed ones become antiquated before they can ossify. All that is solid melts into air, all that is holy is profaned, and man is at last compelled to face with sober senses his real conditions of life, and his relations with his kind.[7]

This formulation contains three important implications.

(a) The direction of history can be read, prior to all philosophical considerations, empirically as it were, in the movement of the flow of history: At the point where the *mobilization* and *revolutionizing* of *life-conditions* experience their greatest acceleration, modernization has advanced furthest. That the modern world has its center of gravity in the West, in France and especially in England, is a historical fact for Marx, who fastens upon this criterion of acceleration. He has a clear notion of the contemporaneous existence of noncontemporaneous conditions. He thinks that the German conditions of 1843 do not even reach the year 1789 according to the French calendar. German conditions are "below the level of history"; the political present is already found to be like a "dusty fact in the historical junk room of modern nations."[8]

(b) When modern society develops a dynamism in which everything solid and constant melts into air, no matter what, that is, without the self-conscious intervention of acting subjects, the character of "second nature," or the "positive" element, changes as well. The perspective of the young Hegel is still that of the young Marx: The spell cast by the past over the present has to be broken; only in the communist future will the present rule over the past.[9] The positive element, however, no longer appears in the form of the fossilized and continuous; it requires a theoretical effort to uncover in the permanence of change the positivity of a compulsion to repetition. A revolutionizing of all life-conditions, performed without consciousness, is the illusion that conceals the tendencies toward a truly revolutionary movement. Only what has, since the start of the nineteenth century, been called a *social movement* can liberate mankind from the curse of *movement dictated from without*. Hence, Marx wants to trace "the more or less veiled civil war, raging within existing society, up to the point where that war breaks out into open revolution."[10] He already postulates a social movement long before this assumed a historically discernible shape in the European labor movement.

(c) Behind both the forced mobility of external life-conditions and the emancipatory impetus of social movements, there lies a conspicuous unleashing of productive forces — the "rapid improvement of all instruments of production, . . . the immensely facilitated means of communications."[11] This explains the *sobering* character of the accelerated process of history — the *profaning of all that is holy*. Because the acceleration of history ultimately goes back to the "progress of industry" — which is almost hymnically celebrated in the *Communist Manifesto* — the sphere of civil society takes the place reserved by the young Hegel of the theological and political writings for "the life of the people." In the eyes of the young Hegel, religious Orthodoxy and Enlightenment had become as isolated from the life of the people as the political institutions of the declining German Empire. For Marx, society — "the modern political-social reality" — is the ground from which religious life, philosophy, and the bourgeois state have become detached as abstractions. The critique of religion carried out in the meantime by Feuerbach, David Friedrich Strauss, and Bruno Bauer holds good as the model for the critique of the bourgeois state.

The positivism of self-alienated life is now also sealed by a philosophy of unification which, by its thought-construction of a sublation of civil society in the state, suggests that the reconciliation has already been realized. Consequently, Marx confronts Hegel's *Philosophy of Right* to show what the sublation of civil society would look like if it were to do justice to Hegel's own idea of an ethical totality.[12] Marx's point — which is no surprise to us today — is that the state (which attains its authentic form in the parliamentary systems of the West and not in the Prussian monarchy) by no means embeds an antagonistic society in a sphere of ethical life; the state merely fulfills the functional imperatives of this society and is itself an expression of its ruptured ethical dimension.[13]

This critique opens up a perspective on a type of self-organization of society that eliminates the split between the public and the private person and destroys both the fiction of the sovereignty of the citizen and the alienated existence of human beings subsumed "under the domination of inhuman conditions": "Human emancipation will only be complete when the individual man has absorbed into himself the abstract citizen . . . , when he has recognized and organized his own powers (*forces propres*) as social powers, so that he no longer separates this social power from himself as political power."[14] This perspective has determined praxis philosophy's interpretation of modernity.[15] Praxis philosophy is guided by the intuition that it still makes sense to try to realize the idea of an ethical totality *even* under the functional constraints set by highly complex social systems.

This is why Marx is particularly tenacious in his discussion of paragraph 308 of the *Philosophy of Right*, where Hegel is carrying on a polemic against the notion "that all, as individuals, should share in deliberating and deciding on political matters of general concern." Nevertheless, Marx came to grief in his self-imposed task of explicating the structure of a formation of will that would do justice to the "striving of civil society to create a political existence for itself, or to make its real existence into a political one."[16] The parallels between Hegel and Marx are striking. In their youth, both thinkers hold open the option of using the idea of uncoerced will formation in a communication community existing under constraints of cooperation as a model for the reconciliation of a divided bourgeois society. But later on, both forsake the use of this option, and they do so for similar reasons. Like Hegel, Marx is weighted down by the basic conceptual necessities of the philosophy of the subject. He distances himself in Hegelian fashion from the importance of the "ought" of a merely utopian socialism. Like Hegel, he thereby relies on the power of a dialectic of enlightenment: The same principle that is behind the achievements and the contradictions of modern society is also supposed to explain the transforming movement, the release of the rational potential of this society. However, Marx connects the modernization of society with an increasingly effective exploitation of natural resources and an increasingly intensive build-up of a global network of commerce and communication. This unfettering of productive forces must therefore be traced back to a principle of modernity that is grounded in the practice of a producing subject rather than in the reflection of a knowing subject.

For this purpose, Marx only needs to shift the accent within the model of modern philosophy. This model singles out two equiprimordial subject-object relationships: Just as the knowing subject forms opinions — capable of being true — about something in the objective world, so too the acting subject carries out purposive activities — monitored in regard to their success — to bring about something in the objective world. Between knowing and acting, furthermore, the concept of a formative process exercises a mediating function. Through the medium of knowing and acting, subject and object enter into ever new constellations, in which both are themselves affected and altered in their form. The philosophy of reflection, which accords to knowledge a privileged status, conceives the self-formative process of the spirit (on the model of relation-to-self) as a process of becoming conscious. Praxis philosophy, which accords privileged status to the relationship between the acting subject and manipulable worldly objects, conceives the self-formative process of the species (on the model of self-externalization) as a process of self-creation. For it, not self-consciousness but labor counts as the principle of modernity.

From this principle the technical-scientific forces of production can be derived without further ado. But Marx may not conceive the principle of labor too narrowly if he wants to accommodate in this concept of praxis the rational content of bourgeois culture and thus the criteria in terms of which regression can be identified within progress. Consequently, the young Marx assimilated labor to creative production by the artist, who in his works externalizes his own essential powers and appropriates the product once again in rapt contemplation. Herder and Humboldt had sketched out the ideal of the all-round self-realizing individual; Schiller and the Romantics, Schelling and Hegel had then grounded this expressivist idea of self-formation in an aesthetics of production.[17] Inasmuch as Marx now transfers aesthetic productivity to the "species-life actuated in work," he can conceive social labor as the collective self-realization of the producers.[18] Only this assimilation of labor to a model with normative content allows him to make the decisive differentiations between an *objectification* of essential powers and their *alienation*, between a satisfied praxis that returns to itself and a praxis that is impeded and fragmented.

In alienated labor, the circuit of externalization and appropriation of objectified essential powers is interrupted. The producer is cut off from the enjoyment of his products, in which he could find himself again, and so he is also alienated from himself.

In the exemplary case of wage-labor, the private appropriation of socially produced wealth interrupts the normal circuit of praxis. The relationship of wage-labor transforms the concrete action of labor into an abstract performance of labor, that is, into a functional contribution to the process of capital self-realization, which, so to speak, seizes the dead labor taken from the producer. The asymmetrical exchange of labor power for wages is the mechanism that is supposed to explain why the sphere of essential powers alienated from wage-laborers becomes systemically autonomous. With this assumption of value theory, the aesthetic-expressivist content of the concept of praxis is enlarged to embrace a moral element. For alienated labor no longer deviates merely from the model — conceived in terms of an aesthetic of production — of a self-satisfying praxis, but also from the natural-right model of an exchange of equivalents.

Lastly, however, the concept of praxis is also supposed to include "critical-revolutionary activity," that is to say, the self-conscious political action by which the associated laborers break the capitalist spell of dead over living labor and appropriate their fetishistically alienated essential powers. If, then, the ruptured ethical totality is thought of as alienated labor, and if the latter is supposed to overcome its alienation *from itself,* then emancipatory praxis can proceed from labor itself. Here Marx is entangled in basic conceptual difficulties similar to Hegel's. Praxis philosophy does not afford the means for thinking dead labor as mediatized and *paralyzed intersubjectivity.* It remains a variant of the philosophy of the subject that locates reason in the purposive rationality of the acting subject instead of in the reflection of the knowing subject. But in the relations between an agent and a world of perceptible and manipulable objects, only cognitive-instrumental rationality can come into its own. The unifying power of reason, which is now presented as emancipatory praxis, is not exhausted by this purposive rationality.

The history of Western Marxism has brought to light the basic conceptual difficulties of praxis philosophy and its concept of reason. These result from lack of clarity about the normative foundations of critique. I want at least to call to mind three of these difficulties.

(a) The assimilation of social labor to the model of autonomous activity in the sense of creative self-realization could derive a certain plausibility at most from the romantically transfigured prototype of handicraft activity — for example, the contemporary reform movement of John Ruskin and William Morris, who promoted handmade art, oriented itself by the same model. Nevertheless, the development of industrial labor grew ever more remote from the model of an integral process of making. Even Marx eventually gave up his orientation to the prototype of craftsmanlike praxis taken from the past. But he still inconspicuously incorporated the questionable normative content of this notion of praxis into the premises of his labor theory of value, making it virtually indiscernible. This explains why the concept of labor as well as its inherently purposive rationality has remained so ambiguous in the Marxist tradition.

Accordingly, *the assessment of the forces of production* oscillates from one extreme to the other. Some welcome the development of productive forces, especially scientific-technical progress, as the driving force behind the rationalization of society. They expect the institutions that articulate the division of social power and regulate differential access to the means of production to be revolutionized under the rationalizing pressure emanating from the forces of production. Others mistrust a rationality of dominating nature that fuses with the irrationality of class domination. Science and technology, for Marx an unambiguous potential for emancipation, are turned into an even more effective means of repression for Lukács, Bloch, and Marcuse. Such differences can arise because Marx did not give any account of how the palpable rationality of purposive activity is related to the intuitively intended rationality of a social praxis that is only vaguely represented in the picture of an association of free producers.

(b) A further difficulty results from the abstract antithesis of dead and living labor. If one starts with the concept of alienated labor, the process of production, torn loose from any orientation to use-value, appears as a shadowy form of the expropriated, anonymous, essential powers of the producers. The approach of praxis philosophy suggests that the systemic interconnection between an economy organized along capitalist lines and its governmental complement is a sheer illusion, which is supposed to melt away into nothing with the abolition of the relations of production. From this standpoint, however, all structural differentiations that cannot be brought into the acting subject's horizon of orientation lose their legitimacy at one blow. The question of whether the media-guided subsystems manifest properties that have their own functional value, independently of the class structure, is not even posed. The theory of revolution awakens instead the expectation that in principle all reified, systemically autonomous social relationships can be brought into the horizon of the lifeworld: The dissipated illusion of capital will give back to a lifeworld rigidified under the dictates of the law of value its spontaneity. But if emancipation and reconciliation are represented only in the mode of a *de-differentiation* of hypercomplex conditions of life, it is quite easy for systems theory, in view of stubborn complexities, to dismiss the unifying power of reason as a sheer illusion.

(c) Both difficulties are thus connected to the fact that the normative foundations of praxis philosophy — particularly the potential of the concept of praxis for accomplishing the tasks of a critical social theory — have never been satisfactorily clarified. Both the revaluation of the concept of social labor from the perspective of an aesthetics of production and its moral-practical expansion require a grounding that cannot be furnished by methodologically questionable investigations, be they anthropological or existential-phenomenological. Those who no longer invest the concept of praxis with any more reason than can be gathered from the purposive rationality of goal-directed action and of self-assertion proceed in a more consistent manner.[19]

To be sure, the principle of labor secures for modernity a singular tie with rationality. But praxis philosophy is confronted with the same task as the philosophy of reflection was in its day. The necessity for self-objectification is immanent in the structure of self-externalization, just as it was in the structure of the relation-to-self. Therefore, the formative process of the species is marked by the tendency for laboring individuals, in proportion to their domination of nature, to gain their identity only at the cost of repressing their own inner nature. To dissolve the self-entrapment of a subject-centered reason, Hegel opposed the absolute self-mediation of the spirit to the absolutization of self-consciousness. Praxis philosophy, which abandoned this route with good reason, is not spared from a corresponding problem; it is even more acute for it. For what can it oppose to the instrumental reason of a purposive rationality puffed up into a social totality, if it has to understand itself in materialist fashion as a component and result of this reified relationship — if the compulsion toward objectification invades the citadel of critical reason itself?

Horkheimer and Adorno, in *their* version of the *Dialectic of Enlightenment*, now want only to develop this aporia and not to lead the way out of it any more. Indeed, they meet instrumental reason with a "mindfulness" or "remembrance" [*Eingedenken*] that seeks out the stirrings of a rebellious nature rising up against its instrumentalization. They even have a name for this resistance: mimesis. The name evokes associations that are intended: empathy and imitation. It calls to mind a relationship between persons in which the accommodating, identifying externalization of one partner in relation to the model of the other does not require the sacrifice of that partner's own identity, but preserves dependency and autonomy at once: "The reconciled condition would not annex what is other, but would find its happiness in the fact that this other retains its distance and its difference within the permitted intimacy, that it remains beyond heterogeneity and sameness."[20] But this mimetic capacity evades any conceptual framework fashioned for subject-object relationships alone; so mimesis appears as sheer impulse, the exact antithesis of reason. The critique of instrumental reason can only denounce as tainted what it cannot explain in its taintedness; for it is caught in concepts that make it possible for a subject to control external and internal nature but are not up to endowing an objectified nature with a language to tell us what is being perpetrated upon it by human subjects.[21] By way of his *Negative Dialectics*, Adorno tries to circumscribe what cannot be presented discursively; and with his *Aesthetic Theory*, he seals the surrender of cognitive competency to art. The aesthetic experience that springs from romantic art (and that the young Marx smuggled into his concept of praxis) was radicalized in avant-garde art. Adorno summons this to be the single witness *against* a praxis that in the course of time has buried everything once meant by reason [*Vernunft*] under its debris. Critique can only exhibit, as a kind of exercise, why that mimetic capacity slips out of our theoretical grasp and finds for the present a refuge in the most advanced works of art.

IV The Neoconservative Response to Praxis Philosophy

The neoconservatism that today dominates a scene disappointed by Marxism,[22] especially in the social sciences, is nourished by motifs from Right Hegelianism. Hegel's official disciples — I shall be referring above all to Rosenkranz, Hinrichs, and Oppenheim — are the somewhat older contemporaries of Marx. They did not react directly to Marx but to the challenge of early socialist doctrines and movements in France and England, which were made known in Germany especially by Lorenz von Stein.[23] These Hegelians of the first generation understood themselves as advocates of (a pre-1848) liberalism. They were concerned to extract from Hegel's *Philosophy of Right* space for politically establishing the liberal constitutional state and certain sociopolitical reforms. They shifted the accent between a reason that, conceptually speaking, is the sole reality and the finite forms of its historical manifestation: Empirical conditions are in need of completion because pasts that in themselves have already been superseded are also reproduced in them. Like the Left Hegelians, the Right Hegelians are convinced that "the present apprehended in thought . . . exists not merely theoretically in thought, but is striving to pervade reality practically."[24] They, too, understand the present as the privileged locus of the realization of philosophy: Ideas have to enter into union with existing interests. They, too, see the political substance of the state drawn into the radically temporalized formation of political will.[25]

Nor does the Hegelian Right close its eyes any more than the Left to the conflict potential of bourgeois society.[26] But they reject the communist path decisively. Between the liberal and the socialist disciples of Hegel, there is a disagreement concerning the differentiation of state and society, which one faction fears and the other desires. Marx is convinced that the self-organization of society, which strips public power of its

political character, will bring to an end the very condition that
his opponents argue it would actually bring to pass — namely,
the complete dissolution of a substantive ethical totality into
the unmediated competition of natural interests. Both sides
judge bourgeois society critically, as a state based on need and
understanding rather than reason [*Not- und Verstandesstaat*], a
state that has only the welfare and the subsistence of the individual as its aim, only the labor and enjoyment of the private
person as its content, only the natural will as its principle, and
only the multiplication of needs as its result. The Right Hegelians see in bourgeois society the realization of the principle
of the social as such; and they assert that this principle would
attain absolute dominance if the difference between the political and the social were abolished.[27] Society is from the outset
a sphere of the inequality of natural needs, talents, and skills;
it forms an objective nexus whose functional imperatives inevitably permeate subjective action orientations. All attempts
to introduce the civic principle of equality into society, and to
subject the latter to the democratic formation of will on the
part of the united producers, are doomed to founder on this
structure and this complexity.[28]

Later on, Max Weber took up this critique and sharpened
it; he has been proven correct in his prognosis that the destruction of private capitalism would by no means signify a bursting
of the iron cage of modern industrial labor. In "really existing
socialism," the attempt to dissolve civil society into political
society actually had only its bureaucratization as a result; it only
expanded economic constraint into an administrative control
pervading all realms of life.

On the other hand, the Hegelian Right suffered its shipwreck on account of its trust in the regenerative capacities of
a strong state. Rosenkranz still defended the monarchy because
it alone could secure the neutrality of a regime standing beyond
parties, could tame the antagonism of interests and guarantee
the unity of the particular and the universal. On his view, the
regime has to remain the final court of appeal, since only it
"can read out of the book of public opinion what is necessary."[29]
From here a line of intellectual history leads via Carl Schmitt
to the constitutional law scholars who believed, in reviewing

the ungovernability of the Weimar Republic, that they should justify a total state.[30] Along this strand of tradition, the concept of the substantive state could be transformed into one that is nakedly authoritarian, because in the meantime the hierarchy of subjective, objective, and absolute spirit, which was still appealed to by the Right Hegelians, had been fundamentally destroyed.[31]

After the end of fascism, the Right Hegelians have begun anew by undertaking two revisions. First, they have come to terms with a theory of science that cedes no rights to reason outside the established culture of the understanding comprised by the natural sciences and the *Geisteswissenschaften*; and on the other hand, they have accepted the result of the sociological enlightenment, to the effect that the state (which is functionally interlaced with the capitalist economy) secures the private and professional existence of the individual in industrial society based on the division of labor, but by no means elevates it ethically. Under these premises, such authors as Hans Freyer and Joachim Ritter have revived the ideas of the Hegelian Right.[32] In the process, the theoretical heritage of a recently departed philosophy now fell to the *Geisteswissenschaften*; and to the traditional forces of ethical life, religion, and art there fell the compensatory role that could no longer be entrusted to the state. This altered mode of argumentation created the foundation for combining an affirmative attitude toward social modernity with a simultaneous devaluation of cultural modernity. This pattern of evaluation today marks neoconservative diagnoses of the age in the United States as well as in Germany.[33] I would like to elucidate this with reference to the influential works of Joachim Ritter.

In a first interpretative step, Ritter separates modernity from the time-consciousness through which it acquired its self-understanding. Because modern society reduces human beings to their subjective nature, to enjoyment and labor, and because it reproduces itself by way of the use and exploitation of external nature, Ritter sees the historical essence of modernity in terms of a relationship to nature without any history. The modern world "dissociates historical orders from social being,"[34] and the diremption of social existence is grounded in this lack of history: "What emerges with the modern age is . . . the end of previous history; the future is without relationship to its origins."[35]

This description suggests two consequences. First, social modernity can develop its own evolutionary dynamism apart from the historical transmission of tradition, and this lends it the stability of a second nature. Connected with this idea is the *technocratic* notion that the process of modernization is guided by material constraints that cannot be influenced from without. Second, citizens of the modern world owe their subjective freedom to this abstraction from the orders of history; without the braking effect of the shredded padding of tradition, they would obviously be delivered over without any protection to the functional imperatives of economy and administration. Connected with this is the *historicist* notion that the subjective freedom that arises in the mode of diremption can only be shielded against the risks of total socialization and bureaucratization if the devalued forces of tradition take on a compensatory role. They have been broken in their objective validity; they ought to be preserved as the privatized powers of belief [*Glaubensmächte*] "of personal life, of subjectivity, and of roots."[36] The continuity of history *outwardly* interrupted in modern society is to be preserved in the sphere of *inward* freedom: "Subjectivity has taken over the task of preserving and keeping vitally present the knowledge of God (in the religious sphere), the beautiful (in the aesthetic sphere), and ethical life (as morality), which, in the reification of the world, have become merely subjective as far as their social basis is concerned. That is its greatness and its world-historical office."[37]

Ritter did indeed sense the difficulty in this theory of compensation; but he did not really grasp the paradoxical nature of his desperate, because historically enlightened, traditionalism. How are traditions, for which truly convincing grounds have gone by the boards with the collapse of religious and metaphysical world views, supposed to live on as subjective powers of belief, if only science still has the authority to ground our holding something. Ritter thinks they can win back their

credibility through the medium of being made present once
again by the *Geisteswissenschaften*.

The modern sciences have renounced the rational claims of
the philosophical tradition. With them, the classical relationship between theory and practice is inverted. Natural sciences
that generate technically usable knowledge have become the
reflective form of praxis, the primary force of production.
They belong within the functional context of modern society.
In a somewhat different sense, this holds true of the *Geisteswissenschaften* also. They certainly do not serve the reproduction
of social life; but they do aid in compensating for social deficits.
Modern society needed "an organ to compensate for its lack
of history and to keep open and present the historical and
spiritual world, which it has set aside."[38] But the theoretical
validity of the contents of the *Geisteswissenschaften* can hardly
be grounded with such a reference to their function. Precisely
if, with Ritter, we start from an objectivistic self-understanding
of the *Geisteswissenschaften*, it cannot be seen why the authority
of the scholarly method should be communicated to the contents historically made present in this way. Historicism is itself
an expression of the very problem that, in Ritter's view, it is
supposed to solve. The museumlike effect accomplished by the
Geisteswissenschaften surely does not give back to the devalued
forces of tradition their binding power; the historical form of
heightening the Enlightenment cannot neutralize the distantiating effect that came on the scene with the unhistorically
minded Enlightenment of the eighteenth century.[39]

Joachim Ritter combines a technocratic interpretation of
modern society with a functionalist revaluation of traditional
culture. His neoconservative disciples have drawn from this the
implication that all unpleasant manifestations that do not fit
into the picture of a compensatorily satisfied modernity have
to be attributed to the cultural-revolutionary activity of "pur-
veyors of meaning." They repeat the old Hegel's critique of
the abstractions put between reality as rational and the consciousness of its critics — of course, in an ironic way. For the
subjectivity of the critics is now no longer supposed to arise
from the fact that they are incapable of apprehending a reason
that has been formed into objectivity. Instead, the critics com-

mit the error of still starting from the expectation that reality could ever take on a rational shape. They have to be instructed by their opponents about the fact that scientific progress has become "uninteresting in relation to political ideas." Empirical scientific knowledge leads to technical novelties or sociotechnical recommendations; interpretations by the *Geisteswissenschaften* secure historical continuities. Those who raise more extensive theoretical claims, who pursue philosophy and social theory in the footsteps of the master thinkers, reveal themselves to be intellectuals — seducers in the garb of enlighteners — who share in the priestly domination by the New Class.

From the need for compensation on the part of an unstable social modernity, the neoconservatives draw the further implication that the explosive contents of modern culture must be defused. They turn off the light of a future-oriented time-consciousness, gather together everything cultural that does not enter directly into the welter of the dynamism of modernization, and place it in the perspective of a rememorative preservation. This traditionalism denies all right to the constructive and critical viewpoints afforded by moral universalism, as well as to the creative and subversive powers of avant-garde art. A retrospectively oriented aesthetics[40] renders harmless especially those motifs which first emerged in early Romanticism and which nourished Nietzsche's aesthetically inspired critique of reason.

Nietzsche wanted to explode the framework of Occidental rationalism within which the competitors of Left and Right Hegelianism still moved. His antihumanism, continued by Heidegger and Bataille in two variations, is the real challenge for the discourse of modernity. Next, I want to investigate in Nietzsche just what lies hidden behind the radical gestures of this challenge. If it should turn out that this way also does not seriously lead beyond the philosophy of the subject, we would have to return to the alternative that Hegel left in the lurch back in Jena — to a concept of communicative reason that places the dialectic of enlightenment in a different light. Perhaps the discourse of modernity took the wrong turn at that first crossroads before which the young Marx stood once again when he criticized Hegel.[41]

Excursus on the Obsolescence of the Production Paradigm

As long as the theory of modernity takes its orientation from the basic concepts of the philosophy of reflection — from ideas of knowledge, conscious awareness, self-consciousness — the intrinsic connection with the concept of reason or of rationality is obvious. This is not as evident with the basic concepts of the philosophy of praxis, such as action, self-generation, and labor. To be sure, within the Marxian theory of value the normative contents of the notions of practice and reason, productive activity and rationality, are still intermeshed, though not in a wholly perspicuous fashion. But this linkage began to come loose, in the 1920s at the latest, as theoreticians such as Gramsci, Lukács, Korsch, Horkheimer, and Marcuse brought the originally practical meaning of the critique of reification to bear against the economism and historical objectivism of the Second International. Two different lines of tradition developed within Western Marxism, one determined by the reception of Max Weber, the other by the reception of Husserl and Heidegger. The early Lukács and Critical Theory conceived of reification as rationalization and developed a critical concept of rationality on the basis of a materialistic appropriation of Hegel, but without appealing to the production paradigm *for this purpose.*[1]

On the other hand, reading the Marx of the *Early Writings* in the light of Husserlian phenomenology and developing a concept of practice with normative content, the early Marcuse and later Sartre renewed the production paradigm, which had become washed out in the meantime, but without appealing to a concept of rationality *for this purpose*. These two traditions start to converge only within the paradigm shift from productive activity to communicative action and the reformulation of the concept of the lifeworld in terms of communications theory — a concept that had been connected in a variety of ways with Marx's concept of practice ever since Marcuse's dissertation on the philosophical concept of labor. That is to say, the theory of communicative action establishes an internal relation between practice and rationality. It studies the suppositions of rationality inherent in ordinary communicative practice and conceptualizes the normative content of action oriented to mutual understanding in terms of communicative rationality.[2] This paradigm shift is motivated by, among other things, the fact that the normative foundations of critical social theory could not be demonstrated along either of the two traditional lines. I have analyzed the aporias of Weberian Marxism elsewhere. Here I would like to discuss the difficulties of a Marxism that renews the production paradigm while depending on phenomenology in connection with two works that have come out of the Budapest School. Ironically enough, the late Lukács already paved the way for an anthropological turn and a rehabilitation of the concept of practice in terms of "the world of everyday life."[3]

Husserl introduced the concept of practice as constitution in the context of his analyses of the lifeworld. It was not from the outset tailored to genuinely Marxian problematics. This can be seen, for instance, in the fact that the theories of the everyday world developed independently by Berger and Luckmann (following Schütz) and by Agnes Heller (following Lukács) exhibit striking similarities. The concept of objectification is central to both: "Human expressivity is capable of objectivation, that is, it manifests itself in products of human activity that are available both to their producers and to other men as elements of a common world."[4]

The phrase "human expressivity" refers to the expressivist model (traced by Charles Taylor back to Herder) of a process of generation and self-formation that came to Marx via Hegel, Romanticism, and, naturally, Feuerbach.[5] The model of the externalization and appropriation of essential powers was derived, on the one hand, from dynamizing Aristotle's concept of form — the individual unfolds his essential powers through his own productive activity — and, on the other hand, from the philosophy of reflection's mediation of the Aristotelian concept of form with an aesthetic one — the objectifications in which subjectivity takes on external shape are at the same time the symbolic expression of both a conscious act of creation and an unconscious process of self-formation. The productivity of the creative genius is thus prototypical for an activity in which autonomy and self-realization are united in such a way that the objectification of human essential powers loses the character of violence in relation to both external and internal nature. Berger and Luckmann connect this idea with the world-constituting productivity of Husserl's transcendental consciousness and conceive of the process of social reproduction in accord with this model: "The process by which the externalized products of human activity attain the character of objectivity is objectivation."[6] But objectification designates only a phase in the circular process of externalization, objectivation, appropriation, and reproduction of essential human powers in which creative acts are integrated with the self-formative process of socialized subjects: "Society is a human product. Society is an objective reality. Man is a social product."[7]

Since this lifeworld practice is still interpreted in terms of the philosophy of consciousness as the achievement of a transcendentally basic subjectivity, the normativity of self-reflection is intrinsic to it. A possibility for error is built into the process of becoming conscious: the hypostatization of one's own accomplishments into independently existing entities. Like Feuerbach in his critique of religion, and Kant in his critique of transcendental illusion, the later Husserl employs this figure of thought in his critique of the sciences. Without forcing anything, Berger and Luckmann can link Husserl's concept of objectivism with that of reification: "Reification is the apprehension of the products of human activity as if they were something else than human products — such as facts of nature, results of cosmic laws, or manifestations of divine will. Reification implies that man is capable of forgetting his own authorship of the human world and, further, that the dialectic between man, the producer, and his products is lost *to consciousness*. The reified world is, by definition, a dehumanized world. It is experienced by man as a strange facticity, an *opus alienum* over which he has no control rather than as the *opus proprium* of his own productive activity."[8] The normative content of the expressivist model is reflected in this concept of reification: What we can no longer be aware of as our own product places constraints on our productivity and at the same time inhibits autonomy and self-realization and alienates the subject both from the world and from himself.

When this idealist figure of thought of producing or constituting a world is conceived materialistically, that is, literally as a process of production, all these determinations stemming from the philosophy of reflection can be immediately transposed in a naturalistic manner by praxis philosophers. In this sense, Agnes Heller defines everyday life as "the totality of activities which are performed by individuals for their reproduction and which create at any given time the possibilities for social reproduction."[9] With the materialist interpretation of the idealist concept of practice in terms of constitution (most recently developed by Husserl), "production" is transformed into the expenditure of labor power, "objectivation" into the objectification of labor power, the "appropriation" of what is "produced" into the satisfaction of material needs (that is, consumption). And "reification," which withholds from the producers their externalized essential powers as something alien and removed from their control, becomes material exploitation caused by the privileged appropriation of socially produced wealth and ultimately by private ownership of the means of production. This shift in interpretation certainly has the advantage of relieving the concept of everyday practice of the foundational obligations and methodological difficulties that come with any foundationalist philosophy of consciousness and that Berger and Luckmann inherit by assimilating the concept of practice of the young Marx to the late Husserl.

However, the production paradigm detached from its roots in the philosophy of reflection brings with it at least three new problems when it is called upon to perform similar tasks in social theory: (1) The production paradigm so restricts the concept of practice that the question arises of how the paradigmatic activity-type of labor or the making of products is related to all the other cultural forms of expression of subjects capable of speech and action. Indeed, Agnes Heller counts institutions and linguistic forms of expression as "objectivations proper to the species" no less than labor products in the narrower sense.[10] (2) The production paradigm gives a naturalistic meaning to the concept of practice in such a way that the question arises of whether any normative content at all can still be derived from the metabolic process between society and nature. Heller unabashedly points to the activity of artists and scientists as the still valid model for a creative break with the routines of alienated everyday life.[11] (3) The production paradigm gives the concept of practice such a clear empirical meaning that the question arises of whether it loses its plausibility with the historically foreseeable end of a society based upon labor. Claus Offe opened a recent conference of German sociologists with this question.[12] I will confine myself to the first two difficulties, both of which have been discussed by György Markus.[13]

With regard to the first difficulty, Markus sets out to explain in what sense not merely fabricated things — the instruments and products of the labor process — but *all* the components of a social lifeworld, and even the context of the lifeworld itself, can be understood as objectifications or objectivations of human labor. He develops his argument in three steps. *First,* Markus shows that objective elements of the lifeworld owe their meaning not only to technical rules of production but also to conventions of use. The use-value of any commodity represents not only the labor power expended in the process of production and the skill deployed in it but also the context of its use and the needs whose satisfaction it serves. Just as Heidegger analyzes the tool character of articles of use, Markus emphasizes the social character that attaches like a "natural" property to any object produced for a specific use: "A product is an objectification only in relation to a process of appropriation, that is, in relation to such activities of any individual in which essential conventions of use are followed and interiorized —

in which the social needs and capacities that it embodies (in the quality of its use-value) are once again transformed into vital desires and skills."[14] In other words, not only the productively expended labor powers but also the socially specified possibilities for appropriation by consumers are objectified in objects.

Second, such practice, which is guided by technical rules of production as well as by utilitarian rules of use, is also mediated by norms for the distribution both of the means of production and of the wealth produced. These norms of action ground differential rights and duties and secure motivations for the exercise of differentially distributed social roles, which in turn determine activities, skills, and the satisfaction of needs. Hence, social practice appears under a twofold aspect: on the one hand, as a *process of production and appropriation*, which proceeds in accord with technical-utilitarian rules and signals the relevant level of exchange between society and nature (that is, the state of the forces of production); and on the other hand, as a *process of interaction*, which is regulated by social norms and brings about a selective access to power and wealth (that is, expresses the relations of production). The latter process pours the material content, namely, the given skills and needs, into the specific form of a structure of privileges and fixes the distribution of positions.

Finally, Markus sees the decisive advantage of the production paradigm in the fact that it permits one to conceive of the "unity of this dual process," that is, to understand social practice simultaneously "as labor and as the reproduction of social relations."[15] It is possible to conceive "the unity of processes of interaction between human beings, and between human beings and nature," from the viewpoint of production.[16] This assertion is astonishing because Markus, with all the clarity one might desire, distinguishes between the technical-utilitarian rules for producing and employing products, on the one hand, and rules of social interaction, that is, norms of action dependent upon intersubjective recognition and sanctions, on the other hand. Correlatively, he proposes a clear analytic separation between "technical" and "social" spheres. He leaves no doubt that practice in the sense of the production and useful employment of products has structure-forming effects only for the metabolic process between human beings and nature. By contrast, practice in the sense of norm-governed interaction cannot be analyzed on the model of the productive expenditure of labor power and the consumption of use-values. Production constitutes only an object or a content for normative rules.

According to Markus, in the course of history up to now the technical and the social spheres can only be separated analytically; empirically the two stay indissolubly fused with one another so long as the forces and relations of production mutually determine one another. Thus, Markus uses the fact that the production paradigm is fit solely for the explanation of labor and not for that of interaction to specify just those social formations that will have brought about an institutional division between technical and social spheres. That is, he sees socialism as characterized precisely by the fact that "it reduces material-productive activities to that *which they are and always were in their specificity*, namely, an active-rational metabolism with nature, purely 'technical' activity, beyond both conventions and social domination."[17]

This brings us to the second difficulty, the question concerning the normative content of the concept of practice as interpreted in terms of production. If one imagines the metabolism between human beings and nature as a circular process in which production and consumption mutually stimulate and expand each other, this presents two criteria for evaluating social evolution: the increase in technically useful knowledge, and the differentiation as well as universalization of needs. Both can be subsumed under the functionalist viewpoint of an increase in complexity. Today, however, no one would wish to assert that the quality of life together in society has to improve along with the increasing complexity of social systems. The metabolic model suggested by the production paradigm has as little normative content as the system-environment model that has replaced it in the meantime.

But what happens to the notions of autonomy and self-realization that were built into the conception of a self-formative process in the philosophy of reflection? Can't these normative contents still be recovered by the philosophy of praxis?

As we have seen, Markus makes normative use of the distinction between a practice that is regulated by technical-utilitarian rules under the constraints of external nature and a practice governed by norms of action in which interests, value-orientations, and goals are sedimented as forms of expression of subjective nature.

As a practical goal, he envisions an institutional separation between the technical moment and the social moment, a division between a sphere of external necessity and a sphere in which we are ourselves ultimately responsible for all "necessitites": "The category of labor, given pride of place by critical social theory as distinct from bourgeois economics, attains to practical truth in a socialist society alone; for only here . . . does human becoming occur in virtue of its own goal-conscious action, as determined solely by that social objectivity that people find ready-made for them and that, as nature, imposes limits on their action."[18] This formulation does not express clearly enough that the emancipatory perspective proceeds precisely not from the production paradigm, but from the paradigm of action oriented toward mutual understanding. It is the form of interaction processes that must be altered if one wants to discover practically what the members of a society in any given situation might want and what they should do in their common interest. The following passage is clearer: "Life is (only) rational when people, in awareness of the constraints and restrictions of their life-situation, determine the collective social goals and values of their action through the articulation and dialogical confrontation of their needs."[19] As to how this idea of reason as something that is in fact built into communicative relations, and that can in practice be seized upon, could be grounded — about this a theory committed to the paradigm of production can say nothing.

IV

The Entry into Postmodernity: Nietzsche as a Turning Point

I

Neither Hegel nor his direct disciples on the Left or Right ever wanted to call into question the achievements of modernity from which the modern age drew its pride and self-consciousness. Above all the modern age stood above all under the sign of subjective freedom. This was realized in society as the space secured by civil law for the rational pursuit of one's own interests; in the state, as the in principle equal rights to participation in the formation of political will; in the private sphere, as ethical autonomy and self-realization; finally, in the public sphere related to this private realm, as the formative process that takes place by means of the appropriation of a culture that has become reflective. Even the forms of the absolute and of the objective spirit, looked at from the perspective of the individual, had assumed a structure in which the subjective spirit could emancipate itself from the naturelike spontaneity of the traditional way of life. In the process, the spheres in which the individual led his life as *bourgeois*, *citoyen*, and *homme* thereby grew ever further apart from one another and became self-sufficient. This separation and self-sufficiency, which, considered from the standpoint of philosophy of history, paved the way for emancipation from age-old dependencies, were experienced at the same time as abstraction, as alienation from the totality of an ethical context of life. Once religion had been the unbreakable seal upon this totality; it is not by chance that this seal has been broken.

The religious forces of social integration grew weaker in the wake of a process of enlightenment that is just as little susceptible of being revoked as it was arbitrarily brought about in the first place. One feature of this enlightenment is the irreversibility of learning processes, which is based on the fact that insights cannot be forgotten at will; they can only be repressed or corrected by better insights. Hence, enlightenment can only make good its deficits by radicalized enlightenment; this is why Hegel and his disciples had to place their hope in a dialectic of enlightenment in which reason was validated as an equivalent for the unifying power of religion. They worked out concepts of reason that were supposed to fulfill such a program. We have seen how and why these attempts failed.

Hegel conceived of reason as the reconciling self-knowledge of an absolute spirit; the Hegelian Left, as the liberating appropriation of productively externalized, but withheld, essential powers; the Hegelian Right, as the rememorative compensation for the pain of inevitable diremptions. Hegel's concept proved too strong; the absolute spirit was posited unperturbed, beyond the process of a history open to the future and beyond the unreconciled character of the present. Against the quietistic withdrawal of the priestly caste of philosophers from an unreconciled reality, therefore, the Young Hegelians invoked the profane right of a present that still awaited the realization of philosophical thought. In doing so, they brought to bear a concept of praxis that fell short. This concept only enhanced the force of the absolutized purposive rationality that it was supposed to overcome. Neoconservatives could spell out for praxis philosophy the social complexity that stubbornly asserted itself in the face of all revolutionary hopes. They in turn altered Hegel's concept of reason in such a way that modern society's need for compensation was brought to the fore at the same time as its rationality. But this concept did not reach far enough to make intelligible the compensatory function of a historicism that was supposed to bring traditional forces back to life through the medium of the *Geisteswissenschaften.*

Against this contemporary culture fed from the springs of an antiquarian historiography, Nietzsche brought the modern time-consciousness to bear in a way similar to that in which the Young Hegelians once did against the objectivism of the Hegelian philosophy of history. In the second of his *Untimely Observations*, "On the Advantage and Disadvantage of History for Life," Nietzsche analyzes the fruitlessness of cultural tradition uncoupled from action and shoved into the sphere of interiority. "Knowledge, taken in excess without hunger, even contrary to need, no longer acts as a transforming motive impelling to action and remains hidden in a certain chaotic inner world . . . and so the whole of modern culture is essentially internal. . . . a 'Handbook of Inner Culture for External Barbarians.'"[1] Modern consciousness, overburdened with historical knowledge, has lost "the plastic power of life" that makes human beings able, with their gaze toward the future, to "interpret the past from the standpoint of the highest strength of the present."[2] Because the methodically proceeding *Geisteswissenschaften* are dependent on a false, which is to say unattainable, ideal of objectivity, they neutralize the standards necessary for life and make way for a paralyzing relativism: "Things were different in all ages; it does not matter how you are."[3] They block the capacity "to shatter and dissolve something [past]" from time to time, in order "to enable [us] to live [in the present]."[4] Like the Young Hegelians, Nietzsche senses in the historicist admiration of the "power of history" a tendency that all too easily turns into an admiration of naked success in the style of *Realpolitik*.

With Nietzsche's entrance into the discourse of modernity, the argument shifts, from the ground up. To begin with, reason was conceived as a reconciling self-knowledge, then as a liberating appropriation, and finally as a compensatory remembrance, so that it could emerge as the equivalent for the unifying power of religion and overcome the diremptions of modernity by means of its own driving forces. Three times this attempt to tailor the concept of reason to the program of an intrinsic dialectic of enlightenment miscarried. In the context of this constellation, Nietzsche had no choice but to submit subject-centered reason yet again to an immanent critique — or to give up the program entirely. Nietzsche opts for the second alternative: He renounces a renewed revision of the concept of reason and *bids farewell* to the dialectic of enlightenment. In particular, the historicist deformation of modern conscious-ness, in which it is flooded with arbitrary contents and emptied of everything essential, makes him doubt that modernity could still fashion its criteria out of itself — "for from ourselves we moderns have nothing at all."[5] Indeed Nietzsche turns the thought-figure of the dialectic of enlightenment upon the his-toricist enlightenment as well, but this time with the goal of exploding modernity's husk of reason as such.

Nietzsche uses the ladder of historical reason in order to cast it away at the end and to gain a foothold in myth as the other of reason: "for the origin of historical education — and its inner, quite radical contradiction with the spirit of a 'new age,' a 'modern consciousness' — this origin *must* itself in turn be historically understood, history *must* itself dissolve the problem of history, knowledge *must* turn its sting against itself — this threefold *must* is the imperative of the new spirit of the 'new age' if it really does contain something new, mighty, original and a promise of life."[6] Nietzsche is thinking here of his *Birth of Tragedy*, an investigation, carried out with historical-philol-ogical means, that led him beyond the Alexandrian world and beyond the Roman-Christian world back to the beginnings, back to the "ancient Greek world of the great, the natural and human." On this path, the antiquarian-thinking "latecomers" of modernity are to be transformed into "firstlings" of a post-modern age — a program that Heidegger will take up again in *Being and Time*. For Nietzsche, the starting situation is clear. On the one hand, historical enlightenment only strengthens the now palpable diremptions in the achievements of modern-ity; reason as manifested in the form of a religion of culture no longer develops any synthetic forces that could renew the unifying power of traditional religion. On the other hand, the path of restoration is barred to modernity. The religious-me-taphysical world views of ancient civilizations are themselves already a product of enlightenment; they are *too rational*, there-fore, to be able to provide opposition to the radicalized enlight-enment of modernity.

Like all who leap out of the dialectic of enlightenment, Nietzsche undertakes a conspicuous leveling. Modernity loses its singular status; it constitutes only a last epoch in the far-reaching history of a rationalization initiated by the dissolution of archaic life and the collapse of myth.[7] In Europe, Socrates and Christ, the founders of philosophical thought and of ecclesiastical monotheism, mark this turning point: "The tremendous historical need of our unsatisfied historical culture, the assembling around one of the countless other cultures, the consuming desire for knowledge — what does all this point to, if not to the loss of myth, the loss of the mythical home?"[8] The modern time-consciousness, of course, prohibits any thoughts of regression, of an unmediated return to mythical origins. Only the future constitutes the horizon for the arousal of mythical pasts: "The past always speaks as an oracle: Only as masterbuilders of the future who know the present will you understand it."[9] This *utopian* attitude, directed to the god *who is coming*, distinguishes Nietzsche's undertaking from the reactionary call of "Back to the origins!" Teleological thought that contrasts origin and goal with each other loses its power completely. And because Nietzsche does not negate the modern time-consciousness, but heightens it, he can imagine modern art, which in its most subjective forms of expression drives this time-consciousness to its summit, as the medium in which modernity makes contact with the archaic. Whereas historicism presents us with the world as an exhibition and transforms the contemporaries enjoying it into blasé spectators, only the suprahistorical power of an art consuming itself in actuality can bring salvation for "the true neediness and inner poverty of man."[10]

Here the young Nietzsche has in mind the program of Richard Wagner, who opened his "Essay on Religion and Art" with the statement: "One could say that wherever religion has become artistic, it is left to art to save the core of religion, in that it grasps the mythic symbols (which religion wants to believe are true in a real sense) in terms of their symbolic values, so that the profound truth hidden in them can be recognized through their ideal representation."[11] The religious festival become work of art is supposed, with a culturally revived public sphere, to overcome the inwardness of privately appropriated historical culture. An aesthetically renewed mythology is supposed to relax the forces of social integration consolidated by competitive society. It will decenter modern consciousness and open it to archaic experiences. This art of the future denies that it is the product of an individual artist and establishes "the people itself as the artist of the future."[12] This is why Nietzsche celebrates Wagner as the "Revolutionary of Society" and as the one who overcomes Alexandrian culture. He expects the effect of Dionysian tragedy to go forth from Bayreuth — "that the state and society and, quite generally, the gulfs between man and man give way to an overwhelming feeling of unity leading back to the very heart of nature."[13]

As we know, later on Nietzsche turned away in disgust from the world of the Wagnerian opera. What is more interesting than the personal, political, and aesthetic reasons for this aversion is the philosophical motive that stands behind the question, "What would a music have to be like that would no longer be of Romantic origin (like Wagner's) — but Dionysian?"[14] The idea of a new mythology is of Romantic provenance, and so also is the recourse to Dionysus as the god who is coming. Nietzsche likewise distances himself from the Romantic use of these ideas and proclaims a manifestly more radical version pointing far beyond Wagner. But wherein does the Dionysian differ from the Romantic?

II

In Hegel's "Oldest System Program" of 1796/97, one encounters already the expectation of a new mythology that establishes poetry as the schoolmistress of humanity. There is already apparent here a motif that both Wagner and Nietzsche will later emphasize: In the forms of a revived mythology, art can reacquire the character of a *public* institution and develop the power to regenerate the ethical totality of the nation.[15] In the same sense, Schelling, at the end of his *System of Transcendental Idealism*, tells us that the new mythology "cannot be the invention of an individual poet, but of a new race representing, as it were, One Poet."[16] In his "Discourse on Mythology," Friedrich Schlegel says something similar: "Our poetry lacks a middle point, the way mythology was for the ancients; and everything essential, in which the modern art of poetry falls short of the ancient, may be summarized in the words: We have no mythology. But . . . we are close to obtaining one."[17] Both publications stem from the year 1800 and spin out the idea of a new mythology in different variations.

Hegel's "Oldest System Program" contains as a further motif the notion that with the new mythology art will take the place of philosophy, because aesthetic intuition is "the highest act of reason": "Truth and goodness [are] intimately related only in beauty."[18] This sentence could stand as a motto over Schelling's "System" of 1800. Schelling finds in aesthetic intuition the solution to the puzzle of how the "I" can be made aware of the identity of freedom and necessity, spirit and nature, conscious and unconscious activity in a product it has itself brought forth. "Hence, for the philosopher art is the most sublime, because it opens up for him the sanctuary, where in eternal and primordial union there burns in one flame, as it were, what is sundered in nature and history, and what must eternally flee from itself in life and action as well as in thought."[19] Under the modern conditions of a reflection driven to extremes, art, and not philosophy, guarded the flame of that absolute identity that had once been enkindled in the festival cults of religious communities of faith. Art was to reacquire its public character in the form of a new mythology; it would no longer be merely the organon, but rather the goal and future of philosophy. After its culmination, the latter could flow back into the ocean of poetry from which it had once come. "It is not difficult to say in general what the 'middle term' for the return of science to poetry will be, because such a thing has existed in mythology. . . . But how a new mythology might be able to emerge is a problem whose illumination is to be awaited from the future destinies of the world."[20]

The difference from Hegel is obvious — not speculative reason, but poetry alone can, as soon as it becomes public in the form of a new mythology, replace the unifying power of religion. To be sure, Schelling does erect an entire philosophical system to reach this conclusion. It is speculative reason

itself that surpasses itself through the program of a new mythology. Schlegel sees things differently; he recommends that
the philosopher "[discard] the warlike adornment of the system
and [share] with Homer a dwelling in the temple of the new
poetry."[21] In Schlegel's hands, the new mythology is transformed from a *philosophically grounded* hope into a *messianic*
hope that can be given wing by historical signs — by signs that
tell us "that humanity is struggling with all its power to find its
center. It must pass away . . . or be rejuvenated. . . . Gray Antiquity will become vital again, and the most remote future
culture will already announce itself in premonitions."[22] This
messianic temporalizing of what for Schelling was a well-
founded historical expectation results from the changed status
Schlegel ascribes to speculative reason.

To be sure, this had already had its center of gravity shifted
with Schelling: Reason could no longer take possession of itself
in its own medium of self-reflection; it could only rediscover
itself in the prior medium of art. But what, according to Schelling, can be intuited in the products of art is nevertheless still
reason become objective — the intimate relationship of the
true and the good in the beautiful. Schlegel calls precisely this
unity into question. He adheres to the autonomy of the beautiful in the sense "that it is separate from the true and the
moral, and that it [has] equal rights with these."[23] The new
mythology is to owe its binding force not to some form of art
in which *all* moments of reason are intimately related, but to a
divinatory gift of poetry that is distinct from philosophy and
science, morals and ethics: "For that is the beginning of all
poetry, namely, to overcome the operation and laws of rationally thinking reason and transpose us again into the lovely
confusion of fantasy, into the primordial chaos of human nature, for which I know of no more beautiful symbol than the
abundant throng of the classical gods."[24] Schlegel no longer
understands the new mythology as the rendering sensuous of
reason, the becoming aesthetic of ideas that are supposed to
be joined in this way with the interests of the people. Instead,
only poetry that has become autonomous, that has been
cleansed of associations with theoretical and practical reason,
opens wide the door to the world of the primordial forces of

myth. Modern art alone can communicate with the archaic sources of social integration that have been sealed off within modernity. On this reading, the new mythology demands of a diremepted modernity that it relate to the "primordial chaos" as the other of reason.

If, however, the creation of the new myth lacked the thrust-power of the dialectic of enlightenment, if the expectation "of that grand process of rejuvenation" could no longer be grounded in a philosophy of history, "Romantic messianism" needed a new figure of thought.[25] In this connection, the fact that Dionysus, the driven god of frenzy, of madness, and of ceaseless transformations, undergoes a surprising revulation in early Romanticism is worthy of note.

The cult of Dionysus could become attractive to an age of enlightenment losing confidence in itself because in the Greece of Euripides and of sophistic critique it had kept awake ancient religious traditions. Manfred Frank singles out as the decisive motive the fact that Dionysus, as *the god who is coming*, could attract redemptive hopes to himself.[26] With Semele, a mortal woman, Zeus gave birth to Dionysus, who was persecuted with divine wrath by Hera, Zeus's wife, and ultimately driven into madness. Since then, Dionysus wanders about with a wild herd of Satyrs and Bacchants throughout North Africa and Asia Minor, a "foreign god," as Hölderlin says, who plunges the West into the "night of the gods" and leaves behind nothing but the gift of intoxication. But Dionysus is supposed to return some day, reborn through the mysteries and freed from insanity. He is distinguished from all the other Greek gods as the one who is absent, whose return is still to come. The parallel to Christ was evident; he, too, died and left behind bread and wine until he would himself return.[27] Dionysus, of course, has the peculiarity that in his cultic excesses he preserves, as it were, that fund of social solidarity which was lost to the Christian West along with the archaic forms of religiosity. So Hölderlin connects the Dionysus myth with a unique figure of historical interpretation that could carry a messianic expectation — a figure that has remained influential down to Heidegger. Since its beginnings, the West has remained in the night of the remoteness of God or of the forgetfulness of being. The god of the future will renew the lost, primordial forces; and the approaching god makes his arrival sensible through his absence, brought painfully to consciousness by "the greatest remoteness." By making those abandoned feel more urgently what was withdrawn from them, he announces his return all the more convincingly: In the greatest peril, what brings salvation waxes as well.[28]

Nietzsche is not original in his Dionysian treatment of history. The historical thesis about the origin of the Greek tragic chorus in the ancient Greek cult of Dionysus acquires its critical point for modernity from a context that was already well developed in early Romanticism. Why Nietzsche distances himself from this Romantic background thus stands all the more in need of explanation. The key is the equation of Dionysus and Christ, which was not only taken up by Hölderlin but was entertained as well by Novalis, Schelling, Creuzer — by the whole early Romantic reception of myth. This identification of the frenzied wine-god with the Christian savior-god is only possible because Romantic messianism aimed at a *rejuvenation* of, but not a departure from, the West. The new mythology was supposed to restore a lost solidarity but not reject the emancipation that the separation from the primordial mythical forces also brought about for the individual as individuated in the presence of the One God.[29] In Romanticism, the recourse to Dionysus was supposed to open up only that dimension of public freedom in which Christian promises were to be fulfilled in a this-worldly manner, so that the principle of subjectivity — deepened and at the same time authoritatively brought to dominance by the Reformation and the Enlightenment — could lose its narrowness.

III

The mature Nietzsche recognizes that Wagner, in whom modernity is almost "summed up," shared with the Romantics the perspective on the still-to-come *fulfillment* of the modern age. Precisely Wagner pushes Nietzsche to "disappointment with everything left for us modern men to be enthusiastic about," because he, a desperate decadent, "suddenly . . . bowed down

before the Christian cross."[30] Thus, Wagner remains captive to
the Romantic union of the Dionysian with the Christian. Just
as little as the Romantics does he esteem in Dionysus the demigod who offers radical redemption from the curse of identity, who rescinds the principle of individuation, who validates
the polymorphous versus the unity of the transcendent God,
and anomie versus precepts. In Apollo, the Greeks divinized
individuation, the observance of the limits of the individual.
But Apollonian beauty and moderation only hid the Titanic
and barbaric underground that erupted in the ecstatic tone of
the Dionysian festival: "The individual, with all his restraint
and proportion, succumbed here to the self-oblivion of the
Dionysian states, and forgot the precepts of Apollo."[31]
Nietzsche recalls Schopenhauer's depiction of the "terror which
seizes man when he suddenly begins to doubt the cognitive
form of phenomena, because the principle of sufficient reason
. . . seems to suffer an exception. If we add to this terror the
blissful ecstasy that wells from the innermost depths of man,
indeed of nature, at this collapse of the *principii individuationis*,
we steal a glimpse into the nature of the Dionysian."[32]

But Nietzsche was not only the disciple of Schopenhauer; he
was the contemporary of Mallarmé and the Symbolists, an
advocate of *l'art pour l'art*. Therefore, as an ingredient in the
description of the Dionysian — as the heightening of the subjective to the point of utter self-oblivion — there is also the
experience (radicalized once again in comparison to the Romantics) of contemporary art. What Nietzsche calls the "aesthetic phenomenon" is disclosed in the concentrated dealings
with itself of a decentered subjectivity set free from everyday
conventions of perceiving and acting. Only when the subject
loses itself, when it sheers off from pragmatic experience in
space and time, when it is stirred by the shock of the sudden,
when it considers "the longing for true presence" (Octavio Paz)
fulfilled and, oblivious to itself, is transported by the moment;
only when the categories of intelligent doing and thinking are
upset, the norms of daily life have broken down, the illusions
of habitual normality have collapsed — only then does the
world of the unforseen and the absolutely astonishing open
up, the realm of aesthetic illusion, which neither hides nor

reveals, is neither appearance nor essence, but nothing other than surface. Nietzsche continues the Romantic purification of the aesthetic phenomenon from all theoretical and practical associations.[33] In the aesthetic experience, the Dionysian reality is shut off by a "chasm of forgetfulness" against the world of theoretical knowledge and moral action, against the everyday. Art opens access to the Dionysian only at the cost of ecstasy — at the cost of a painful de-differentiation, a de-delimitation of the individual, a merging with amorphous nature within and without.

Consequently, the mythless human beings of modernity can expect from the new mythology only a kind of redemption that eliminates all mediations. This Schopenhauerian conception of the Dionysian principle gives a twist to the program of the new mythology that was foreign to Romantic messianism — it is now a question of totally turning away from the nihilistic void of modernity. With Nietzsche, the criticism of modernity dispenses for the first time with its retention of an emancipatory content. Subject-centered reason is confronted with reason's absolute other. And as a counterauthority to reason, Nietzsche appeals to experiences that are displaced back into the archaic realm — experiences of self-disclosure of a decentered subjectivity, liberated from all constraints of cognition and purposive activity, all imperatives of utility and morality. A "break-up of the principle of individuation" becomes the escape route from modernity. Of course, if it is going to amount to more than a citation of Schopenhauer, this can only gain credibility through the most advanced art of modernity. Nietzsche can blind himself to this contradiction because he splits off the rational moment that comes to expression in the inner logic of avant-garde art from any connection with theoretical and practical reason and shoves it into the realm of metaphysically transfigured irrationality.

Already in the *Birth of Tragedy*, standing *behind* art is life. We already find there the peculiar theodicy according to which the world can be justified only as an aesthetic phenomenon.[34] Profound cruelty and pain, as well as joy and delight, count as the projections of a creative spirit who surrenders himself unhesitatingly to the diffuse enjoyment of the power and arbitrariness of his illusory appearances. The world appears as a network of distortions and interpretations for which no intention and no text provides a basis. Together with a sensibility that allows itself to be affected in as many different ways as possible, the power to create meaning constitutes the authentic core of the *will to power*. This is at the same time a *will to illusion*, a will to simplification, to masks, to the superficial; art counts as man's genuine metaphysical activity, because life itself is based on illusion, deception, optics, the necessity of the perspectival and of error.[35]

Of course, Nietzsche can shape these ideas into a "metaphysics for artists" only if he reduces everything that is and should be to the aesthetic dimension. There can be neither ontic nor moral phenomena — at least in the sense in which Nietzsche speaks of aesthetic phenomena. The famous sketches for a pragmatic theory of knowledge and for a natural history of morality that trace the distinctions between "true" and "false," "good" and "evil," back to preferences for what serves life and for the noble, are meant to demonstrate this.[36] According to this analysis, behind apparently universal normative claims lie hidden the subjective power claims of value appraisals. Even in these power claims, it is not the strategic wills of individual subjects that obtain. Instead, the transsubjective will to power is manifested in the ebb and flow of an anonymous process of subjugation.

The theory of a will to power operating in every event provides the framework within which Nietzsche explains how the fictions of a world comprised of entities and of goods arise, as well as the illusory identities of knowing and morally acting subjects; how, with the soul and self-consciousness, a sphere of inwardness is constituted; how metaphysics, science, and the ascetic ideal achieved dominance — and, finally, how subject-centered reason owes this entire inventory to the occurrence of an unsalutary, masochistic inversion of the very core of the will to power. The nihilistic domination of subject-centered reason is conceived as the result and expression of a perversion of the will to power.

Since, then, the undistorted will to power is merely a metaphysical conception of the Dionysian principle, Nietzsche can grasp the nihilism of the present age as the night of the remoteness of the gods, in which the proximity of the absent god is proclaimed. His being "apart" and "beyond" is misunderstood by the people as a flight from reality — "while it is only his absorption, immersion, penetration into reality, so that, when he one day emerges into the light, he may bring home the redemption of this reality."[37] Nietzsche designates the time of the return of the Anti-Christ as "the bell-stroke of noon" — in a remarkable agreement with the aesthetic time-consciousness of Baudelaire. In the hour of Pan the day holds its breath, time stands still — the transitory moment is wed to eternity.

Nietzsche owes his concept of modernity, developed in terms of his theory of power, to an unmasking critique of reason that sets itself outside the horizon of reason. This critique has a certain suggestiveness because it appeals, at least implicitly, to criteria borrowed from the basic experiences of aesthetic modernity. Nietzsche enthrones taste, "the Yes and the No of the palate," as the organ of a knowledge beyond true and false, beyond good and evil. But he cannot legitimate the criteria of aesthetic judgment that he holds on to because he transposes aesthetic experience into the archaic, because he does not recognize as a moment of reason the critical capacity for assessing value that was sharpened through dealing with modern art — a moment that is still at least procedurally connected with objectifying knowledge and moral insight in the processes of providing argumentative grounds. The aesthetic domain, as the gateway to the Dionysian, is hypostatized instead into the other of reason. The disclosures of power theory get caught up in the dilemma of a self-enclosed critique of reason that has become total. In a retrospective glance back at the *Birth of Tragedy*, Nietzsche admits the youthful naiveté of his attempt "to present science in the context of art, to look at science in the perspective of the artist."[38] Even at an older age, though, he could muster no clarity about what it means to pursue a critique of ideology that attacks its own foundations.[39] In the end, he oscillates between two strategies.

On the one hand, Nietzsche sees the possibility of an artistic contemplation of the world carried out with scholarly tools but in an antimetaphysical, antiromantic, pessimistic, and sceptical attitude. Because it serves the philosophy of the will to power, a historical science of this kind is supposed to be able to escape the illusion of belief in truth.[40] Then, of course, the validity of that philosophy would have to be presupposed. That is why Nietzsche must, on the other hand, assert the possibility of a critique of metaphysics that digs up the roots of metaphysical thought without, however, itself giving up philosophy. He proclaims Dionysus a philosopher and himself the last disciple and initiate of this god who does philosophy.[41]

Nietzsche's critique of modernity has been continued along both paths. The sceptical scholar who wants to unmask the perversion of the will to power, the revolt of reactionary forces, and the emergence of a subject-centered reason by using anthropological, psychological, and historical methods has successors in Bataille, Lacan, and Foucault; the initiate-critic of metaphysics who pretends to a unique kind of knowledge and pursues the rise of the philosophy of the subject back to its pre-Socratic beginnings has successors in Heidegger and Derrida.

IV

Heidegger wants to take over the essential motifs of Nietzsche's Dionysian messianism while avoiding the aporias of a self-enclosed critique of reason. Nietzsche, operating in a "scholarly" mode, wanted to catapult modern thinking beyond itself by way of a genealogy of the belief in truth and of the ascetic ideal; Heidegger, who espies an uncleansed remnant of enlightenment in this power-theoretical strategy of unmasking, would rather stick with Nietzsche the "philosopher." The goal that Nietzsche pursued with a totalized, self-consuming critique of ideology, Heidegger wants to reach through a destruction of Western metaphysics that proceeds immanently. Nietzsche had spanned the arch of the Dionysian event between Greek tragedy and a new mythology. Heidegger's later philosophy can be understood as an attempt to displace this even from the area of an aesthetically revitalized mythology to that of philosophy.[42] Heidegger is faced first of all with the task of putting philosophy in the place that art occupies in Nietzsche (as a countermovement to nihilism), in order then to transform philosophical thinking in such a way that it can become the area for the ossification and the renewal of the Dionysian forces — he wants to describe the emergence and overcoming of nihilism as the beginning and end of metaphysics.

Heidegger's first Nietzsche lecture is entitled "The Will to Power as Art." It is based above all on the posthumous fragments, which in their compilation by Elisabeth Foerster-Nietzsche were puffed up into an unwritten magnum opus, *The Will to Power*.[43] Heidegger attempts to substantiate the thesis that "Nietzsche moves in the orbit of Western philosophy."[44] He does call the thinker who "in his metaphysics . . . reverts to the beginnings of Western philosophy"[45] and leads the countermovement to nihilism an "artist-philosopher." However, Nietzsche's ideas about the saving power of art are supposed to be "aesthetic" only "at first glance" but "metaphysical . . . according to [their] innermost will."[46] Heidegger's classicist understanding of art requires this interpretation. Like Hegel, he is convinced that art reached its essential end with Romanticism. A comparison with Walter Benjamin would show how little Heidegger was influenced by genuine experiences of avant-garde art. And so he was also unable to grasp why it is that only a subjectivistically heightened and radically differentiated art, which consistently develops the meaning proper to the aesthetic dimension out of the self-experience of a decentered subjectivity, recommends itself as the inaugurator of a new mythology.[47] Thus, he has little difficulty in imagining the leveling of the "aesthetic phenomenon" and the assimilation of art to metaphysics. The beautiful allows Being to show forth: "Both beauty and truth are related to Being, indeed by way of unveiling the Being of beings."[48]

Later on this will read: The poet proclaims the holy, which reveals itself to the thinker. Poetry and thinking are of course interdependent, but in the end it is poetry that stems from thinking in its initial stages.[49]

Once art has been ontologized in this way,[50] philosophy must again take on the task that it had handed over to art in Romanticism, namely, creating an equivalent for the unifying power of religion, in order effectively to counter the diremptions of modernity. Nietzsche had entrusted the overcoming of nihilism to the aesthetically revived Dionysian myth. Heidegger projects this Dionysian happening onto the screen of a critique of metaphysics, which thereby takes on world-historical significance.

Now it is Being that has withdrawn itself from beings and that announces its indeterminate arrival by an absence made palpable and by the mounting pain of deprival. Thinking, which stalks Being through the destiny of the forgetfulness of Being to which Western philosophy has been doomed, has a catalytic function. The thinking that simultaneously emerges out of metaphysics, inquires into the origins of metaphysics, and transcends the limits of metaphysics from inside no longer shares in the self-confidence of a reason boasting of its own autonomy. To be sure, the different strata within which Being is buried have to be excavated. But the work of destruction, in contrast with the power of reflection, serves to train one in a new heteronomy. It focuses its energy singlemindedly on the self-overcoming and the self-renunciation of a subjectivity that has to learn perseverance and is supposed to dissolve in humility. As for reason itself, it can only be exercised in the baleful activity of forgetting and expelling. Even memory lacks the power to promote the return of what has been exiled. As a result, Being can only come about as a fateful dispensation; those who are in need can at most hold themselves open and prepared for it. Heidegger's critique of reason ends in the distancing radicality of a change in orientation that is all-pervasive but empty of content — away from autonomy and toward a self-surrender to Being, which supposedly leaves behind the opposition between autonomy and heteronomy.

Bataille's Nietzsche-inspired critique of reason takes another tack. It, too employs the concept of the sacred for those decentering experiences of ambivalent rapture in which a hardened subjectivity transgresses its boundaries. The actions of religious sacrifice and of erotic fusion, in which the subject seeks to be "loosed from its relatedness to the I" and to make room for a reestablished "continuity of Being," are exemplary for him.[51] Bataille, too, pursues the traces of a primordial force that could heal the discontinuity or rift between the rationally disciplined world of work and the outlawed other of reason. He imagines this overpowering return to a lost continuity as the eruption of elements opposed to reason, as a breath-taking act of self-de-limiting. In this process of dissolution, the monadically closed-off subjectivity of self-assertive and mutually objectifying individuals is dispossessed and cast down into the abyss.

Bataille does not approach this Dionysian violence directed against the principle of individuation by way of the restrained path of a self-overcoming of knowledge that is caught up in metaphysics, but by way of an empirical and analytic grasp of phenomena associated with the self-transgression and self-extinction of the purposive-rational subject. He is obviously interested in the Bacchanalian traits of an orgiastic will to power — the creative and exuberant activity of a mighty will manifested as much in play, dance, rapture, and giddiness as in the kinds of stimulation aroused by destruction, by viewing pain that incites cruelty and pleasure, by witnessing violent death. The curious gaze with which Bataille patiently dissects the limit experiences of ritual sacrifice and sexual love is guided and informed by an aesthetics of terror. The years-long follower and later opponent of André Breton does not, like Heidegger, pass by the foundational aesthetic experience of Nietzsche, but follows out the radicalization of this experience into surrealism. Like one possessed, Bataille investigates those ambivalent, offputting emotional reactions of shame, loathing, shock; he analyzes the sadistic satisfaction released by sudden, injurious, intrusive, violently intervening impressions. In these explosive stimuli are joined the countervailing tendencies of longing and of horrified withdrawal into paralyzing fascination. Loathing, disgust, and horror fuse with lust, attraction, and craving. The consciousness exposed to these rending ambivalences enters a sphere beyond comprehension. The Surrealists wanted to arouse this state of shock with aggressively employed aesthetic means. Bataille pursues the traces of this "profane illumination" (Benjamin) right back to the taboos regarding the human corpse, cannibalism, naked bodies, menstrual bleeding, incest, and so on.

These anthropological investigations, which we shall consider below, provide the starting point for a theory of sovereignty. Just as Nietzsche did in the *Genealogy of Morals*, so Bataille studies the demarcating and ever fuller extirpating of everything heterogeneous by which the modern world of purposively rational labor, consumption, and domination is constituted. He does not avoid constructing a history of Western reason which, like Heidegger's critique of metaphysics, portrays modernity as an epoch of depletion. But in Bataille's account the heterogeneous, extraneous elements appear not in the guise of an apocalyptically fateful dispensation, mystically tacked on, but as subversive forces that can only be convulsively released if they are unfettered within a libertarian socialistic society.

Paradoxically, Bataille fights for the rights of this renewal of the sacral with the tools of scientific analysis. By no means does he regard methodical thought as suspect. "No one [can] pose the problem of religion if he starts out from arbitrary solutions not allowed by the present *climate of exactitude*. Insofar as I talk about internal experience and not about objects, I am not a man of science; but the moment I talk about objects, I do so with the unavoidable rigor of the scientist."[52]

Bataille is separated from Heidegger both by his access to a genuinely aesthetic experience (from which he draws the concept of the sacred) and by his respect for the scientific character of the knowledge that he would like to enlist in the service of his analysis of the sacred. At the same time, if one considers their respective contributions to the philosophical discourse of modernity, there are parallels between the two thinkers. The structural similarities can be explained by the fact that Heidegger and Bataille want to meet the same challenge in the wake of Nietzsche. They both want to carry out a radical critique of reason — one that attacks the roots of the critique itself. Similar constraints on argumentation result from this agreement about the posing of the problem.

To begin with, the object of the critique has to be determined sharply enough so that we can recognize in it subject-centered reason as the principle of modernity. Heidegger picks the objectifying thought of the modern sciences as his point of departure; Bataille, the purposively rational behavior of the capitalist enterprise and of the bureaucratized state apparatus as his. The one, Heidegger, investigates the basic ontological concepts of the philosophy of consciousness in order to lay bare the will to technical control of objectified processes as the underlying impulse governing the train of thought from Descartes to Nietzsche. Subjectivity and reification distort our view of the unmanipulable. The other, Bataille, investigates the imperatives to utility and efficiency, to which work and consumption have been ever more exclusively subordinated, in order to identify within industrial production an inherent tendency toward self-destruction in all modern societies. Rationalized societies hinder the unproductive spending and generous squandering of accumulated wealth.

Since such totalizing critique of reason has given up all hope of a dialectic of enlightenment, what falls under this totalizing critique is so comprehensive that the other of reason, the counterforce of *Being* or of *sovereignty*, can no longer be conceived of only as repressed and split-off moments of reason itself. Consequently, like Nietzsche, Heidegger and Bataille must reach beyond the origins of Western history back to archaic times in order to rediscover the traces of the Dionysian, whether in the thought of the pre-Socratics or in the state of excitement surrounding sacred rites of sacrifice. It is here that they have to identify those buried, rationalized-away experiences that are to fill the abstract terms "Being" and "sovereignty" with life. Both are just names to start with. They have to be introduced as concepts contrasting with reason in such a way that they remain resistant to any attempts at rational incorporation. "Being" is defined as that which has *withdrawn* itself from the totality of beings that can be grasped and known as something in the objective world; "sovereignty" as that which has been *excluded* from the world of the useful and calculable. These primordial forces appear in images of a plenitude that is to be bestowed but is now withheld, missing — of a wealth that awaits expending. Whereas reason is characterized by calculating manipulation and valorization, its counterpart can only be portrayed negatively, as what is simply unmanipulable and not valorizable — as a medium into which the subject can plunge if it gives itself up and transcends itself *as* subject.

The two moments — that of reason and that of its other — stand not in opposition pointing to a dialectical *Aufhebung*, but in a relationship of tension characterized by mutual repugnance and exclusion. Their relationship is not constituted by the dynamics of repression that could be reversed by countervailing processes of self-reflection or of enlightened practice. Instead, reason is delivered over to the dynamics of withdrawal and of retreat, of expulsion and proscription, with such impotence that narrow-minded subjectivity can never, by its own powers of anamnesis and of analysis, reach what escapes it or holds itself at a remove from it. Self-reflection is sealed off from the other of reason. There reigns a play of forces of a metahistorical or cosmic sort, which calls for an effort of a *different* observance altogether. In Heidegger, the paradoxical effort of a reason transcending itself takes on the chiliastic form of an urgent meditation conjuring up the dispensation of Being, whereas, with his heterological sociology of the sacred, Bataille promises himself enlightenment about, but ultimately no influence over, the transcendent play of forces.

Both authors develop their theory by way of a narrative reconstruction of the history of Western reason. Heidegger, who interprets reason as self-consciousness in line with motifs from the philosophy of the subject, conceives of nihilism as the expression of a technical world-mastery loosed in totalitarian fashion. The ill fate of metaphysical thought is supposed to culminate in this way — a thought that was set in motion by the question about Being, but that more and more loses sight of what is essential in view of the totality of reified entities. Bataille, who interprets reason as labor in line with motifs from praxis philosophy, conceives of nihilism as the consequence of a compulsive accumulation process. The ill fate of surplus production that at first still served celebratory and sovereign exuberance, but then uses up ever more resources for the purpose of just raising the level of productivity, culminates in this way: Extravagance changes into productive consumption and removes the basis for creative, self-transcending sovereignty.

Forgetfulness of Being and the expulsion of the outlawed part are the two dialectical images that have till now inspired all those attempts to dissociate the critique of reason from the pattern of a dialectic of enlightenment and to raise the other of reason to a court of appeal before which modernity can be called to order. In what follows, I will examine whether Heidegger's later philosophy (and the productive continuation of his philosophical mysticism by Derrida), on the one hand, and Bataille's general economy (and Foucault's genealogy of knowledge grounded on a theory of power), on the other — these two ways suggested by Nietzsche — really lead us out of the philosophy of the subject.

Heidegger has resolutely ontologized art and bet everything on the one card: a movement of thought that liberates by destroying, that is supposed to overcome metaphysics on its own ground. He thereby evades the aporias of a self-referential critique of reason that is bound to undermine its own foundations. He gives an ontological turn to Dionysian messianism; with this he ties himself to the style of thought and the mode of reasoning of *Ursprungsphilosophie* in such a way that he can only overcome the foundationalism of Husserlian phenomenology at the price of a foundationalizing of history, which leads into a void. Heidegger tries to break out of the enchanted circle of the philosophy of the subject by setting its foundations aflow temporally. The superfoundationalism of a history of Being abstracted from all concrete history shows that he remains fixated on the thinking he negates. By contrast, Bataille remains faithful to an authentic aesthetic experience and opens himself to a realm of phenomena in which subject-centered reason can be opened up to its other. To be sure, he cannot admit the modern provenance of this experience out of surrealism; he has to transplant it into an archaic context with the help of anthropological theories. Thus, Bataille pursues the project of a scientific analysis of the sacred and of a general economy, which are supposed to illuminate the world-historical process of rationalization and the possibility of a final reversal. In this way, he gets into the same dilemma as Nietzsche: His theory of power cannot satisfy the claim to scientific objectivity and, at the same time, put into effect the program of a total and hence self-referential critique of reason that also affects the truth of theoretical propositions.

Before I follow the two paths opened up by Nietzsche and traveled by Heidegger and Bataille into postmodernity, I would like to pause to consider a course of thought which, viewed from that perspective, would seem to retard development: Horkheimer and Adorno's ambiguous attempt at a dialectic of enlightenment that would satisfy Nietzsche's radical critique of reason.

V

The Entwinement of Myth and Enlightenment: Max Horkheimer and Theodor Adorno

The "dark" writers of the bourgeoisie, such as Machiavelli, Hobbes, and Mandeville, always had an appeal for Max Horkheimer, who was influenced by Schopenhauer early in his career. These writers still thought in a constructive way; and there were lines leading from their disharmonies to Marx's social theory. The "black" writers of the bourgeoisie, foremost among them the Marquis de Sade and Nietzsche, broke these ties. In their blackest book, *Dialectic of Enlightenment*, Horkheimer and Theodor Adorno joined with these writers to conceptualize the Enlightenment's process of self-destruction. On their analysis, it is no longer possible to place hope in the liberating force of enlightenment. Inspired by Benjamin's now ironic hope of the hopeless, they still did not want to relinquish the now paradoxical labor of conceptualization. We no longer share this mood, this attitude. And yet under the sign of a Nietzsche revitalized by poststructuralism, moods and attitudes are spreading that are confusingly like those of Horkheimer and Adorno. I would like to forestall this confusion.

Dialectic of Enlightenment is an odd book. A substantial part of it is composed of notes taken by Gretel Adorno during discussions between Horkheimer and Adorno in Santa Monica, California. The text was completed in 1944 and published three years later by the Querido Press in Amsterdam. Copies of the first edition were available for almost twenty years. The impact of this book — through which Horkheimer and Adorno exercised a special influence upon the intellectual development of the Federal Republic of Germany, especially in its first two decades — stands in a curious relation to the number of its purchasers. Odd, too, is the composition of the book. It comprises an essay of something over fifty pages, two excursuses, and three appendixes. The latter take up more than half the text. This rather unperspicuous form of presentation renders the clear structure of its train of thought almost undiscernible at first glance.

I shall therefore begin by explaining its two central theses (I). What interests me in regard to the contemporary situation stems from Horkheimer and Adorno's appreciation of modernity — why they want to enlighten the Enlightenment about itself in a radical way (II). Nietzsche was the great model for the critique of ideology's totalizing self-overcoming. Comparing Horkheimer and Adorno with Nietzsche is not only instructive in regard to the contrary orientations with which the two sides pursue their critiques of culture (III); but it also raises doubts about the repeated self-reflection on the part of the Enlightenment itself (IV).

I

In the tradition of the Enlightenment, enlightened thinking has been understood as an opposition and counterforce to myth. As *opposition*, because it opposes the unforced force of the better argument to the authoritarian normativity of a tradition interlinked with the chain of the generations; as *counterforce*, because by insights gained individually and transposed into motives, it is supposed to break the spell of collective powers. Enlightenment contradicts myth and thereby escapes its violence.[1] Horkheimer and Adorno put forward the thesis of a secret complicity to challenge this opposition, of which enlightened thinking is so certain: "Myth is already enlightenment; and enlightenment reverts to mythology."[2] This thesis, announced in the preface, is developed in the title essay and documented in the form of an interpretation of the *Odyssey*.

The anticipated objection of philologists to the effect that the authors incur a *petitio principii* with their choice of a late elaboration in epic form of a mythic tradition already distantiated by Homer is turned to methodological advantage: "The myths have been deposited in the various layers of the Homeric narrative. But the account given of them there, the unity wrested from the diffuse sagas, is also a description of the retreat of the individual from the mythic powers" (DE, p. 46). The primal history of a subjectivity that wrests itself free from the power of mythic forces is reflected in the adventures of Odysseus, who has been driven off course in a double sense. The mythic world is not the homeland, but the labyrinth from which one has to escape for the sake of one's own identity: "It is homesickness that gives rise to the adventures through which subjectivity (whose fundamental history is presented in the *Odyssey*) escapes from the prehistoric world. The quintessential paradox of the epic resides in the fact that the notion of the homeland is opposed to myth — which the fascist would falsely present as homeland" (DE, p. 78).

To be sure, the mythic narratives call the individual back to genealogical origins mediated by generational chains; but the ritual enactments that are supposed to bridge over and heal the guilt-laden remoteness of the origins simultaneously deepen the rift.[3] The myth of origin involves the *double meaning* of "springing from": a shudder at being uprooted and a sigh of relief at escaping. Consequently, Horkheimer and Adorno pursue the cunning of Odysseus into the intimacy of sacrificial acts; a moment of deception is intrinsic to the latter inasmuch as, by offering a symbolically revalued vicarious victim, people buy off the curse of vengeful powers.[4] This layer of myth marks the ambivalence of a mode of consciousness for which ritual practice is both reality and illusion. The regenerative force of a ritual return to origins (which, as Durkheim has shown, guarantees social solidarity) is vitally necessary for collective consciousness. But the sheerly illusionary character of the return to origins, from which at the same time the member of the tribal collectivity has to escape by being formed into an ego, is no less necessary. Thus, the primal powers, which are hallowed and outsmarted at the same time, already occupy a first stage of enlightenment in the primal history of subjectivity (DE, p. 60).

It would amount to successful enlightenment if distantiation from origins meant liberation. But mythic power proves to be a retarding moment that checks the emancipation striven for and keeps on prolonging ties to one's origins that are also experienced as imprisonment. Hence, Horkheimer and Adorno call the entire process, suspended between the two sides, "enlightenment." And this process of gaining mastery over mythic forces is supposed to call forth, in fateful fashion, the return of myth at each new stage. Enlightenment is supposed to relapse into mythology. The authors also attempt to confirm this thesis in connection with the *Odyssey*'s stage of consciousness.

They go through the *Odyssey* episode by episode to discover the price paid by the experienced Odysseus for his ego to issue from the adventures he has undergone just as strengthened and stabilized as Spirit does from the experiences of consciousness, as reported by Hegel the phenomenologist (with the same intent as Homer the epic writer). The episodes tell of danger, cunning, and escape, and of the self-imposed renunciaton by which the ego, learning to master danger, gains its own identity and takes leave of the bliss of archaic union with internal and external nature. The Sirens' song recalls happiness once guaranteed by the "fluctuating relationship with nature"; Odysseus surrenders to their seductions as one who already knows himself in chains: "Man's domination over himself, which grounds his selfhood, is almost always the destruction of the subject in whose service it is undertaken; for the substance which is dominated, suppressed and dissolved through self-preservation is none other than that very life as a function of which the achievements of self-preservation are defined; it is, in fact, what is to be preserved" (DE, p. 54). This figure of human beings shaping their identity by learning to dominate external nature at the cost of repressing their internal nature supplies the model for a description under which the process of enlightenment reveals its Janus-face; the price of renunciation, of self-concealment, of interrupted communication between the ego and its own nature (now anonymous, as the id) is construed as a consequence of the introversion of sacrifice. The ego, which had once outsmarted mythic destiny, is again overtaken by the latter as soon as it finds it necessary to introject the sacrifice: "The identically persistent self which arises in the abrogation of sacrifice immediately becomes an unyielding, rigidified sacrificial ritual that man celebrates upon himself by opposing his consciousness to the natural context" (DE, p. 54).

The human race has removed itself even further from its origins in the world-historical process of enlightenment, and yet it has not dissolved the mythic compulsion to repetition. The modern, fully rationalized world is only seemingly disenchanted; there rests upon it the curse of demonic reification and deadly isolation. In the paralyzing effects of an idling emancipation is expressed the revenge of primordial forces upon those who had to emancipate themselves and yet could not escape. The compulsion toward rational domination of externally impinging natural forces has set the subject upon the course of a formative process that heightens productive forces without limit for the sake of sheer self-preservation, but lets the forces of reconciliation that transcend mere self-preservation atrophy. The permanent sign of enlightenment is domination over an objectified external nature and a repressed internal nature.

Thus, Horkheimer and Adorno play a variation on the well-known theme of Max Weber, who sees the ancient, disenchanted gods rising from their graves in the guise of depersonalized forces to resume the irreconcilable struggles between the demons.[5]

The reader who resists being overwhelmed by the rhetoric of the *Dialectic of Enlightenment*, who steps back and takes seriously the thoroughly philosophic claim of the text, can get the impression that the thesis treated here is no less risky than Nietzsche's similarly posed diagnosis of nihilism; that the authors are aware of this risk and, contrary to first appearances, make a consistent attempt to ground their critique of culture; but that in doing so they bring abstractions and simplifications into the bargain that make the plausibility of their cause problematic. First of all, I want to examine whether this impression is correct.

Reason itself destroys the humanity it first made possible — this far-reaching thesis, as we have seen, is grounded in the first excursus by the fact that *from the very start* the process of enlightenment is the result of a drive to self-preservation that mutilates reason, because it lays claim to it only in the form of a purposive-rational mastery of nature and instinct — precisely as instrumental reason. This does not yet prove that reason remains subordinated to the dictates of purposive rationality right into its most recent products — modern science, universalistic ideas of justice and morality, autonomous art. The title essay on the concept of enlightenment, the excursus on enlightenment and morality, and the appendix on the culture industry are devoted to demonstrating just this.

Adorno and Horkheimer are convinced that *modern science* came into its own in logical positivism, that it has rejected any emphatic claim to theoretical knowledge in favor of technical utility: "What is abandoned is the whole claim and approach of knowledge: to comprehend the given as such; not merely to determine the abstract spatiotemporal relations of the facts, which allow us to come to grips with them, but on the contrary to conceive them as the superficies, as mediated conceptual moments which come to fulfillment only in the development of their social, historical, and human significance" (DE, pp. 26–27). The critique of the positivist understanding of science deployed earlier is heightened here into the totalized reproach that the sciences themselves have been absorbed by instrumental reason. In addition, Horkheimer and Adorno want to show, along lines furnished by the *Histoire de Juliette* and the *Genealogy of Morals*, that reason has been driven out of *morality and law* because, with the collapse of religious-metaphysical world views, all normative standards have lost their credit before the single remaining authority — science: "Not to have glossed over or suppressed but to have trumpeted far and wide the impossibility of deriving from reason any fundamental argument against murder is what fired the hatred which progressives (and they precisely) still direct against Sade and Nietzsche" (DE, p. 118). And again: "They have not pretended that formalistic reason is more closely allied to morality than to immorality" (DE, pp. 117–118). Their earlier critique of metaethical reinterpretations of morality turns into a sarcastic agreement with ethical scepticism.

Finally, Horkheimer and Adorno want to demonstrate with their analysis of mass culture that *art* fused with entertainment has been hobbled in its innovative force and emptied of all critical and utopian content: "That factor in a work of art which enables it to transcend reality certainly cannot be detached from style; but it does not consist of the harmony actually realized, of any doubtful unity of form and content, within and without, of individual and society; it is to be found in those features in which discrepancy appears — in the necessary failure of the passionate striving for identity. Instead of exposing itself to this failure in which the style of the great work of art has always achieved self-negation, the inferior work has always relied on its similarity with others — on a surrogate identity. In the culture industry this imitation finally becomes absolute" (DE, pp. 130–131). Their earlier critique of the merely affirmative character of bourgeois culture mounts up to impotent rage at the ironic justice of the putatively nonrevisable judgment that mass culture passes on an art that has always also been ideological.

Thus, in respect to science, morality, and art, the argument follows the same figure: Already the separation of cultural domains, the collapse of the substantive reason still incorporated in religion and metaphysics, so greatly disempowers the moments of reason (as isolated and robbed of their coherence) that they regress to a rationality in the service of self-preservation gone wild. In cultural modernity, reason gets definitively stripped of its validity claim and assimilated to sheer power. The critical capacity to take up a "Yes" or "No" stance and to distinguish between valid and invalid propositions is *undermined* as power and validity claims enter into a turbid fusion.

If one reduces the critique of instrumental reason to this core, it becomes clear just why the *Dialectic of Enlightenment* has to oversimplify its image of modernity so astoundingly. Cultural modernity's specific dignity is constituted by what Max Weber called the differentiation of value spheres in accord with their own logics. The power of negation and the capacity to discriminate between "Yes" and "No" is not so much crippled by this as reinforced. For now questions of truth, of justice, and of taste can be worked out and unfolded in accord with their own proper logics. It is true that with the capitalist econ-omy and the modern state the tendency to incorporate all questions of validity into the limited horizon of purposive ra-tionality proper to subjects interested in self-preservation and to self-maintaining systems is also strengthened. But the far from contemptible compulsion toward the progressive differ-entiation of a reason that, moreover, assumes a procedural form — a compulsion induced by the rationalization of world views and lifeworlds — competes with this inclination toward a social regression of reason. The formation of expert cultures, within which carefully articulated spheres of validity help the claims to propositional truth, normative rightness, and authen-ticity, attain *their own logic* (as well, of course, as *their own life*, esoteric in character and endangered in being split off from ordinary communicative practice); and this development com-petes with the naturalistic assimilation of validity claims to power claims and the destruction of our critical capacities.

The *Dialectic of Enlightenment* does not do justice to the ra-tional content of cultural modernity that was captured in bour-geois ideals (and also instrumentalized along with them). I am thinking here of the specific theoretical dynamic that contin-ually pushes the sciences, and even the self-reflection of the sciences, *beyond* merely engendering technically useful knowl-edge; I am referring, further, to the universalistic foundations of law and morality that have *also* been incorporated (in how-ever distorted and incomplete a fashion) into the institutions of constitutional government, into the forms of democratic will formation, and into individualist patterns of identity forma-tion; I have in mind, finally, the productivity and explosive power of basic aesthetic experiences that a subjectivity liberated from the imperatives of purposive activity and from conven-tions of quotidian perception gains from its own decentering — experiences that are presented in works of avant-garde art, that are articulated in the discourses of art criticism, and that also achieve a *certain measure* of illuminating effect (or at least contrast effects that are instructive) in the innovatively en-riched range of values proper to self-realization.

If these key terms were to be sufficiently elaborated for the purposes of my argument, they could support the intuitive impression of, to put it cautiously, the incompleteness and one-sidedness left by a first reading of this book. The reader correctly gets the feeling that the oversimplified presentation fails to notice essential characteristics of cultural modernity. But then a question arises as to *motives* that could have led Horkheimer and Adorno to commence their critique of enlightenment at such a *depth* that the project of enlightenment itself is endangered. *Dialectic of Enlightenment* holds out scarcely any prospect for an escape from the myth of purposive rationality that has turned into objective violence. To clarify this question, I want first to identify the place assumed by Marx's critique of ideology in the process of enlightenment as a whole, in order to find out why Horkheimer and Adorno believed they had both to give up and to supersede this type of critique.

II

Up to this point we have become familiar with the mythic mode of thought only under the aspect of the ambiguous comportment of the subject toward the primordial powers, that is, from the viewpoint central to the formation of identity — *emancipation*. Horkheimer and Adorno conceive of enlightenment as the unsuccessful attempt to spring from the powers of fate. The curse of mythic violence still overtakes the one escaping in the guise of the desolate emptiness of emancipation. A *different dimension* to the description both of mythic and of enlightened thinking is articulated only in a few passages where the path of demythologization is defined as a transformation and *differentiation of basic concepts*. Myth owes the totalizing power with which it integrates all superficially perceived phenomena into a network of correspondences, similarities, and contrasts to basic concepts that render consistent with one another categories that are no longer compatible in the modern understanding of the world. For example, language, the medium of presentation, is not yet abstracted from reality to such an extent that the conventional sign is completely separate from its semantic content and its referents; the linguistic world view remains interwoven with the order of the world. Mythic traditions cannot be revised without danger to the order of things and to the identity of the tribe set within it. Categories of validity such as "true" and "false," "good" and "evil," are still blended with empirical concepts like exchange, causality, health, substance, and wealth. Magical thinking does not allow for basic conceptual distinctions between things and persons, inanimate and animate; between objects that can be manipulated and agents to whom we ascribe actions and linguistic utterances. Only demythologization dispels this enchantment, which appears to *us* to be a confusion between nature and culture. The process of enlightenment leads to the desocialization of nature and the denaturalization of the human world; we can conceive of this with Piaget as a *decentering of world view.*

The traditional world view ultimately gets temporalized and can be distinguished as a variable interpretation from the world itself. This external world is differentiated into the objective world of entities and the social world of norms (or normatively regulated interpersonal relations); they both stand in contrast to each person's own internal world of subjective experiences. As Max Weber has shown, this process proceeds by the rationalization of world views that, as religion and metaphysics, are themselves the result of demythologization. Where (as in the Western tradition) rationalization does not stop at basic theological and metaphysical concepts, the sphere of validity relations is not only purified of empirical admixtures but also gets internally differentiated in terms of the viewpoints proper to truth, normative rightness, and subjective truthfulness or authenticity.[6]

If one describes the process suspended between myth and enlightenment in this way, as the formation of a decentered understanding of the world, the place where the procedure of ideology critique enters into this drama can also be specified. Only when contexts of meaning and reality, when internal and external relationships have been unmixed, only when science, morality, and art are each specialized in *one* validity claim, when each follows its *own* respective logic and is cleansed of all cosmological, theological, and cultic dross — only then can the suspicion arise that the autonomy of validity claimed by a theory (whether empirical or normative) is an illusion because secret interests and power claims have crept into its pores.

Critique, which is inspired by such a suspicion, attempts to supply the proof that the *suspected* theory expresses *a tergo*, and within the very propositions for which it frontally makes validity claims, dependencies it could not admit without a loss of credibility. Critique becomes ideology critique when it attempts to show that the validity of a theory has not been adequately dissociated from the context in which it emerged; that behind the back of the theory there lies hidden an inadmissible *mixture of power and validity*, and that it still owes its reputation to this. Ideology critique wants to show how, on a level for which this painstaking distinction between contexts of meaning and contexts of reality is constitutive, precisely these internal and external relationships are confused — and that they are confused because validity claims are determined by relationships of power. Ideology critique itself is not a theory competing with some other theory; it simply makes use of certain theoretical assumptions. Thus equipped, it *disputes* the *truth* of a suspicious theory by *exposing its untruthfulness*. It advances the process of enlightenment by showing that a theory presupposing a demythologized understanding of the world is still ensnared by myth, by pointing out a putatively overcome category mistake.

With this kind of critique, enlightenment becomes reflective for the first time; it is performed with respect to its own products — theories. Yet the drama of enlightenment first arrives at its climax when ideology critique *itself* comes under suspicion of not producing (any more) truths — and the enlightenment attains second-order reflectiveness. Then doubt reaches out to include reason, whose standards ideology critique had found already given in bourgeois ideals and had simply taken at their word. *Dialectic of Enlightenment* takes this step — it renders critique independent even in relation to its own foundations. Why do Horkheimer and Adorno see themselves compelled to take this step?

Critical Theory was intitially developed in Horkheimer's circle to think through political disappointments at the absence of revolution in the West, the development of Stalinism in Soviet Russia, and the victory of fascism in Germany. It was supposed to explain mistaken Marxist prognoses, but without breaking with Marxist intentions. Against this background it becomes intelligible how the impression could indeed get established in the darkest years of the Second World War that the last sparks of reason were being extinguished from this reality and had left the ruins of a civilization in collapse without any hope. The idea of a natural history, which the young Adorno had taken up from Benjamin,[7] seemed to have been realized in an unforeseen manner. In the moment of its most extreme acceleration, history congealed into nature and faded into the Golgotha of a hope become unrecognizable.

Such explanations in terms of contemporary history and psychology can be of interest in theoretical contexts only to the extent that they provide hints of a systematic motive. As a matter of fact, political experiences had to affect the basic assumptions of historical materialism upon which the Frankfurt circle was based in the 1930s.

In one of the "Notes and Drafts" concerning "Philosophy and the [Scientific] Division of Labor," which is unsystematically tacked on, there is a passage that reads like an interloper from the classical period of Critical Theory. Philosophy, it says, "knows of no workable abstract rules or goals to replace those at present in force. It is immune to the suggestion of the status quo precisely because *it accepts bourgeois ideals without making any allowances.* These ideals may be those still proclaimed, though in distorted form, by the representatives of the status quo; or those which, however much they may have been tinkered about with, are still recognizable as the objective meaning of existing institutions, whether technical or cultural" (DE, p. 243). Thus, Horkheimer and Adorno recall the figure from Marx's ideology critique which set out from the fact that the potentiality for reason expressed in "bourgeois ideals" and sedimented in the "objective meaning of institutions" manifests a double face: On the one side, it bestows on the ideologies of the dominant class the deceptive appearance of being convincing theories; on the other, it offers the starting point for an immanent critique of structures that elevate to the status of the general interest what actually only serves the dominant part of society. [Classical] ideology critique deciphered in such misused ideas a piece of extant reason hidden from itself; it read these ideas as a directive that could be cashed in by social movements to the extent that surplus forces of production were developed.

In the 1930s, critical theorists had retained a portion of the trust (grounded in a philosophy of history) in the rational potential of bourgeois culture that was supposed to be released under the pressure of developed forces of production. The kind of interdisciplinary research program set forth in the volumes of the *Zeitschrift für Sozialforschung* (1932–1941) was founded on this basis. With reference to the development of earlier Critical Theory, Helmut Dubiel has exhibited just why this fund of confidence was exhausted at the beginning of the 1940s, why Horkheimer and Adorno considered Marxian ideology critique bankrupt and no longer believed it possible to redeem the promise of a critical theory of society with the tools of the social sciences.[8] Instead of this, they pushed for a radicalization and self-overcoming of ideology critique, which was supposed to enlighten the Enlightenment about itself. The preface to *Dialectic of Enlightenment* begins with this admission: "Even though we had known for many years that the great discoveries of applied science are paid for with an increasing diminution of theoretical awareness, we still thought that in regard to scientific activity our contribution could be restricted to the criticism or extension of specialist contributions. Thematically, at any rate, we were to keep to the traditional disciplines: to sociology, psychology and epistemology. However, the fragments united in this volume show that we were forced to abandon this conviction" (DE, p. xi).

If the cynical consciousness of the "black" writers speaks the truth about bourgeois culture, ideology critique does not have anything in reserve to which it might appeal; and when the forces of production enter into a baneful symbiosis with the relations of production that they were supposed to blow wide open, there is no longer any dynamism upon which critique could base its hope. Horkheimer and Adorno regard the foundations of ideology critique as shattered — and yet they would still like to hold on to the basic figure of enlightenment. So what enlightenment has perpetrated on myth, they apply to the process of enlightenment as a whole. Inasmuch as it turns against reason as the foundation of its own validity, critique becomes total. How is this totalization and independence of critique to be understood?

III

The suspicion of ideology becomes *total*, but without any change of direction. It is turned not only against the irrational function of bourgeois ideals, but against the rational potential of bourgeois culture itself, and thus it reaches into the foundations of any ideology critique that proceeds immanently. But the goal remains that of producing an effect of unmasking. The thought-figure, into which a scepticism regarding reason is now worked, remains unchanged: Now reason itself is suspected of the baneful confusion of power and validity claims, but still with the intent of enlightening. With their concept of "instrumental reason" Horkheimer and Adorno want to add up the cost incurred in the usurpation of reason's place by a calculating intellect.[9] This concept is simultaneously supposed to recall that when purposive rationality, overblown into a totality, abolishes the distinction between what claims validity and what is useful for self-preservation, and so tears down the barrier between validity and power, it cancels out those basic conceptual differentiations to which the modern understanding of the world believed it owed the definitive overcoming of myth. As instrumental, reason assimilated itself to power and thereby relinquished its critical force — that is the *final* disclosure of ideology critique applied to itself. To be sure, this description of the self-destruction of the critical capacity is paradoxical, because in the moment of description it still has to make use of the critique that has been declared dead. It denounces the Enlightenment's becoming totalitarian with its own tools. Adorno was quite aware of this performative contradiction inherent in totalized critique.

Adorno's *Negative Dialectics* reads like a continuing explanation of why we have to circle about within this *performative contradiction* and indeed even remain there; of why only the insistent, relentless unfolding of this paradox opens up the prospect of that magically invoked "mindfulness of nature in the subject in whose fulfillment the unacknowledged truth of all culture lies hidden" (DE, p. 40). Twenty-five years after the conclusion of *Dialectic of Enlightenment*, Adorno remained faithful to its philosophical impulse and never deviated from the paradoxical structure of thinking as totalizing critique. The grandeur of this consistency is shown by a comparison with Nietzsche, whose *Genealogy of Morals* had been the great model for a second level of reflection on the Enlightenment. Nietzsche suppressed the paradoxical structure and explained the complete assimilation of reason to power in modernity with a *theory of power* that was remythologized out of arbitrary pieces and that, in place of the claim to truth, retains no more than the rhetorical claim proper to an aesthetic fragment. Nietzsche showed how one totalizes critique; but what comes out in the end is only that he finds the fusion of validity and power scandalous because it impedes a glorified will to power that has taken on the connotations of artistic productivity. The comparison with Nietzsche makes manifest that no direction is inscribed in totalized critique as such. Nietzsche is the one among the steadfast theoreticians of unmasking who radicalizes the counter-Enlightenment.[10]

The stance of Horkheimer and Adorno toward Nietzsche is ambivalent. On the one hand, they attest of him that he was "one of the few after Hegel who recognized the dialectic of enlightenment" (DE, p. 44). Naturally, they accept the "merciless doctrine of the identity of domination and reason" (DE, p. 119), which is to say, the *approach* toward a totalizing self-overcoming of ideology critique. On the other hand, they cannot overlook the fact that Hegel is also Nietzsche's great antipode. Nietzsche gives the critique of reason such an affirmative twist that even determinate negation — which is to say, the very procedure that Horkheimer and Adorno want to retain as the sole exercise, since reason itself has become so shaky — loses its sting. Nietzsche's critique consumes the critical impulse itself: "As a protest against civilization, the masters' morality conversely represents the oppressed. Hatred of atrophied instincts actually denounces the true nature of the taskmasters — which comes to light only in their victims. But as a Great Power or state religion, the masters' morality wholly subscribes to the civilizing powers that be, the compact majority, resentment and everything that it formerly opposed. The realization of Nietzsche's assertions both refutes them and at the same time reveals their truth, which — despite all his affirmation of life — was inimical to the spirit of reality" (DE, p. 101).

This ambivalent attitude toward Nietzsche is instructive. It also suggests that *Dialectic of Enlightenment* owes more to Nietzsche then just the strategy of an ideology critique turned against itself. Indeed, what is unexplained throughout is their certain lack of concern in dealing with the (to put it in the form of a slogan) achievements of Occidental rationalism. How can these two men of the Enlightenment (which they both remain) be so unappreciative of the rational content of cultural modernity that all they perceive everywhere is a binding of reason and domination, of power and validity? Have they also let themselves be inspired by Nietzsche in drawing their criteria for cultural criticism from a basic experience of aesthetic modernity that has now been *rendered independent?*

The similarities in content are at first startling.[11] Point-for-point correspondences with Nietzsche are found in the construction by which Horkheimer and Adorno underpin their "primal history of subjectivity." As soon as humans were robbed of their detached instincts, claims Nietzsche, they had to rely on their "consciousness," namely, on their apparatus for objectifying and manipulating external nature: "They were reduced to thinking, inferring, reckoning, co-ordinating cause and effect, these unfortunate creatures."[12] In the same stroke, however, the old instincts had to be tamed, and feelings and desires, no longer finding a spontaneous outlet, had to be repressed. In the course of this process of reversal of conative direction and of internalization, the subjectivity of an inner nature was formed under the sign of renunciation or of "bad conscience": "All instincts that do not discharge themselves outwardly *turn inward* — this is what I call the *internalization* of man: thus it was that man first developed what was later called his 'soul'. The entire inner world, originally as thin as if it were stretched between two membranes, expanded and extended itself, acquired depth, breadth, and height, in the name of measure as outward discharge was *inhibited.*"[13] Finally, the two elements of

domination over external and internal nature were bound together and fixed in the institutionalized dominion of human
beings over other humans: "The curse of society and of peace"
is based in all institutions, because they coerce people into
renunciation: "Those fearful bulwarks with which the political
organization protected itself against the old instincts of freedom — punishments belong among these bulwarks — brought
about that all these instincts of wild, free, prowling man turned
backward *against man himself.*"[14]

Similarly, Nietzsche's critique of knowledge and morality anticipates an idea that Horkheimer and Adorno develop in the
form of the critique of instrumental reason: Behind positivism's ideals of objectivity and claims to truth, behind universalistic morality's ideals of asceticism and claims to rightness,
lurk imperatives of self-preservation and domination. A pragmatist epistemology and a moral psychology unmask theoretical and practical reason as pure fictions in which power claims
furnish themselves an effective alibi — with the help of imagination and of the "drive to metaphorize," for which external
stimuli provide only the occasion for projective responses and
for a web of interpretations behind which the text disappears
altogether.[15]

Nietzsche brings out the perspective from which he handles
modernity in a way different from that of *Dialectic of Enlightenment.* And only this angle explains why objectified nature and
moralized society sink to correlative forms of appearance of
the same mythic force, be it of a perverted will to power or of
instrumental reason.

This perspective was inaugurated with aesthetic modernity
and that stubborn self-disclosure (forced by avant-garde art)
of a decentered subjectivity liberated from all constraints of
cognition and purposiveness and from all imperatives of labor
and utility. Nietzsche is not just a contemporary and kindred
spirit of Mallarmé;[16] he not only imbibed the late Romantic
spirit of Richard Wagner; he is the first to conceptualize the
attitude of aesthetic modernity before avant-garde consciousness assumed objective shape in the literature, painting, and
music of the twentieth century — and could be elaborated by
Adorno into an *Aesthetic Theory.* In the upgrading of the tran-

sitory, in the celebration of the dynamic, in the glorification of the current and the new, there is expressed an aesthetically motivated time-consciousness and a longing for an unspoiled, inward presence. The anarchist intention of the Surrealists *to explode* the continuum of the story of decline is already operative in Nietzsche. The subversive force of aesthetic resistance that would later feed the reflections of Benjamin and even of Peter Weiss, already arises from the experience in Nietzsche of rebellion against everything normative. It is this same force which neutralizes both the morally good and the practically useful, which expresses itself in the dialectic of secret and scandal and in the pleasure derived from the horror of profanation. Nietzsche builds up Socrates and Christ, those advocates of belief in truth and the ascetic ideal, as his great opponents; they are the ones who negate the aesthetic values! Nietzsche trusts only in art, "in which precisely the *lie* is sanctified, the will to deception,"[17] and in the terror of the beautiful, not to let themselves be imprisoned by the fictive world of science and morality.

Nietzsche enthrones *taste*, "the Yes and No of the palate,"[18] as the sole organ of "knowledge" beyond truth and falsehood, beyond good and evil. He elevates the judgment of taste of the art critic into the model for value judgment, for "evaluation." The legitimate meaning of critique is that of a value judgment that establishes an order of rank, weighs things, and measures forces. And all interpretation is evaluation. "Yes" expresses a high appraisal; "No" a low one. The "high" and the "low" indicate the dimension of yes/no positions in general.

It is interesting to see how coherently Nietzsche *undermines* the taking of "Yes" and "No" positions on criticizable validity claims. First, he devalues the truth of assertive statements and the rightness of normative ones, by reducing validity and invalidity to positive and negative *value judgments*. He reduces "p is true" and "h is right" (that is, the complex statements by which we claim validity for propositional statements or for ought statements) to simple evaluative statements by which we express value appraisals, by which we state that we prefer the true to the false and good over evil. Thus, Nietzsche reinterprets validity claims into preferences and then poses the question: "Suppose that we prefer truth (and justice): why not rather untruth (and injustice)?"[19] The responses to questions about the "value" of truth and justice are judgments of taste.

Of course, there could still be an architectonic lurking behind these fundamental value appraisals that, as in Schelling, anchors the unity of theoretical and practical reason in the faculty of aesthetic judgment. Nietzsche can carry out his complete assimilation of reason to power only by removing any cognitive status from value judgments and by demonstrating that the yes/no positions of value appraisals no longer express validity claims, but pure power claims.

Viewed in terms of language analysis, the next step in the argument therefore has the aim of assimilating judgments of taste to imperatives, and value appraisals to expressions of will. Nietzsche disputes Kant's analysis of judgments of taste in order to ground the thesis that evaluations are necessarily subjective and cannot be linked with a claim to intersubjective validity.[20] The illusion of disinterested pleasure and of the impersonal character and universality of aesthetic judgment arises only from the perspective of the spectator; but from the perspective of the producing artist we realize that value *appraisals* are induced by innovative value *positings*. The aesthetics of production unfolds the experience of the genial artist who *creates* values: From his perspective, value appraisals are dictated by his "value-positing eye."[21] Value-positing productivity prescribes the law for value appraisal. What is expressed in the validity claimed by the judgment of taste is only "the excitement of the will by the beautiful." One will responds to another; one force takes hold of another.

This is the route by which Nietzsche arrives at the concept of the will to power from the yes/no positions of value appraisals, after he has cleansed them of all cognitive claims. The beautiful is "the stimulant of the will to power." The aesthetic core of the will to power is the capacity of a sensibility that lets itself be affected in the greatest possible multiplicity of modes.[22]

However, if thinking can no longer operate in the element of truth, or of validity claims in general,[23] contradiction and criticism lose their meaning. *To contradict*, to negate, now has only the sense of "*wanting to be different.*" Nietzsche cannot really be satisfied with this in his critique of culture. The latter is not supposed to be merely a form of agitation, but *to demonstrate* why it is false or incorrect or bad to recognize the sovereignty of the ideals of science and universalistic morality, which are inimical to life. But once all predicates concerning validity are devalued, once it is power and not validity claims that is expressed in value appraisals — by what criterion shall critique still be able to propose discriminations? It must at least be able to discriminate between a power that *deserves* to be esteemed and one that *deserves* to be devalued.

A *theory of power* that distinguishes between "active" and merely "reactive" forces is supposed to offer a way out of this aporia. But Nietzsche cannot admit of the theory of power as a theory that can be true or false. He himself moves about, according to his own analysis, in a world of illusion, in which lighter shadows can be distinguished from darker ones, but not reason from unreason. This is, as it were, a world fallen back into myth, in which powers influence one another and no element remains that could transcend the battle of the powers. Perhaps it is typical of the ahistorical mode of perception proper to aesthetic modernity that particular epochs lose their own profile in favor of a heroic affinity of the present with the most remote and the most primitive: The decadent strives to relate itself in a leap to the barbaric, the wild, and the primitive. In any case, Nietzsche's renewal of the framework of the myth of origins is suited to this mentality: *Authentic* culture has been in decline already for a long time; the curse of remoteness from origins lays upon the present; and so Nietzsche conceives of the gathering of a still dawning culture in antiutopian terms — as a comeback and a return.

This framework does not have a merely metaphorical status; it has the systematic role of making room for the paradoxical business of a critique disburdened of the mortgages of enlightened thought. That is to say, totalized ideology critique for Nietzsche turns into what he calls "genealogical critique." Once the critical sense of saying "No" is suspended and the procedure of negation is rendered impotent, Nietzsche goes back to the very dimension of the myth of origins that permits a distinction which affects *all other* dimensions: What is *older* is *earlier* in the generational chain and nearer to the origin. The *more primordial* is considered the more worthy of honor, the preferable, the more unspoiled, the purer: It is deemed better. *Derivation* and *descent* serve as criteria of rank, in both the social and the logical senses.

In this manner, Nietzsche bases his critique of morality on *genealogy*. He traces the moral appraisal of value, which assigns a person or a mode of action a place within a rank ordering based on criteria of validity, back to the descent and hence to the social rank of the one making the moral judgment: "The signpost to the *right* road was for me the question: what was the real etymological significance of the designations for 'good' coined in the various languages? I found they all led back to the *same conceptual transformation* — that everywhere 'noble', 'aristocratic' in the social [*ständisch*] sense, is the basic concept from which 'good' in the sense of 'with aristocratic soul', 'noble', 'with a soul of a high order', 'with a privileged soul' necessarily developed: a development which always runs parallel to that other in which 'common', 'plebeian', 'low' are finally transformed into the concept 'bad'."[24] So the genealogical localization of powers takes on a critical sense: Those forces with an earlier, more noble descent are the active, creative ones, whereas a perverted will to power is expressed in the forces of later, lower, and reactive descent.[25]

With this, Nietzsche has in hand the conceptual means by which he can denounce the prevalence of the belief in reason and of the ascetic ideal, of science and of morality, as a merely factual victory (though of course decisive for the fate of modernity) of lower and reactionary forces. As is well known, they are supposed to have arisen from the resentment of the weaker and "the protective and healing instinct of a degenerating life."[26]

IV

We have pursued totalizing critique applied to itself in two variants. Horkheimer and Adorno find themselves in the same embarrassment as Nietzsche: If they do not want to renounce the effect of a final unmasking and still want to *continue with critique*, they will have to leave at least one rational criterion intact for their explanation of the corruption of *all* rational criteria. In the face of this paradox, self-referential critique loses its orientation. It has two options.

Nietzsche seeks refuge in a theory of power, which is consistent, since the fusion of reason and power revealed by critique abandons the world to the irreconcilable struggle between powers, as if it *were* the mythic world. It is fitting that Nietzsche, mediated by Gilles Deleuze, has become influential in structuralist France as a theoretician of power. Foucault, too, in his later work, replaces the model of domination based on repression (developed in the tradition of enlightenment by Marx and Freud) by a plurality of power strategies. These power strategies intersect one another, succeed one another; they are distinguished according to the type of their discourse formation and the degree of their intensity; but they cannot be *judged* under the aspect of their validity, as was the case with consciously working through conflicts in contrast to unconsciously doing so.[27]

The doctrine of active and merely reactive forces also fails to provide a way out of the embarrassment of a critique that attacks the presuppositions of its own validity. At best, it paves the way for breaking out of the horizon of modernity. It is without basis as a theory, if the categorial distinction between power claims and truth claims is the ground upon which *any* theoretical approach has to be enacted. The effect of unmasking is also transformed as a result: It is not the lightning flash of *insight* into some confusion threatening identity that causes shock, the way *understanding* the point of a joke causes liberating laughter; what produces shock is affirmative de-differentiation, an affirmative overthrow of the very categories that can make an act of mistaking, of forgetting, or of misspeaking into a category mistake threatening to identity — or art into illusion. This regressive turn still places the forces of emancipation at the service of counterenlightenment.

Horkheimer and Adorno adopt another option by stirring up, holding open, and no longer wanting to overcome theoretically the performative contradiction inherent in an ideology critique that outstrips itself. Any attempt to develop a theory at this level of reflection would have to slide off into the groundless; they therefore eschew theory and practice determinate negation on an ad hoc basis, thus standing firm against that fusion of reason and power that plugs all crevices: "Determinate negation rejects the defective ideas of the absolute, the idols, differently than does rigorism, which confronts them with the idea they cannot match up to. Dialectic, on the contrary, interprets every image as writing. It shows how the admission of its falsity is to be read in the lines of its features — a confession that deprives it of its power and appropriates it for truth. Thus language becomes more than just a sign system. With the notion of determinate negativity, Hegel revealed an element that distinguishes the Enlightenment from the positivist degeneracy to which he attributes it" (DE, p. 24). A practiced spirit of contradiction is all that remains of the "spirit of . . . unrelenting theory." And this practice is like an incantation seeking "to turn . . . to its end" the negative spirit of relentless progress (DE, p. 42).

Anyone who abides in a paradox on the very spot once occupied by philosophy with its ultimate groundings is not just taking up an uncomfortable position; one can only hold that place if one makes it at least minimally plausible that there is *no way out*. Even the retreat from an aporetic situation has to be barred, for otherwise there is a way — the way back. But I believe this is precisely the case.

The comparison with Nietzsche is instructive inasmuch as it draws our attention to the aesthetic horizon of experience that guides and motivates the gaze of contemporary diagnosis. I have shown how Nietzsche detaches that moment of reason, which comes into its own in the logic proper to the aesthetic-expressive sphere of value, and especially in avant-garde art and art criticism, from its connection with theoretical and practical reason; and how he stylizes aesthetic judgment, on the model of a "value appraisal" exiled to irrationality, into a capacity for discrimination beyond good and evil, truth and falsehood. In this way, Nietzsche gains criteria for a critique of culture that unmasks science and morality as being in similar ways ideological expressions of a perverted will to power, just as *Dialectic of Enlightenment* denounces these structures as embodiments of instrumental reason. This confirms our suspicion that Horkheimer and Adorno perceive cultural modernity from a similar experiential horizon, with the same heightened sensibility, and even with the same cramped optics that render one insensible to the traces and the existing forms of communicative rationality. The architectonics of Adorno's later philosophy, in which his *Negative Dialectics* and *Aesthetic Theory* mutually support one another, are also evidence of this — the one, which develops the paradoxical concept of the nonidentical, points to the other, which deciphers the mimetic content hidden in avant-garde works of art.

Did the state of the question by which Horkheimer and Adorno saw themselves confronted at the beginning of the 1940s leave no way out? To be sure, the theory upon which they had earlier based themselves and their procedure of ideology critique was no longer viable — because the forces of production no longer developed any explosive force; because crises and class conflicts promoted not a revolutionary, or even a unified consciousness, but a fragmentary one instead; finally, because bourgeois ideals began to retire, or at least to assume forms that eluded the cutting edge of an immanent critique. On the other hand, at that time Horkheimer and Adorno did not expend any more effort on a social-scientific revision of theory, since scepticism regarding the truth content of bourgeois ideas seemed to call the criteria of ideology critique itself into question.

Faced with this second element, Horkheimer and Adorno made the really problematic move; like historicism,[28] they surrendered themselves to an uninhibited scepticism regarding reason, instead of weighing the grounds that cast doubt on this scepticism itself. In this way, perhaps, they could have set the normative foundations of critical social theory so deep[29] that they would not have been disturbed by the decomposition of bourgeois culture that was then being enacted in Germany for all to see.

In one respect, ideology critique had in fact continued the undialectical enlightenment proper to ontological thinking. It remained caught up in the purist notion that the devil needing exorcism was hiding in the internal relationships between genesis and validity, so that theory, purified of all empirical connotations, could operate in its own element. Totalized critique did not discharge this legacy. The intention of a "final unmasking," which was supposed to draw away with one fell swoop the veil covering the confusion between power and reason, reveals a purist intent — similar to the intent of ontology to separate being and illusion categorially (that is, with one stroke). However, just as in a communication community the researcher, the context of discovery, and the context of justification are so entwined with one another that they have to be separated procedurally, by a *mediating* kind of thinking — which is to say, continuously — the same holds for the two spheres of being and illusion. In argumentation, critique is constantly entwined with theory, enlightenment with grounding, even though discourse participants always *have to suppose* that only the unforced force of the better argument comes into play under the unavoidable communication presuppositions of argumentative discourse. But they know, or they can know, that even this idealization is only necessary because convictions are formed and confirmed in a medium that is not "pure" and not removed from the world of appearances in the style of Platonic "pure" and not removed from the world of appearances in the style of Platonic Ideas. Only a discourse that admits this might break the spell of mythic thinking without incurring a loss of the light radiating from the semantic potentials also preserved in myth.

The Undermining of Western Rationalism through the Critique of Metaphysics: Martin Heidegger

I

Horkheimer and Adorno battled with Nietzsche; Heidegger and Bataille gather under Nietzsche's banner for the final confrontation. Taking as my point of departure Heidegger's Nietzsche lectures from the 1930s and early 1940s, I would like to examine, step by step, how he absorbs Dionysian messianism into his attempt to step over the threshold to postmodern thought by internally overcoming metaphysics. In so doing, he arrives at a temporalized philosophy of origins. What I mean by this latter expression can be spelled out provisionally in terms of four operations that Heidegger undertakes in his confrontation with Nietzsche.

(1) First of all, Heidegger puts philosophy back in the dominant position from which it had been driven by the critique of the Young Hegelians. At that time, the desublimation of the spirit was carried out by using Hegel's own concepts — as a rehabilitation of the external over against the internal, of the material over against the spiritual, of being as against consciousness, of the objective as against the subjective, of the senses in relation to the intellect, and of the empirical in relation to reflection. The critique of Idealism had resulted in a disempowering of philosophy — not only in relation to the independent logics of science, morality, and art, but also in relation to the independent right of the political-social world. In his countermove, Heidegger returns to philosophy its lost

plenitude of power. On his view, the historical destiny of a culture or society is determined by a collectively binding preunderstanding of the things and events that can appear in the world at all. This ontological preunderstanding depends on horizon-forming basic concepts, which to a certain extent prejudice the meaning of any beings: "However any being may be interpreted, whether as spirit in the sense of Spiritualism, or as matter and force in the sense of Materialism, or as becoming and life, or as will, or as substance or subject, or as *energeia*, or as the eternal recurrence of the same — in every case the being appears as a being in the light of Being."[1]

In the West, metaphysics is the place where this preunderstanding is articulated most clearly. The epochal changes in the understanding of Being are reflected in the history of metaphysics. The history of philosophy had already become a key to philosophy of history for Hegel. The history of metaphysics holds a comparable rank for Heidegger; through it the philosopher masters the sources from which each epoch fatefully receives its own light.

(2) This idealistic perspective has consequences for Heidegger's critique of modernity. At the beginning of the 1940s — during the same period when Horkheimer and Adorno were composing the separate fragments that were later published as *Dialectic of Enlightenment* — Heidegger sees in the political and military forms in which the totalitarian appears "the completion of the European-modern dominance of the world." He speaks of the "struggle for the domination of the earth," of the "struggle for the unlimited exploitation of the earth as a domain of raw materials, and for the illusion-free deployment of human material in the service of an unconditional empowerment of the 'will to power.'"[2] In a tone that is still not entirely free of admiration, Heidegger characterizes the overman in accord with the image of the ideal-type of the SA-man: "The overman is the striking [or stamping: *Schlag*] of that mankind which wills itself for the first time as a striking [*Schlag*] and sets itself to this striking [*selbst zu diesem Schlag sich schlägt*]. . . . This breed of men [*Menschenschlag*] posits within the meaningless whole the will to power as the 'meaning of the earth.' The final stage of European nihilism is the 'catastrophe' in the sense of

the affirmative turnabout."[3] Heidegger sees the totalitarian essence of his epoch characterized by the global techniques for mastering nature, waging war, and racial breeding. In them is expressed the absolutized purposive rationality of the "calculation of all acting and planning." But this in turn is grounded in the specifically modern understanding of Being, which has been radicalized from Descartes down to Nietzsche: "That period we call modern . . . is defined by the fact that man becomes the center and measure of all beings. Man is the *subjectum*, that which lies at the bottom of all beings, that is, in modern terms, at the bottom of all objectification and representation."[4] Heidegger's originality consists in delineating the modern dominance of the subject in terms of a history of metaphysics. Descartes stands in the center, as it were, between Protagoras and Nietzsche. He conceives of the subjectivity of self-consciousness as the absolutely certain foundation of representation; being as a whole is thereby transformed into the subjective world of represented objects, and truth is transformed into subjective certitude.[5]

With this critique of modern subjectivism, Heidegger takes up a motif that has been one of the enduring themes of the discourse of modernity since Hegel. The ontological turn Heidegger gives the theme is less interesting than the lack of ambiguity with which he places subject-centered reason on trial. Heidegger hardly pays any attention to the difference between reason [*Vernunft*] and understanding [*Verstand*], out of which Hegel still wanted to develop the dialectic of enlightenment. He can no longer glean from self-consciousness any reconciling dimension in addition to its authoritarian aspect. It is Heidegger himself — and not the narrow-minded Enlightenment — that levels reason to the understanding. The same understanding of Being that spurs modernity to the unlimited expansion of its manipulative power over objectified processes of nature and society also forces this emancipated subjectivity into bonds that serve to secure its imperative activity; these self-made normative obligations remain hollow ideals. From this perspective, Heidegger can so fundamentally de-struct modern reason that he no longer distinguishes between the universalistic contents of humanism, enlightenment, and even positivism, on the one side, and the particularistic, self-assertive representations of racism and nationalism, or of retrospectively oriented typological doctrines in the style of Spengler and Jünger, on the other side.[6] No matter whether modern ideas make their entry in the name of reason or of the destruction of reason, the prism of the modern understanding of Being refracts *all* normative orientations into the power claims of a subjectivity crazed with self-aggrandizement.

To be sure, the critical reconstruction of the history of metaphysics cannot get along without its *own* standard. This it borrows from the implicitly normative concept of the "completion" of metaphysics.

(3) The idea of the origin and end of metaphysics owes its critical potential to the circumstance that Heidegger moves about within the modern time-consciousness no less than Nietzsche. For him, the beginning of the *modern period* is marked by the epochal incision of the philosophy of consciousness starting with Descartes; and Nietzsche's radicalizing of this understanding of Being marks the *most recent period* determining the constellation of the present.[7] The present, in turn, appears as the moment of crisis; it stands under the pressure of a decision as to "whether this end period is the close of Western history or the counterpart to another beginning."[8] This is a matter of the decision "whether the West still trusts itself to create a goal beyond itself and history; or whether it prefers to sink down into preserving and heightening the interests of life and commerce, and to be satisfied with the appeal to what went before, as if this were the absolute."[9] The necessity of another beginning[10] draws our gaze into the maelstrom of the future. Turning back to the origins, to the "provenance of essence," is only thinkable in the mode of striding forward into the "future of essence." This future enters under the category of the absolutely new: "The completion of an age . . . is the installation — unconditional for the first time and complete in advance — of the unexpected and the never to be expected . . . the new."[11] However, Nietzsche's messianism, which still left room for "compelling salvation" (as it is called in Jewish mysticism), is inverted by Heidegger into the apocalyptic expectation of a catastrophic entry of the new. At the same time,

Heidegger borrows from the Romantic models, especially Hölderlin, the thought-figure of the absent God, so as to be able to conceive of the end of metaphysics as a "completion," and hence as the unmistakable sign of "another beginning."

Just as Nietzsche once expected from Wagnerian opera a tiger's leap into the futural past of ancient Greek tragedy, so Heidegger would like to be transported by Nietzsche's metaphysics of the will to power back to the pre-Socratic origins of metaphysics. But before Heidegger can describe the history of the West, between the beginnings of metaphysics and its end, as the night of the remoteness of the Gods, before he can describe the completion of metaphysics as the return of the God that disappeared, he has to establish a correspondence between Dionysus and the concern of metaphysics, which has to do with the Being of beings. The demigod Dionysus had offered himself to the Romantics as well as to Nietzsche as the absent God, as the one who enables a modernity forsaken by God to understand, by means of his "greatest remoteness," what was taken from it by way of energy for social bonds in the wake of its own progress. The idea of the ontological difference serves as the bridge between this Dionysian thought and the fundamental question of metaphysics. Heidegger separates Being, which had always been understood as the Being of beings, from the beings. For Being can only function as a carrier of the Dionysian happening if — as the historical horizon within which beings first come to appearance — it becomes autonomous to a certain extent. Only Being, as distinguished from beings by way of hypostatization, can take over the role of Dionysus. "The being is abandoned by Being itself. The abandonment of Being applies to beings as a whole, not only to that being that takes the shape of man, who represents being as such, a representing in which Being itself withdraws from him in its truth."[12]

Heidegger tirelessly elaborates the positive power of this withdrawal of Being as an event of refusal. "The staying away of Being is Being itself as this very default."[13] In modernity's total forgetfulness of Being, the negativity of the abandonment by Being is no longer even felt. This explains the central significance of an anamnesis of the history of Being which now discloses itself as the destruction of the self-forgetfulness of metaphysics.[14] Heidegger's whole effort is aimed at "experienc[ing] the default of Being's unconcealment as such for the first time as an advent of Being itself, and [of] ponder[ing] what is thus experienced."[15]

(4) Heidegger cannot, however, understand the destruction of the history of metaphysics as unmasking critique, or the overcoming of metaphysics as a final act of disclosure, for the self-reflection that achieves this still belongs to the epoch of modern subjectivity. Thus, the thinking that uses the ontological difference as a guide must claim a cognitive competence *beyond* self-reflection, beyond discursive thought. Nietzsche could still invoke putting philosophy "on the basis of art"; for Heidegger, there remains only the reassuring gesture that for the initiate "there is a thinking more rigorous than the conceptual."[16] Wholesale devaluation befalls scientific thinking and methodically pursued research, because they move within modernity's understanding of Being prescribed by the philosophy of the subject. As long as it does not renounce argument, even philosophy stays inside the enchanted circle of objectivism. It, too, has to be reminded that "all refutation in the field of essential thinking is foolish."[17]

To make his claims of necessity, of a special knowledge, that is, of a privileged access to truth, plausible, even if only superficially, Heidegger has to level the differentiated developments of the sciences and of philosophy *after* Hegel in a bewildering manner.

In the 1939 lectures on Nietzsche, there is an interesting chapter bearing the heading "Mutual Understanding and Calculation." In it, Heidegger turns as always against the monological approach of the philosophy of consciousness, which takes as its point of departure the individual subject who in knowing and acting stands over against an objective world of things and occurrences. The self-maintenance of the subject appears as a calculated dealing with perceivable and manipulable objects. Within this model, even the prior dimension of mutual understanding among subjects appears under the category of "being able to count on [other] people."[18] In contrast to this, Heidegger stresses the nonstrategic meaning of the intersubjectively achieved agreement on which, indeed, "the relationship to the other, to the thing, and to oneself" is truly based. "To reach mutual understanding about something means: to think *the same thing* about it and, in case of a divergence of opinions, to establish the respects in which there is agreement or division of opinion. . . . Because misunderstanding and lack of understanding are only degenerate species of mutual understanding . . . the approach of human beings toward one another in their selfsameness and selfhood has first to be grounded through mutual understanding."[19] The resources required for the continued existence of social groups — among others, those springs of social integration that are drying up in modernity — are also to be found in this dimension of mutual understanding.[20]

Oddly enough, Heidegger believes that insights of *this kind* are exclusively reserved to his critique of metaphysics. He ignores the fact that altogether similar considerations are the starting point both for the methodology of the interpretative *Geisteswissenschaften* and social sciences and for influential philosophical trends (such as the Pragmatism of Peirce and Mead and, later, the linguistic philosophy of Wittgenstein and Austin and the philosophical hermeneutics of Gadamer). The philosophy of the subject is by no means an absolutely reifying power that imprisons all discursive thought and leaves open nothing but a flight into the immediacy of mystical ecstasy. There are *other* paths leading out of the philosophy of the subject. The fact that Heidegger sees in the history of philosophy and the sciences after Hegel nothing but a monotonous spelling out of the ontological pre-judgments [*Vor-Urteile*] of the philosophy of the subject can only be explained by the fact that, even in rejecting it, he still remains caught in the problems that the philosophy of the subject in the form of Husserlian phenomenology had presented to him.

II

In their attempts to overcome the philosophy of the subject, Hegel and Marx had been ensnared in its own basic concepts. This objection cannot be leveled at Heidegger, but a similarly telling one can be. So little does Heidegger free himself from the pregiven problematics of transcendental consciousness that he can burst the conceptual cage of the philosophy of consciousness in no other way than by abstract negation. Even in the "Letter on Humanism," which sums up the results of the Nietzsche interpretations of the previous decade, Heidegger cannot characterize his own procedure otherwise than through implicit reference to Husserl: He wants, as he puts it there, "[to] retain the essential help of the phenomenological way of seeing and [to] dispense with the inappropriate concern with 'science' and 'research.'"[21]

Husserl understood his transcendental reduction as a procedure that was supposed to allow the phenomenologist to draw a clear line between the world of beings given in the natural attitude and the sphere of the pure constituting consciousness which first lends beings their meaning. His whole life long, Heidegger held on to the *intuitionism* of this *procedure*; in the late philosophy, his manner of proceeding is simply relieved of the claims to be methodical and set free for a privileged "inherence in the truth of being." Husserl's way of *posing problems* also remains normative for Heidegger, inasmuch as he merely turns the basic epistemological question into an ontological one. In both cases, the phenomenological gaze is directed upon the world as the correlate of the knowing subject. In contrast to, say, Humboldt, Mead, or the later Wittgenstein, Heidegger does not free himself from the traditional granting of a distinctive status to theoretical activity, to the constative use of language, and to the validity claim of propositional truth. He also remains attached, in a negative way, to the *foundationalism* of the philosophy of consciousness. In the introduction to *What Is Metaphysics?* he compares philosophy to a tree that branches out into the sciences and itself grows out of the main root of metaphysics. The thoughtful remembrance [*Andenken*] of Being that he propagates does not call into question the foundationalist starting point: "To speak in images, it does not tear out the root of philosophy. It digs up the ground and plows the soil for it."[22] Because Heidegger does not gainsay the hierarchical orderings of a philosophy bent on self-grounding, he can only counter foundationalism by excavating a still more deeply laid — and henceforth unstable — ground. The idea of the destining of Being remains chained to its abstractly negated antithesis in this respect. Heidegger passes beyond the horizon of the philosophy of consciousness only to stay in the shadows. Before turning to *Being and Time* to work out this twilight position more clearly, I would like to point out three rather awkward consequences.

(a) Since the close of the eighteenth century, the discourse of modernity has had a single theme under ever new titles: the weakening of the forces of social bonding, privatization, and diremption — in short, the deformations of a one-sidedly rationalized everyday praxis which evoke the need for something equivalent to the unifying power of religion. Some place their hope in the reflective power of reason, or at least in a mythology of reason; others swear by the mythopoetic power of an art that is supposed to form the focal point of a regenerated public life. What Hegel called the need for philosophy was transformed from Schlegel until Nietzsche into the need — critical of reason — for a new mythology. But only Heidegger vaporized this concrete need by ontologizing it and foundationalizing it into a Being that is withdrawn from beings. Through this shift, Heidegger makes unrecognizable not only the source of this need in the pathologies of an ambiguously rationalized lifeworld but also a resolutely subjectivistic art as the experiential background for the radicalized critique of reason. Heidegger enciphers the palpable distortions of everyday communicative practice into an impalpable destining of Being [*Seinsgeschick*] administered by philosophers. At the same time, he cuts off the possibility of any deciphering by the fact that he shoves aside the defective everyday practice of mutual understanding as a calculation-oriented practice of self-maintenance — oblivious of Being and vulgar — and deprives the diremped ethical totality of the lifeworld of any essential interest.[23]

(b) A further implication of Heidegger's later philosophy is that the critique of modernity is made independent of scientific analysis. "Essential thinking" renounces all empirical and normative questions that can be treated by social-scientific or historical means, or can be at all handled in argumentative form.

Abstract insights into essences thus range all the more freely within an unreflected horizon of prejudices of bourgeois culture critique. Heidegger's critical judgments on "*das Man*," on the dictatorship of the public realm and the impotence of the private sphere, on technocracy and mass civilization, are without any originality whatsoever, because they belong to a repertoire of opinions typical of a certain generation of German mandarins.[24] Certainly, in the Heideggerian school, more serious attempts have been made to focus more precisely the ontological concepts of technique, the totalitarian dimension, and the political sphere in general, for purposes of analyzing the present age; but these efforts evince the irony that the thinking of Being falls all the more into the trap of contemporary scientific fashions, the more it thinks itself removed from the business of science.

(c) Finally, the indeterminacy of the fate that Heidegger holds in prospect as a result of the overcoming of metaphysics is problematic. Because Being withdraws itself from the assertive grasp of descriptive statements, because it can only be encircled in indirect discourse and "rendered silent," the destinings of Being remain undiscoverable. The propositionally contentless speech about Being has, nevertheless, the illocutionary sense of demanding resignation to fate. Its practical-political side consists in the perlocutionary effect of a diffuse readiness to obey in relation to an auratic but indeterminate authority. The rhetoric of the later Heidegger compensates for the propositional content that the text itself refuses: It attunes and trains its addressees in their dealings with pseudo-sacral powers.

Human beings are the "shepherds of Being" [*Hirte des Seins*]. Thinking is a meditative "letting oneself be claimed" [*Sichinanspruchnehmenlassen*]. It "belongs to" [*gehört*] Being. The thoughtful remembrance of Being is subject to "the laws of fittingness" [*Gesetzen der Schicklichkeit*]. Thinking "heeds" [*achtet*] the destining of Being. The humble shepherd is called [*gerufen*] by Being itself to preservation [*Wahrnis*: safekeeping] of the truth. In this way, Being "vouchsafes" [*gewärt*] to healing [*dem Heilen*] its upsurge [*Aufgang*] into favor [*Huld*] and to raging [*dem Grimm*] its compulsion [*Andrang*] to malignancy [*Unheil*].

These are well-known formulations from the "Letter on Humanism" that have been repeated stereotypically since then. The language of *Being and Time* had suggested the decisionism of empty resoluteness; the later philosophy suggests the submissiveness of an equally empty readiness for subjugation. To be sure, the empty formula of "thoughtful remembrance" can also be filled in with a different attitudinal syndrome, for example with the anarchist demand for a subversive stance of refusal, which corresponds more to present moods that does blind submission to something superior.[25] But the arbitrariness with which the same thought-figure can be given contemporary actualization remains irritating.

When one ponders these implications, one may well doubt that Heidegger's later philosophy, which outdoes Nietzsche's critique of metaphysics, actually leads us out of the discourse of modernity. It results from a "turn" that is supposed to lead out of the dead end of *Being and Time*. But this work — which is argumentatively the most rigorous by Heidegger the philosopher — can be understood as a dead end only if one views it in a thought context different from the one that Heidegger retrospectively arranges for himself.

III

Heidegger has repeatedly emphasized that he had already carried out his existential analysis of Dasein with the single goal of renewing the question of the meaning of Being, which had been buried over since the beginnings of metaphysics. He wanted to occupy the exposed point at which the history of metaphysics makes itself known in its unifying meaning and at the same time comes to a culmination.[26] This imperious claim of the later Heidegger conceals the proximate context in which *Being and Time* actually arose. I am speaking not only of the post-Idealism of the nineteenth century, but especially of the neo-ontological wave that captured German philosophy after the First World War, from Rickert through Scheler down to Hartmann. In terms of the history of philosophy, this era is marked by the collapse of neo-Kantianism — at that time the only philosophy of worldwide note — and not by a return to pre-Kantian ontology. Instead, ontological thought forms were employed to expand transcendental subjectivity beyond the realm of cognition and to "concretize" it. Historicism and *Lebensphilosophie* had already disclosed the ordinary and the extraordinary realms of experience of the transmission of tradition, of aesthetic creativity, of bodily, social, and historical existence, and had raised them to the level of philosophical interest. These realms of experience overburdened the constitutive performances of the transcedental ego and burst asunder at least the classical concept of the transcendental subject. Dilthey, Bergson, and Simmel replaced the generative performances of transcendental synthesis with the vague, vitalistically toned productivity of life or the stream of consciousness; but in doing so they had not yet freed themselves from the expressivistic model. For them, too, the idea of a subjectivity that externalizes itself, in order to melt down these objectifications into experience, remained standard.[27] Heidegger takes up these impulses but recognizes the inadequacy of the basic concepts of the philosophy of consciousness dragged along with them. He faces the problem of dissolving the concept of transcendental subjectivity dominant since Kant, but without leveling down the wealth of differentiations that the philosophy of the subject had worked out, most recently in Husserl's phenomenology.

Heidegger himself mentions the context of the problem in which *Being and Time* arose in section 10, where he refers to Husserl and Scheler: "The person is not a thing, not a substance, not an object. Here Scheler is emphasizing what Husserl suggests when he insists that the unity of the person must have a constitution essentially different from that required for the unity of things of nature. . . . Essentially the person exists only in the performance of intentional acts. . . . Thus psychical being has nothing to do with personal being. Acts get performed; the person is a performer of acts."[28] Heidegger is not satisfied with this approach and inquires: "What, however, is the ontological meaning of 'performance'? How is the kind of being which belongs to a person to be ascertained ontologically in a positive way?" (p. 73). He makes use of the vocabulary of the neo-ontological turn in order to advance further the dissolution of the concept of the transcendental subject; but even in this radicalization he holds on to the transcendental attitude of a reflective illumination of the conditions of the possibility of the being of the person as a being-in-the-world. Otherwise the articulated profusion of structures would sink into the undifferentiated conceptual whirl of *Lebensphilosophie*. The philosophy of the subject is to be overcome by the equally sharp and systematic, but far more profound, conceptual framework of an existential ontology proceeding in a transcendental fashion. Under this head, Heidegger forces together in an original way theoretical approaches that were hitherto incompatible but now indicate a meaningful perspective of inquiry in view of the goal of systematically replacing the basic concepts of the philosophy of the subject.

In the introductory chapter of *Being and Time*, Heidegger makes three weighty strategic decisions that free the way for fundamental ontology. *First*, he confers upon the transcendental problematic an *ontological* sense. The positive sciences are concerned with ontic questions; they make statements about nature and culture, about something in the world. The transcendental analysis of the conditions for these ontic modes of knowledge then clarifies the categorial constitution of these realms of objects as regions of Being. Accordingly, Heidegger understands Kant's *Critique of Pure Reason* not primarily as epistemology, but as "an a priori logic for the subject matter of that area of Being called 'nature'" (p. 31). This ontologizing coloration of transcendental philosophy becomes intelligible if one considers that the sciences themselves do not derive from free-floating cognitive performances, as the neo-Kantians had affirmed, but are embedded within concrete life-contexts: "Sciences are Dasein's ways of being" (p. 33). Husserl called this the founding of the sciences in the lifeworld. The meaning of the categorial makeup of scientific object-domains or regions of Being is only disclosed by going back to the understanding of Being of those who, in their *everyday existence*, are already comporting themselves toward entities in the world, and who are able then to stylize this naive intercourse into the precision-form of doing science. There belongs to situated, bodily-historical existence a comprehension, however diffuse, of a world, from the horizon of which the meaning of the entities later capable of being objectified by the sciences is always already interpreted. We encounter this preontological understanding of Being when, in the transcendental attitude, we inquire back *behind* the categorial makeup of entities disclosed by transcendental philosophy as it follows the guiding thread of the sciences. The analysis of the prior world-understanding grasps those structures of the lifeworld or of "being-in-the-world" that Heidegger calls existentials. Because these are prior to the categories of entities as a whole, and especially to the regions of being toward which the the scientist comports himself in an objectifying mode, the existential analytic of being-in-the-world earns the name of fundamental ontology. This is to say that the latter makes transparent for the first time the lifeworld or existential foundations of the regional ontologies elaborated in the transcendental attitude.

In a *second* step, Heidegger bestows on the phenomenological method the sense of an ontological *hermeneutics*. A phenomenon is, in Husserl's sense, anything that shows itself as itself of its own accord. Translating "the evident" with "the manifest," Heidegger plays on such opposite meanings as the hidden, the concealed, the covered over, and the like. It is only indirectly that phenomena come to appearance. What appears is the entity that covers over the "how" of its givenness. Phenomena escape our direct grasp because in their appearances as ontic they do not show themselves as what they are in themselves. Thus, phenomenology is distinguished from the sciences in that it does not have to do simply with particular species of appearances, but with the explication of what is concealed in every appearance — of what can only come to speak through phenomenology. The domain of phenomenology is the Being that has been displaced by entities. This is why it requires a special apophantic effort to make phenomena really present. The model for this effort is no longer intuition, as it was for Husserl, but the interpretation of a text — not the intuitive making-present of ideal essences that brings phenomena to self-givenness, but the hermeneutical understanding of complex meaning-contexts that discloses Being. In this fashion, Heidegger clears the way for an apophantic concept of truth and inverts the methodological meaning of the phenomenology of essential intuitions into its existentially hermeneutical opposite: In lieu of the description of an immediately intuited entity, we have the interpretation of a meaning that escapes all *Evidenz*.

In a *final* step, Heidegger links this analytic of Dasein (which proceeds transcendentally and hermeneutically at once) with a motif of *existentialist philosophy*. Human Dasein understands itself in terms of the possibility of either being or not being itself. It stands before the inescapable alternative of authenticity or inauthenticity. It is an entity of the kind that "has to be" its being. Human Dasein has to apprehend itself in terms of the horizon of its possibilities and take a hand in its own existence. Anyone who tries to avoid this alternative has already opted for a life in the mode of drivenness and of fallenness. This motif of responsibility for one's own salvation (heightened in an existentialist manner by Kierkegaard), Heidegger translates into the formula about care for one's own existence. "Dasein is an entity for which, in its being, that being is an issue" (p. 236).

Heidegger now employs this secularized salvational motif in such a way that care for one's own existence, heightened to anxiety, provides the guidelines for the analysis of the temporal constitution of human existence. However, the methodological use to which Heidegger puts this motif is equally important. It is not just the philosopher who, in posing the Being question, is referred to the preontological understanding of world and Being in his bodily-historical existence; no, it is a determination of this existence itself to be concerned about its being, to secure hermeneutically the existential possibilities of "his ownmost capacity to be." Precisely to this extent, the human being is an entity with an ontological nature for whom the Being-question is an inbuilt existential necessity. The existential analytics arises from the most deepset drive of human existence itself. Heidegger calls this the ontic rootedness of the existential analytic: "If to interpret the meaning of Being becomes our task, Dasein is not only the primary entity to be interrogated; it is also that entity which already comports itself, in its being, towards what we are asking about when we ask this question. But in that case the question of Being is nothing other than the radicalization of an essential tendency-of-Being which belongs to Dasein itself" (p. 15).

The three conceptually strategic decisions can be summarized successively by stating that Heidegger first couples transcendental philosophy with ontology in order to be able to characterize his existential analytic as fundamental ontology; that he goes on to shift the meaning of phenomenology into ontological hermeneutics in order to be able to carry out his fundamental ontology as an existential hermeneutics; that, finally, he endows his existential hermeneutics with motifs from existentialist philosophy in order to be able to embed the enterprise of fundamental ontology in contexts of interest otherwise degraded to the level of the merely ontic. At this single locus, the ontological difference is put out of play and the rigorous methodological distinction between the universal (of transcendentally accessible existentials) and the particular (of concretely experienced problems of existence) is broken through.

By these couplings, Heidegger seems to have succeeded in taking from the subject-object relationship its paradigmatic significance. The turn to ontology explodes the primacy of epistemology without giving up the transcendental problematic. Because the being of entities remains related internally to the prior understanding of Being, because Being comes into play only within the horizon of human Dasein, fundamental ontology does not mean a fall back beyond transcendental philosophy, but rather a radicalization of it.

The turn to existential hermeneutics at the same time puts an end to the methodological distinctiveness of self-reflection, which Husserl still needed for the procedure of transcendental reduction. In place of the knowing subject's relationship to itself — which is to say, of self-consciousness — enters the interpretation of a preontological understanding of Being and hence the explication of meaning-contexts within which one already finds oneself in everyday existence. Finally, Heidegger integrates existentialist motifs in such a way that the elucidation of the structures of being-in-the-world (which have replaced the conditions of the objectivity of experience) simultaneously affords an answer to the practical question about the right life. An emphatic concept of truth as manifestation founds the validity of judgments in the authenticity of a human existence that comports itself toward entities prior to all science.

This concept of truth serves as the guideline in terms of which Heidegger introduces the key term of fundamental ontology — the concept of *world*. World shapes the meaning-disclosing horizon within which entities are at once withdrawn from and manifested to the Dasein existentially concerned with its being. World is always prior to the subject that relates itself to objects in knowing and acting. For it is not the subject that assumes relationships toward something in the world, but the world that first of all establishes the context out of whose preunderstanding entities can be encountered. Through this preontological understanding of Being, the human being is admitted from the outset into frameworks of the world and privileged in relation to all the other entities in the world. It is the very entity that cannot simply be come across in the world; thanks to its special mode of being in the world, the human being is so interwoven with the context-shaping, space-giving, temporalizing processes of world-disclosure that Heidegger characterizes its existence as Da-sein (there-being), which "lets be" every entity by comporting itself toward it. The Da (there) of Dasein is the locale where the lighting-up process of Being [*Lichtung des Seins*] opens up.

The strategic conceptual gain relative to the philosophy of the subject is plain: Knowing and acting no longer have to be conceived in terms of subject-object relationships. "A *commercium* of the subject with a world (of representable or manipulable objects) does not get created for the first time by knowing, nor does it arise from some way in which the world acts upon a subject. Knowing is a mode of Dasein founded upon being-in-the-world" (p. 90). instead of the subject who in knowing or acting confronts the objective world as the totality of existing states of affairs, the acts of knowing and doing performed in the objectifying attitude can now be conceived as derivatives from basic modes of standing within a lifeworld, within a world intuitively understood as context and background. Heidegger characterizes these modes of being-in the lifeworld, in view of their temporal structure, as so many modes of caring, of having concern for something; as instances, he names "having to do with something, producing, attending to something and looking after it, giving up something and letting it go, undertaking, accomplishing, evincing, interrogating, considering, discussing, determining, and so forth" (p. 83).

At the center of the first section of *Being and Time* stands the analysis of the concept of world. From the perspective of manipulation, and in general of nonobjectifying, practical dealings with physical components of the lifeworld, Heidegger explicates a concept of world as a network of involvements reminiscent of Pragmatism. This is then generalized beyond the domain of the ready-at-hand and elucidated as a sign-context. Only by means of a distantiating change of attitude does nature get taken out of its horizon in the lifeworld and objectified. Only this de-worlding of a region of entities as sheerly represented gives rise to an objective world of objects and occurrences to which a subject (in the sense of the philosophy of consciousness) can relate itself through knowing and acting.

IV

I do not need to go into these analyses (sections 14–24) since they do not really advance beyond what was elaborated in Pragmatism from Peirce to Mead and Dewey. What is original, of course, is the use Heidegger makes of this concept of world for a critique of the philosophy of consciousness. But this undertaking immediately comes to a standstill. This becomes clear in the "question of the 'who' of Dasein" (section 25), which Heidegger at first answers by saying that Dasein is the entity that I always am myself: "The question of the 'who' answers itself in terms of the 'I' itself, the 'subject,' the 'self.' The 'who' is what maintains itself as something identical throughout changes in its experiences and ways of behaviour, and which relates itself to this changing multiplicity in so doing" (p. 150). This response would naturally itself lead straightaway back to the philosophy of the subject. This is why Heidegger extends his analysis of the tool-world, as it was presented from the perspective of the actor operating alone as a context of involvements, to the world of social relationships among several actors: "In clarifying being-in-the-world we have shown that a bare subject without a world never . . . is . . . given. And so . . . an isolated 'I' without others is just as far from being proximally given" (p. 152). Heidegger expands his world-analysis from the angle of interpersonal relations that I enter into with others.

As we shall see in another connection, the change in perspective from solitary rational purposiveness to social interaction does promise to illuminate the very processes of mutual understanding [*Verständigung*] — and not merely of understanding [*Verstehen*] — that keep present the world as an intersubjectively shared lifeworld background. We can find in language used communicatively the structures that explain how the lifeworld is reproduced even without subjects, so to speak, through the subjects and their activity orientated toward mutual understanding. In this way, the question concerning the "who" of Dasein would take care of itself — a question that Heidegger actually traces back again to a subject that constitutes the world of being-in-the-world by the authentic project of his possibilities for existing. The lifeworld in which human existence is embedded is by no means generated by the existential efforts of a Dasein that has tacitly assumed the place of transcendental subjectivity. It is suspended, as it were, in the structures of linguistic intersubjectivity and is maintained in the same medium in which subjects capable of speech and action come to a mutual understanding about something in the world.

Heidegger does not take the path to a response in terms of a theory of communication because from the start he degrades the background structures of the lifeworld that reach beyond the isolated Dasein as structures of an average everyday existence, that is, of inauthentic Dasein. To be sure, the co-Dasein of others first appears to be a constitutive feature of being-in-the-world. But the priority of the lifeworld's intersubjectivity over the mineness of Dasein escapes any conceptual framework still tinged with the solipsism of Husserlian phenomenology. The idea that subjects are individuated and socialized in the same stroke cannot be accommodated in the latter framework. In *Being and Time*, Heidegger does not construct intersubjectivity any differently than Husserl does in the *Cartesian Meditations*: Dasein as in each case mine constitutes being-with in the same way that the transcendental ego constitutes the intersubjectivity of the world shared by myself and others. Consequently, Heidegger cannot make his analysis of being-with fruitful for the question of how the world itself is constituted and maintained. He only takes up the theme of language after heading his analysis in another direction (section 34).

The communicative practice of everyday life is only supposed to make being-onself possible in the mode of a "dictatorship of the others": "One belongs to the others oneself and enhances their power. . . . The 'who' is not for this one, not that one, not oneself, not some people, and not the sum of them all. The 'who' is the neuter, the 'they'" (p. 164). The "they" now serves as a foil before which a Kierkegaardian existence, radically isolated in the face of death — the authentic existence of the human being in need of redemption — can be identified as the "who" of Dasein. Only as my own is the capacity for being open to authenticity and inauthenticity. Unlike Kierkegaard, of course, Heidegger no longer wants to think the totality of finite Dasein "ontotheologically" out of an empowering relationship to some highest entity or to entities taken as a whole; but rather only out of itself — that is, as a self-affirmation that is paradoxical because it is without any basis. W. Schulz correctly characterized the self-understanding of *Being and Time* as the heroic nihilism of self-affirmation in the impotence and finitude of Dasein.[29]

Although Heidegger in his *first* step de-structs the philosophy of the subject in favor of a frame of reference that first makes possible subject-object relationships, in his *second* step he falls back into the conceptual constraints of the philosophy of the subject, as he endeavors to make the world intelligible on its own terms as a process of world-occurrence. For the solipsistically posited Dasein once again occupies the place of transcendental subjectivity. To be sure, the latter no longer appears in the shape of an omnipotent *Ur-Ich* (primal I), but still as "the ultimate pursuit of human existence . . . in which all existing in the midst of being must be rooted."[30] To Dasein is ascribed the authorship of the projecting of the world. The authentic capacity to be whole on Dasein's part, or the freedom whose temporal structures Heidegger traces in the second part of *Being and Time*, is actuated in the transcending disclosure of entities: "The selfhood of the self, which lies at the basis of all spontaneity, lies in transcendence. Freedom is what lets world govern — by projecting and throwing world over being."[31] The classic demand of *Ursprungsphilosophie* for self-grounding and ultimate grounding is not deflected but answered in the sense of a Fichtean act [*Tathandlung*] that has been modified into a world-project. Dasein grounds itself from itself: "Dasein grounds (establishes) world only insofar as it grounds itself in the midst of being."[32] Heidegger once again grasps the world as a process out of the subjectivity of a will to self-affirmation. The two works following immediately after *Being and Time* — *What Is Metaphysics?* and *The Essence of Reasons* — demonstrate this.

Why fundamental ontology had to run off into the blind alley of the philosophy of the subject it was supposed to be steering clear of is easy to see. Ontology with a transcendental twist is guilty of the same mistake that it attributes to classical epistemology: Whether one gives primacy to the Being-question or to the knowledge-question, in either case the cognitive relation to the world and fact-stating discourse — theory and propositional truth — hold a monopoly as what is genuinely human and in need of clarification. This ontological/epistemological primacy of entities as what is knowable levels off the complexity of relations to the world sedimented in the multiplicity of illocutionary forces proper to natural languages, in favor of the *one* privileged relation to the objective world. This relation remains normative for practice, too; the monological execution of plans (that is, rational purposiveness) holds good as the primary form of action.[33] The objective world, even though conceived of as a derivative of contexts of involvements, remains the reference point even for fundamental ontology, under the heading of entities taken as a whole. The analytic of Dasein follows the architectonic structure of Husserlian phenomenology in that it grasps comporting oneself toward entities in accord with the model of the cognitive relationship — just as phenomenology analyzes all intentional acts on the model of the perception of elementary properties of objects. Within this architectonic, there is necessarily a place for the subject that constitutes objective realms by way of the transcendental conditions of knowledge. Heidegger fills this place with something that is productive in another way, namely, by the creation of meanings that disclose the world. Just as Kant and Husserl contrast the transcendental with the empirical, so Heidegger distinguishes the ontological from the ontic, or the *Existential* from the *Existentiell*.

Heidegger notes the breakdown of his attempt to tear away from the enchanted circle of the philosophy of the subject, but he does not note that this is a consequence of the sort of Being-question that can only be posed within the horizon of an *Ursprungsphilosophie*, however transcendentally turned it may be. The only way out of this impasse is afforded by an operation with which he often enough found fault in respect to Nietzsche's "rotation of Platonism": He stands *Ursprungsphilosophie* on its head without dissociating himself from any of its prior problems.

We have already become acquainted with the rhetoric by which the reversal is announced. The human being is no longer the placeholder of nothingness, but the shepherd of Being; being extended out toward anxiety gives way to joy and gratitude for the gift of Being; hanging on in spite of fate yields to self-surrender to the destining of Being; self-affirmation cedes to self-donation. The change in position can be described under three aspects: (a) Heidegger renounces the claim ascribed to metaphysics of self-grounding and ultimate grounding. The foundation that was formerly supposed to be laid by fundamental ontology in the form of a transcendentally executed analysis of the basic constitution of Dasein loses its significance in favor of a contingent occurrence to which Dasein is delivered over. The event of Being can only be meditatively experienced and presented narratively, but not argumentatively retrieved and explained. (b) Heidegger rejects existential ontology's concept of freedom. Dasein is no longer considered the author of world-projects in light of which entities are at once manifested and withdrawn; instead, the *productivity* of the creation of meaning that is disclosive of world passes over to *Being* itself.

Dasein bows to the authority of an unmanipulable meaning of Being and rids itself of any will to self-affirmation that is suspect of subjectivity. (c) Heidegger negates in the end the foundationalism of a thinking that has recourse to a first principle, whether it occurs in the traditional patterns of metaphysics or in the patterns of transcendental philosophy from Kant to Husserl. This refusal does not, of course, extend to the hierarchy of levels of knowledge that rest on a foundation beyond which we cannot go, but only to the atemporal character of this origin. Heidegger temporalizes the origins, which, in the shape of an unfathomable destiny, certainly retain the sovereignty of a first principle. The temporality of Dasein is now only the cornice of a self-temporalizing dispensation of Being. The first principle of *Ursprungsphilosophie* is temporalized. This is revealed in the undialectical nature of Being: The holy — as which Being supposedly comes to language in poetry — is considered to be the absolutely unmediated, just as it had been for metaphysics.

A consequence of this inverted foundationalism is the shift in meaning of "fore-having" [*Vorhabe*], which Heidegger announced for the never written second volume of *Being and Time*: According to the self-understanding of *Being and Time*, it belonged to the province of a phenomenological destruction of the history of ontology to loosen up rigid traditions and to awaken the contemporary awareness of problems to the buried experiences of ancient ontology. Aristotle and Hegel treated the history of philosophy no differently — as a prehistory of their own system. After the reversal, this at first *propaedeutically intended* task mounts up to almost *world-historical* significance, since the history of metaphysics — and of the poetry deciphered against its backdrop — advances to the status of the single intelligible medium of the dispensations of Being itself. From this perspective, Heidegger seizes upon Nietzsche's critical reflections on metaphysics in order to integrate him into the history of metaphysics as its ambiguous culmination and to take up the legacy of his Dionysian messianism.

Nevertheless, Heidegger could not have turned Nietzsche's radical critique of reason into a destruction of the history of ontology, he could not have projected Nietzsche's Dionysian messianism apocalyptically onto Being, if an uprooting of propositional truth and a devaluation of discursive thought did not go hand in hand with his historicization of Being. Only for these reasons can the critique of reason in terms of the history of Being give the illusion, in spite of its radicality, of avoiding the paradoxes connected with any self-referential critique of reason. It reserves the title of truth for the so-called truth-occurrence, which no longer has anything to do with a validity-claim transcending space and time. The truths (emerging in the plural) of this temporalized *Ursprungsphilosophie* are in each case provincial and yet total; they are more like the commanding expressions of some sacral force fitted out with the aura of truth. As for the apophantic concept of truth developed in *Being and Time* (section 44), Ernst Tugendhat shows how Heidegger "precisely by the fact that he turns the word 'truth' into a basic term, . . . passes over the problem of truth."[34] Already at this point, the world-project disclosive of meaning, which is inscribed in the totality of a linguistic world view (as in Humboldt) or in the grammar of a language game (as in Wittgenstein), is raised above any and every critical forum: The luminous force of world-disclosing language is hypostatized. It no longer has to prove itself by its capacity to throw light on beings in the world. Heidegger supposes that beings can be opened up in their Being with equal ease by any given approach. He fails to see that the horizon of the understanding of meaning brought to bear on beings is not prior to, but rather subordinate to, the question of truth.[35]

Of course, when the rule system of a language changes, the validity conditions of the sentences formulated in it also change. But whether the validity conditions are in fact satisfied to such an extent that the sentences can also function is not a matter of the world-disclosing power of the language, but of the innerworldly success of the practice it makes possible. The Heidegger of *Being and Time* was still enough a phenomenologist to fend off the idea that his argumentatively performed existential hermeneutics was removed from all claims of grounding. He was already prevented from taking this position by the idea (laden with strong normative connotations) of the authentic capacity to be that he linked with an existentialist interpretation of individual conscience (sections 54–60).

But even this check by a (surely problematic, because reducible to an empty formula) decisionistic resoluteness loses its force after the *Kehre*. That dimension of unconcealment prior to propositional truth passes over from the conscientious project of the individual concerned about his existence to an anonymous dispensation of Being that demands subjection, is contingent, and prejudices the course of concrete history. The heart of the reversal is the fact that Heidegger misleadingly furnishes the metahistorical authority of a primordial force set temporally aflow with the attribute of being an occurrence of truth.

V

This step is so bereft of plausibility that it cannot be satisfactorily explained in terms of the internal motifs discussed up to this point. I suspect that Heidegger could find his way to the temporalized *Ursprungsphilosophie* of the later period only by way of his temporary identification with the National Socialist movement — to whose inner truth and greatness he still attested in 1935.

It is not Heidegger's "Profession of Faith in Adolf Hitler and the National Socialist Movement" (the title under which his address to the election rally of German scholars and scientists held at Leipzig on 11 November 1933 was disseminated) that calls for a judgment by those born later — who cannot know whether in a similar situation they, too, would not have failed. What is irritating is the unwillingness and the inability of this philosopher, after the end of the Nazi regime, to admit his error with so much as *one* sentence — an error fraught with political consequences. Instead, Heidegger embraces the maxim that it is not the perpetrators but the victims themselves who are guilty: "Certainly — it is always presumptuous when men add up and attribute guilt to other men. But when one seeks out the guilty and measures their guilt: Is there not also a guilt of essential omission? Those who were then so prophetically gifted that they saw everything coming just as it did —

I was not that wise — why have they waited almost ten years to take action against the malignancy? Why didn't those who thought they knew in 1933, why didn't they rise up then to turn everything toward the good, from the ground up?"[36] What is irritating is the repression of guilt in a man who, when it was all over, wrote out a denazification certificate justifying his option for fascism from the valet's perspective of petty university intrigues. Just as Heidegger immediately pins the blame for his assumption of the rectorship and the quarrels that followed on the "essentially metaphysical condition of science,"[37] so he detaches his actions and statements altogether from himself as an empirical person and attributes them to a fate for which one cannot be held responsible. He viewed his own theoretical development from this perspective as well; he did not understand the so-called *Kehre* as the outcome of an effort of thought to solve problems, the result of a process of investigation, but always as the objective event of an anonymous overcoming of metaphysics staged by Being itself. Up to this point I have reconstructed the transition from fundamental ontology to the meditative thinking of Being as an internally motivated way out of the philosophy of the subject, that is, as a *solution to a problem*. Heidegger would emphatically reject this reconstruction. There is also some truth in this protest. As a matter of fact, the reversal is the result of his historical experience with National Socialism, that is, of an event that Heidegger to a certain extent ran up against. Only this moment of truth within a metaphysically enraptured self-understanding can render plausible what would have to remain unintelligible from the internal perspective of a theoretical development guided by problems: how Heidegger could understand the history of Being as truth-occurrence and keep it immune from any simple historicism of world views or epochal interpretations of the world. Thus, I am interested in the question of how fascism played into the very development of Heidegger's theory.

So little did Heidegger perceive the position worked out in *Being and Time* — and elucidated many times in the succeeding years until 1933 — as problematic that after the takeover of power he made an original use precisely of the implications, in terms of the philosophy of the subject, of self-assertive Dasein in its finitude. To be sure, it was a use that significantly shifted the connotations and the original meaning of the existential analytic. The basic concepts (left unchanged) of fundamental ontology were given a new content by Heidegger in 1933. If he had hitherto used "Dasein" in an unmistakable way for the existentially isolated individual on his course toward death, now he substitutes for this "in-each-case-mine" Dasein the collective Dasein of a fatefully existing and "in-each-case-our" people [*Volk*].[38] All the existential categories stay the same and yet with one stroke they change their very meaning — and not just the horizon of their expressive significance. The connotations they owe to their Christian origins, especially Kierkegaard, are transformed in the light of a New Paganism prevalent at that time.[39] The obscene intonation of its semantics can be made evident by citations that have long been familiar. In an election manifesto, Rector Heidegger writes in the *Freiburger Studentenzeitung* of 10 November 1933: "The German people is called by the Führer to an election; but the Führer asks nothing of the people. Rather he gives them the most direct possibility of the highest free choice: whether the entire people wills its own Dasein or not. . . . This election simply cannot be compared to previous elections. Its unique quality is the simple greatness of the decision to be made. . . . This final decision reaches out to the uttermost boundaries of the Dasein of our people. . . . The election choice that the German people now makes is — apart from its outcome — already the occurrence of and the strongest testimony to the new German reality of the National Socialist State. Our will to the self-responsibility of the people wills that each people find the greatness and truth of its determination. . . . The Führer has awakened this will in the whole people and has fused it into a single decision."[40] Whereas earlier the ontology was rooted ontically in the existence of the individual in the lifeworld,[41] now Heidegger singles out the historical existence of a nation yoked together by the Führer into a collective will as the locale in which Dasein's authentic capacity to be whole is to be decided. The first Reichstag elections, taking place in the shadow of KZs filled with Communists and Social Democrats, shift into the

aura of some final existential decision. What has actually degenerated into an empty acclamation Heidegger stylizes into a
decision that, in the light of *Being and Time*'s conceptual framework, takes on the character of a project: the project of a new,
authentic form of life for the people.

On the occasion of the aforementioned election rally by scientists and scholars for the Führer, *Being and Time* again provides the script for a speech that is supposed to stir up not
individual existence but now the whole people, and to push
them to a heroic truth: "The people is winning back the truth
of its will to exist [*Daseinswille*], for truth is the manifestness of
what a people makes secure, clear, and strong in its action and
knowledge." The formal determination of provisional resoluteness heard by students since 1927 gets concretized into the
outbreak of a national revolution — and into a break with the
world of Occidental rationalism: "We have completely broken
with idolizing a thinking that has no ground and no power.
We see the end of all philosophy that could serve it. We are
certain of this — that the clear toughness and the certainty that
does justice to achievement, which are proper to simple, uncompromising questioning about the nature of Being, are coming back to us. The primordial courage to either grow from or
break under the confrontation with what is [*dem Seienden*] is
the innermost motivation of a national science [*einer völkischen
wissenschaft*]. . . . Questioning bids us not to shut ourselves off
from the terror of the untamed and the chaos of darkness. . . .
And so we — who will henceforth be entrusted with the preservation of our people's desire to know — proclaim: The
National Socialist revolution is not simply the assumption of
existing power in the state by another party that has become
equal to the task; rather, this revolution brings with it a complete upheaval of our German existence Dasein."[42]

As the lectures for the summer semester of 1935 demonstrate, Heidegger held fast to this profession of faith beyond
the time span of his short term as rector. Once he at last could
no longer be deluded about the true character of the National
Socialist regime, he had maneuvered himself philosophically
into a difficult situation. Because he identified "Dasein" with
the Dasein of the nation, authentic capacity to be with the

seizure of power, and freedom with the will of the Führer, and because he had read into the question of Being the National Socialist revolution, including labor service, military service, and scholarly service, an internal and not easily touched up connection between his philosophy and contemporary events was established. A plain, political-moral revaluation of National Socialism would have attacked the foundations of the renewed ontology and called into question the entire theoretical approach. But if, on the contrary, the disappointment with National Socialism could be elevated beyond the foreground sphere of responsible judgment and action and stylized into an objective error, to an error gradually revealing itself in history, the continuity with the point of departure of *Being and Time* need not be endangered. Heidegger works up his historical experience with National Socialism in a manner that does not call into question the elitist claim to a privileged access to the truth on the part of philosophers. He interprets the untruth of the movement by which he had let himself be dragged along not in terms of an existential fallenness into the "they" for which one is subjectively responsible, but as an objective withholding of the truth. That the eyes of the most resolute philosopher were only gradually opened up to the nature of the regime — for this astoundingly delayed reading of world history — the course of the world itself is supposed to assume authorship, not concrete history, indeed, but a sublimated history promoted to the lofty heights of ontology. Thus was born the concept of the history of Being.

Within the frame of this concept, Heidegger's fascist error takes on a significance related to the history of metaphysics.[43] In 1935 Heidegger still saw the inner truth and greatness of the National Socialist movement in the "encounter between global technology and modern man."[44] At that time, he still trusted in the National Socialist movement to enlist the potential of technology in the service of the project of the new German Dasein. Only in the later course of the debate with Nietzsche's theory of power does Heidegger develop the concept of technology in terms of the history of ontology as that of *Gestell*. From that time, he was able to view fascism itself as a symptom and to classify it, alongside Americanism and communism, as an expression of the metaphysical domination of technology. It is only after this turn that fascism, like Nietzsche's philosophy, belongs to the objectively ambiguous phase of the overcoming of metaphysics.[45] With this shift in meaning, the activism and decisionism of self-assertive Dasein, in both its versions, the existentialist and the national revolutionary, also lose their meaning-disclosing function; only now does the pathos of self-assertion become a basic trait of the subjectivity that holds sway over modernity. In the later philosophy, the pathos of letting be and of readiness to listen takes its place.

Our recapitulation of the motivation behind the *Kehre* in terms of the history of that period confirms the outcome of our reconstruction of its internal theoretical development. Inasmuch as he propagates a mere inversion of the thought patterns of the philosophy of the subject, Heidegger remains caught up in the problematic of that kind of philosophy.

VII
Beyond a Temporalized Philosophy of Origins: Jacques Derrida's Critique of Phonocentrism

I

Insofar as Heidegger was received in postwar France as the author of the "Letter on Humanism," Derrida is correct in claiming for himself the role of an authentic disciple who has critically taken up the teaching of the master and productively advanced it. Not without a feeling for the *kairos* of the situation in contemporary history, Derrida made this claim in May of 1968 just as the riots had reached their highpoint.[1] Like Heidegger, Derrida takes into consideration "the Occident in its entirety" and confronts it with its "other," which announces itself in "radical upheavals" — economically and politically (that is, manifestly) by new constellations between Europe and the Third World, metaphysically by the end of anthropocentric thought. The human being as the being toward death has always lived in relation to its natural end. But now it is a matter of the end of its humanistic self-understanding: In the homelessness of nihilism it is not the human being but the essence of the human that wanders blindly about. And this end is supposed to be disclosed in the thinking about Being initiated by Heidegger. Heidegger prepares the completion of an epoch that will perhaps never end in a historical-ontic sense.[2] The familiar melody of the self-overcoming of metaphysics also sets the tone for Derrida's enterprise; destruction is renamed deconstruction: "Within the closure, by an oblique and always perilous movement, constantly risking falling back within what is being deconstructed, it is necessary to surround the critical concepts with a careful and thorough discourse . . . to designate rigorously their intimate relationship to the machine whose deconstruction they permit; and, in the same process, to designate the crevice through which the unnameable glimmer beyond the closure of our epoch can be glimpsed."[3] To this point we are on familiar ground.

To be sure, Derrida distances himself from Heidegger's later philosophy, especially from its network of metaphors. He defends himself against the regressively innocuous "metaphorics of proximity, of simple and immediate presence . . . associating the proximity of Being with the values of neighboring, shelter, house, service, guard, voice, and listening."[4] Whereas Heidegger decks out his history-of-Being fatalism in the style of Schultze-Naumburg with its sentimental homely pictures of a preindustrial peasant counterworld,[5] Derrida moves about instead in the subversive world of the partisan struggle — he would even like to take the house of Being apart and, out in the open, "to dance . . . the cruel feast of which the *Genealogy of Morals* speaks."[6] We shall have to see whether the concept of the history of Being changes along with the tenor, or whether under Derrida's hands the same idea merely takes on a different coloring.

Heidegger purchases the temporalization of *Ursprungsphilosophie* with a concept of truth made historically dynamic, but deracinated. When one lets oneself be as affected by the circumstances of contemporary history as Heidegger does, and nonetheless progresses, as if with the force of gravity, into the dimension of essential concepts, the truth claim of inverted foundationalism becomes rigidified into a prophetic gesture. At least it remains unclear how the normative core of a *truth claim* that transcends space and time could be maintained within the mobility of a happening of truth that is not at our disposal. With his concept of the Dionysian, Nietzsche had still pointed to a sphere of normative experience; and even Heidegger, in his existentialist period, could orient himself in terms of the normative content of an authentic Dasein. By contrast, the gracious gift of unfathomable Being lacks any structure whatsoever; the concept of the holy is ultimately no less diffuse than that of life. Distinctions we associate with the meaning of validity do not find any support within a dispensation of Being removed from all verification. Only religious connotations furnish any points of support — but they are immediately rejected as ontotheological remnants.

Derrida, too, perceives this situation as unsatisfactory; structuralism seems to provide a way out. For Heidegger, language constitutes the medium of the history of Being; the grammar of linguistic world views directs the preontological understanding of Being dominant at any given time. Heideggger rests content with characterizing language globally as the house of Being; despite the privileged status accorded it, he never systematically studied language. This is where Derrida starts. A scholarly climate shaped by the structuralism of Saussure encourages him to enlist linguistics, too, in the service of the critique of metaphysics. He then redoes the step from philosophy of consciousness to philosophy of language in a methodical way and, with grammatology, opens up a field of research for analyses that could no longer have existed for Heidegger on the level of his history of Being. For reasons we still need to explain, Derrida does not make use of the analyses of ordinary language carried out in the Anglo-Saxon world; he does not concern himself with the grammar of language or with the logic of its use. Instead, in a countermove to structuralist phonetics, he sets out to study the foundations of grammatology, that is, the science of writing. He cites from Littré the lexical entry for "grammatology" — "A treatise upon letters, upon the alphabet, syllabation, reading, and writing" — and names as a relevant study I. J. Gelb's book *A Study of Writing: The Foundations of Grammatology*.[7]

Grammatology recommends itself as a guide for the critique of metaphysics because it goes to the roots of phonetic writing, that is, of writing that copies the sound of words; and this is not only coextensive but also equiprimordial with metaphysical thought. Derrida is convinced "that phonetic writing, the medium of the great metaphysical, scientific, technical, and economic adventure of the West, is limited in space and time" — and in our day has reached its limit.[8] The early Derrida hopes to carry out the enterprise of the self-overcoming of metaphysics in the form of a grammatological study that reaches back beyond the beginnings of phonetic writing. It inquires beyond any writing that remains within the enchanted circle of the phonetic as a sheer fixation of sound patterns. Grammatology is supposed to explain instead why what is essential to language has to be grasped on the model of writing and not that of speech: "The 'rationality' — but perhaps that word should be abandoned for reasons that will appear at the end of this sentence — which governs a writing thus enlarged and radicalized, no longer issues from a logos. Further, it inaugurates the destruction, not the demolition but the de-sedimentation, the de-construction, of all the significations that have their source in that [signification] of the logos. Particularly the signification of truth. All the metaphysical determinations of truth, and even the one beyond metaphysical ontotheology that Heidegger reminds us of, are more or less immediately inseparable from the instance of the logos."[9] Since the logos, as we shall see, constantly indwells the spoken word, Derrida wants to confront the logocentrism of the West in the form of phonocentrism.

To understand this startling turn to grammatology it is useful to recall the metaphor of the book of nature or the book of the world, which points to the hard-to-read, painstakingly to be deciphered handwriting of God. Derrida quotes a saying of Jaspers: "The world is the handwriting of another, never fully legible world, which only existence deciphers." There are only books in the plural because the original text has been lost. Yet Derrida removes any optimistic note from this picture by radicalizing the notion of the lost book in a Kafkaesque manner. This book written in God's handwriting never existed, but only traces of it, and even they have been obliterated. This awareness has left its imprint on the self-understanding of modernity, at least since the nineteenth century: "It is not only to have lost the theological certainty of seeing every page bind itself into the unique text of the truth, . . . the genealogical anthology, the Book of Reason this time, the infinite manuscript read by a God who, in a more or less deferred way, is said to have given us the use of this pen. This lost certainty, this absence of divine writing, that is to say, first of all, the absence of the

Jewish God (who himself writes, when necessary), does not solely and vaguely define something like 'modernity.' As the absence and haunting of the divine sign, it regulates all modern criticism and aesthetics."[10] Modernity is in search of the traces of a writing that no longer holds out the prospect of a meaningful whole as the book of nature or the Holy Scripture had done.

Within a traditional context marked by catastrophe, the substrate of written signs is the only thing that survives corruption. The text is often damaged and fragmented so that it denies any access to interpreters in succeeding generations. But the signification remains upon even unintelligible texts, the signs last — matter survives as the trace of a spirit that has vanished.

It is obvious that Derrida, taking up from Levinas, is inspired by the Jewish understanding of tradition, which is more removed than the Christian from the idea of the book and precisely for this reason remains more rigorously bound to erudition in scripture. The program of a scripture scholarship with claims to a critique of metaphysics is nourished from religious sources. By the same token, Derrida does not want to think theologically; as an orthodox Heideggerian, he is forbidden any thought about a supreme entity. Instead, similarly to Heidegger, Derrida sees the modern condition as constituted by phenomena of deprival that are not comprehensible within the horizon of the history of reason and of divine revelation. As he assures us at the start of his essay on "différance," he does not want to do any theology, not even negative theology. Even less does he want whatever thus deprives us of itself to just trickle away through our fingers like the fluid of an intrinsically paradoxical history of Being.

The medium of writing provides, for this reason as well, a model in terms of which the aura is to be removed from the happening of truth, the Being distinguished from entities taken in sum and also from any supreme entity, and it is to be given a certain playful consistency. Consequently, Derrida has in mind here not the "solid permanence of the written," but primarily the circumstance that the written form detaches any given text from the context in which it arose. Writing makes what is said independent from the mind of the author, from the breath of the audience, as well as from the presence of the objects under discussion. The medium of writing lends the text a stony autonomy in relation to all living contexts. It extinguishes the concrete connections with individual subjects and determinate situations, and yet the text still retains its readability. Writing guarantees that a text can always repeatedly be read in arbitrarily changing contexts. What fascinates Derrida is this thought of an *absolute readability*: Even in the absence of every possible audience, after the death of all beings with an intelligent nature, the writing holds open in heroic abstraction the possibility of a repeatable readability that transcends everything in this world. Because writing mortifies the living connections proper to the spoken word, it promises salvation for its semantic content even beyond the day on which all who can speak and listen have fallen prey to the holocaust.[11] "All graphemes are of a testamentary essence."[12]

Of course, this idea is merely a variation on the motif of the dependency of living discourse upon self-sufficient structures of language. Inasmuch as Derrida replaces grammar as the science of language with grammatology as the science of writing, he intends to make the basic insight of structuralism even more pointed. Heidegger lacked the concept of a self-stabilized linguistic medium. This is why in *Being and Time* he had to base the constitution and maintenance of the world initially on the productivity of a world-projecting and self-grounding Dasein, which is to say, on an equivalent for the creative activity of transcendental subjectivity. Derrida is spared the detour through *Being and Time*. Backed by structuralism, he can forge a direct route from Husserl's earlier philosophy of consciousness to the late Heidegger's philosophy of language. I want to test whether his grammatologically distanced conception of the history of Being avoids the objection that was raised by Heidegger against Nietzsche and that recoils upon Heidegger himself: "The Nietzschean demolition remains dogmatic and, like all reversals, a captive of that metaphysical edifice which it professes to overthrow."[13] To anticipate my thesis: Even Derrida does not extricate himself from the constraints of the paradigm of the philosophy of the subject. His attempt to go beyond Heidegger does not escape the aporetic structure of a truth-occurrence eviscerated of all truth-as-validity. Derrida passes beyond Heidegger's inverted foundationalism, but remains in its path. As a result, the temporalized *Ursprungsphilosophie* takes on clearer contours. The remembrance of the messianism of Jewish mysticism and of the abandoned but well-circumscribed place once assumed by the God of the Old Testament preserves Derrida, so to speak, from the political-moral insensitivity and the aesthetic tastelessness of a New Paganism spiced up with Hölderlin.

II

The text through which we can examine in detail Derrida's attempt to break out of the philosophy of the subject is the critique of Husserl's theory of meaning that was published in 1967, at the same time as *Of Grammatology*.[14] From the standpoint of a deconstruction of the philosophy of consciousness, Derrida could scarcely have chosen a more fitting target than the section on "Expression and Meaning" from the second volume of the *Logical Investigations*.[15] Here Husserl energetically defends the sphere of pure consciousness against the intermediate domain of linguistic communication; he pushes meaning emphatically to the side of ideal essence and of the intelligible, in order to purify it from the empirical associations of the linguistic expression without which we cannot get hold of the meaning.

Husserl distinguishes the *sign*, which expresses a linguistic meaning, from a mere *indication*. Fossil bones attest to the existence of antediluvian animals; flags or banners testify to the nationality of their bearers; knots in a handkerchief remind one of a not yet carried out plan. In all these cases, the signal calls a situation to consciousness. It is immaterial whether the indicator is connected with the existence of the situation indicated by causal, logical, iconic, or purely conventional connections; it functions as an indication when, like the knots in the handkerchief, the sign-perception evokes the thought of a non-present state of affairs in virtue of an association effective in the psyche. The linguistic expression represents its meaning (or the object to which it is related when it appears with a referential function) in a different mode. Unlike the signal, the linguistic expression has its meaning on the basis of an ideal connection and not in virtue of association. Interestingly enough, Husserl reckons mimicry and gesture as indications because he misses in these spontaneous bodily expressions the act of will or the communicative intent — in brief, the intentionality of the speaker. They take on a meaning, to be sure, as soon as they substitute for linguistic expressions. Expressions can be set off from indications by reason of their genuinely linguistic structure. "Each expression not only has a meaning, but refers to certain objects."[16] In other words, an expression can always be expanded into a sentence that refers the content of what is said to something about which something is stated. In contrast, the indication lacks this differentiation into object reference and predicated content — and hence that independence of situation which is specifically characteristic of the linguistic expression.

Husserl's theory of meaning — like that of Saussure — adopts a semiotic and not a semantic approach. He does not expand the semiotic distinction between sign-types (indication versus expression) into a grammatical distinction between signal language and propositionally differentiated language.[17] Derrida's critique confines itself to semiotic considerations as well. He refers especially to the peculiar use Husserl makes of his distinction between sign and indication to devalue expressions employed communicatively as against linguistic expressions *strictu sensu*. Husserl expounds the thesis that linguistic expressions, which arise pure, as it were, in the internal forum of the "solitary mental life," have to take on the additional function of indication as soon as they are to serve the pragmatic function of communication and pass over into the external sphere of speech. In the course of communicative speech, expressions are supposed to be "intertwined" with indications. It is common practice in analytic philosophy as well to prescind from the pragmatic aspects of the use of expressions in utterances and to concentrate only on the semantic structure of sentences and components of sentences. This conceptual cut can be clarified in relation to the transition from intersubjective discourse to internal monologue — the semantic point of view is satisfied with just the aspects constitutive of a monological use of linguistic expressions. But the semanticist position, which denies the intrinsic connection of language in its semantic dimension with speech, and proceeds as if the pragmatic functions of speech were extrinsic, does not necessarily follow from choosing formal semantics as one's level of analysis. Within the framework of phenomenology, Husserl espouses just this (semanticist) position; given the premises of the philosophy of consciousness, he has no other choice.[18]

The monadological start from the transcendental ego forces Husserl to reconstruct intersubjective relationships produced in communication from the perspective of the individual consciousness directed toward intentional objects. The process of coming to an understanding breaks down into "informing," on the part of a speaker who produces sounds and links them with meaning-engendering acts, and the "being informed" of a hearer, for whom the signs perceived *indicate* the "informative" psychic experiences: "What first makes mental commerce possible, and turns connected speech into discourse, lies in the correlation among the corresponding physical and mental experiences of communicating persons."[19] Since at first the subjects stand immediately before one another and perceive one another as objects, communication between them is portrayed on the model of signaling contents of experience, that is, in expressivistic terms. The mediating *signs* function as *indications* for acts that the speaker performs in his solitary mental life: "If one surveys these interconnections, one sees at once that all expressions in communicative speech function as indications. They serve the hearer as signs of the 'thoughts' of the speaker, i.e. of his sense-giving inner experiences."[20]

Because Husserl posits as originary the subjectivity of sense-giving acts rather than the linguistically created intersubjectivity of mutual understanding, the process of reaching understanding between subjects has to be represented on the model of transmitting and deciphering experiential signals. Taking recourse in the distinction between expression and indication, he describes the communicative use of *signs* in such a fashion that they take on the function of external *indications* of the inwardly performed acts of the speaker. However, if linguistic expressions are joined to indications only in communication, that is, secondarily, expressions as such have to be ascribed to the sphere of solitary mental life — and only when they depart the sphere of interiority do they enter among the determinations of the indication. Then, however, the physical sign-substrate is devalued in relation to the meaning of the linguistic expression and demoted to a virtual state; its existence is, so to speak, canceled. Everything external is relegated to the category of the indication. Since the expression gets sublimated into pure meaning, released from any communicative function and shed of anything bodily, one is not at all sure why it is that meanings still need to be expressed with the help of word and sentence signs. In the internal monologue, there is no need for the subject in interchange only with itself to manifest to itself something of its inner experience: "Shall one say that in soliloquy one speaks to oneself, and employs words as signs, i.e. as indications, of one's own inner experience? I cannot think such a view acceptable."[21] In the inward monologue, the sign-substrate of the meaning expressed liquefies into something "essentially indifferent." "The expression seems to direct interest away from itself towards its sense, and to point to the latter. But this pointing is not an indication in the sense previously discussed. . . . What we are to use as an indication, must be perceived by us as existent. This also holds for expressions used in communication, but not for expressions used in soliloquy. . . . In imagination a spoken or printed word floats before us, though in reality it has no existence."[22]

This rendering virtual of the interiorized sign that issues from the philosophy of the subject has an important implication. That is to say, Husserl finds himself forced to anchor the identity of the meaning in something *other* than rules for sign-usage. This latter conception, subsequently developed by Wittgenstein, would presuppose an instrinsic connection between the identity of meaning and the intersubjective validity of the rules of meaning. Husserl, too, compares the signs we use in calculating with figures we move in accord with the rules of a chess game. But in contrast to Wittgenstein, Husserl has to postulate the primacy of pure meanings; only by virtue of our acquaintance with these originary meanings can we know how to proceed with the chess figures: "and so arithmetical signs have, besides their *original* meaning, their so-to-say games-meaning, ... If one treats arithmetical signs as mere counters in the rule-sense, to solve the tasks of the reckoning games leads to numerical signs or formulae whose interpretation in their original, *truly* arithmetical senses also represents the solution of corresponding arithmetical problems."[23]

The meaning of an expression is grounded in acts of meaning-intention and of intuitive fulfillment of this intention — this is meant not psychologically, but in the sense of a transcendental grounding. The content of meaning is an ideal something-in-itself that Husserl wants to get from the intentional nature of the meaning-bestowing act, and ultimately from the nature of the meaning-fulfilling act of a correlative ideal intuition. However, no necessary connection exists "between the ideal unities which in fact operate as meanings, and the signs to which they are tied, i.e. through which they become real in human mental life."[24] This *Platonism of meaning*, which unites Husserl with Frege, is what ultimately permits the distinction between meanings "in themselves" and merely "expressed" meanings, which recalls Popper's equivalent distinction between the third and second worlds. The expression that emerges in the interior monologue as a "sign fantasy" serves the cognitive appropriation of ideal unities, which are available for knowing subjects only as expressed: "Wherever a new concept is formed, we see how a meaning becomes realized that was previously unrealized."[25]

I have gone through Husserl's theory of meaning step by step in order to show exactly the point at which Derrida's critique begins. Against the Platonizing of meaning and against the disembodying interiorization of its linguistic expression, Derrida wants to bring out the indissoluble interweave of the intelligible with the sign-substrate of its expression, one might even say: the transcendental primacy of the sign as against the meaning. Interestingly, his reflections are not aimed at those premises of the philosophy of consciousness that make it impossible to identify language as an intersubjectively constituted intermediate domain that has a share in both the transcendental character of world-disclosure and the empirical character of the innerworldly experienceable. Derrida does not take as his point of departure that nodal point at which the philosophy of language and of consciousness branch off, that is, the point where the paradigm of linguistic philosophy separates from that of philosophy of consciousness and renders the identity of meaning dependent upon the intersubjective practice of employing rules of meaning. Instead, Derrida follows Husserl along the path of separating off (in terms of transcendental philosophy) every innerworldly thing from the performances of the subject that are constitutive of the world, in order to take up the battle against the sovereignty of ideally intuited essences within its innermost precincts.

III

Derrida's critique approaches Husserl's concept of evidence in a manner similar to Heidegger's earlier critique of Husserl's concept of phenomenon. To secure the status of meanings existing "in themselves" beyond all embodiments, Husserl has to have recourse to an intuition in which these essences show themselves "of their own accord" and attain to givenness as pure phenomena. He constructs this intuition as the fulfillment of a meaning-intention, as the self-givenness of the "object" intended by the linguistic expression. The act intending meaning is related to the act fulfilling meaning as an image is to the actual perception of an object. The intuition makes good the promissory note issued by the expressed meaning. With this conception, however, Husserl trims down a priori all linguistically expressible meanings to their cognitive dimension.

Derrida rightly takes exception to the fact that language is then reduced to those components useful for knowing or for stating facts. Logic takes precedence over grammar, the cognitive function over the function of reaching understanding. To Husserl this seems obvious: "If we ask what an expression means, we naturally recur to cases where it actually contributes to knowledge."[26] Husserl himself remarks that, for example, the significance of singular terms could not be explained without further ado in accord with this model — there are "subjective expressions" whose meaning shifts along with the speech situation. But he meets this difficulty with the assertion that "each subjective expression is replaceable by an objective expression which will preserve the identity of each momentary meaning-intention."[27] Individual names are supposed to be replaceable by specification of distinguishing characteristics, deictic expressions of place and time by specification of spatiotemporal points, and so forth. As Tugendhat has shown, this program of translating subjective expressions into situation-independent objective expressions cannot be carried through; singular terms, like performative expressions, are examples of genuinely pragmatic meanings that cannot be explained independently of an intersubjective practice of applying rules. Derrida, to be sure, interprets this state of affairs completely differently. He understands the fact that Husserl has to couple *all* linguistic meanings with truth-related objective expressions, which are tied to fulfillment by actual intuition and hence are foreshortened to their cognitive function, as a symptom of a logocentrism with a long pedigree and by no means remediable through linguistic analysis: "Clearly, in fact, to say that each subjective expression could be replaced by an objective expression, is no more than to assert the unbounded range of objective reason."[28] It is this prior metaphysical bounding of language by reason, of meaning by knowledge, that evokes Derrida's resistance. In Husserl's evidential concept of truth, he sees a metaphysics at work that necessitates thinking Being as presence, as making-present or presentment.

This is where Derrida brings into play the exteriority of the sign that was pushed aside as inessential in Husserl's argument — a semiotic insight, but by no means one based on the pragmatics of speech. For Derrida, the idea of the identity of an experience as certified by presence reveals the metaphysical heart of phenomenology — metaphysical inasmuch as the model of an intuitively fulfilled meaning-intention does away with the *temporal difference* and otherness that are constitutive for the act of intuitively re-presenting [*Vergegenwärtigung*] the same object and thus also for the identity of the meaning of a linguistic expression. In Husserl's suggestion of the simple presence of something given in itself, the structure of repetition is lost, without which nothing can be torn out of the flux of time and the stream of experiences and made present as the same, which is to say, can be represented [*repräsentiert*].

In the central chapter 5 of *Speech and Phenomena*, Derrida goes back to Husserl's analyses of internal time-consciousness to work out — with Husserl and against Husserl — the differential structure of the intuition of what is actually given, an intuition that is made possible only through primary expectation and remembrance. The simple presence of an undivided object that is identical with itself falls apart as soon as we become conscious of the net of protentions and retentions in which every actual experience is embedded. The experience that is present "at the moment" is indebted to an act of re-presentation, perception is indebted to a reproducing recognition, such that the difference of a temporal interval and thus also an element of otherness is inherent in the spontaneity of the living moment. The intimately fused unity of what is intuitively given proves in fact to be something compounded and produced. Because the Husserl of the *Logical Investigations* failed to appreciate this original process of temporizing and spacing at the heart of transcendental subjectivity, he could also misconstrue the role of the sign in the constitution of objects and meanings identical with themselves. The sign is indispensable for every representation that relates past and present to one another: "A phoneme or grapheme is necessarily always to some extent different each time that it is presented in an operation or a perception. But it can function as a sign, and in general as language, only if a formal identity enables it to be issued again and to be recognized. This identity is necessarily ideal."[29] In place of the ideal character of some meaning in itself, which Husserl separates as rigorously from the acts of intending and of communication as from the sign-substrate of the expression and of the referent, Derrida has recourse to the "ideality of the sensible form of the signifier."[30] Nevertheless he does not explain this pragmatically from rule-usage, but by setting it off from what he calls Husserl's metaphysics of presence.

According to Derrida's central objection, Husserl permitted himself to be blinded by the fundamental idea of Western metaphysics: that the ideal nature of self-identical meaning is only guaranteed by the living presence of the unmediated, intuitively accessible, actual experience in the interiority of a transcendental subjectivity purified of all empirical associations. Otherwise he could not have deluded himself about the fact that, at the very source of this apparently absolute presence, a temporal difference and otherness looms on the horizon, which Derrida characterizes both as a *passive difference* and as a *deferral that produces difference.* This not-yet of a temporarily withheld, potential, still outstanding present forms the foil of references without which nothing at all could be experienced *as* something present. Derrida disputes that any meaning-intention can ever be wholly absorbed in the fulfilling intention, can be congruent with it, can ever melt away into it. An intuition can never make good that promissory note of meaning-intention issued by the expression. Rather, temporal difference and otherness are constitutive for both — for the meaning-function of a linguistic expression, which has to remain intelligible precisely in the absence of that to which the intended and the said refer; and for the structure of the experience of an object, which can be identified and held on to as something presently perceived only in anticipation of an interpretative expression, an expression, that is to say, that transcends actual experience and to that extent is not present.

A structure of repeatability investigated by Husserl himself in the concepts of protention and retention lies at the basis of every perception. Husserl did not recognize that the structure of re-presentation is only made possible by the symbolizing power or representative function of the sign. Only the expression, in its substratelike, nonsublimatable externality of the sign-character, brings forth the irrevocable difference, on the one hand, between itself and that for which it stands — its meaning — and, on the other hand, between the sphere of linguistically articulated meanings and the innerworldly sphere to which the speaker and hearer belong, together with their experiences and their speech, and above all the objects of the latter. Derrida interprets the internally differentiated relationship between expression, meaning, and experience as a crevice through which shines the light of language in which something can first be present as something in the world. Expression and meaning represent something — and Derrida grasps this symbolic representation as a process of temporalization, as a deferring, as an active being absent and withheld that comes into play in the structure of making-present and coming-to-the-light-of-day characteristic of the act of intuition.

Husserl was mistaken about the internal connection between this structure of repetition and the representative function of the linguistic sign. To explain this, Derrida refers to a casual remark of Husserl's: "that I imagine the verbal presentations which accompany and support my silent thinking sometimes involve picturings of words *spoken by my own voice*."[31] Derrida is convinced that Husserl could only neglect the substrate character of the linguistic sign as an inessential moment because in the Western tradition the sound pattern has enjoyed a questionable primacy over the written pattern, as has the phonetic embodiment over the graphic inscription. The fleeting transparency of the voice promotes the assimilation of the word to the expressed meaning. Herder already pointed out the unique relation to self that resides in listening to oneself talk. Like Herder (and Gehlen), Derrida emphasizes the intimacy and transparency, the absolute proximity of the expression animated simultaneously by my breath and my meaning-intention.

Inasmuch as the speaker hears himself, he performs three almost indistinguishable acts together: He produces sound patterns; inasmuch as he affects himself, he perceives the sensual form of the phoneme; and at the same time he understands the intended meaning. "Every other form of auto-affection must either pass through what is outside the realm of 'ownness' or forego any claim to universality."[32] This property explains not merely the primacy of the spoken word but also the suggestion that the being of the intelligible is, as it were, incorporeally present and is authenticated through what is present and experienced with immediate evidence. To this degree, phonocentrism and logocentrism are akin to one another: "[The voice] can show the ideal object or the ideal *Bedeutung* . . . without venturing outside ideality, ouside the interiority of self-present life."[33] This then becomes the starting thesis of grammatology as a critique of metaphysics: "Within the closure of this experience, the word is lived as the elementary and undecomposable unity of the signified and the voice, of the concept and a transparent substance of expression."[34]

However, if phonocentrism is the ground for the metaphysical privileging of the present, and if this metaphysics of presence in turn explains why Husserl remained closed to the basic semiotic insights into the representative function of the sign and its world-disclosing power, then it makes sense no longer to explicate the sign-structure of the linguistic expression and of its representative structure from the horizon of listening to oneself talk, but to select instead *writing* as the point of departure for the analysis. The written expression reminds us more insistently that the linguistic sign, "despite the total absence of a subject and beyond the subject's death," makes possible the decipherability of a text and, if it does not exactly guarantee its intelligibility, at least holds it in prospect. Writing is the testamentary promise of understanding. Derrida's critique of Husserl's theory of meaning aims at this strategic point: Till Husserl (and even Heidegger), metaphysics thought of Being as presence — Being is the "production and recollection of beings in presence, in knowledge and mastery."[35] The history of metaphysics culminates in a phenomenological intuitionism that annihilates the original difference of temporal separation and otherness that first makes possible the identity of objects and meanings, in the suggestive self-affection by one's own voice, a voice without differance: "A voice without differance, a voice without writing, is at once absolutely alive and absolutely dead."

The German translator uses the artificial word "Differänz" [translated "differance" above] to capture Derrida's word-play with the (French) homophonic expressions "différence" and "différance." The sign-structure that is at the basis of the repetition-structure of experience is combined with the temporal meaning of deferral, of circuitous hesitation, of calculative holding back, of the hint of a later payoff. The reference-structure of substitution, of representation, or of one thing's taking the place of another thereby gains a dimension of *temporizing* and of making-place-for in a *differentiated way*. "*Différer* in this sense is to temporize, to take recourse, consciously or unconsciously, in the temporal and temporizing mediation of a detour that suspends the accomplishment or fulfillment of 'desire' or 'will.'"[36] With the help of this concept of "differance," so loaded with a temporal dynamism, Derrida wants simultaneously to undermine by radicalizing Husserl's attempt to elaborate the ideal sense of meaning "in itself" and purified of all empirical associations. Derrida pursues Husserl's idealizations right to the most inward point of transcendental subjectivity in order to make plain here, at the source of the spontaneity of experience that is present to itself, the ineradicable difference which, if it is presented on the model of the referential structure of a written text, as an operation dissociated from the performing subject, can thus be conceived precisely as an *event without any subject*. Writing counts as the absolutely originary sign, abstracted from all pragmatic contexts of communication, independent of speaking and listening subjects.

This writing, which is prior to any subsequent fixing of sound patterns, this *Urschrift* (archewriting) makes possible — so to speak, without the help of the transcendental subject, in advance of any accomplishments of this subject — the world-disclosing differentiations between the intelligibility of meanings and the empirical element that comes to appearance within its horizon, between the world and what is within the world. This "making-possible" is a process of deferring that goes on inside the act of distinguishing: From this perspective, the intelligible that is distinguished from the sensible appears simultaneously as the postponed sensible; the concept distinguished from intuition as the postponed intuition; the culture distinguished from nature as postponed nature. Thus, Derrida achieves an inversion of Husserlian foundationalism inasmuch as the originative transcendental power of creative subjectivity passes over into the anonymous, history-making productivity of writing. The presence of whatever shows itself in actual intuition becomes directly dependent on the representative power of the sign.

It is important to note that in the course of pursuing this line of thought Derrida by no means breaks with the foundationalist tenacity of the philosophy of the subject; he only makes what it had regarded as fundamental dependent on the still profounder — though now vacillating or oscillating — basis of an originative power set temporally aflow. Unabashedly, and in the style of *Ursprungsphilosophie*, Derrida falls back on this *Urschrift*, which leaves its traces anonymously, without any subject: "New names indeed will have to be used if we are to conceive as 'normal' and pre-primordial what Husserl believed he could isolate as a particular and accidental experience, something dependent and secondary — that is, the indefinite drift of signs, as errance and change of scene, and linking representations one to another without beginning or end."[37] What is first and last is not the history of Being, but a picture-puzzle: The labyrinthine mirror-effects of old texts, each of which points to another, yet older text without fostering any hope of ever attaining the archewriting. As Schelling once did in speculating about the timelessly temporalizing internesting of the past, present, and future ages of the world, so Derrida clings to the dizzying thought of a past that has never been present.

IV

To get a purchase on these ideas about the model of an archewriting prior to all identifiable inscriptions, Derrida takes up themes from Saussure's *Course in General Linguistics* to cast light on his thesis that writing is in a certain respect the primary medium of expression in language. Again and again he charges into the seemingly trivial idea that in its structure language is oriented toward the spoken word and that writing merely imitates phonemes. Of course, Derrida does not espouse the empirical assertion that writing emerged chronologically sooner than speech. He even bases his argument on the usual idea that writing is *par excellence* the sign become reflective. And yet writing is not parasitic; the spoken word is by its very nature meant to be supplemented by the written word, so that the essence of language — fixing and "institutionalizing" meanings *conventionally* in sign substrata — can be explained in connection with the constitutive properties of writing. Every means of expression is essentially "writing." Every linguistic sign is arbitrary, stands in a conventional relationship to the meaning that it symbolizes; and "the idea of institution . . . is unthinkable before the possibility of writing and outside of its horizon."[38]

Derrida makes use of the basic notion of structuralist phonetics that the defining characteristics of every single phoneme are determined only by the systematically established relationship of a phoneme to all the other phonemes. The individual sound pattern is then constituted not by its substance as phonetic, but by a bundle of systematically interrelated abstract characteristics. With a sense of satisfaction, Derrida cites the following passage from Saussure's *Course*: "The linguistic signifier . . . is not (in essence) phonic but immaterial — constituted not by its material substance but the differences that separate its sound-image from all others."[39] He looks to the structural properties of the sign that can be realized as well in the substance of ink as in that of air; in these abstract expressive forms, which are indifferent to the various media of expression in phonetic and written forms, he recognizes the character of language as writing. This archewriting is at the basis of both the spoken and the written word.

The archewriting takes on the role of a subjectless generator of structures that, according to structuralism, are without any author. It establishes the differences between sign elements that are reciprocally related to one another in an abstract order. Not without some violence, Derrida combines these "differences," in the structuralist sense of the term, with the "differance" worked out in connection with Husserl's theory of meaning, which is supposed to go beyond Heidegger's ontological difference: "It [the differance] permits the articulation of spoken speech and writing — in the colloquial sense — as it founds the metaphysical opposition between the sensible and the intelligible, then between signifier and signified, expression and content, etc."[40] Whether they emerge as phonemes or as graphemes, all linguistic expressions are to a certain extent set in operation by an archewriting not itself present. The latter fulfills the function of world-disclosure by preceding every process of communication and every participating subject; and it does so, of course, by withholding itself, resisting parousia, and leaving behind no more than its trace in the referential structure of the produced text, in the "general text." In the metaphor of the archewriting and its trace, we see again the Dionysian motif of the god making his promised presence all the more palpable to the sons and daughters of the West by means of his poignant absence: "But the movement of the trace is necessarily occulted, it produces itself as occultation. When the other announces itself as such, it presents itself in the dissimulation of itself."[41]

Derrida's deconstructions faithfully follow the movement of Heidegger's thought. Against his will, he lays bare the inverted foundationalism of this thought by once again going beyond the ontological difference and Being to the differance proper to writing, which puts an origin already set in motion yet one level deeper. Thus, the advantage that Derrida may have hoped to gain from grammatology and an apparent concretizing/textualizing of the history of Being remains insignificant. As a participant in the philosophical discourse of modernity, Derrida inherits the weaknesses of a critique of metaphysics that does not shake loose of the intentions of first philosophy. Despite his transformed gestures, in the end he, too, promotes only a mystification of palpable social pathologies; he, too, disconnects essential (namely, deconstructive) thinking from scientific analysis; and he, too, lands at an empty, formulalike avowal of some indeterminate authority. It is, however, not the authority of a Being that has been distorted by beings, but the authority of a no longer holy scripture, of a scripture that is in exile, wandering about, estranged from its own meaning, a scripture that testamentarily documents the absence of the holy. Derrida initially distinguished himself from Heidegger by what looked like a scientific claim; but then with his new science he only placed himself above the deplored incompetency of the sciences in general and of linguistics in particular.[42]

Derrida develops the history of Being — which is encoded in writing — in another variation from Heidegger. He, too, degrades politics and contemporary history to the status of the ontic and the foreground, so as to romp all the more freely, and with a greater wealth of associations, in the sphere of the ontological and the archewriting. But the rhetoric that serves Heidegger for the initiation into the fate of Being, in Derrida comes to the aid of a different, rather more subversive orientation. Derrida stands closer to the anarchist wish to explode the continuum of history than to the authoritarian admonition to bend before destiny.[43]

This contrasting stance may have something to do with the fact that Derrida, all denials notwithstanding, remains close to Jewish mysticism. He is not interested in going back, in the fashion of the New Paganism, beyond the beginnings of monotheism, beyond the concept of a tradition that sticks to the traces of the lost divine scripture and keeps itself going through heretical exegesis of the scriptures. Derrida cites approvingly the saying of Rabbi Eliezer passed on by Emanuel Levinas: "If all the seas were of ink, and all ponds planted with reeds, if the sky and the earth were parchments and if all human beings practised the art of writing — they would not exhaust the Torah I have learned, just as the Torah itself would not be diminished any more than is the sea by the water removed by a paint brush dipped in it."[44] The Cabalists already had an interest in upgrading the value of the oral Torah, which goes back to human words, in relation to the presumptive divine word of the Bible. They conferred a high rank on the commentaries with which each generation appropriates the revelation anew. For the truth has not been fixed; it has not been made positive once and for all in some well-circumscribed set of statements. This cabalist conception was later radicalized again. Now even the written Torah is considered a problematic translation of the divine word into the language of human beings — as a mere, that is, a disputable, interpretation. *Everything* is oral Torah, no syllable is authentic, transmitted, as it were, in archewriting. The Torah of the Tree of Knowledge is a concealed Torah from the beginning. It keeps changing its clothes permanently, and these clothes *are* the tradition.

Gershom Scholem reports on discussions enkindled by the question of whether all ten commandments were transmitted by Moses to the people of Israel unadulterated. Some Cabalists were of the opinion that only the first two, those constitutive of monotheism, stemmed directly from God; others doubted the authenticity of even the first two commandments handed over by Moses. Rabbi Mendel of Rymanow puts an even sharper point on an idea of Maimonides: "In Rabbi Mendel's view not even the first two commandments were revealed directly to the whole people of Israel. All that Israel heard was the *aleph* with which in the Hebrew text the first commandment begins. . . . This strikes me," Scholem adds, "as a highly remarkable statement, providing much food for thought. For in Hebrew the consonant *aleph* represents nothing more than the position taken by the larynx when a word begins with a vowel. Thus the *aleph* may be said to denote the source of all articulate sound. . . . To hear the *aleph* is to hear next to nothing; it is the preparation for all audible language, but in itself contains no determinate, specific meaning. Thus, with his daring statement . . . Rabbi Mendel transformed the revelation on Mount Sinai into a mystical revelation, pregnant with infinite meaning, but *without specific meaning*. In order to become a foundation of religious authority, it had to be translated into human language, and that is what Moses did. In this light every statement on which authority is grounded would become a human interpretation, however valid and exalted, of something that transcends it."[45] The *aleph* of Rabbi Mendel is akin to the soundless "a" of *différance*, discriminated only in writing, for in the indeterminacy of this fragile and ambiguous sign is concentrated the entire wealth of the promise.

Derrida's grammatologically circumscribed concept of an archewriting whose traces call forth all the more interpretations the more unfamiliar they become, renews the mystical concept of tradition as an ever *delayed* event of revelation. Religious authority only maintains its force as long as it conceals its true face and thereby incites the frenzy of deciphering interpreters. Earnestly pursued deconstruction is the paradoxical labor of continuing a tradition in which the saving energy is only renewed by expenditure: The labor of deconstruction lets the refuse heap of interpretations, which it wants to clear away in order to get at the buried foundations, mount ever higher.

Derrida means to go beyond Heidegger; fortunately, he goes back behind him. Mystical experiences were able to unfold their explosive force, their power of liquefying institutions and dogmas, in Jewish and Christian traditions because they remained related in these contexts to a hidden, world-transcendent God. Illuminations cut off from this concentrated font of light become peculiarly diffuse. The path of their consistent secularization points into the domain of radical experiences that avant-garde art has opened up. Nietzsche had taken his orientations from the purely aesthetic rapture of ecstatic subjectivity, gone out from itself. Heidegger took his stand halfway down this path; he wanted to retain the force of an *illumination without direction* and yet not pay the price of its secularization. So he toyed with an aura that the sacred had lost. Within a mysticism of Being, illuminations retrogress back into the magical. In the mysticism of the New Paganism, the unbounded charisma of what is outside the everyday does not issue in something liberating, as it does with the aesthetic; nor in something renewing, as with the religious — it has at most the stimulus of charlatanry. Derrida purifies the mysticism of Being of this stimulus, taking it back into the context of the monotheistic tradition.[46]

If this suspicion is not utterly false, Derrida returns to the historical locale where mysticism once turned into enlightenment. His whole life long, Scholem traced this upheaval that took place in the eighteenth century. As Adorno has remarked, mysticism and enlightenment have been found together under the conditions of the twentieth century for "one last time" in Benjamin, and in this case with the conceptual tools of historical materialism. It seems to me doubtful that this unique movement of thought could be repeated with the tools of a negative foundationalism; in any case, it could only lead us deeper into the very modernity that Nietzsche and his followers wanted to overcome.

Excursus on Leveling the Genre Distinction between Philosophy and Literature

I

Adorno's "negative dialectics" and Derrida's "deconstruction" can be seen as different answers to the same problem. The totalizing self-critique of reason gets caught in a performative contradiction since subject-centered reason can be convicted of being authoritarian in nature only by having recourse to its own tools. The tools of thought, which miss the "dimension of nonidentity" and are imbued with the "metaphysics of presence," are nevertheless the only available means for uncovering their own insufficiency. Heidegger flees from this paradox to the luminous heights of an esoteric, special discourse, which absolves itself of the restrictions of discursive speech generally and is immunized by vagueness against any specific objections. He makes use of metaphysical concepts for purposes of a critique of metaphysics, as a ladder he casts away once he has mounted the rungs. Once on the heights, however, the late Heidegger does not, as did the early Wittgenstein, withdraw into the mystic's silent intuition; instead, with the gestures of the seer and an abundance of words, he lays claim to the authority of the initiate.

Adorno operates differently. He does not slip out of the paradoxes of the self-referential critique of reason; he makes the performative contradiction within which this line of thought has moved since Nietzsche, and which he acknowledges to be unavoidable, into the organizational form of indirect communication. Identity thinking turned against itself becomes pressed into continual self-denial and allows the wounds it inflicts on itself and its objects to be seen. This exercise quite rightly bears the name negative dialectics because Adorno practices determinate negation unremittingly, even though it has lost any foothold in the categorial network of Hegelian Logic — as a fetishism of demystification, so to speak. This fastening upon a critical procedure that can no longer be sure of its foundations is explained by the fact that Adorno (in contrast to Heidegger) bears no elitist contempt for discursive thought. Like exiles, we wander about lost in the discursive zone; and yet it is only the insistent force of a groundless reflection turned against itself that preserves our connection with the utopia of a long since lost, uncoerced and intuitive knowledge belonging to the primal past.[1] Discursive thought cannot identify itself as the decadent form of this knowledge by means of its own resources; for this purpose, the aesthetic experience gained in contact with avant-garde art is needed. The promise for which the surviving philosophic tradition is no longer a match has withdrawn into the mirror-writing of the esoteric work of art and requires a negativistic deciphering. From this labor of deciphering, philosophy sucks the residue of that paradoxical trust in reason with which negative dialectics executes (in the double sense of this word) its performative contradiction.

Derrida cannot share Adorno's aesthetically certified, residual faith in a de-ranged reason that has been expelled from the domains of philosophy and become, literally, utopian [having no place]. He is just as little convinced that Heidegger actually escaped the conceptual constraints of the philosophy of the subject by using metaphysical concepts in order to "cancel them out." Derrida does, to be sure, want to advance the already forged path of the critique of metaphysics; he, too, would just as soon break out of the paradox as broodingly encircle it. But like Adorno, he guards against the gestures of profundity that Heidegger unhesitatingly imitates from his opposite number, the philosophy of origins. And so there are also parallels between Derrida and Adorno.

This affinity in regard to their thought gestures calls for a more precise analysis. Adorno and Derrida are sensitized in the same way against definitive, totalizing, all-incorporating models, especially against the organic dimension in works of art. Thus, both stress the primacy of the allegorical over the symbolic, of metonymy over metaphor, of the Romantic over the Classical. Both use the fragment as an expository form; they place any system under suspicion. Both are abundantly insightful in decoding the normal case from the point of view of its limit cases; they meet in a negative extremism, finding the essential in the marginal and incidental, the right on the side of the subversive and the outcast, and the truth in the peripheral and the inauthentic. A distrust of everything direct and substantial goes along with an intransigent tracing of mediations, of hidden presuppositions and dependencies. The critique of origins, of anything original, of first principles, goes together with a certain fanaticism about showing what is merely produced, imitated, and secondary in everything. What pervades Adorno's work as a materialist motif — his unmasking of idealist positings, his reversal of false constitutive connections, his thesis about the primacy of the object — even for this there is a parallel in Derrida's logic of the supplement. The rebellious labor of deconstruction aims indeed at dismantling smuggled-in basic conceptual hierarchies, at overthrowing foundational relationships and conceptual relations of domination, such as those between speech and writing, the intelligible and the sensible, nature and culture, inner and outer, mind and matter, male and female. Logic and rhetoric constitute one of these conceptual pairs. Derrida is particularly interested in standing the primacy of logic over rhetoric, canonized since Aristotle, on its head.

It is not as though Derrida concerned himself with these controversial questions in terms of viewpoints familiar from the history of philosophy. If he had done so, he would have had to relativize the status of his own project in relation to the tradition that was shaped from Dante to Vico, and kept alive through Hamann, Humboldt, and Droysen, down to Dilthey and Gadamer. For the protest against the Platonic-Aristotelian primacy of the logical over the rhetorical that is raised anew by Derrida was articulated in this tradition. Derrida wants to expand the sovereignty of rhetoric over the realm of the logical in order to solve the problem confronting the totalizing critique of reason. As I have indicated, he is satisfied neither with Adorno's negative dialectics nor with Heidegger's critique of metaphysics — the one remaining tied to the rational bliss of the dialectic, the other to the elevation of origins proper to metaphysics, all protestations to the contrary notwithstanding. Heidegger only escapes the paradoxes of a self-referential critique of reason by claiming a special status for *Andenken*, that is, its release from discursive obligations. He remains completely silent about the privileged access to truth. Derrida strives to arrive at the same esoteric access to truth, but he does not want to admit it as a privilege — no matter for what or for whom. He does not place himself in lordly fashion above the objection of pragmatic inconsistency, but renders it *objectless*.

There can only be talk about "contradiction" in the light of consistency requirements, which lose their authority or are at least subordinated to other demands — of an aesthetic nature, for example — if logic loses its conventional primacy over rhetoric. Then the deconstructionist can deal with the works of philosophy as works of literature and adapt the critique of metaphysics to the standards of a literary criticism that does not misunderstand itself in a scientistic way. As soon as we take the *literary* character of Nietzsche's writings seriously, the suitableness of his critique of reason has to be assessed in accord with the standards of rhetorical success and not those of logical consistency. Such a critique (which is more adequate to its object) is not immediately directed toward the network of discursive relationships of which arguments are built, but toward the figures that shape style and are decisive for the literary and rhetorical power of a text. A literary criticism that in a certain sense merely *continues* the literary process of its objects cannot end up in science. Similarly, the deconstruction of great philosophical texts, carried out as literary criticism in this broader sense, is not subject to the criteria of problem-solving, purely cognitive undertakings.

Hence, Derrida *undercuts* the very problem that Adorno acknowledged as unavoidable and turned into the starting point of his reflectively self-transcending identity-thinking. For Derrida, this problem has no object since the deconstructive enterprise cannot be pinned down to the discursive obligations of philosophy and science. He calls his procedure deconstruction because it is supposed to *clear away* the ontological *scaffolding* erected by philosophy in the course of its subject-centered history of reason. However, in his business of deconstruction, Derrida does not proceed analytically, in the sense of identifying hidden presuppositions or implications. This is just the way in which each successive generation has critically reviewed the works of the preceding ones. Instead, Derrida proceeds by a critique of style, in that he finds something like indirect communications, by which the text itself denies its manifest content, in the rhetorical surplus of meaning inherent in the literary strata of texts that present themselves as nonliterary. In this way, he compels texts by Husserl, Saussure, or Rousseau to confess their guilt, against the explicit interpretations of their authors. Thanks to their rhetorical content, texts combed against the grain contradict what they state, such as the explicitly asserted primacy of signification over the sign, of the voice in relation to writing, of the intuitively given and immediately present over the representative and the postponed-postponing. In a philosophical text, the blind spot cannot be identified on the level of manifest content any more than it can in a literary text. "Blindness and insight" are rhetorically interwoven with one another. Thus, the constraints constitutive for knowledge of a philosophical text only become accessible when the text is handled as what it would not like to be — as a literary text.

If, however, the philosophical (or scholarly) text were thereby only *extraneously turned* into an apparently literary one, deconstruction would still be an arbitrary act. Derrida can only attain Heidegger's goal of bursting metaphysical thought-forms from the inside by means of his essentially rhetorical procedure if the philosophical text is *in truth* a literary one — if one can *demonstrate* that the genre distinction between philosophy and literature dissolves upon closer examination. This demonstration is supposed to be carried out by way of deconstruction itself; in every single case we see anew the impossibility of so specializing the language of philosophy and science for cognitive purposes that they are cleansed of everything metaphorical and merely rhetorical, and kept free of literary admixtures. The frailty of the genre distinction between philosophy and literature is evidenced in the practice of deconstruction; in the end, *all* genre distinctions are submerged in one comprehensive, all-embracing context of texts — Derrida talks in a hypostatizing manner about a "universal text." What remains is self-inscribing writing as the medium in which each text is woven together with everything else. Even before it makes its appearance, every text and every particular genre has already lost its autonomy to an all-devouring context and an uncontrollable happening of spontaneous text production. This is the ground of the primacy of rhetoric, which is concerned with the qualities of texts in general, over logic, as a system of rules to which only certain types of discourse are subjected in an exclusive manner — those bound to argumentation.

II

This — at first glance inconspicuous — transformation of the "destruction" into the "deconstruction" of the philosophical tradition transposes the radical critique of reason into the domain of rhetoric and thereby shows it a way out of the aporia of self-referentiality: Anyone who still wanted to attribute paradoxes to the critique of metaphysics after this transformation would have misunderstood it in a scientistic manner. This argument holds good only if the following propositions are true:

1. Literary criticism is not primarily a scientific (or scholarly: *wissenschaftliches*) enterprise but observes the same rhetorical criteria as its literary objects.

2. Far from there being a genre distinction between philosophy and literature, philosophical texts can be rendered accessible in their essential contents by literary criticism.

3. The primacy of rhetoric over logic means the overall responsibility of rhetoric for the general qualities of an all-embracing context of texts, within which all genre distinctions are

ultimately dissolved; philosophy and science no more constitute their own proper universes than art and literature constitute a realm of fiction that could assert its autonomy vis-à-vis the universal text.

Proposition 3 explicates propositions 2 and 1 by despecializing the meaning of "literary criticism." Literary criticism does serve as a model that clarifies itself through a long tradition; but it is considered precisely as a model case of something more universal, namely, a criticism suited to the rhetorical qualities of everyday discourse as well as of discourse outside the everyday. The procedure of deconstruction deploys this generalized criticism to bring to light the suppressed surpluses of rhetorical meaning in philosophical and scientific texts — against their manifest sense. Derrida's claim that "deconstruction" is an instrument for bringing Nietzsche's radical critique of reason out of the dead end of its paradoxical self-referentiality therefore stands — or falls — along with thesis number 3.

Just this thesis has been the centerpoint of the lively reception Derrida's work has enjoyed in the literature faculties of prominent American universities.[2] In the United States, literary criticism has for a long time been institutionalized as an academic discipline, that is, within the scholarly-scientific enterprise. From the very start, the self-tormenting question about the scholarly-scientific character of literary criticism was institutionalized along with it. This endemic self-doubt forms the background for the reception of Derrida, along with the dissolution of the decades-long domination of the New Criticism, which was convinced of the autonomy of the literary work of art and drew nourishment from the scientific pathos of structuralism. The idea of "deconstruction" could catch on in this constellation because it opened up to literary criticism a task of undoubted significance, under exactly the opposite premises: Derrida disputes the autonomy of the linguistic work of art and the independent meaning of the aesthetic illusion no less energetically than he does the possibility of criticism's ever being able to attain scientific status. At the same time, literary criticism serves him as the model for a procedure that takes on an almost world-historical mission with its overcoming of the thinking of the metaphysics of presence and of the age of logocentrism.

The leveling of the genre distinction between literary criticism and literature frees the critical enterprise from the unfortunate compulsion to submit to pseudo-scientific standards; it simultaneously lifts it above science to the level of creative activity. Criticism does not need to consider itself as something secondary; it gains literary status. In the texts of Hillis Miller, Geoffrey Hartman, and Paul de Man we can find the new self-awareness: "that critics are no more parasites than the texts they interpret, since both inhabit a host-text of pre-existing language which itself parasitically feeds on their host-like willingness to receive it." Deconstructionists break with the traditional Arnoldian conception of criticism's function as a mere servant: "Criticism is now crossing over into literature, rejecting its subservient, Arnoldian stance and taking on the freedom of interpretive style with a matchless gusto."[3] Thus, in perhaps his most brilliant book, Paul de Man deals with critical texts by Lukács, Barthes, Blanchot, and Jakobson with a method and finesse that are usually reserved only for literary texts: "Since they are not scientific, critical texts have to be read with the same awareness of ambivalence that is brought to the study of non-critical literary texts."[4]

Just as important as the equation of literary criticism with creative literary production is the increase in significance enjoyed by literary criticism as sharing in the business of the critique of metaphysics. This upgrading to the critique of metaphysics requires a counterbalancing supplement to Derrida's interpretation of the leveling of the genre distinction between philosophy and literature. Jonathan Culler recalls the strategic meaning of Derrida's treatment of philosophical texts through literary criticism in order to suggest that, in turn, literary criticism treat literary texts also as philosophical texts. Simultaneously maintaining and relativizing the distinction between the two genres "is essential to the demonstration that the most truly philosophical reading of a philosophical text . . . is one that treats the work as literature, as a fictive, rhetorical construct whose elements and order are determined by various textual exigencies." Then he continues: "Conversely, the most powerful and opposite readings of literary works may be those that treat them as philosophical gestures by teasing out the implications of their dealings with the philosophical oppositions that support them."[5] Proposition 2 is thus varied in the following sense:

2'. Far from there being a genre distinction between philosophy and literature, literary texts can be rendered accessible in their essential contents by a critique of metaphysics.

Of course, the two propositions, 2 and 2', point in the direction of the primacy of rhetoric over logic, which is asserted in proposition 3. Consequently, American literary critics are concerned to develop a concept of *general* literature, equal in overall scope to rhetoric, which would correspond to Derrida's "universal text." The notion of literature as confined to the realm of the fictive is deconstructed at the same time as the conventional notion of philosophy that denies the metaphorical basis of philosophical thought: "The notion of literature or literary discourse is involved in several of the hierarchical oppositions on which deconstruction has focussed: serious/non-serious, literal/metaphorical, truth/fiction. . . . Deconstruction's demonstration that these hierarchies are undone by the working of the texts that propose them alters the standing of literary language." There now follows, in the form of a conditional statement, the thesis on which everything depends — both the self-understanding of a literary criticism upgraded to the critique of metaphysics and the deconstructionist dissolution of the performative contradiction of a self-referential critique of reason: "If serious language is a special case of non-serious, if truths are fictions whose fictionality has been forgotten, then literature is not a deviant, parasitical instance of language. On the contrary, other discourses can be seen as cases of a generalized literature, or archi-literature."[6] Since Derrida does not belong to those philosophers who like to argue, it is expedient to take a closer look at his disciples in literary criticism within the Anglo-Saxon climate of argument in order to see whether this thesis really can be held.

Jonathan Culler reconstructs in a very clear way the somewhat impenetrable discussion between Derrida and Searle in order to show by the example of Austin's speech-act theory that any attempt to demarcate the ordinary domain of normal speech from an "unusual" use of language, "deviating" from the standard cases, is doomed to failure. Culler's thesis is expanded and indirectly confirmed in a study of speech-act theory by Mary Louise Pratt, who wants to prove, by the example of the structuralist theory of poetics, that even the attempt to delimit the extraordinary domain of fictive discourse from everyday discourse fails (see section III below). But first let us take a look at the debate between Derrida and Searle.[7]

From this complex discussion, Culler selects as the central issue the question of whether Austin does in fact, as it seems he does, make a totally unprejudiced, provisory, and purely methodical move. Austin wants to analyze the rules intuitively mastered by competent speakers, in accordance with which typical speech acts can be successfully executed. He undertakes this analysis with respect to sentences from *normal* everyday practice that are uttered *seriously* and used as *simply* and *literally* as possible. Thus, the unit of analysis, the standard speech act, is the result of certain abstractions. The theoretician of speech acts directs his attention to a sample of normal linguistic utterances from which all complex, derivative, parasitic, and deviant cases have been filtered out. A concept of "usual" or normal linguistic practice underpins this isolation, a concept of "ordinary language" whose harmlessness and consistency Derrida puts in doubt. Austin's intention is clear: He wants to analyze the universal properties of "promises," for example, with respect to cases in which the utterance of corresponding sentences actually *functions* as a promise. Now there are contexts in which the same sentences lose the illocutionary force of a promise. Spoken by an actor on the stage, as part of a poem, or even in a monologue, a promise, according to Austin, becomes "null and void in a unique manner." The same holds true for a promise that comes up in a quotation, or one merely mentioned. In these contexts, there is no *serious* or *binding* use, and sometimes not even a *literal* use, of the respective performative sentence, but a derivative or parasitic use instead. As

Searle constantly repeats, these fictive or simulated or indirect modes of use are "parasitic" in the sense that logically they presuppose the possibility of a serious, literal, and binding use of sentences grammatically appropriate for making promises. Culler extracts what are in essence three objections from Derrida's texts; they point toward the impossibility of such an operation and are meant to show that the common distinctions between serious and simulated, literal and metaphorical, everyday and fictional, usual and parasitic modes of speech break down.

(a) In his initial argument, Derrida posits a not very clear link between quotability and repeatability on the one hand, and fictionality on the other. The quotation of a promise is only apparently something secondary in comparison to the directly made promise, for the indirect rendition of a performative utterance in a quote is a form of repetition, and as quotability presupposes the possibility of repetition in accord with a rule, that is, conventionality, it belongs to the nature of any conventionally generated utterance (including performative ones) that it can be quoted — and fictively imitated, in a broader sense: "If it were not possible for a character in a play to make a promise, there could be no promise in real life, for what makes it possible to promise, as Austin tells us, is the existence of a conventional procedure, of formulas one can repeat. For me to be able to make a promise in real life, there must be iterable procedures or formulas such as are used on stage. Serious behavior is a case of role-playing."[8]

In this argument, Derrida obviously already presupposes what he wants to prove: that any convention which permits the repetition of exemplary actions possesses from the outset not only a symbolic, but also a fictional character. But it must first be shown that the conventions of a game are ultimately indistinguishable from norms of action. Austin introduces the quotation of a promise as an example of a derivative or parasitic form because the illocutionary force is removed from the quoted promise by the form of indirect rendition; it is thereby taken out of the context in which it "functions," that is, in which it coordinates the actions of the different participants in interaction and has consequences relevant to action. Only the actually performed speech act is *effective as action*; the promise mentioned or reported in a quote depends grammatically upon this. A setting that deprives it of its illocutionary force constitutes the bridge between quotation and fictional representation. Even action on the stage rests on a basis of everyday action (on the part of the actors, director, stage-workers, and theater people); and in the context of this framework, promises can function *in another mode* than they do "on stage," that is, with obligations and consequences relevant for action. Derrida makes no attempt to "deconstruct" this distinctive functional mode of ordinary speech within communicative action. In the illocutionary binding force of linguistic utterances Austin discovered a mechanism for coordinating action that places normal speech, as part of everyday practice, under constraints different from those of fictional discourse, simulation, and interior monologue. The constraints under which illocutionary acts develop a force for coordinating action and have consequences relevant to action define the domain of "normal" language. They can be analyzed as the kinds of idealizing suppositions we have to make in communicative action.

(b) The second argument brought forward by Culler, with Derrida, against Austin and Searle relates to just such idealizations. Any generalizing analysis of speech acts has to be able to specify general contextual conditions for the illocutionary success of standardized speech acts. Searle has been especially occupied with this task.[9] Linguistic expressions, however, change their meanings depending on shifting contexts; moreover, contexts are so constituted as to be open to ever wider-reaching specification. It is one of the peculiarities of our language that we can separate utterances from their original contexts and transplant them into different ones — Derrida speaks of "grafting." In this manner, we can think of a speech act, such as a "marriage vow," in ever new and more improbable contexts; the specification of universal contextual conditions does not run into any natural limits: "Suppose that the requirements for a marriage ceremony were met but that one of the parties were under hypnosis, or that the ceremony were impeccable in all respects but had been called a 'rehearsal,' or finally, that while the speaker was a minister licensed to perform weddings and the couple had obtained a license, that three of them were on this occasion acting in a play that, coincidentally, included a wedding ceremony."[10] These variations of context that change meaning cannot in principle be arrested or controlled, because contexts cannot be exhausted, that is, they cannot be theoretically mastered once and for all. Culler shows clearly that Austin cannot escape this difficulty by taking refuge in the intentions of speakers and listeners. It is not the thoughts of bride, bridegroom, or priest that decide the validity of the ceremony, but their actions and the circumstances under which they are carried out: "What counts is the plausibility of the description: whether or not the features of the context adduced create a frame that alters the illocutionary force of the utterances."[11]

Searle reacted to this difficulty by introducing a qualification to the effect that the literal meaning of a sentence does not completely fix the validity conditions of the speech act in which it is employed; it depends, rather, on tacit supplementation by a system of background assumptions regarding the normality of general world conditions. These parareflective background certainties have a holistic nature; they cannot be exhausted by a countably finite set of specifications. Meanings of sentences, however well analyzed, are thus valid only relative to a shared background knowledge that is constitutive of the lifeworld of a linguistic community. But Searle makes clear that the addition of this relational moment does not bring with it the relativism of meaning that Derrida is after. As long as language games are functioning and the preunderstanding constitutive of the lifeworld has not broken down, participants rightly count on world conditions being what is understood in their linguistic community as "normal." And in cases where individual background convictions do become problematic, they assume that they could reach a rationally motivated agreement. Both are strong, that is to say idealizing, suppositions; but these idealizations are not arbitrary, logocentric acts brought to bear by theoreticians on unmanageable contexts in order to give the illusion of mastery; rather, they are presuppositions that the participants themselves have to make if communicative action is to be at all possible.

(c) The role of idealizing suppositions can also be clarified in connection with some other consequences of this same state of affairs. Because contexts are changeable and can be expanded in any desired direction, the same text can be open to different readings; it is the text itself that makes possible its uncontrollable effective history. Still, Derrida's purposely paradoxical statement that any interpretation is inevitably a false interpretation, and any understanding a misunderstanding, does not follow from this venerable hermeneutic insight. Culler justifies the statement "Every reading is a misreading" as follows: "If a text can be understood, it can in principle be understood repeatedly, by different readers in different circumstances. These acts of reading or understanding are not, of course, identical. They involve modifications and differences, but differences which are deemed not to matter. We can thus say that understanding is a special case of misunderstanding, a particular deviation or determination of misunderstanding. It is a misunderstanding whose misses do not matter."[12] Yet Culler leaves one thing out of consideration. The productivity of the process of understanding remains unproblematic only so long as all participants stick to the reference point of possibly achieving a mutual understanding in which the *same* utterances are assigned the same meaning. As Gadamer has shown, the hermeneutic effort that would bridge over temporal and cultural distances remains oriented toward the idea of a possible consensus being brought about in the present.

Under the pressure for decisions proper to the communicative practice of everyday life, participants are dependent upon agreements that coordinate their actions. The more removed interpretations are from the "seriousness of this type of situation," the more they can prescind from the idealizing supposition of an achievable consensus. But they can never be wholly absolved of the idea that wrong interpretations must in principle be criticizable in terms of consensus to be aimed for ideally. The interpreter does not impose this idea on his object; rather, with the performative attitude of a participant observer, he takes it over from the direct participants, *who can act communicatively only under the presupposition of intersubjectively identical ascriptions of meaning.* I do not mean to marshal a Wittgensteinian positivism of language games against Derrida's thesis. It is not habitual linguistic practice that determines just what meaning is attributed to a text or an utterance.[13] Rather, language games only work because they presuppose idealizations that transcend any particular language game; as a necessary condition of possibly reaching understanding, these idealizations give rise to the perspective of an agreement that is open to criticism on the basis of validity claims. A language operating under these kinds of constraints is subject to an ongoing test. Everyday communicative practice, in which agents have to reach an understanding about something in the world, stands under the need to prove its worth, and it is the idealizing suppositions that make such testing possible in the first place. It is in relation to this need for standing the test within ordinary practice that one may distinguish, with Austin and Searle, between "usual" and "parasitic" uses of language.

III

Up to this point, I have criticized Derrida's third and fundamental assumption only to the extent that (against Culler's reconstruction of Derrida's arguments) I have defended the possibility of demarcating normal speech from *derivative* forms. I have not yet shown how fictional discourse can be separated from the normal (everyday) use of language. This aspect is the most important for Derrida. If "literature" and "writing" constitute the model for a universal context of texts, which cannot be surpassed and within which all genre distinctions are ultimately dissolved, they cannot be separated from other discourses as an autonomous realm of fiction. For the literary critics who follow Derrida in the United States, the thesis of the autonomy of the linguistic work of art is, as I mentioned, also unacceptable, because they want to set themselves off from the formalism of the New Criticism and from structuralist aesthetics.

The Prague Structuralists originally tried to distinguish poetic from ordinary language in view of their relations to extralinguistic reality. Insofar as language occurs in *communicative functions*, it has to produce relations between linguistic expression and speaker, hearer, and the state of affairs represented. Bühler articulated this in his semiotic scheme as the sign-functions of expression, appeal, and representation.[14] However, when language fulfills a poetic function, it does so in virtue of a reflexive relation of the linguistic expression to itself. Consequently, reference to an object, informational content, and truth-value — conditions of validity in general — are extrinsic to poetic speech; an utterance can be poetic to the extent that it is directed to the linguistic medium itself, to its own linguistic form. Roman Jakobson integrated this characterization into an expanded scheme of functions; in addition to the basic functions — expressing the speaker's intentions, establishing interpersonal relations, and representing states of affairs — which go back to Bühler, and two more functions related to making contact and to the code, he ascribes to linguistic utterances a poetic functon, which directs our attention to "the message as such."[15] We are less concerned here with a closer characterization of the poetic function (in accord with which the principle of equivalence is projected from the axis of selection to the axis of combination) than with an interesting consequence that is important for our problem of delimiting normal from other instances of speech: "Any attempt to reduce the sphere of the poetic function would be a deceptive oversimplification. The poetic function is not the only function of verbal artistry, merely a *predominant* and *structurally determinative* one, whereas in all other linguistic activities it plays a subordinate and supplementary role. Inasmuch as it *directs our attention to the sign's perceptibility*, this function deepens the fundamental dichotomy between signs and objects. For this reason, linguistics should not, when it studies the poetic function, restrict itself solely to the field of poetry."[16] Poetic speech, therefore, is to be distinguished only in virtue of the primacy and structure-forming force of a certain function that is always fulfilled together with other linguistic functions.

Richard Ohmann makes use of Austin's approach to specify poetic language in this sense. For him, the phenomenon in need of clarification is the fictionality of the linguistic work of art, that is, the generation of aesthetic illusion by which a second, specifically de-realized arena is opened up on the basis of a continued everyday practice. What distinguishes poetic language is its "world-generating" capacity: "A literary work creates a world . . . by providing the reader with *impaired* and incomplete speech acts which he completes by supplying the appropriate circumstances."[17] The unique *impairment* of speech acts that generates fictions arises when they are robbed of their illocutionary force, or maintain their illocutionary meanings only as in the refraction of indirect repetition or quotation: "A literary work is a discourse whose sentences lack the illocutionary forces that would normally attach to them. Its illocutionary force is mimetic. . . . Specifically, a literary work purportedly imitates a series of speech acts, which in fact have no other existence. By doing so, it leads the reader to imagine a speaker, a situation, a set of ancillary events, and so on."[18] The bracketing of illocutionary force virtualizes the relations to the world in which the speech acts are involved due to their illocutionary force, and releases the participants in interaction from reaching agreement about something in the world on the basis of idealizing understandings in such a way that they coordinate their plans of action and thus enter into obligations relevant to the outcomes of action: "Since the quasi-speech acts of literature are not *carrying on the world's business* — describing, urging, contracting, etc. — the reader may well attend to them in a non-pragmatic way."[19] Neutralizing their binding force releases the disempowered illocutionary acts from the pressure to decide proper to everyday communicative practice, removes them from the sphere of usual discourse, and thereby empowers them for the playful creation of new worlds — or, rather, for the pure demonstration of the world-disclosing force of innovative linguistic expressions. This specialization in the world-disclosive function of speech explains the unique self-reflexivity of poetic language to which Jakobson refers and which leads Geoffrey Hartman to pose the rhetorical question: "Is not literary language the name we give to a diction whose frame of reference is such that the words stand out as words (even as sounds) rather than being, at once, assimilable meanings?"[20]

Mary L. Pratt makes use of Ohmann's studies[21] to refute, by means of speech-act theory, the thesis of the independence of the literary work of art in Derrida's sense. She does not consider fictionality, the bracketing of illocutionary force, and the disengagement of poetic language from everyday communicative practice to be adequate selective criteria, because fictional speech elements such as jokes, irony, wish-fantasies, stories, and parables pervade our everyday discourse and by no means constitute an autonomous universe apart from "the world's business." Conversely, nonfiction works, memoirs, travel reports, historical romances, even *romans à clef* or thrillers that, like Truman Capote's *In Cold Blood*, adapt a factually documented case, by no means create an unambiguously fictional world, even though we often relegate these productions, for the most part at least, to "literature." Pratt uses the results of studies in sociolinguistics by W. Labov[22] to prove that natural narratives, that is, the "stories" told spontaneously or upon request in everyday life, follow the same rhetorical laws of construction as and exhibit structural chracteristics similar to literary narratives: "Labov's data make it necessary to account for narrative rhetoric in terms that are not exclusively literary; the fact that fictive or mimetically organized utterances can occur in almost any realm of extraliterary discourse requires that we do the same for fictivity or mimesis. In other words, the relation between a work's fictivity and its literariness is indirect."[23]

Nonetheless, the fact that normal language is permeated with fictional, narrative, metaphorical, and, in general, with rhetorical elements does not yet speak against the attempt to explain the autonomy of the linguistic work of art by the bracketing of illocutionary forces, for, according to Jakobson, the mark of fictionality is suited for demarcating literature from everyday discourses only to the degree that the world-disclosing function of language predominates over the other linguistic functions and determines the structure of the linguistic artifact. In a certain respect, it is the refraction and partial elimination of illocutionary validity claims that distinguishes the story from the statement of the eyewitness, teasing from insulting, being ironic from misleading, the hypothesis from the assertion, wish-fantasy from perception, a training maneuver from an act of warfare, and a scenario from a report of an actual catastrophe. But in none of these cases do the illocutionary acts lose their binding force for coordinating action. Even in the cases adduced for the sake of comparison, the communicative functions of the speech acts remain intact insofar as the fictive elements cannot be separated from contexts of life practice. The world-disclosive function of language does not gain independence over against the expressive, regulative, and informative functions. By contrast, in Truman Capote's literary elaboration of a notorious and carefully researched incident, precisely this may be the case. That is to say, what grounds the *primacy* and the structuring force of the poetic function is not the deviation of a fictional representation from the documentary report of an incident, but the exemplary elaboration that takes the case out of its context and makes it the occasion for an innovative, world-disclosive, and eye-opening representation in which the rhetorical means of representation depart from communicative routines and take on a life of their own.

It is interesting to see how Pratt is compelled to work out this poetic function against her will. Her sociolinguistic counterproposal begins with the analysis of a speech situation that poetic discourse shares with other discourses — the kind of arrangement in which a narrator or lecturer turns to a public and calls its attention to a text. The text undergoes certain procedures of preparation and selection before it is ready for delivery. Before a text can lay claim to the patience and discretion of the audience, it has also to satisfy certain criteria of relevance: it *has to be worth telling*. The tellability is to be assessed in terms of the manifestation of some significant exemplary experience. In its content, a tellable text reaches beyond the local context of the immediate speech situation and is open to further elaboration: "As might be expected, these two features — contextual detachability and susceptibility to elaboration — are equally important characteristics of literature." Of course, literary texts share these characteristics with "display texts" in general. The latter are characterized by their special communicative functions: "They are designed to serve a purpose I have described as that of verbally representing states of affairs and experiences which are held to be *unusual* or *problematic* in such a way that the addressee will respond affectively in the intended way, adopt the intended evaluation and interpretation, take pleasure in doing so, and *generally find the whole undertaking worth it*."[24] One sees how the pragmatic linguistic analyst creeps up on literary texts from outside, as it were. The latter have still to satisfy a final condition; in the case of literary texts, tellability must gain a preponderance over other functional characteristics: "In the end, tellability can take precedence over assertability itself."[25] Only in this case do the functional demands and structural constraints of everyday communicative practice (which Pratt defines by means of Grice's conversation postulates) lose their force. The concern to give one's contribution an informative shape, to say what is relevant, to be straightforward and to avoid obscure, ambiguous, and prolix utterances are idealizing presuppositions of the communicative action *of normal speech*, but not of poetic discourse: "Our tolerance, indeed propensity, for elaboration when dealing with the tellable suggests that, in Gricean terms, the standards of quantity, quality and manner for display texts differ from those Grice suggests for declarative speech in his maxims."

In the end, the analysis leads to a confirmation of the thesis it would like to refute. To the degree that the poetic, world-disclosing function of language gains primacy and structuring force, language escapes the structural constraints and communicative functions of everyday life. The space of fiction that is opened up when linguistic forms of expression become reflexive results from suspending illocutionary binding forces and those idealizations that make possible a use of language oriented toward mutual understanding — and hence make possible a coordination of plans of action that operates via the intersubjective recognition of criticizable validity claims. One can read Derrida's debate with Austin also as a denial of this independently structured domain of everyday communicative practice; it corresponds to the denial of an autonomous realm of fiction.

IV

Because Derrida denies both, he can analyze any given discourse in accord with the model of poetic language, and do so as if language generally were determined by the poetic use of language specialized in world-disclosure. From this viewpoint, language as such converges with literature or indeed with "writing." This *aestheticizing of language, which is purchased with the twofold denial of the proper senses of normal and poetic discourse*, also explains Derrida's insensitivity toward the tension-filled polarity between the poetic-world-disclosive function of language and its prosaic, innerworldly functions, which a modified version of Bühler's functional scheme takes into consideration.[26]

Linguistically mediated processes such as the acquisition of knowledge, the transmission of culture, the formation of personal identity, and socialization and social integration involve mastering problems posed by the world; the independence of learning processes that Derrida cannot acknowledge is due to the independent logics of these problems and the linguistic medium tailored to deal with them. For Derrida, linguistically mediated processes within the world are embedded in a *world-constituting* context that prejudices everything; they are fatalistically delivered up to the unmanageable happening of text production, overwhelmed by the poetic-creative transformation of a background designed by archewriting, and condemned to be provincial. An aesthetic contextualism blinds him to the fact that everyday communicative practice makes learning processes possible (thanks to built-in idealizations) in relation to which the world-disclosive force of interpreting language has in turn to prove its worth. These learning processes unfold an independent logic that transcends all local constraints, because experiences and judgments are formed only in the light of criticizable validity claims. Derrida neglects the potential for negation inherent in the validity basis of action oriented toward reaching understanding; he permits the capacity to solve problems to disappear behind the world-creating capacity of language; the former capacity is possessed by language as the medium through which those acting communicatively get involved in relations to the world whenever they agree with one another about something in the objective world, in their common social world, or in the subjective worlds to which each has privileged access.

Richard Rorty proposes a similar leveling; unlike Derrida, however, he does not remain idealistically fixated upon the history of metaphysics as a transcendent happening that determines everything intramundane. According to Rorty, science and morality, economics and politics, are delivered up to a process of language-creating protuberances *in just the same way* as art and philosophy. Like Kuhnian history of science, the flux of interpretations beats rhythmically between revolutions and normalizations of language. He observes this back-and-forth between two situations in all fields of cultural life: "One is the sort of situation encountered when people pretty much agree on what is wanted, and are talking about how best to get it. In such a situation there is no need to say anything terribly unfamiliar, for argument is typically about the truth of assertions rather than about the utility of vocabularies. The contrasting situation is one in which everything is up for grabs at once — in which the motives and terms of discussions are a central subject of argument. . . . In such periods people begin to toss around old words in new senses, to throw in the occasional neologism, and thus to hammer out a new idiom which initially attracts attention to itself and only later gets put to work."[27] One notices how the Nietzschean pathos of a *Lebensphilosophie* that has made the linguistic turn beclouds the sober insights of pragmatism; in the picture painted by Rorty, the renovative process of linguistic world-disclosure no longer has a *counterpoise* in the testing processes of intramundane practice. The "Yes" and "No" of communicatively acting agents is so prejudiced and rhetorically overdetermined by their linguistic contexts that the anomalies that start to arise during the phases of exhaustion are taken to represent only symptoms of waning vitality, or aging processes analogous to processes of nature — and are not seen as the result of *deficient* solutions to problems and *invalid* answers.

Intramundane linguistic practice draws its power of negation from validity claims that go beyond the horizons of any currently given context. But the contextualist concept of language, laden as it is with *Lebensphilosophie*, is impervious to the very real force of the counterfactual, which makes itself felt in the idealizing presuppositions of communicative action. Hence

Derrida and Rorty are also mistaken about the unique status of discourses differentiated from ordinary communication and tailored to a single validity dimension (truth or normative rightness), or to a single complex of problems (questions of truth or justice). In modern societies, the spheres of science, morality, and law have crystallized around these forms of argumentation. The corresponding cultural systems of action administer *problem-solving capacities* in a way similar to that in which the enterprises of art and literature administer *capacities for world-disclosure*. Because Derrida overgeneralizes this one linguistic function — namely, the poetic — he can no longer see the complex relationship of the ordinary practice of normal speech to the two extraordinary spheres, differentiated, as it were, in opposite directions. The polar tension between world-disclosure and problem-solving is held together within the functional matrix of ordinary language; but art and literature on the one side, and science, morality, and law on the other, are specialized for experiences and modes of knowledge that can be shaped and worked out within the compass of *one* linguistic function and *one* dimension of validity at a time. Derrida holistically levels these complicated relationships in order to equate philosophy with literature and criticism. He fails to recognize the special status that both philosophy and literary criticism, each in its own way, assume as mediators between expert cultures and the everyday world.

Literary criticism, institutionalized in Europe since the eighteenth century, has contributed to the differentiation of art. It has responded to the increasing autonomy of linguistic works of art by means of a discourse specialized for questions of taste. In it, the claims with which literary texts appear are submitted to examination — claims to "artistic truth," aesthetic harmony, exemplary validity, innovative force, and authenticity. In this respect, aesthetic criticism is similar to argumentative forms specialized for propositional truth and the rightness of norms, that is, to theoretical and practical discourse. It is, however, not merely an esoteric component of expert culture but, beyond this, has the job of mediating between expert culture and everyday world.

This *bridging function* of art criticism is more obvious in the cases of music and the plastic arts than in that of literary works, which are already formulated in the medium of language, even if it is a poetic, self-referential language. From this second, exoteric standpoint, criticism performs a translating activity of a unique kind. It brings the experiential content of the work of art into normal language; the innovative potential of art and literature for the lifeworlds and life histories that reproduce themselves through everyday communicative practice can only be unleashed in this maieutic way. This is then deposited in the changed configuration of the evaluative vocabulary, in a renovation of value orientations and need interpretations, which alters the color of modes of life by way of altering modes of perception.

Philosophy also occupies a position with two fronts similar to that of literary criticism — or at least this is true of modern philosophy, which no longer promises to redeem the claims of religion in the name of theory. On the one hand, it directs its interest to the foundations of science, morality, and law and attaches theoretical claims to its statements. Characterized by universalist problematics and strong theoretical strategies, it maintains an intimate relationship with the sciences. And yet philosophy is not simply an esoteric component of an expert culture. It maintains just as intimate a relationship with the totality of the lifeworld and with sound common sense, even if in a subversive way it relentlessly shakes up the certainties of everyday practice. Philosophical thinking represents the lifeworld's interest in the whole complex of functions and structures connected and combined in communicative action, and it does so in the face of knowledge systems differentiated out in accord with particular dimensions of validity. Of course, it maintains this relationship to totality with a reflectiveness lacking in the intuitively present background proper to the lifeworld.

If one takes into consideration the two-front position of criticism and philosophy that I have only sketched here — toward the everyday world on the one side, and on the other toward the specialized cultures of art and literature, science and morality — it becomes clear what the leveling of the genre

distinction between philosophy and literature, and the assimilation of philosophy to literature and of literature to philosophy, as affirmed in propositions 2 and 2', mean. This leveling
and this assimilation confusedly jumble the constellations in
which the rhetorical elements of language assume *entirely different* roles. The rhetorical element occurs in its *pure form* only
in the self-referentiality of the poetic expression, that is, in the
language of fiction specialized for world-disclosure. Even the
normal language of everyday life is ineradicably rhetorical; but
within the matrix of different linguistic functions, the rhetorical elements recede here. The world-disclosive linguistic
framework is almost at a standstill in the routines of everyday
practice. The same holds true of the specialized languages of
science and technology, law and morality, economics, political
science, etc. They, too, live off of the illuminating power of
metaphorical tropes; but the rhetorical elements, which are by
no means expunged, are tamed, as it were, and enlisted for
special purposes of problem-solving.

The rhetorical dimension plays a different and far more
important role in the language of literary criticism and philosophy. They are both faced with tasks that are paradoxical in
similar ways. They are supposed to feed the contents of expert
cultures, in which knowledge is accumulated under one aspect
of validity at a time, into an everyday practice in which all
linguistic functions and aspects of validity are intermeshed to
form one syndrome. And yet literary criticism and philosophy
are supposed to accomplish this task of mediation with means
of expression taken from languages specialized in questions of
taste or of truth. They can only resolve this paradox by rhetorically expanding and enriching their special languages to
the extent that is required to link up indirect communications
with the manifest contents of statements, and to do so in a
deliberate way. That explains the strong rhetorical strain characteristic of studies by literary critics and philosophers alike.
Significant critics and great philosophers are also noted writers.
Literary criticism and philosophy have a family resemblance to
literature — and to this extent to one another as well — in
their rhetorical achievements. But their family relationship
stops right there, for in each of these enterprises the tools of

rhetoric are subordinated to the discipline of a *distinct* form of argumentation.

If, following Derrida's recommendation, philosophical thinking were to be relieved of the duty of solving problems and shifted over to the function of literary criticism, it would be robbed not merely of its seriousness, but of its productivity. Conversely, the literary-critical power of judgment loses its potency when, as is happening among Derrida's disciples in literature departments, it gets displaced from appropriating aesthetic experiential contents into the critique of metaphysics. The false assimilation of one enterprise to the other robs both of their substance. And so we return to the issue with which we started. Whoever transposes the radical critique of reason into the domain of rhetoric in order to blunt the paradox of self-referentiality, also dulls the sword of the critique of reason itself. The false pretense of eliminating the genre distinction between philosophy and literature cannot lead us out of this aporia.[28]

VIII
Between Eroticism
and General Economics:
Georges Bataille

I

After Bataille's death in 1962, his companion of many years, Michel Leiris, described his friend with these words: "After he had been the impossible one, fascinated by everything he could discover about what was really unacceptable . . . he expanded his field of vision (in line with his old idea of getting beyond the 'No!' of a child stamping around in a rage) and, in the consciousness that a human being is only really a human being when, in this state of being without measure or standard, he seeks his own standard, he made himself into the man of the impossible, desirous of reaching the point where above and below become blurry in a Dionysian vertigo and where the distance between totality and nothingness is eliminated."[1] The salient attribute of "the impossible one" refers on the surface to the author of the "obscene work" who carried on the black writing of the Marquis de Sade; but it also refers to the philosopher and scholar who tried to take up the impossible heritage of Nietzsche as critic of ideology.

Bataille read Nietzsche relatively early on (1923), a year before Leiris introduced him to the circle of André Masson and to the leading Surrealists. To be sure, Bataille gave the philosophical discourse of modernity a direction similar to Heidegger's; but for his departure from modernity he chose a completely different path. He developed his concept of the holy from an anthropologically grounded critique of Christianity that forms a counterpart to Nietzsche's *Genealogy of Morals*. He did not get into an immanent critique of metaphysics at all. An initial glance at the double life of this archivist of the Bibliothèque Nationale and bohemian author in the midst of the Parisian intellectual scene reveals that Bataille and the philosophy professor from Marburg and Freiburg lived on different stars. What separates them especially are two central experiences: aesthetic experience in the circle of surrealism and political experience in connection with left radicalism.

At the end of the 1920s, the group associated with the journal *La révolution surréaliste* broke up. Breton raised severe objections against the apostates in his *Second Surrealist Manifesto*; they responded with a massive counterattack. From then on, there was an all-out war between Breton's "Association" and Bataille's "Cercle Communiste Démocratique." Together with Michel Leiris and Carl Einstein, Bataille founded at the same time the famous journal *Documents*, in which important studies by the editor were published. This is when Bataille first developed the concept of "the heterogeneous," the name he gave to all those elements that resist assimilation to the bourgeois form of life and to the routines of everyday life, just as they evade the methodical grasp of the sciences. In this concept, Bataille condensed the basic experience of the surrealist writers and artists who wanted shockingly to proclaim the ecstatic forces of intoxication, of dreamlife, of the instinctive and impulsive generally, against the imperatives of utility, normality, and sobriety, in order to shake up conventionally set modes of perception and experience. The realm of the heterogeneous is opened up only in explosive moments of fascinated shock, when those categories fall apart that guarantee in everyday life the confident interaction of the subject with himself and with the world. From the start, Bataille applied the concept of the heterogeneous to social groups, to the outcasts and the marginalized, to the counterworld — familiar since Baudelaire — of those elements that are placed outside the boundaries of social normality — be they the pariahs and the untouchables, the prostitutes or the lumpen proletariat, the crazies, the rioters, and revolutionaries, the poets or the bohemians. Thus, this aesthetically inspired concept also became an instrument for the analysis of Italian and German fascism: Bataille ascribed to fascist leaders a heterogeneous existence.

The contrary biographical orientations, the contradictory political options, and the obvious differences between erotic writing and scholarly essays on the one side and philosophical investigation and Being-mysticism on the other — these contrasts make it difficult at first glance to see the common project that links Bataille with Heidegger. The one, like the other, is concerned to break out of the prison of modernity, out of the closed universe of an Occidental rationalism that has been victorious on the scale of world history. Both want to overcome subjectivism, which covers the world with its reifying violence and lets it harden into a totality of technically manipulable and economically realizable goods. So much do both thinkers agree in this project that what Foucault says about Bataille's idea of transgression might as well be said of the later Heidegger's concept of transcendence: "In our day, is not the play of limit and transgression the essential test for a thought that centers on the 'origin,' for a form of thought to which Nietzsche dedicated us from the beginning of his works and one which would be, absolutely and in the same motion, a Critique and an Ontology, an understanding that comprehends both finitude and being?"[2] In the next sentence, the name Bataille might just as well be replaced by that of Heidegger. "And perhaps to all those who strive above all to maintain the unity of the philosopher's grammatical function . . . we could oppose Bataille's exemplary enterprise: his desperate and relentless attack on the preeminence of the philosophical subject. His experience and his language became an ordeal, a deliberate drawing and quartering of that which speaks in philosophical language, a disposition of stars that come out at midnight, allowing voiceless words to be born."[3]

Nevertheless, serious differences result from the fact that Bataille does not attack reason at the foundations of *cognitive* rationalization or at the *ontological* presuppositions of objectifying science and technology. He concentrates instead on the foundations of an *ethical* rationalization, which, as Max Weber has shown, made possible the capitalist system and hence subjected social life as a whole to imperatives of alienated labor and processes of accumulation. Bataille establishes the principle of modernity not in relation to a rootlessly autonomous self-consciousness puffed up in an authoritarian pose, not in relation to cognition, but in relation to the success-oriented utilitarian action that serves the realization of any given subjective purpose. To be sure, Heidegger and Bataille have in mind the same tendencies by which objectifying thought and purposive-rational action unleash their historical power; but the critique that is supposed to go to the roots of the malaise takes a different tack in each: Heidegger's procedure of critique of metaphysics digs into the frozen ground of transcendental subjectivity in order to lay bare the true foundations of an origin set temporally aflow; in contrast, Bataille's approach of moral critique is concerned not with discovering still deeper *foundations* of subjectivity, but with *unbounding* it — with the form of expression that leads the monadically self-encapsulated subject back again into the intimacy of a life-context that has become alien, confined, cut off, and fragmented. For Bataille, a completely different perspective from Heidegger's is opened up with this idea of unbounding: The self-transcendent subject is not dethroned and disempowered in favor of a superfoundationalist destining of Being; rather, spontaneity is given back its outlawed drives. Opening toward the sacral domain does not mean subjugation to the authority of an indeterminate fate only hinted at in its aura; transgressing boundaries toward the sacral does not imply the humble self-surrender of subjectivity, but liberation to true sovereignty.

It is no accident that not *Being* but *sovereignty* has the last word: In it, we see a proximity (unthinkable for Heidegger) to Nietzsche's aesthetically inspired concept of freedom and superhuman self-assertion. For Bataille, as for Nietzsche, there is a convergence between the self-aggrandizing and meaning-creating will to power and a cosmically moored fatalism of the eternal return of the same. A basically anarchist trait links Bataille with Nietzsche: Because the latter's thought is aimed against any authority whatsoever, even against the holy as an authority, the teaching about the death of God is intended in a strictly atheistic sense. On the other hand, for Heidegger, who repeats this thesis in noble tones, it loses all its radicality.

To be sure, God as an ontic entity is denied; but the ontologically restored event of revelation hovers ambiguously about the grammatical place left unoccupied by the demolished God-projection — as if all we lacked in the meantime was the language for naming the one whose name is ineffable. So Foucault's question has a point only for Bataille, not Heidegger: "But what does it mean to kill God if he does not exist, to kill God who has never existed?"[4] Foucault recognizes that Bataille must seek the excess of self-transgressing subjectivity in the experience of the erotic, because he conceives of the holy in rigorously atheistic terms. Indeed, the profanation of the holy is the model for transgression; but Bataille does not delude himself about the fact that there is nothing left to profane in modernity — and that it cannot be the job of philosophy to fashion a substitute for this in a mysticism of Being with a capital B. Bataille posits an intrinsic link between the sexual horizon of experience and the death of God — "not that it proffers any new content for our age-old acts; rather, it permits a profanation without object, a profanation that is empty and turned inward upon itself and whose instruments are brought to bear on nothing but each other."[5]

I want now to consider the significance for his construction of modernity of Bataille's analysis of fascism in terms of the concepts of the homogeneous and the heterogeneous. Bataille sees modernity embedded in a history of reason in which the forces of sovereignty and labor are in conflict with one another. The history of reason extends from the archaic beginnings of sacral society to the totally reified world of Soviet society from which the last feudal traces of sovereignty have been expunged. This complete unmixing of homogeneous and heterogeneous components, however, opens up perspectives on a formation of a future society that reconciles social equality with the sovereignty of individuals. Bataille's anthropological explanation of the heterogeneous as the discriminated against and the outlawed breaks with all dialectical figures of thought. Hence, the question arises as to how Bataille would explain the revolutionary transition from the cooled-off, totally reified society to a renewal of sovereignty. The project of a general economics extrapolated to the energy ecology of nature as a whole can be understood as an answer to this question. This enterprise gets caught up in the paradoxes of self-referential reason. Thus, in the end Bataille oscillates between an incoherent reattachment to the Hegelian project of a dialectic of enlightenment, on the one hand, and an unmediated juxtaposition of scholarly analysis and mysticism, on the other.

II

The victory of the Fascist movement in Italy and the National Socialist takeover of power in the German Reich were — long before Auschwitz — phenomena from which issued waves not only of irritation, but also of fascinated excitement. There was no theory of contemporaneity not affected to its core by the penetrating force of fascism. This holds true especially of the theories that were in their formative period in the late 1920s and early 1930s — of Heidegger's fundamental ontology, as we have seen, no less than of Bataille's heterology or Horkheimer's Critical Theory.[6] In November 1933, when Heidegger was making his campaign speeches for the "Führer," Bataille published a study of *The Psychological Structure of Fascism*.[7] In contrast with Marxist attempts, he directs his attention not to economic and social-structural causes accessible only to theory, but to the most visible effects, especially to the palpable social-psychological phenomena of the new political movements. He is particularly interested in the connection between the masses mobilized by plebiscites and their charismatic Führer-figures, and generally in the show aspect of fascist leadership (brought to mind by Fest's Hitler film) — the cultic honoring of leaders as sacred personages, the artfully staged mass rituals, the manifestly violent and hypnotic elements, the breach of legality, the renunciation of even the appearance of democracy and all egalitarian values: "The affective stream that connects the Führer with his followers in the form of moral identification . . . is a function of a common awareness of mounting energies, growing violently into a state without measure or standard, which are accumulating and becoming available without limit in the person of the Führer."[8]

Bataille was Marxist enough at the time to recognize the objective conditions of crisis of which fascism was only the exploiter. The capitalist economy and its apparatus have first to "collapse because of internal contradictions" before a kind of violence that has no affinity whatsoever with the structure of existing society could inject itself into the functional gaps. The principle of freedom of choice was incorporated in democratically constituted industrial capitalism, a subjective freedom of choice for private entrepreneurs and for workers as well as for citizens (isolated in the election booths): "The movement and ultimate triumph of National Socialism owe not a little to the fact that some German capitalists became aware of how risky for them this principle of individual freedom could become in a crisis."[9] To be sure, the functional imperative for a totalitarian abolition of this principle remains "an empty wish" taken by itself; the resources on which fascism feeds — which is to say, the "inexhaustible wealth of forms of affective life" — cannot be explained in functionalist terms. That these forces taken over by the fascist state obviously spring from a realm that is heterogeneous in relation to the existing society gives Bataille the motivation to study heterogeneous elements. He is not satisfied with psychoanalytic explanations that derive from Freud's study, *Mass Psychology and Ego Analysis*;[10] he is convinced instead that the roots of fascism go deeper than the unconscious that is still accessible to the analytic force of self-reflection. The model on which Bataille conceives the splitting off of the heterogeneous is not the Freudian model of repression. It is one of exclusion and of the stabilization of boundaries that can only be penetrated by excess, that is, *violently*. Bataille seeks an economics of the total social ecology of drives; this theory is supposed to explain why modernity continues its life-endangering exclusions *without alternatives*, and why hope in a dialectic of enlightenment, which has accompanied the modern project right down to Western Marxism, is in vain: "The homogeneous society is incapable of discovering in itself a meaning and purpose for action. Consequently it enters into dependency upon imperative forces it has excluded."[11]

Bataille stands in the tradition of the Durkheim school. He traces the heterogeneous aspects of social as well as of psychic and mental life back to the sacred element that Durkheim had defined by contrasting it with the world of the profane. Sacred objects possess an auratic power that simultaneously entices and attracts even as it terrifies and repulses. If stimulated, they release shocking effects and represent a different, higher level of reality. They are incommensurable with profane things and evade any homogenizing treatment that would liken the strange to the familiar and explain the unexpected with the help of what one is well acquainted with. Bataille also adds the distinction of unproductive expenditure: The heterogeneous is related to the profane world as what is superfluous — from refuse and excrement, through dreams, erotic temptations, and perversions, to contaminating, subversive ideas; from palpable luxury to exuberantly electrifying hopes and transcendences pronounced holy. In opposition to this, the homogeneous and conformist elements of everyday life are the result of the metabolism with a resistant external nature. In capitalist society, labor measured abstractly in time and money (that is, wage labor) is effective as a homogenizing power, which increases when combined with science and technology. Technology is the link between science and production, and Bataille contends, like Adorno, that "the laws created by science produce relationships of identity between the various elements of a produced and measurable world."[12]

Into this rationalized world irrupt the fascist Führer and his entranced masses. It is not without admiration that Bataille speaks of their heterogeneous existence. Against the background of interest-oriented mass democracy, Hitler and Mussolini appear to be "the totally other." He is fascinated by the violence "that raises them [Hitler and Mussolini] above the people, the parties, and even the laws, a violence that penetrates the normal course of affairs, the peaceful but boring homogeneity that is impotent when it comes to maintaining itself by its own force."[13] In a fascist regime, homogeneous and heterogeneous elements are fused in a novel way — on the one hand, those characteristics such as readiness to perform, discipline, and love of order, which pertain to the functional demands of homogeneous society; and on the other, the mass ecstasy and authority of the Führer that reflect the splendor of true sovereignty. The fascist state merges the heterogeneous with homogeneous elements; it is governmentalized sovereignty. It inherits a kind of sovereignty that in traditional societies assumed religious and military forms. In the sovereignty of the Führer, both these elements remain undifferentiated. In fascism, the essential moment of rule by men over men is, so to speak, achieved in its purity. The aura of the Führer assures a mass loyalty that is drawn upon independently of any quest for legitimation. In terms reminiscent of Carl Schmitt, Bataille explains this unconditional acceptance by the fact that the power of a leader is at its core charismatic — rooted precisely in the heterogeneous: "The simple fact of rule by men over men implies the heterogeneity of the ruler, at least to the extent that he is the ruler; to the extent that he appeals to his nature or to his personal qualities for the legitimation of his authority, he characterizes this nature as totally other, without being able to give a rational account of it."[14] Bataille traces the captivating, sensational moment in the exercise of power by the fascist Führer back to sovereignty, to which he ascribes authenticity — this is where the difference from Horkheimer and Adorno's theory of fascism, which has a similar point of departure, becomes clear.

Like Bataille, they concentrate on the psychological surface of fascism — at least in "The Elements of Anti-Semitism."[15] In the arrangement of the highly ritualized mass demonstrations, Horkheimer and Adorno decipher "the false counterfeit of frightened mimesis" — thus, the arousal and manipulation of age-old patterns of reaction. Fascism uses the mimetic behavior (eliminated by civilization) for its own purposes. The suppression of the archaic ambivalence between flight and self-surrender, disgust and allure, becomes reflexive in an ironic way: "In modern fascism, rationality has reached a point at which it is no longer satisfied with simply repressing nature; rationality now exploits nature by incorporating into its own system the rebellious potentialities of nature."[16] To this extent, Bataille's analysis can be still translated into the concepts of Critical Theory: Fascism ultimately only serves to render inner nature's revolts against instrumental reason adaptable to the imperatives of the latter. The decisive difference between the two

approaches, however, lies in the way they specify the suppressed or excluded and outlawed parts of subjective nature.
For Horkheimer and Adorno, the mimetic impulse carries with
it the promise of a "happiness without power,"[17] whereas for
Bataille happiness and power are indissolubly fused in the
heterogeneous: In the erotic and in the sacred, Bataille celebrates an "elemental violence."[18] With the help of the same
idea, he also justifies in fascism that element (so characteristic
of Carl Schmitt) of groundless or "pure" leadership, against
which Horkheimer and Adorno most clearly set the force of
the mimetic.

Even Benjamin, who in an early essay seems to anticipate
Bataille's conception of an immaculate sovereign power in appealing to Sorel's myth of the general strike, ultimately holds
fast to the reference point of a constraint-free intersubjectivity
of mutual understanding. The fateful power of revolutionary,
corrective acts, which are essentially anarchical and yet lie at
the basis of all institutions of freedom (and have to be kept
present in them), is projected by Benjamin into a politics of
"pure means." This is separated by only a hair's breadth from
what fascist power would like to be. And yet this power, as an
end in itself that does not mediate justice instrumentally but
manifests and fulfills it, remains, according to Benjamin, always
tied to a sphere of agreement free of violence. This sphere of
human agreement which "is wholly inaccessible to violence"
remains for Benjamin "the proper sphere of 'understanding'
and of language."[19] By his enterprise of redemptive critique,
Benjamin is so committed to this idea that he even wants to
see the nonviolence of "pure means" exemplified in the pro-
letarian general strike.

Without such a violence-transcending point of reference,
Bataille runs into difficulty making plausible the distinction
that remains so important for him — namely, that between the
socialist revolution and the fascist takeover of power, which
merely seems to be like the former. What Benjamin affirms of
the enterprise of surrealism as a whole — that it wanted "to
win the energies of intoxication for the revolution"[20] — Bataille
also has in mind; it is the dream of an aestheticized, poetic
politics purified of all moral elements. Indeed, this is what

fascinates him about fascism: "The example of fascism, which today calls into question even the existence of the labor movement, suffices to demonstrate what we might expect from a favorable recourse to renewed affective forces."[21] But then the question arises as to how the subversively spontaneous expression of these forces and the fascist canalizing of them really differ. The question becomes uncomfortable if, with Bataille, one proceeds from the assumption that the difference should be identified already in the forms and patterns of politics and not merely in their concrete material consequences. In his 1933 writing, Bataille attempts to draw a boundary within the world of the heterogeneous between higher and lower elements. So little does this attempt succeed that Bataille is finally satisfied with suggesting a change in the function of the fascist politics that he is struggling against. He recommends the elaboration of a science of heterology that "would permit us to foresee the effective social reactions that convulse the superstructure — and perhaps even to manipulate them to a certain degree. . . . A systematic knowledge of the social movements of attraction and repulsion [that is, of emotional ambivalences released by the heterogeneous] proves itself a weapon at the moment when fascism stands opposed not so much to communism as to radically imperative forms . . . of subversion."[22]

In the three subsequent decades, Bataille finished the basic outlines of the science postulated at that time. I want to consider first his historico-philosophical distantiation from modernity, in order then to look at the General Economics from which he hoped for a response to the still open question of how the final transition from reification to sovereignty should be conceived.

III

As early as 1933, Bataille published a treatise on the concept of waste in which we can recognize a philosophy of history with a Manichaean turn.[23] As a communist, Bataille moves within the argumentative space of praxis philosophy: Labor, in the sense of social production, is the form of reproduction specific to the human species. He begins by describing modern class antagonisms in terms of the *Economic and Philosophic Manuscripts* of the early Marx: "The goal of the worker is to produce in order to live, but that of the entrepreneur is to produce in order to deliver the laboring producers into abject misery."[24] Yet Bataille denies the implicit consequence that the "life" for the sake of which production occurs is intrinsic to labor as its rational telos. The goal of the type of production Bataille has in mind instead transcends the circuit of productive expenditure of labor power and the consumptive appropriation of those use-values into which the labor process is objectified. Bataille gives the expressivist model of human activity from which he takes off a twist that negates the very foundations of praxis philosophy. This is to say, he sees a deep ambivalence embedded in consumption itself between the reproduction of labor power directly necessary for life and a consumption of luxury that removes the products of labor from the sphere of vital necessities in a wasteful way and hence from the dictates of the processes of sheer metabolism. Only this unproductive form of expenditure, which from the economic perspective of individual commodity owners represents a loss, can simultaneously make possible and confirm the sovereignty of human beings and their authentic existence.

To be sure, Marx, too, speaks of a sphere of freedom *beyond* the sphere of necessity, beyond the realm of production determined by the metabolism with external nature. But Marx also subsumes even the creative use of leisure time under the model of externalization and reappropriation of the essential powers of the individual — the reference point remains the total individual, universally realizing himself. With utter realism, Bataille sees in this the danger that the habitualized necessities of nature merely continue under the cover of a seemingly autonomous freedom; he fears that true sovereignty would also be suppressed in a world of material abundance as long as the rational — according to the principle of balancing payments — use of material and spiritual goods did not leave room for a radically different form of consumption — namely, of wasteful expenditure in which the consuming subject expresses himself. This unproductive form of expenditure places Bataille in proximity with the toxic state of self-surrender, of self-transcendence, of frenzy. This unbounding of the self also leaves its economic traces in luxury consumption: "Human activity is not to be reduced wholly to processes of production and reproduction; and consumption is to be divided into two different domains. The first, which is reducible, comprises the minimal amount necessary for individuals of a society to preserve their lives and to continue their productive activity. . . . The second domain embraces the so-called unproductive expenses: luxury, mourning ceremonies, wars, cults, the erection of splendid buildings, games, theater, the arts, perverse sexuality (that is, detached from genitality) represent activities that at least originally have their end in themselves."[25] The self-sufficient activity performed for its own sake (Aristotle), as displayed in the luxury of the leisure classes, still reveals something of primordial sovereignty.

However, capitalism is characterized by the fact that all surpluses get reinvested, that is, they are spent again productively; the process of accumulation is guided by imperatives of the self-realization of capital. In this regard, Marx criticized only the growing independence of the production of exchange-values from the production of use-values. Bataille deplores the fact that the productive investment of surpluses replaces their unproductive use. "With their wealth," capitalists have "taken on the obligation to expend it in a functional way"[26]: Hence modern society does without the public display of luxury — "exhibition of wealth occurs now behind private walls in accord with boring and oppressive conventions."[27] The generous, the orgiastic, the lack of measure that still marked feudal waste, has disappeared.

Along the lines of this concept of expenditure, Bataille developed his major theoretical work, the first part of which appeared in 1949, after eighteen years of preparatory labor, under the title *La Part maudite*; a section from the third part was published in 1956 under the title *La Souveraineté*. In the intervening years the distance from the problems and concepts of praxis philosophy had grown even greater. In a certain way, Bataille's theory can be understood as a counterpart to the theory of reification developed by Lukács, Horkheimer, and Adorno along the lines of a Weberian Marxism. Sovereignty stands in opposition to the principle of reifying, instrumental reason that issues from the sphere of social labor and attains dominance in the modern world. To be sovereign means not to let oneself be reduced, as in labor, to the condition of an object, but to free subjectivity from bondage: The subject removed from labor and obsessed by the fulfillment of the present is wholly given up to the consumption of self. The essence of sovereignty consists of useless consumption, of "whatever pleases me."[28] This sovereignty falls to the verdict of a world-historical process of disenchantment and reification. The sovereign nature gets spiritualized in modern societies and excluded from a universe that subsumes everything under the form of valorizable and manipulable objects, that is, of private property: "At the beginning of industrial society, which is based on the primacy and autonomy of goods — of things — there stands the opposed will, the one thing essential — what makes us tremble violently in the presence of the horrifying and the enticing — outside the world of activity, the world of objects."[29]

The parallels with the early Lukács are striking. For at first it looks as if this process of excluding a sacred element removed from the world were only the consequence of the capitalist mode of production: "On the basis of the accumulation of riches for the purpose of an ever expanding industrial production, bourgeois society is the society of things. It is, in comparison with the shape of feudal society, not a society of persons. . . . The object translatable into money is worth more than the subject who, since he is dependent upon objects (to the extent that he owns them), no longer exists for himself and possesses no real value."[30] As a matter of fact, the fetishism of the commodity form promotes only the universal spread of the dominion of a calculative reason anthropologically rooted in the structures of labor. The tendency toward the reification of society goes back to archaic times and extends beyond capitalism into the future of bureaucratic socialism, which will finally put into effect the testament of the world-historical process of disenchantment.

This is already more reminiscent of later Critical Theory than of early Lukács; but both comparisons fall short. What Bataille has in mind is not a theory of reification at all, but a philosophy that redescribes history as one great process of proscription, that is, of the progressive extraterritorialization of sacred powers. He wants to expound the world-historical destiny of sovereignty, that unfathomable freedom which consists of "consuming without profit what might have remained tied to useful works."[31]

The purest, still empirically graspable form of this sovereignty Bataille finds in ritual sacrifice, which he carefully analyzes using ethnological accounts of human sacrifice among the Aztecs: "The sacrifice immolates what it consecrates. It does not need to destroy the way fire does; only the bond that ties the sacrificial gift to the world of useful activity is cut off. But this separation has the significance of a decisively final consumption; the consecrated sacrificial gift cannot be given back to the real order. This principle opens the way for the release from bondage; it sets violence free by liberating a domain for it in which it can rule undividedly."[32] The meaning of sacrifice, as of all religion, reveals that the ritual core of the sacred is not primordial, but is already a reaction to the loss of an originally intimate unity of human beings with nature. We can infer this only if we recall what first became of the universe of innocent things through the labor of human hands, which is to say, with the first act of purposive objectification. Bataille's version of the expulsion from paradise reads as follows: "By the introduction of labor, intimacy, the depth of desire, and its free unleashing were replaced from the start by rational concatenation, in which the truth of the moment is no longer of import, but only the end result of any set of operations — in short, the first labor establishes the world of objects. . . . Since the foundation of the world of objects, the human being himself becomes one among the objects of this world, at least for the period during which one labors. Human beings of all ages have sought to escape this fate. In his unique myths and cruel rites, the human being is after his lost intimacy. . . . It is always a matter of tearing something away from the real order, from the poverty of objects, and of returning something to the divine order."[33] Just as religion already stands under the curse of labor, and only restores the destroyed order of things and makes possible a wordless communication with it for brief moments of ritual renunciation of the self, so, too, is pure sovereignty to be won back only in moments of ecstasy.

What became effective as sovereign violence in history, what first gained a lasting shape in the sacred power of the priests, then in the military power of the nobility, and finally in the absolutist power of the monarch and his court (already based on the apparatus of government) is a derivative of sovereignty made *impure* by its connection with profane power. All historical forms of sovereignty can be recognized from their differentiating power to ground distinctions of rank. The social rank of the ruler and of those who participate in domination is a mixed phenomenon in which we can see both aspects: its origin out of a sphere beyond labor and objects, as well as the repressive and exploitative function of domination within the system of social labor. The world-historical changes in the appearances of sovereignty do exhibit a tendency toward a dedifferentiation of distinctions of rank: "In archaic society, rank is tied to the consecrated presence of a subject whose sovereignty does not depend upon objects but integrates things into its movement. In bourgeois society, it still depends on ownership of objects that are neither sacral nor sovereign."[34] Now this does not mean that sovereignty has completely disappeared from the bourgeois world. The circumstances that private disposition over the means of production not only splits the society objectively into classes, but also grounds a system of privileges that distributes statuses and life-opportunities differentially, already speaks against its utter loss. Differences of rank merely lose their political character; but they do not disappear as such because they are derived from one's position in the production process rather than from one's share in political authority.

Even politicians in Western democracies retain something of the radiance proper to the sovereign nature in the form of personal prestige produced by public relations, even though this image is derived only from disposition over media-enhanced organizational power and not from charismatic qualities. The democratic politician stands midway between the subjectivity of being as it is present in the sovereign ruler, and even in the fascist Führer, on the one hand, and the objectivity of power on the other: "Only the seriousness of a communist statesman enables us to recognize something that is merely a constantly thwarted possibility in bourgeois society: the power promoted by the increase in things, independently of the striving for rank for which human beings seek to squander it."[35] According to the somewhat unrealistic picture of Stalinism put forth by Bataille in the early 1950s, in the bureaucratic socialism of Soviet Russia, social de-differentiation is supposed to have been complete; with the abolition of ranks, sovereignty is finally expelled root and branch from the sphere of social labor.

In all historical forms of domination, sovereignty was always alloyed with power. In the Soviet regime, for the first time, a power purified of all associations with sovereignty emerges, so to speak, unmixed, and in this sense "objective," and dispenses with the last attributes of religion. Without any certification through the authenticity of charisma, this objective power is exclusively functional, defined by the system of social labor, in short, by the goal of the development of the forces of production: "Whoever exercises supreme power in its objectivity has it as his end to prevent the rule of sovereignty over things; he has to liberate things from all particular subjugation; they should be subordinate to undifferentiated human beings" — which means to the collective will of a strictly egalitarian society.[36] Objective power that has cast off the mantle of a disenchanted sovereignty is included in the universe of a completely reified society — we could also say, a society that has congealed into a system. The fictitious picture of a coagulated Soviet domination is meant to be equivalent to the idea Engels had taken over from Saint-Simon: In place of the rule by men over men, we have the administration of things. This point is all the more surprising when Bataille's lament over the bourgeois negation of the brilliance, pomp, and wasteful extravagance of the feudal world sounds like a slick reversal of Saint-Simon's famous parable.[37] With Bataille, of course, Saint-Simon does not have the last word.

The celebration of a militant communism that subordinates all human spontaneity to the sociopolitical goal of industrialization and affirms a heroic materialism even in the respect "that the work of liberation will reduce the human being utterly into a thing"[38] — this paradoxical twist only becomes comprehensible if one considers Bataille's deprecatory judgment of bourgeois society's potential for a critique of civilization. Here the protest against the reification of the modern world and the romantic transfiguration of traditional forms of sovereignty contradict most profoundly precisely the subversive impulse behind heterogeneous existences — namely the radicality peculiar to the aesthetic avant-garde "of going in every direction to the very end of the possibilities of the world."[39] Fascism merely let out the secret of capitalism; the latter could erect its rational edifices of bondage only on the subterranean foundation of the remnants of sacred and military domination. These concealed but functionally necessary leftovers from prebourgeois sovereignty are finally set aside by Soviet Marxism's total assimilation of human beings to their products: "The perfection of things can only have a liberating aspect if old values associated with unproductive tasks get condemned and dismantled, as did Catholic values during the Reformation."[40]

Bataille treats Stalinism as the last stage in a process in which the two distinct spheres of a reified practice and of a pure sovereignty, cleansed in the end of all practical functions, are progressively separated from one another. Whether consciously or not, Stalin pursues the esoteric message that Bataille hears in Marx's exoteric doctrine: "Inasmuch as Marx reserved practice to the activity of transforming material conditions [that is, reduced practice to labor and the structure of purposive rational activity], he *explicitly* asserted what Calvinism only hinted at, namely, the radical independence of things (of the economy) from other strivings (of a religious or, in general, of an affective nature); however, he thus *implicitly* affirms the independence of the return of humanity to itself (to the depth and intimacy of its essential nature) from all productive activity. This return is, however, only possible when liberation is completed; it can begin only when action reaches a closure"[41] — and hence the project of a laboring society formed into a totality that has been set forth by Marx's philosophy.

This world-historical process, suspended between reification and sovereignty, which is supposed to end with a separation of spheres, an unmixing of homogeneous and heterogeneous elements, of labor and sacrifice, can no longer be thought dialectically — at any rate, not in accord with subject-philosophy's model of a dialectic of enlightenment, which relies on the constellation of moments of reason. Sovereignty is conceived of as the other of reason. Bataille cannot make his construction of modernity plausible by giving it the semblance of being dialectical. Above all, he must explain two things: For one, the world-historical process of societal rationalization; for another, the expectation that total reification will be overturned into freedom. Bataille makes it his scientific ambition to answer these two questions.

IV

From the beginning of his anthropological studies, Bataille repeatedly returns to the phenomenon of potlatch, the festival of waste at which North American Indians heap gifts upon their rivals in order, by this ostentatious squandering of wealth, to challenge them, to humiliate them, and to place them under obligation.[42] Actually, he is not interested in the socially integrating functions of the exchange of gifts as establishing reciprocal obligations. He neglects this aspect in favor of the more prominent aspect of expenditure, of destruction, and of the intended loss of property which, as a gift without immediate reciprocation, is squandered. Potlatch is an example of unproductive consumption in tribal societies. It is undeniable, however, that the one giving by no means spends his wealth selflessly. By outdoing rivals, who in turn are competing with their gifts, he secures prestige and power and earns or stabilizes his social rank within the given collective. Thus, sovereign disdain for use-values is already overtaken at this level by the calculative acquisition of power. This practice bears within itself the contradiction between sovereignty and purposive rationality: It places the "value, prestige, and truth of life in the negation of the utilitarian use of goods, but at the same time makes a utilitarian use of this negation."[43] Because precisely this contradiction is implanted structurally in *all* forms of historically embodied sovereignty, Bataille would like to use it to explain why it is that the sovereignty that expresses itself in acts of waste is more and more used for the exploitation of labor power and why it is that this source of true authority shrivels up into a "disgraceful source of profit."

However, the fact that sovereignty and power have been amalgamated from the very beginning and that this amalgam *can* be employed for the purpose of appropriating surplus value by no means already explains why the historical tendency toward the expansion and reification of the profane sphere and toward the exclusion of the sacred has actually prevailed. Bataille cannot adopt a politico-economic explanation in the Marxist style because the latter is related to changes *within* the system of social labor — and not to the interplay of the economy with a violence that is not rooted in economic domains or in those of calculating reason at all, but transcends the process of material exchange between human beings and external nature from the very start, as the other of reason. So Bataille is only being consistent when he plugs into Max Weber's religious-ethical explanation of capitalism and traces this in terms of the history of religions back to those beginnings of the moral regulation of drives prior to all historical forms of sovereignty and exploitation. This approach can be summarized in three steps.

The *first* idea has a biblical simplicity about it. In the process of hominization, the human beings that emerge out of the animal life-context are constituted not just in virtue of labor, but also by prohibitions. Humans are distinguished from animals by the fact that their vital drives are subordinated to constraints. Sexual shame and consciousness of mortality arise equiprimordially with labor. Such things as burial rites, costumes, and the incest taboo demonstrate that the most ancient taboos hold good for the human corpse and sexuality — the body as dead and as naked. If one also considers the prohibition of murder, a more general aspect comes to the fore: What is taboo is the violence associated with death and sexuality — a violence also expressed in the ritual climax of the festival and of the religious sacrifice. The excess that issues from generation and the excess associated with death as suffered or as violently enacted are related to cultic excesses, whereby Bataille understands "excess" quite literally as the transgression of those boundaries drawn by individuation. The most primitive norms are like dams set up against the swamp of a luxuriously exuberant nature that assures abundance and continuity of life by entwining individual existences: "When we perceive in the basic prohibitions the denial that the individual sets in opposition to nature as a waste of vital energy and an orgy of annihilation, we can discern no difference between death and sexuality. Death and sexuality are only the climax of a festival celebrated by nature with the inexhaustible masses. Both amount to a boundless squandering performed by nature in contradiction to the deep desire of each being [as individuated] for its own self-preservation."[44] The sphere of labor has to be bounded by limits that "banish" the violence of an exuberant nature "from the ordinary course of affairs."[45]

In a *second* step, Bataille makes clear, however, that the normative foundations of social life remain incomprehensible if one interprets them only from the perspective of what they achieve for the preservation of the system of social labor. From a functionalist perspective, it cannot be explained whence prohibitions draw their obligatory force. Durkheim already saw that the validity of norms could not be reduced in empiricist fashion to sanctions attached conventionally (that is, extrinsically) to the prohibitions. Rather, norms owe their binding force to the authority of something sacred that we approach with the ambivalence of terror and attraction without ever touching it. Bataille interprets this situation from his horizon of aesthetic experience in such a way that a deep ambiguity is constitutive for the most primitive norms: The validity claim of norms is founded in the experience of transgressing norms, which is forbidden and — precisely for this reason — *enticing*, that is to say, in the experience of sacrilege, in which the feelings of anxiety, loathing, and horror fuse with those of charm and benumbing happiness. Bataille speaks of the profound intimacy between law and transgression of the law. Because the rational world of labor is bounded and established within the frame of prohibitions, these prohibitions themselves are not at all laws of reason. Instead, they open the door to the sacred for the profane world and draw from it the illuminating force of fascination. "In the beginning, a calm opposition [of prohibitions] against the violence [of internal nature] would not have sufficed to separate the two worlds. If the opposition did not itself have its share of violence, . . . reason alone would not have possessed enough authority to determine the limits of transgression. Only unthinking fear and horror could offer resistance in the face of boundless unbridledness. That is the nature of the taboo: It makes possible a world of tranquillity and reason, but it is itself and in its very principle in the nature of a shudder that befalls not the intelligence but the spirit."[46] Erotic experience is related to religious experience in that they both link concurrence with the most primitive prohibitions to the ecstasy of terror overcome that follows upon profanation. "The inner experience of eroticism requires of the one undergoing it a no less great sensitivity toward the anxiety that establishes the prohibition than toward the desire that leads to its transgression. It is the religious sensitivity that continuously connects desire and terror, intense pleasure and anxiety, with one another."[47] In another passage, Bataille describes the phases of dizzying excess as loathing, then the overcoming of loathing, upon which giddiness follows.[48]

In a *third* step Bataille, finally reaches a critique of morality that forms a bridge to Max Weber's sociology of religion. It covers the development of religion from archaic rites to world religions, from the Jewish origins of monotheism to Protestantism, and interprets it as a path of ethical *rationalization*. Luther and Calvin mark a watershed in a religious evolution in which basic religious concepts are moralized and, along with this, religious experiences are spiritualized. The holy, which ambivalently releases repulsion and attraction, is domesticated and at the same time split apart. The archangel Lucifer is cast out of heaven. Opposed to heaven's blessings stands profane evil; along with the diabolical part of the sacred, the erotic is charged to the world and condemned as a sin of the flesh. When *all ambiguity is removed from the holy*, the consciousness of sin takes on a purely moral character. But if neither religious nor sensuous excess can any longer provide access to the sacred, the normative validity of the law is dissociated from the experience of excess (that is, of the risky, experimental transgressions of the law) from which it got its authority. Within the Judeo-Christian tradition, an autonomous morality can take shape only because the dialectic of prohibition and transgression is brought to a standstill, because the sacred no longer penetrates the profane world with its lightning flashes. Bataille's critique of morality is not aimed against morality as such — for this is only the outcome of a rationalization of religious world views that licenses access to a sacred that has been robbed of its complexity, spiritualized, and made unequivocal, individuated, and concentrated as the personal God in a beyond. The believer develops a merely moral consciousness to the extent that he is cut off from religious and sexual experiences of ecstatic self-transcendence. To this degree, then, the rise of autonomous morality explains the tendency toward progressive differentiation between the realms of religion and of economics, of sacrifice and of labor — it explains the expansion and reification of profane spheres of life under the ever thinner cover of sovereign powers that are further and further removed from the sources of sovereignty. Weber's interpretation of the Protestant ethic can be integrated without strain into this perspective: "In one and the same movement, religion and economics are liberated from what burdens them, namely, religion from profane calculation and economics from extraeconomic constraints."[49]

Even if we were to suppose that this explanatory strategy might be fruitful in relation to capitalism, it is not clear how it could be rendered fertile for the analysis of the utterly secularized enterprise of Soviet industrialization under authoritarian direction. The question remains open, therefore, why the predicted unmixing — the radically executed separation of the spheres of a completely rationalized society of labor, on the one side, and of a sovereignty become utterly extraterritorial, dissociated, and inaccessible, on the other side — is supposed, under conditions of advanced industrial society, to change abruptly into a condition that once again releases the energies of primordial sovereignty: "Were the complete formation that Stalin wanted to give to the perfect human being of communism at all worthy of its name, then this person would approximate, in an age in which the works of material civilization could not be relinquished, to that kind of sovereignty which, combined with voluntary respect for the sovereignty of the other, characterized the primitive shepherds and hunters. Of course, when the latter respected the sovereignty of the other, they did so only as a matter of fact"[50] — whereas, it should be added, a liberated mankind would make the reciprocal respect for the sovereignty of each by all into the moral foundation of common life. Bataille has to explain the adventuresome upheaval of Stalinism into a libertarian socialism without recourse to the thought-figure of an intrinsically dialectical movement of reason. This challenge he meets with his project of a General Economics.

Economics, including political economy and its critique, has until now been pursued under the restricted viewpoint of how scarce resources can be effectively deployed within the energy cycle of the reproduction of social life. Bataille opposes to this particular scarcity-based viewpoint the *general* viewpoint of a *cosmically expanded* energy ecology. On the basis of this change in perspective — which he executes on analogy with the change from the perspective of the microeconomic actor to that of the macroeconomic system — the fundamental economic question is inverted: The key problem is no longer the use of scarce resources but the unselfish expenditure of superfluous resources. That is, Bataille proceeds from the biological assumption that the living organism collects more energy than it uses to reproduce its life. The surplus energy is used for growth. When this comes to a standstill, the unabsorbed surplus of energy has to be spent unproductively — the energy must be lost without gain. This can occur in either a "glorious" or a "catastrophic" form. Sociocultural life also stands under the pressure of surplus energy.

This surplus energy can be canalized in different ways, for example, into the demographic, geographic, or social expansion of collectivities, into raising production and the standard of living, or, in general, into the increase of complexity — here organic growth finds a social equivalent. More conspicuous is the absorption of surplus vital energies by death and procreation, by the annihilation of individual existences and the begetting of new generations, which fall prey once again to annihilation. Corresponding to this luxury of nature is the luxury of the dominant social strata. Sovereign waste, whether in the economic forms of unproductive consumption or in the erotic and religious forms of excess, maintains in this way a central place in the economics of the universe interpreted in terms of a cosmic *Lebensphilosophie*. On the other hand, the unleashing of productive forces and capitalist growth, of industrial growth in general, increases the surpluses that cannot be absorbed by productive use alone. The disciplining power of morality, the abhorrence of luxury, the prohibition of sovereign violence, and the exclusion of the heterogeneous work in the same direction. When superfluous wealth is not squandered in a glorious, life-enhancing, and exalting way, however, the catastrophic forms of squandering present themselves as the only alternative — imperialistic adventures, global wars, and in our day we can add ecological pollution and nuclear destruction.

Bataille adduces speculations about equilibrium in the energy ecology of the cosmos and of the world society to support his expectation that total reification must turn into a resurrection of pure sovereign power. For the universe of a laboring society will increase the unabsorbed surpluses so immensely that the staging of orgies of waste and expenditures in the grand style will become inevitable — whether in the form of predictable catastrophes or precisely in the form of a libertarian society that frees its wealth for sovereign waste, that is, for excesses, for the self-transcendence of the subject, for the unbounding of subjectivity in general.

I do not need to go into the details of this metaphysical (in a pejorative sense) world view, which is presented in the anthropologically motivated form of an overcoming of the economy. But whether it is science or merely a substitute for metaphysics, Bataille is faced in any case with the same difficulty as Nietzsche, who proceeded in terms of a scientific critique of ideology: If sovereignty and its source, the sacred, are related to the world of purposive-rational action in an absolutely heterogeneous fashion, if the subject and reason are constituted only by excluding all kinds of sacred power, if the other of reason is more than just the irrational or the unknown — namely, the *incommensurable*, which cannot be touched by reason except at the cost of an explosion of the rational subject

— then there is no possibility of a theory that reaches beyond the horizon of what is accessible to reason and thematizes, let alone analyzes, the interaction of reason with a transcendent source of power. Bataille sensed this dilemma but did not resolve it. He experimented with the idea of a nonobjectifying science and speculated about the extreme where the knowing subject not only plays a part in constituting the object domain, not only is connected with it and communicates with it by virtue of prior structures, not only is implicated in it by intervening in it, but where he reaches his "boiling point." At this point, however, the knowing subject would — paradoxically — have to surrender his own identity and yet retrieve those experiences to which he was exposed in ecstasy — to catch them like fish from the decentered ocean of emotions. In spite of this paradox, Bataille stubbornly makes a claim to objectivity of knowledge and impersonality of method — even for this science "from within," for the grasp of "inner experience." Thus, in regard to this central question, there remains an inconclusive to-and-fro.

In many passages, Bataille glides imperceptibly back into the wake of the dialectic of enlightenment — especially when he ties his philosophic and scientific concerns to the goal of gaining reflective insights that can attain practical power by transforming dumb passivity into self-conscious participation. Here again he gets into the paradoxes of a totalized, self-referential critique: "We cannot penetrate to the ultimate object of knowledge without dissolving the sort of knowledge that reduces people to subordinate and useful things. . . . No one can know and at the same time preserve himself from annihilation."[51]

At the end of his life, Bataille appears to have wanted to use the possibility opened to him by his double life as a writer and theoretician to withdraw from philosophy and science. Eroticism led him to the insight that knowledge of what is essential is reserved for mystical experience, for silence with eyes closed. Discursive knowledge remains hopelessly caught in the circle of linguistic sequences: "Language assembles the totality of what has meaning for us, but fragments it at the same time. . . . Our attention remains directed toward that whole which slips away from us in a series of statements, but we cannot reach the point at which the flashes of successive statements yield to the grand illumination."[52]

The erotic writer can still use language in a poetic way, such that the reader, assaulted by obscenity, gripped by the shock of the unexpected and unimaginable, is jolted into the ambivalence of loathing and pleasure. But philosophy cannot in the same way break out of the universe of language: "It deploys language in such a fashion that silence never follows. So that the supreme moment necessarily transcends the philosophical problematic."[53] With this statement, however, Bataille undercuts his own efforts to carry out the radical critique of reason with the tools of theory.

IX

The Critique of Reason as
an Unmasking of the Human
Sciences: Michel Foucault

I

Foucault does not stand to Bataille, as Derrida does to Heidegger, in a relationship of disciple and successor. Even the external bond of a discipline within whose tradition both grew up together is lacking. Bataille took up ethnology and sociology without ever holding an academic post; Foucault was until his recent death Professor of the History of Systems of Thought at the Collège de France. Yet Foucault still calls Bataille one of his mentors. He is fascinated by Bataille as someone who stems the tide against the denaturing flood of enlightened discourse about sexuality and who wants to give back to both sexual and religious ecstasy their proper, specifically erotic meaning. But, above all, Foucault admires Bataille as someone who ranges texts in fiction and analysis, novels and reflection, alongside one another; someone who enriches the language with gestures of waste and excess and transgression of limits, in order to break out of the language of triumphant subjectivity. To a question about his mentors, Foucault gave the instructive response: "For a long time I was dominated by a badly resolved conflict between a passion for Blanchot and Bataille on the one hand, and an interest in certain positive studies like those of Dumézil and Lévi-Strauss on the other. But actually, both these directions, whose single common denominator is perhaps the religious problem, have contributed in the same fashion toward leading me to the idea of the disappearance of the subject."[1]

Like many of his contemporaries, Foucault was also taken with the structuralist revolution; it turned him, as it did Derrida, into a critic of the phenomenological-anthropological thought prevalent from Kojève till Sartre; and it was what first determined him in his choice of methods. He understood this "negative discourse about the subject" introduced by Lévi-Strauss to be at the same time a critique of modernity. But Nietzsche's motif of a critique of reason reached Foucault not via Heidegger, but through Bataille. Finally, he worked out these impulses not as a philosopher but as a student of Bachelard, and indeed as a historian of science who, in contrast to what is usual in that specialty, was more interested in the human sciences than in the natural sciences.

These three lines of tradition indicated by the names of Lévi-Strauss, Bataille, and Bachelard are joined together in the first book that made Foucault known outside the narrower circle of his fellow specialists. *Madness and Civilization* (1961) is a study of the prehistory and early history of psychiatry. The model of structuralist ethnology is noticeable in the means of analyzing discourse and in the methodical distantiation from one's own culture. The subtitle already lays claim to a critique of reason: *The History of Madness in the Age of Reason.* Foucault wants to show how the phenomenon of madness has been constituted as a mental illness since the end of the eighteenth century. With this goal in mind, he reconstructs the history of the rise of the discourse in which psychiatrists of the nineteenth and twentieth centuries talk about madness. What makes this book more than a wide-ranging study of cultural history by a historian of science is a philosophical interest in madness as a phenomenon complementary to reason. A reason that has become monological holds madness at arm's length from itself so as safely to gain mastery of it as an object cleansed of rational subjectivity. Making madness clinical, which first renders mental illness a medical phenomenon, is analyzed by Foucault as an example of those processes of exclusion, proscription, and outlawing in whose traces Bataille had read the history of Western rationality.

In Foucault's hands, the history of science is enlarged into a history of reason because it studies the constituting of madness as a reflex image of the constituting of reason. Foucault declares programmatically that he wants "to write the history of the boundaries . . . by which a culture reprobates something that lies *outside* it."[2] He classifies insanity among those limit experiences in which Western logos sees itself, with extreme ambivalence, faced with something heterogeneous. Boundary-transgressing experiences include contact with and even immersion in the Oriental world (Schopenhauer); rediscovery of the tragic element and of the archaic in general (Nietzsche); penetration of the dream sphere (Freud) and of archaic prohibitions (Bataille); even the exoticism nourished by anthropological reports. Foucault omits Romanticism from this list, aside from one mention of Hölderlin.[3]

And yet in *Madness and Civilization* a Romantic motif comes through that Foucault will later give up. Just as Bataille discovers in the paradigmatic experience of ecstatic self-unbounding and orgiastic self-dissolution the eruption of heterogeneous forces into the homogeneous world of an everyday life that has been compulsively normalized, so Foucault suspects that behind the psychiatrically engendered phenomenon of mental illness, and indeed behind the various masks of madness at that time, there is something authentic whose sealed mouth need only be opened up: "One would have to bend an attentive ear to the whispers of the world and try to perceive the many images that have never been set down in poetry and the many fantasies that have never reached the colors proper to the waking state."[4]

Foucault recognizes immediately the paradoxicalness of the task of catching the truth of madness "as it bubbles up long before it gets apprehended by erudition," for "the act of perception that tries to apprehend these words in their unfettered state necessarily belongs to a world that already has it in its grip." Nonetheless, the author still has in mind an analysis of discourse that, in the manner of depth hermeneutics, probes its way back to the original point of the initial branching off of madness from reason in order to decipher what is unspoken in what is said.[5] This intention points in the direction of a negative dialectics that tries to break out of the enchanted circle of identifying thought by means of such thought itself, that pursues the history of the rise of instrumental reason back to the point of the primordial usurpation and of the split of a monadically hardening reason from mimesis, and then circles round this point, even if only in an aporetic fashion. But then Foucault would have to clamber about archeologically among the debris of an objective reason that had been destroyed, from the mute testimony of which we might still retrospectively shape the perspective of a (long since revoked) hope for reconciliation. But this is Adorno's approach, not Foucault's.

One who desires to unmask nothing but the naked image of subject-centered reason cannot abandon himself to the dreams that befall this reason in its "anthropological slumber." Three years later, in the foreword to *The Birth of the Clinic*, Foucault calls himself to order. In the future, he will abstain from dealing with texts through commentary and give up all hermeneutics, no matter how deeply it may penetrate below the surface of the text. He no longer seeks madness itself behind discourse about madness, or the mute contact of body with eyes, which seemed to precede any discourse, behind the archeology of the medical gaze. Unlike Bataille, he rejects any evocative access to the excluded and outlawed — heterogeneous elements no longer promise anything. A hermeneutics of unveiling always still connects a promise with its critique; a chastened archeology should be rid of that: "Is it not possible to make a structural analysis of discourses that would evade the fate of commentary by supposing no remainder, nothing but the fact of its historical appearance? The facts of discourse would then have to be treated not as autonomous nuclei of multiple significations, but as events and functional segments gradually coming together to form a system. The meaning of a statement would be defined not by the treasure of intentions that it might contain, revealing and concealing at the same time, but by the difference that articulates it upon other real or possible statements, which are contemporary to it or to which it is opposed in a linear series of time. A systematic history of discourses would then become possible."[6] There is already a suggestion here of a conception of historical writing that Foucault, under the influence of Nietzsche, from the late 1960s set over against the human sciences — which are integrated into the history of reason and hence degraded — as a kind of antiscience. In the light of this conception, Foucault would assess his earlier work on madness (and the rise of clinical psychology) as well as on sickness (and the development of clinical medicine) as in part "blind attempts." Before getting into this, I want to point out some themes that establish a continuity in subject matter between the earlier and the later works.

II

In *Madness and Civilization,* Foucault already investigates the peculiar connection between discourses and practices. It is not a matter of the familiar attempt to explain the internally reconstructed evolution of science from conditions external to science. In place of the internal perspective of a problem-oriented theory of science, we find from the very beginning a structural description of selected conspicuous discourses which starts out in the gaps that are covered over by the approach of historians of ideas and problems; it is in such gaps that a new paradigm begins to establish itself in opposition to an old one. Moreover, the discourses of scientists are related to other discourses — those of philosophers and those of academically trained professionals such as physicians, judges, administrative officials, theologians, and educators. Of course, the human sciences, which form the stubbornly maintained reference point of Foucault's studies, do not only stand in the context of other discourses; far more important for the history of their emergence are the mute practices into which they are admitted. By the latter, Foucault understands the institutionally fixed and often even architecturally embodied or ritually sedimented regulations of modes of action and customs. Foucault builds into the concept of "practice" the moment of coercive, asymmetric influence over the freedom of movement of other participants in interaction. Legal judgments, police measures, pedagogical instructions, internment, discipline, checks and controls, forms of corporal and intellectual drill are examples of the intrusion of socializing, organizing forces into the quasi-natural substrate of bodily creatures. Foucault allows himself an altogether unsociological concept of the social. From the outset, he is interested in the human sciences as media that in modernity strengthen and promote the mysterious process of this socialization, that is, the investment with power of concrete, bodily mediated interactions. There is some unclarity, to begin with, regarding the problem of how discourses — scientific and non-scientific — are related to practices: whether one governs the other, whether their relationship is to be conceived as that of base to superstructure, or on the model of a circular causality, or as an interplay of structure and event.

Foucault also retained to the end the epochal divisions that articulate the history of madness. Against the background of a diffuse and not very clearly portrayed high middle ages, which in turn point toward the origins of Greek logos,[7] the contours of the Renaissance stand out more clearly. The latter, in turn, serves as a foil for the Classical age (from the middle of the seventeenth until the end of the eighteenth century), portrayed lucidly and with sympathy. Thus, the end of the eighteenth century marks the peripeteia in the drama of the history of reason. It is the threshold of modernity shaped by Kantian philosophy and the new human sciences. Foucault bestows on these epochs, whose conventional names are due more to shifts in cultural and social history, a deeper meaning in accord with the changing constellations of reason and madness. He ascribes to the sixteenth century a certain self-critical restlessness and openness in dealing with the phenomenon of insanity. Reason still has an osmotic porosity — madness is still linked with the tragic and the prophetic and is a place of apocryphal truths; it has the function of a mirror that ironically unmasks the weaknesses of reason. To be disposed toward illusions pertains to the character of reason itself. During the Renaissance, all reversibility has not yet been expunged from the relation of reason to its other. Against this background, two processes take on the significance of watershed events in the history of reason: the great rash of confinements around the middle of the seventeenth century, when, for example, within a few months during the year 1656 every hundredth inhabitant of Paris was arrested and put into an institution; and then, at the close of the eighteenth century, the transformation of these places of incarceration and asylums into closed institutions with supervision by doctors for medically diagnosed mental illness — that is, the birth of the kind of psychiatric establishments that still exist today (and the dismantling of which is promoted by the antipsychiatry movement).

These two events (first, the involuntary confinement of the mad, the criminal, those without housing, libertines, the poor, and the eccentric of every kind, and later on, the erection of clinics for the treatment of mentally ill patients) signal two types of practices. Both serve to delimit heterogeneous elements out of that gradually stabilized monologue that the subject, raised in the end to the status of universal human reason, holds with itself through making everything around it into an object. As in later studies, the comparison of the Classical age with the modern age is central. Both types of exclusionary practices agree in forcing a separation and in rigorously erasing from the picture of madness those traits that are similar to reason. It is just that the indiscriminate confinement of every deviant only means a spatial segmentation of the wild and the fantastic, which are left to themselves; it does not yet mean a domesticating confrontation with a chaos that gives rise to anxiety and that has to be integrated into the order of nature and of humanity as suffering and pathology: "What the classical period had confined was not only an abstract unreason which mingled madmen and libertines, invalids, and criminals, but also an enormous reservoir of the fantastic, a dormant world of monsters supposedly engulfed in the darkness of Hieronymus Bosch which had spewed them forth."[8] Only in the late eighteenth century does the fear of a madness that could force its way outside through the cracks in the asylums grow, along with a compassion for those with nervous disorders and a feeling of guilt for associating them with dirty criminals and abandoning them to their fate. The clinical cleansing of asylums henceforth reserved for the sick goes hand in hand with the scientific objectification of insanity and the psychiatric treatment of the insane. This means at once a humanizing of suffering and a naturalizing of illness.[9]

Here we touch on a further theme that Foucault will pursue with ever greater intensity: the constitutive connection between the human sciences and the practices of supervisory isolation.

The birth of the psychiatric institution and of the clinic in general is exemplary for a form of disciplining that Foucault will describe later on purely and simply as the modern technology of domination. The archetype of the closed institution, which Foucault initially discovers in the clinically transformed world of the asylum, turns up again in the forms of the factory, the prison, the barracks, the school, and the military academy. In these total institutions, which extinguish the quasi-natural differentiations of old European life and elevate the exceptional case of internment into a kind of normal form of "boarding," Foucault perceives the monuments to victory of a regulatory reason that no longer subjugates only madness, but also the needs and desires of the individual organism as well as the social body of an entire population.

A *gaze* that objectifies and examines, that takes things apart analytically, that monitors and penetrates everything, gains a power that is structurally formative for these institutions. It is the gaze of the rational subject who has lost all merely intuitive bonds with his environment and torn down all the bridges built up of intersubjective agreement, and for whom in his monological isolation, other subjects are only accessible as the objects of nonparticipant observation. This gaze is, as it were, architecturally congealed in the Panopticon sketched out by Bentham.[10]

The same structure is to be found at the cradle of the human sciences. It is no accident that these sciences, especially clinical psychology, but also pedagogy, sociology, political science, and cultural anthropology, can, as it were, frictionlessly intermesh in the overall technology of power that finds its architectural expression in the closed institution. They are translated into therapies and social techniques, and so form the most effective medium of the new, disciplinary violence that dominates modernity. They owe this to the fact that the penetrating gaze of the human scientist can occupy that centralized space of the panopticon from which one can look without being seen. In his study on the birth of the clinic, Foucault already conceived of the gaze of the anatomist, trained on the human corpse, as the "concrete apriori" of the sciences of man. In his history of madness, he already sensed the primordial affinity between the setup of the asylum and the doctor-patient relationship. In both, in the organization of the supervised institution and in the clinical observation of the patient, there is effected a division between seeing and being seen that links the idea of the clinic with the idea of the science of man. It is an idea that attains dominance at the same time as subject-centered reason: that killing off dialogical relationships transforms subjects, who are monologically turned in upon themselves, into objects for one another, and only objects.

Using the example of the reform movements that gave rise to psychiatric institutions and clinical psychology, Foucault works out the internal kinship between humanism and terror that endows his critique of modernity with its sharpness and mercilessness. In connection with the birth of the psychiatric institute from humanitarian ideas of the Enlightenment, Foucault demonstrates for the first time that "double movement of liberation and enslavement" which he later recognizes along a broad front in the reforms of the penal system, the educational system, the health establishment, social welfare, and so forth. The freeing of the insane from the neglect of their places of confinement on humanitarian grounds, the creation of hygienic clinics under medical direction, the psychiatric treatment of the mentally ill, the right won by the latter to psychological understanding and therapeutic care — this was all made possible through an institutional ordinance preparing the patient to be an object of continuous supervision, manipulation, isolation, and regulation, and especially the object of medical research. The practices institutionally stabilized in the internal organization of life within these establishments are the basis for a knowledge of madness that first endows it with the objectivity of a fully conceptualized pathology and thus integrates it into the universe of reason. Psychiatric knowledge means an *ambiguous liberation*, in the sense of emancipation and elimination, not only for the patient, but also for the doctor, the practicing positivist: "The knowledge of madness presupposed on the part of those who possess it a specific way of ridding themselves of madness, of freeing themselves from the start from its dangers and its magic. . . . Originally this meant the fixation of a certain way of not being mad."[11]

I will not deal with these four themes in any detail. Instead, I will take up the question of whether Foucault succeeds in bringing off a radical critique of reason in the form of a historiography of the human sciences, which starts as archeology and is expanded into genealogy, without getting caught in the aporias of this self-referential undertaking. The methodological problem of how a history of the constellations of reason and madness can be written at all, if the labor of the historian must in turn move about within the horizon of reason, remained just as unexplained in the early works as that of the relationship between discourses and practices. In the prefaces to his studies published at the start of the 1960s, Foucault poses himself this question without answering it; however, when he delivers his inaugural lecture at the Collège de France in 1970, it seems to have been solved in the meantime. Drawing a boundary between reason and madness turns up again here as one of the three mechanisms of exclusion in virtue of which rational speech is constituted. The elimination of madness stands midway between the more conspicuous operations of keeping refractory speakers away from discourse, suppressing unpleasant themes, censoring certain expressions, and so on, on the one hand, and, on the other hand, the altogether inconspicuous operation of distinguishing within the interaction of discourse between valid and invalid statements. Foucault concedes that at first glance it is implausible to conceive the rules for the elimination of false statements on the model of the delimitation of madness and the proscription of the heterogeneous: "How could one reasonably compare the constraints of the truth with those other divisions, arbitrary in origin if not developing out of historical contingency, in a state of continual flux, supported by a system of institutions imposing them and manipulating them, acting not without constraint, nor without an element, at least, of violence?"[12]

Naturally, Foucault does not allow himself to be influenced by the ostensible lack of coercion of the cogent argument by which truth claims, and validity claims in general, prevail. The appearance of nonviolence on the part of the better argument disappears as soon as one "considers it at a different level," by assuming the attitude of the archeologist who directs his gaze at the buried foundations of meaning, at the infrastructures to be painstakingly excavated, which indeed first establish what is going to be considered true and false *inside* any discourse. Truth is an insidious mechanism of exclusion, because it only functions on condition that the *will to truth* prevalent within it remains hidden: "As though the will to truth were masked by truth itself and its necessary unfolding. . . . *True* discourse, liberated by the nature of its form from *desire* and *power*, is incapable of recognizing the *will to truth* that pervades it; and the will to truth, having imposed upon us for so long, is such that the truth it seeks to reveal cannot fail to mask it."[13]

The criteria of validity according to which what is true gets discriminated from what is false within a discourse abide in a unique transparency and appearance of having no origin whatsoever — validity has to strip away every element of the sheerly genetic, even its derivation from the basic rules constitutive of the discourse, which the archeologist lays bare. So little can the structures that make truth possible themselves be true or false that one can only inquire about the function of the will that attains expression in them, and about the genealogy of this will from some network of the practices of power. From the early 1970s, Foucault distinguished the archeology of knowledge that uncovers the truth-constitutive rules of exclusion in any discourse from the genealogical investigation of the pertinent practices. Genealogy studies how discourses are formed and why they emerge and disappear again, by tracing the historically variable conditions of validity right to their institutional roots. Whereas archeology follows the style of erudite ingenuity, genealogy cherishes a "felicitous positivism."[14] However, if archeology could proceed in learned fashion and genealogy in the mode of innocent positivism, then the methodological paradox of a science that writes the history of the human sciences with the goal of a radical critique of reason would be solved.

III

Foucault owes the concept of an erudite-positivistic historiography in the appearance of an antiscience to his reception of

Nietzsche, which is set down in the introduction to *The Archeology of Knowledge* (1969) and in the essay "Nietzsche, Genealogy, History" (1971). Philosophically considered, this concept seems to offer a promising alternative to the kind of critique of reason that had assumed the form of a temporalized *Ursprungsphilosophie* in Heidegger and Derrida. Now, of course, the entire weight of the problematic rests on the basic concept of power that lends both the archeological prospecting and the genealogical disclosures their dimension of being a critique of modernity. Nietzsche's authority, from which this utterly unsociological concept of power is borrowed, is not enough to justify its systematic usage. The political context of Foucault's reception of Nietzsche — disappointment with the failure of the 1968 revolt — makes the concept of a historiography of the human sciences as a critique of reason biographically intelligible; but even this cannot ground the specific use of the concept of power with which he loads his paradoxical undertaking. The turn to a theory of power must, rather, be understood as an internally motivated attack on problems with which Foucault saw himself confronted after he had carried out his unmasking of the human sciences in *The Order of Things* using only the tools of discourse analysis. But let us first look at Foucault's appropriation of the concept of "genealogy."

Genealogical historiography can only take over the role of a critique of reason qua antiscience if it escapes from the horizon of just those historically oriented sciences of men whose hollow humanism Foucault wants to unmask in his theory of power. The new history has to negate all those presuppositions that have been constitutive for the historical consciousness of modernity and for philosophy of history and the historical Enlightenment since the end of the eighteenth century. This explains why Nietzsche's "Second Untimely Meditation" is a mine for Foucault. For, with a similar purpose in mind, Nietzsche had subjected the historicism of his time to a relentless attack.

Foucault wants (a) *to leave behind modernity's presentist consciousness of time*. He wants to break with the privileging of a present which is singled out under the pressure of the problems of facing the future responsibly, and to which the past is narcissistically related. Foucault settles accounts with the presentism of the kind of historiography that does not get beyond its hermeneutical initial situation and permits itself to be enlisted for the stabilizing assurance of an identity long since shattered. Consequently, genealogy is not supposed to search for an *origin*, but to uncover the contingent *beginnings* of discourse formations, to analyze the multiplicity of factual histories of derivation, and to dissolve the illusion of identity, especially the putative identity of the history-writing subject himself and of his contemporaries: "Where the soul pretends unification or the self fabricates a coherent identity, the genealogist sets out to study the beginning. . . . The analysis of descent permits the dissociation of self, its recognition and displacement as an empty synthesis, in liberating a profusion of lost events."[15]

There results from this (b) the methodological consequence of *a parting with hermeneutics*. The new history makes use not of *Verstehen* but of the destruction and dismantling of that context of effective history which putatively links the historian with his object and with which he enters into communication only to find himself in it: "History must be detached from the image . . . through which it found its anthropological justification: that of an age-old collective consciousness that made use of material documents to refresh its memory."[16] Hermeneutical effort is aimed at the appropriation of meaning; in each document, it hunts out a voice reduced to silence that should be roused into life again. This idea of a *document* pregnant with meaning has to be called into question just as radically as the business of interpretation itself. The "commentary" and its cognate fictions of the "work" and of the "author" as the originator of texts, as well as the tracing back of secondary to primary texts and in general the production of causal chains in intellectual history, are all instruments of an impermissible reduction of complexity; they are procedures for damming up the spontaneous upsurge of discourses which the later interpreter just wants to tailor to his own size and accommodate to his own provincial horizon of understanding. In contrast, the archeologist is going to change talkative documents into mute *monuments*, objects that have to be freed from their own context in order to become accessible to a structuralist description. The genealogist approaches the archeologically excavated monuments from outside, in order to explain their derivation from the contingent ups and downs of battles, victories, and defeats. Only the historian who sovereignly disdains whatever discloses itself to the interpretation of meaning can undermine the foundational function of the knowing subject. He sees through, as sheer deceit, "the guarantee that everything that has eluded him may be restored to him; . . . the promise that one day the subject — in the form of historical consciousness — will once again be able to appropriate, to bring back under his sway, all those things that are kept at a distance by difference."[17]

The basic concepts of the philosophy of the subject dominate not only the type of access to the object domain, but also history itself. Hence, Foucault wants above all (c) *to put an end to global historiography* that covertly conceives of history as a macroconsciousness. History in the singular has to be dissolved, not indeed into a manifold of narrative histories, but into a plurality of irregularly emerging and disappearing islands of discourse. The critical historian will first dissolve *false continuities* and pay attention to ruptures, thresholds, and changes in direction. He does not produce teleological contexts; he is not interested in the large causal chains; he does not count on syntheses and rejects out of hand principles of articulation such as progress and evolution; he does not divide history into epochs: "The project of a total history is one that seeks to constitute the overall form of a civilization, the principle — material or spiritual — of society, the significance *common* to all the phenomena of a period, the law that accounts for their cohesion — what is metaphorically the 'face' of a period."[18] Instead of this, Foucault borrows from the "serial history" of the *Annales* school the programmatically deployed notions of a structuralist procedure that deals with a plurality of noncontemporaneous histories of systems and that shapes their analytic unities in terms of indicators remote from consciousness, that renounces in many cases the conceptual tools issued from the synthetic performances of a supposed consciousness, in other words, that abstains from the formation of totalities.[19] Thus also excluded is the idea of reconciliation, a legacy of the philosophy of history on which the critique of modernity stemming from Hegel still uninhibitedly nourished itself. The kind of history "whose function is to compose the finally reduced diversity of time into a totality fully closed upon itself; a history that always . . . attributes a form of reconciliation to all the displacements of the past; a history whose perspective on all that precedes it implies the end of time,"[20] receives a harsh denunciation.

From this destruction of a historiography that remains captive to anthropological thinking and basic humanistic convictions, there emerges the outline of a *transcendental historicism* at once inherited from and going beyond Nietzsche's critique of historicism. Foucault's radical historiography remains "transcendental" in a weak sense inasmuch as it understands the objects of the historical-hermeneutical interpretation of meaning as constituted — as objectivations of underlying discourse practices that are to be grasped by structuralist methods. The old history concerned itself with totalities of meaning that it made accessible from the internal perspectives of the participants. From this viewpoint, what *constitutes* such a world of discourse never comes into view. Only an archeology that unearths a discursive practice down to its very roots sees what looks from the inside to be a totality from the outside, as something particular that could also be otherwise. Whereas participants understand themselves as subjects who relate to objects in general in accord with universal criteria of validity, without ever being able to transcend the perspicuous horizon of their world, the archeologist approaching from outside brackets this self-understanding. By going back to the rules constitutive of discourses, he ascertains the limits of any given universe of discourse; its form is *bounded* by the kinds of elements that it unconsciously *excludes* as heterogeneous — and to this degree, the rules constitutive of discourses also function as a mechanism of exclusion. What is defined as out of bounds for any given discourse first makes possible the specific subject-object relations that are, however, viewed from within the discourse as universally valid, without any alternatives. In this respect, Foucault takes up the heritage of Bataille's heterology in his archeology of knowledge. What differentiates him from Bataille is the merciless historicism before which even the pre-discursive reference point of sovereignty dissolves. As little as the term "madness" (from the Renaissance down to positivistic psychiatry in the nineteenth century) indicates an authentic experiential potential this side of all the discourses about madmen, just as little does the other of reason, what is excluded as heterogeneous, retain the role of a prediscursive referent that could point to the coming arrival of a lost origin.[21]

Instead, the space of history is seamlessly filled by the absolutely contingent occurrence of the disordered flaring up and passing away of new formations of discourse. No place is left for any *overarching* meaning in this chaotic multitude of past totalities of discourse. The transcendental historicist looks as if into a kaleidoscope: "This kaleidoscope hardly reminds one of successive forms of a dialectical development; it is not explained by a progression of consciousness, nor yet by its descent, nor by the struggle between two principles: desire and repression — each flourish owes its bizarre shape to the space left it by the adjacent practices."[22]

Under the *stoic* gaze of the archeologist, history hardens into an iceberg covered with the crystalline forms of arbitrary formations of discourses. But since the autonomy proper to a totality without origin accrues to every single one of these formations, the only job left for the historian is that of the genealogist who explains the accidental provenance of these bizarre shapes from the hollow forms of bordering formations, that is, from the proximate circumstances. Under the *cynical* gaze of the genealogist, the iceberg begins to move: Discourse formations are displaced and regrouped, they undulate back and forth. The genealogist explains this to-and-fro movement with the help of countless events and a single hypothesis — the only thing that lasts is power, which appears with ever new masks in the change of anonymous processes of overpowering: "An 'event,' consequently, is not a decision, a treaty, a reign, or a battle, but the reversal of a relationship of forces, the usurpation of power, the appropriation of a vocabulary turned against those who had once used it, a feeble domination that poisons itself as it grows lax, the entry of a masked other."[23] What the synthetic power of transcendental consciousness was hitherto supposed to accomplish for the one and general universe of the objects of possible experience — this synthesis —

is now degraded into the subjectless will of a power effective in the contingent and disordered to-and-fro of discursive formations.

IV

Just as "life" was once elevated by Bergson, Dilthey, and Simmel to the basic transcendental concept of a philosophy (which still formed the background to Heidegger's analytics of Dasein), so Foucault now raises "power" to a basic transcendental-historicist concept of historiography as critique of reason. This characteristic is by no means trivial, and certainly not to be grounded on Nietzsche's authority alone. Using the concept of the history of Being as a contrasting background, I want first to study the role assumed by this vexing basic concept in Foucault's critique of reason.

Heidegger and Derrida want to advance Nietzsche's program of a critique of reason by way of a destruction of metaphysics; Foucault wants to do so by way of a destruction of historiography. Whereas the former surpass philosophy through an exorcising, evocative thinking beyond philosophy, Foucault oversteps the human sciences through a historiography that appears as an antiscience. Both sides neutralize the straightforwardly raised validity claims of the types of philosophical and scientific discourses they study by referring either to an epochal understanding of Being or to the formation rules for a given discourse. It is these that are supposed to first make possible the meaning of entities and the validity of statements within the horizon of a given world or of an established discourse. Both also agree that world horizons or discourse formations undergo change; but in these changes they maintain their transcendental power over whatever unfolds *within* the totalities shaped by them. This excludes a dialectical or circular feedback effect of either the ontic occurrence or the referents upon the history of the conditions of their possibility — whether these conditions are construed ontologically or in terms of discourse formation. The history of the transcendentals and the change in world-disclosing horizons require concepts *different* from those appropriate for the ontic and historical dimensions. It is at this point that there is a parting of the ways.

Heidegger radicalizes the figures of thought of *Ursprungs-philosophie*, in which he preserves a vestige of confidence. He transfers the epistemic authority proper to the validity of truth to the process of the formation and transformation of world-disclosing horizons. The conditions making truth possible can themselves be neither true nor false, and yet a paravalidity is ascribed to the process of their changing; this is supposed to be conceived on the model of the validity of truth, as a heightened, historicized form of truth. Viewed in the light of day, Heidegger is proposing a curious alloy with his concept of the history of Being as a truth-occurrence. The authority of the history of Being is due to a fusion of meaning between validity claims free of coercion and imperious claims to power. This fusion lends to the subversive force of the insightful the imperative force of an illumination compelling one to one's knees. With a tiny vestige of confidence in the human sciences, Foucault avoids such a pseudo-religious twist by activating for his own purposes Bataille's heterological idea of de-limitation. He strips the history of discourse-constitutive rules of any authority based on validity and treats the transformation of transcendentally powerful discourse formations just as conventional historiography treats the ups and downs of political regimes. Whereas the archeology of knowledge (and in this it is similar to the destruction of the history of metaphysics) reconstructs the stratum of rules constitutive of discourse, genealogy strives to explain "the discontinuous succession of the sign-systems (ungrounded in themselves) that coerce people into the semantic framework of a determinate interpretation of the world"[24] — and indeed it explains the provenance of discourse formations from practices of power that are entwined with one another in the "risky game of overpowering."

In his later studies, Foucault will fill out this abstract concept of power in a more tangible way; he will comprehend power as the interaction of warring parties, as the decentered network of bodily, face-to-face confrontations, and ultimately as the productive penetration and subjectivizing subjugation of a bodily opponent. In our context, however, it is important to note how Foucault *joins* these palpable meanings of power *together* with the transcendental meaning of synthetic performances that Kant still ascribed to a subject and that structuralism now understands as an anonymous occurrence, namely, as a pure, decentered, rule-guided operation with the ordered elements of a suprasubjectively constructed system.[25] In Foucault's genealogy, "power" is initially a synonym for this *purely structuralistic activity*; it takes the same place that "différance" does in Derrida. But this power constitutive of discourse is supposed to be a power of transcendental generativity *and* of empirical self-assertion simultaneously. Like Heidegger, Foucault also undertakes a fusion of opposed meanings; but here an amalgam results that allows him to follow in the footsteps of Bataille and connect up with Nietzsche's critique of ideology. Heidegger wanted to hold onto the validity-grounding meaning of transcendental world disclosure in his concept of Being as a temporalized power of origin; but at the same time he wanted to eliminate the idealist element of something invariant that points beyond everything historical, beyond everything that is of the nature of a mere event — an element that is also usually found in the concept of the transcendental. Foucault owes his basic transcendental-historical concepts of power not only to this *one* paradoxical operation, which brings synthetic performances a priori back into the realm of historical events; he also undertakes three additional, equally paradoxical operations.

On the one hand, Foucault has to retain for his concept of power — which ironically conceals itself in discourse as the will to truth and at the same time makes itself felt therein — the transcendental meaning of a condition of the possibility of truth. On the other hand, he not only brings to bear against the Idealism of the Kantian concept a temporalizing of the a priori — so that new discourse formations, which push out the old, can emerge like *events* — but also strips this transcendental power of the connotations that Heidegger prudently leaves to an auratic history of Being. Foucault not only historicizes; his approach is at the same time nominalist, materialist, and empiricist. He thinks of the transcendental practices of power as something particular that strives against all universals, and further as the lowly corporeal-sensual that undermines everything intelligible, and finally as the contingent that could also have been otherwise because it is not governed by any regulative order. In Heidegger's later philosophy, it is not easy to pin down the paradoxical consequences of a fundamental concept contaminated by contrary meanings, because meditation upon a Being from time immemorial eludes assessment on the basis of testable criteria. In contrast, Foucault exposes himself to palpable objections, because his historiography, despite its antiscientific tenor, seeks to proceed both "eruditely" and "positivistically." As a result, genealogical historiography can scarcely hide the paradoxical consequences of a basic concept that is similarly contaminated, as we shall see below. There is all the more need to explain why Foucault resolves upon heading his theory of science oriented to a critique of reason onto the path of a theory of power.

From a biographical standpoint, Foucault's motives for taking up Nietzsche's theory of power could be different from Bataille's. Both started out on the political left, and both put increasingly more distance between themselves and Marxist orthodoxy. But only Foucault experienced *sudden* disappointment with a political engagement. In interviews of the early 1970s, Foucault revealed the vehemence of his break with earlier convictions. At that time, he joined the choir of disappointed Maoists of 1968 and was taken by the moods to which one must look if one wants to explain the remarkable success of the New Philosophers in France.[26] Were one to believe it possible to reduce his central ideas to this context, one would surely be underestimating Foucault's originality. At any rate, these external political impulses could not have set anything in motion at the innermost core of the theory, if the dynamism of the theory itself had not (long before his experiences with the revolt of 1968) given rise to the idea that discursive mechanisms of exclusion not only reflect self-sufficient structures of discourse, but carry out imperatives for heightening power. The idea arose in the problematic situation that Foucault faced after the conclusion of his work on the archeology of the human sciences.

In *The Order of Things* (1966), Foucault investigates the modern forms of knowledge (or epistemes) that establish for the sciences their unsurpassable horizons of basic concepts (one could also say: that establish the historical a priori of the understanding of Being). In the history of modern thought, just as in the history of madness, the two historical thresholds of the transition from the Renaissance to the Classical age and from the Classical age to the modern age are at the center of interest. The internal motivations behind the transition to a theory of power can be understood in connection with the difficulties that emerged from this ingenious study itself.

V

The thought of the Renaissance was still guided by a cosmological world view in which things were ordered in, so to speak, a physiognomic way according to relations of similarity, since in the great Book of Nature each signature refers to other signatures. The rationalism of the seventeenth century imports a completely different order into things. The logic of Port Royale is structurally formative; it projects a semiotics and a general combinatory system. Nature is transformed for Descartes, Hobbes, and Leibniz into the totality of what can be "represented" in a twofold sense — that is, what can be represented and can also, as a representation, be presented by means of conventional signs. Foucault contends that the decisive paradigm for this is neither the mathematization of nature nor the mechanistic perspective, but the system of ordered signs. The latter is no longer grounded in a *prior* order of things, but is what first produces a taxonomic order by way of the representation of things. Combined signs or language form a fully transparent medium by which the representation is linked with whatever is represented. The signifier retreats behind the indicated thing signified; it functions like a glass instrument for representation without having a life of its own: "The profound vocation of Classical language has always been to create a table — a 'picture': whether it be in the form of natural discourse, the accumulation of truth, descriptions of things, a body of exact knowledge, or an encyclopaedic dictionary. It exists, therefore, only to be transparent.... The possibility of knowing things and their order passes, in the

Classical experience, through the sovereignty of words: words are, in fact, neither marks to be deciphered (as in the Renaissance period) nor more or less faithful and masterable instruments (as in the positivist period); they form rather a colourless network on the basis of which ... representations are ordered."[27] Thanks to its autonomy, the sign *selflessly* serves the representation of things; in it, the representation of the subject encounters the represented object and they form an order in the chain of representations.

Language is wholly given up to its function of picturing facts, as we would put it today, and depicts everything that can be represented on the *same* level — the nature of the subject doing the representing no differently from that of the objects being represented. On its tableau, the nature of man enjoys no privilege over the nature of things. Internal and external nature are classified, analyzed, and combined in the same manner — words of language in the universal grammar, wealth and needs in political economy, no differently than species of plants and animals in the Linnaean system. Precisely this is the limit of the nonreflexive form of knowledge proper to the Classical age; knowledge is completely dependent on the representational structure of language, without being able to integrate the process of representation itself (the synthetic performance of the subject doing the representing). Foucault elaborates this limit in his surprising interpretation of a famous picture by Velasquez, *Las Meninas*.[28]

This picture portrays the painter in front of a canvas not visible to the spectator; the painter is evidently looking, as are the two ladies-in-waiting next to him, in the direction of his two models, King Philip IV and his spouse. These two personages standing as models are found outside the frame of the picture; they can be identified by the spectator only with the help of a mirror pictured in the background. The point that Velasquez apparently had in mind is a confusing circumstance of which the spectator becomes aware by inference: The spectator cannot avoid assuming the place and the direction of the gaze of the counterfeit but absent royal pair — toward which the painter captured in the picture gazes — as well as the place and the perspective of Velasquez himself, which is to say, of the painter who actually produced this picture. For Foucault, in turn, the real point lies in the fact that the Classical picture frame is too limited to permit the representation of the act of representing as such — it is this that Velasquez makes clear by showing the gaps within the Classical picture frame left by the lack of reflection on the process of representing itself.[29] None of the persons who are involved in the Classical scene of a painted representation of the royal pair (of human beings as sovereign) appear in the depiction as the sovereign subject capable of self-representation, or in other words, as subject and object at once, as simultaneously representing and being represented, as an entity present to itself in the process of representation: "In Classical thought, the personage for whom the representation exists, and who represents himself within it, recognizing himself therein as an image or reflection, he who ties together all the interlacing threads of the 'representation in the form of a picture or table' — he is never to be found himself. Before the end of the eighteenth century, *man* did not exist. . . . Of course, it is possible to object that general grammar, natural history, and the analysis of wealth were all . . . ways of recognizing the existence of man. . . . But there was no *epistemological* consciousness of man as such."[30]

With Kant, the modern age is inaugurated. As soon as the metaphysical seal on the correspondence between language and world breaks down, the representational function of language itself becomes a problem. The subject doing the representing has to objectify himself to gain some clarity about the problematic process of representation itself. The concept of self-reflection takes over, and the relationship to self of the subject doing the representing becomes the single foundation of ultimate certainties. The end of metaphysics is the end of an objective coordination of things and representations that is performed by language itself and thus remains unproblematic. The human person, become present to himself in self-consciousness, has to assume the superhuman task of establishing an order of things as soon as he becomes aware of himself as an existence at once autonomous and finite. This is why Foucault regards the modern form of knowledge as marked from the very start by the aporia that the knowing subject raises itself

up out of the ruins of metaphysics in order, in the consciousness of his finite powers, to solve a task requiring infinite power.
Kant turns this aporia straightaway into a principle of construction of his epistemology by shifting the meaning of the constraints proper to a finite cognitive capacity into that of
transcendental conditions of a knowledge that advances without limit: "Modernity begins with the incredible and ultimately
unworkable idea of a being who is sovereign precisely by virtue
of being enslaved, a being whose very finitude allows him to
take the place of God."[31]

Foucault develops his basic idea that modernity is characterized by the self-contradictory and anthropocentric form of
knowledge proper to a structurally overloaded subject (a finite
subject transcending itself into the infinite) in a wide arc that
stretches from Kant and Fichte to Husserl and Heidegger.
Philosophy of consciousness is subject to conceptual constraints
under which it must "double" the subject and continually treat
it in terms of two contrary and mutually incompatible aspects.
The pressure to break out of this unstable to and fro between
aspects of self-thematization that are just as irreconcilable as
they are inevitable makes itself felt as the intractable will to
knowledge and ever more knowledge. This will pretentiously
shoots beyond anything the structurally overburdened and ov-
erstrained subject is capable of performing. In this way, the
modern form of knowledge is determined by the unique dynamism of a *will to truth* for which any frustration is only a
spur to the renewed production of knowledge. This will to
truth, then, is for Foucault the key to the internal nexus between knowledge and power. The human sciences occupy the
terrain opened up by the aporetic self-thematization of the
cognitive subject. With their pretentious and never redeemed
claims, they erect a facade of universally valid knowledge behind which lurks the facticity of a sheer will to cognitive self-
mastery, a will to a boundlessly productive increase of knowledge in the wake of which both subjectivity and self-consciousness are first formed.

Foucault traces the compulsion toward the problematic "doubling" of the self-related subject primarily in connection with
three sets of oppositions: between the transcendental and the

empirical; between the act of becoming reflectively aware and the reflectively unsurpassable and irretrievable; and finally between the a priori perfect of an "always already" prior origin and the adventlike future of the still-to-come return of the origin. Foucault would have been able to exhibit these oppositions in connection with Fichte's *Wissenschaftslehre*, since it is precisely a matter of those kinds of conceptual constraints of the philosophy of consciousness that are condensed paradigmatically into the *Tathandlung* [reflective conscious activity] of the absolute I. The I can only take possession of itself and "posit" itself by positing, as it were unconsciously, a not-I and trying gradually to retrieve this thing posited by the I. This act of mediated self-positing can be understood under three different aspects: as a process of self-knowledge, as a process of growing reflective awareness, and as a process of self-formation. In each of these dimensions, European thought of the nineteenth and twentieth centuries sways between theoretical approaches that mutually exclude one another — and in each case the attempt to evade unhappy alternatives ends in the snares of a self-deifying subject consuming itself in acts of vain self-transcendence.

Since Kant, the I assumes simultaneously the status of an empirical subject in the world, where it is available as one object among others, and the status of a transcendental subject over against the world as a whole, which it constitutes as the totality of the objects of possible experience. By reason of this double status,[32] the knowing subject sees itself provoked to analyze the same performances that one time get grasped reflectively as performances of transcendental synthesis, and a second time empirically as a process governed by natural laws — no matter whether our cognitive apparatus is explained in terms of psychology or cultural anthropology, biology or history. Naturally, thought cannot rest satisfied with these irreconcilable alternatives. The attempts at overcoming this dilemma in a discipline uniting both aspects and conceiving the concrete history of the a priori forms as a process of the self-creation of the spirit or of the species reaches from Hegel to Merleau-Ponty. Because these hybrid enterprises chase after the utopia of complete self-knowledge, they flip-flop again and again into positivism.[33]

Foucault uncovers the same dialectic in the second dimension of self-positing. Since Fichte, the I, as the reflecting subject, undergoes the twofold experience of encountering itself in the world "always already" as something that has become itself contingently, as something opaque, on the one hand; but, on the other hand, as being endowed by precisely this reflection with the ability to make that "in itself" transparent and to elevate it into consciousness "for itself." The attempts to advance this process of making oneself conscious of what is pre-given and to find a methodological standpoint from which anything that prima facie resists consciousness as something stubbornly extraterritorial (be it the body, needs and desires, labor, or language) might still be retrieved in reflection, made familiar, and transformed into something transparent, extend from Hegel via Freud to Husserl. Freud puts forward the imperative that where Id is, Ego shall be. Husserl sets pure phenomenology the goal of explaining and bringing under conscious control everything merely implicit, prepredicative, already sedimented, not actually present — in brief, the unthought and hidden foundation of the performing subjectivity. These hybrid attempts at emancipation from what is unconsciously in the background fall prey to the utopia of complete self-transparency and hence flip over into nihilistic despair and radical scepticism.

The desire to elude the third double — of the subject as something originally creative and at the same time as alienated from this origin — leads in the end to the same dialectic. The human being knows itself as the remote product of a history reaching back into the archaic, of which it is not master, even though this history refers in turn to the authorship of producing human beings. The more energetically modern thought pursues them, the further back these origins retreat: "Paradoxically it proposes the solution of advancing even further in the direction of this ever-deepening retreat." To this, the philosophy of history from Schelling via Marx to Lukács responds with the idea of an enriching return from alien lands, of an Odyssey of the spirit; on the other hand, Dionysian thought from Hölderlin via Nietzsche to Heidegger responds with the idea of the God who recedes, "who frees the origin in exactly that degree to which he recedes."³⁴ But these hybrid notions of history can only become practical in the form of terror, self-manipulation, and enslavement, since they live from a false eschatological impulse.

Foucault also classifies the human sciences with that anthropocentric thinking which was set in motion by Kant and which, with its utopias of liberation, gets implicated in the practice of enslavement. He cautiously leaves to the experimental natural sciences a special status; they have obviously extricated themselves from the web of practices from which they issued (primarily the practices of the judicial hearing) and have been able to attain a certain autonomy. It is different with the human sciences. Grammar, natural history, and economics, which arose already in the Classical age as taxonomic sciences, were the first to come under the sway of the anthropological turn. General grammar gives way to the history of national languages, tables of natural history to the evolution of species, and the analysis of wealth to a theory that traces use-value and exchange-value back to the expenditure of labor power. A perspective arose in which *the human being* was perceived as a *speaking* and *laboring* creature. The human sciences made use of this perspective; they analyzed the human being as the being that relates itself to objectivations engendered by itself, the speaking and laboring creature. Inasmuch as psychology, sociology, and political science on the one hand, and the cultural sciences and humanities on the other, got involved with object domains for which subjectivity (in the sense of the relation to self of experiencing, acting, and speaking human beings) is constitutive, they found themselves in the wake of the will to knowledge, on the escape route of a boundless productive increase in knowledge. They were delivered up to the dialectic of liberation and enslavement, more defenselessly than the science of history, which at least had control over the sceptical potential of historical relativization; but especially more defenselessly than ethnology or psychoanalysis, for these have (since Lévi-Strauss and Lacan) moved about reflectively in the jungle of the structural and of the individual unconscious.

Because the human sciences — psychology and sociology above all — with their *borrowed* models and *alien* ideals of objectivity, became involved with a human being that was for the first time turned into an object of scientific investigation by the modern form of knowlege, an impulse could prevail in them unawares, which they could not admit without risking their claim to truth: just that restless pressure for knowledge, self-mastery, and self-aggrandizement with which the subject — metaphysically isolated and structurally overburdened, abandoned by God and self-deifying — of the post-Classical age sought to avoid the aporias of its self-thematization. "We are inclined to believe that man has emancipated himself from himself since his discovery that he is not at the center of creation, nor in the middle of space, nor even, perhaps, the summit and culmination of life; but though man is no longer sovereign in the kingdom of the world, though he no longer reigns at the center of being, the human sciences are dangerous intermediaries."[35] Mere intermediaries because they, unlike the reflective sciences and philosophy, do not directly promote that self-destructive dynamic of the self-positing subject, but get unconsciously instrumentalized for it. The human sciences are and remain pseudo-sciences because they do not see through the compulsion to a problematic doubling of the self-relating subject; they are not in a position to acknowledge the structurally generated will to self-knowledge and self-reification — and thus they are also unable to free themselves from the power that drives them. Foucault already depicted this in *Madness and Civilization* in connection with the example of psychiatric positivism.

What, then, are the grounds that determine Foucault to shift the meaning of this specific will to knowledge and to truth that is constitutive for the modern form of knowledge in general, and for the human sciences in particular, by *generalizing* this will to knowing self-mastery into a will to power per se and to postulate that *all* discourses (by no means only the modern ones) can be shown to have the character of hidden power and derive from practices of power? It is this assumption that first marks the turning from an archeology of knowledge to a genealogical explanation of the provenance, rise, and fall of those discourse formations that fill the space of history, without gaps and without meaning.

X

Some Questions Concerning the Theory of Power: Foucault Again

I

With the dynamism of self-mastery through the production of knowledge, the archeology of the human sciences not only furnishes the starting point for intertwining knowledge with the will to knowledge; *The Order of Things* raises problems to which Foucault responds some years later by developing out of the will to knowledge the basic concept of power on which his genealogical historiography is based. Let me indicate three such difficulties.

(a) First of all, Foucault must have been irritated by the affinity that obviously existed between his archeology of the human sciences and Heidegger's critique of the metaphysics of the modern age. The epistemes or forms of knowledge of the Renaissance, Classicism, and Modernity indicate epochal divisions and at the same time stages in the formation of the same subject-centered understanding of Being that Heidegger, using similar concepts, analyzed from Descartes via Kant to Nietzsche. Foucault, however, could not take the path of overcoming subjectivity through a critique of metaphysics; he had shown that even the concept of the history of Being does not lead out of the circle of the third self-thematization of the self-referential subject, that is, its attempt to master an ever-receding origin. The thesis was that Heidegger's later philosophy is still caught in the Chinese puzzle that Foucault discussed under the title "Recession and Return of the Origin." For this reason,

Foucault will henceforth have to do without the concept of episteme altogether.

(b) Just as problematic as his proximity to Heidegger is his nearness to structuralism. In *The Order of Things*, Foucault wanted to respond with a liberating philosophical laugh to all "those who refuse to formalize without anthropologizing, who refuse to mythologize without demystifying," and in general to "all these warped and twisted forms of reflection."[1] With this gesture, reminiscent of the laughter of Zarathustra, he wanted to rouse from their anthropological slumbers all "who refuse to think without immediately thinking that it is man who is thinking." They were supposed to rub their eyes and ask the simple question whether man exists at all.[2] Evidently Foucault then regarded contemporary structrualism (Lévi-Strauss's ethnology and Lacan's psychoanalysis) as alone capable of thinking "the void left by man's disappearance." The originally planned subtitle for the book, "Archeology of Structuralism," was by no means intended critically. But this perspective had to dissolve as soon as it became clear that structuralism had covertly already supplied the model for the description of the Classical form of knowledge (semiotic representationalism).[3] Thus, overcoming anthropocentric thought by means of structuralism would not have meant a surpassing of Modernity, but only an explicit renewal of the protostructuralist form of knowledge of the Classical age.

(c) A further embarrassment arose from the circumstance that Foucault carried out his study of the rise of the human sciences in the form — and only in the form — of an archeology of knowledge. How could this analysis of scientific discourse be combined with the investigation of relevant practices familiar from earlier studies without endangering the self-sufficiency of forms of knowledge rounded off into totalities? Foucault deals with this problem in his methodological considerations on *The Archeology of Knowledge* (1969). He does not reach a completely unequivocal position there, but tends toward the superordination of discourses over the practices on which they are based. The structuralist requirement that each unity of discourse be understood strictly in terms of itself seems to be satisfied only if the rules constitutive of discourse assume control, as it were, of their institutional basis. Discourse is what first links the technological, economic, social, and political conditions to the functioning network of practices that then serve to reproduce it.

Such discourse — totally autonomous, detached from contextual constraints and functional conditions, guiding the underlying practices — clearly suffers from a conceptual difficulty. What then counts as fundamental are the rules (accessible to archeology) that make possible the ongoing discursive practice. However, these rules can make a discourse comprehensible only as regards its conditions of possibility; they do not suffice to explain the discourse practice in its actual functioning — for there are no rules that could govern their own application. A rule-governed discourse cannot itself govern the context in which it is implicated: "Thus, although nondiscursive influences in the form of social and institutional practices, skills, pedagogical practices and concrete models (e.g., Bentham's Panopticon) constantly intrude into Foucault's analysis . . . he must locate the productive power revealed by discursive practices in the regularity of these same practices. The result is the strange notion of regularities which regulate themselves."[4]

Foucault escapes this difficulty when he gives up the autonomy of the forms of knowledge in favor of their foundation within power technologies and *subordinates* the archeology of knowledge to the genealogy that explains the emergence of knowledge from practices of power.

This theory of power also recommends itself for the solution of the two other problems: Foucault can thereby relinquish the philosophy of the subject without depending on models from structuralism or the history of Being, which, according to his own analysis, are themselves captive to either the Classical or the modern form of knowledge. Genealogical historiography clears away the autonomy of self-regulating discourses as well as the epochal and linear succession of global forms of knowledge. The danger of anthropocentrism is banished only when, under the incorruptible gaze of genealogy, discourses emerge and pop like glittering bubbles from a swamp of anonymous processes of subjugation. With his energetic reversal of the relationships of dependency among forms of knowledge and practices of power, Foucault opens up a problematic of social theory in contrast to the rigorously structuralist history of systems of knowledge, and a naturalistic problematic in contrast to the history of the understanding of Being (as a critique of metaphysics). The disourses of the sciences, and in general the discourses in which knowledge is shaped and transmitted, lose their privileged status; together with other discursive practices, they form power complexes that offer a domain of objects sui generis. In going through the types of discourse and forms of knowledge, the point now is to uncover the technologies of subjugation around which a dominant power complex draws together, achieves domination, and is ultimately suppressed by the next power complex. Historical research into the power technologies that instrumentalize systems of knowledge right down to their criteria of validity is supposed to move now on the firm ground of a naturalistic theory of society.

Of course, Foucault only gains this basis by not thinking genealogically when it comes to his *own* genealogical historiography and by rendering unrecognizable the derivation of this transcendental-historicist concept of power.

As we have seen, with respect to the human sciences, Foucault had studied the form of knowledge that appears with the claim of purifying the intelligible from everything empirical, accidental, and particular, and that becomes especially suitable as a medium of power precisely on account of this pretended separation of validity from genesis: Because it thus posits itself absolutely, modern knowledge can conceal from itself and others that impulse which first spurs on a metaphysically isolated subject, thrown back relectively upon itself, toward restless self-mastery. This will to knowledge was supposed to intervene in the constitution of scientific discourse and explain why scientifically prepared knowledge of man can congeal directly into disciplinary violence in the form of therapies, expert opinions, social technologies, curricula, tests, research reports, data banks, proposals for reform, etc. This modern will to knowledge determines "the ensemble of rules according to which the true and the false are separated and specific effects of power attached to the true."[5] With his transition to a theory of power, however, Foucault detaches this will to knowledge from the context of the history of metaphysics and lets it merge into the category of power in general. This transformation is due to two operations. To begin with, Foucault postulates a will constitutive of truth for *all* times and *all* societies: "Every society has its regime of truth, its 'general politics' of truth: that is, the types of discourse which it accepts and makes function as true."[6] Beyond this spatiotemporal generalization, Foucault undertakes a substantive neutralization: He de-differentiates the will to knowledge into a will to power that is supposed to be inherent in all discourses, not just those that specialize in truth, in a manner similar to that in which the will to self-mastery specific to modern subjectivity inheres in the human sciences. Only after the traces of this transformation are erased can the will to knowledge show up again (in the subtitle to *The History of Subjectivity*, 1976), now of course demoted to a special case — the "dispositive of truth" now appears as one among many "dispositives of power."

The *concealed* derivation of the concept of power from the concept of the will to knowledge (originally formulated in terms of a critique of metaphysics) also explains the systematically ambiguous use of the category of "power." On the one hand, it retains the innocence of a concept used descriptively and serves the *empirical analysis* of power technologies; considered from a methodological perspective, this analysis is not obviously different from a historically oriented sociology of knowledge that employs functionalist procedures. On the other hand, the category of power preserves from its covert historical sources the meaning of a basic concept within a *theory of constitution* as well; this is what lends the empirical analysis of technologies of power their significance as a critique of reason and secures for genealogical historiography its unmasking effect.

II

This systematic ambiguity explains but does not justify the paradoxical linking of a positivist attitude with a critical claim that is characteristic of Foucault's works during the 1970s. In *Discipline and Punish* (1976), Foucault treats (preponderantly in connection with French materials) the technologies of domination that arose in the Classical age (more or less in the age of Absolutism) and in Modernity (that is, since the end of the eighteenth century). The corresponding forms of inflicting punishment serve as guidelines for an investigation centered upon "the birth of the prison." The complex of power that, in the Classical age, was concentrated around the sovereignty of a state with a monopoly on violence, is sedimented in the legal language games proper to modern natural law, which operate with the basic concepts of contract and law. The actual task of the absolutist theory of the state is not so much to legitimize human rights as to ground the concentration of all violence in the hands of the sovereign. For him, it is a question of constructing a centralized apparatus of public administration and of gathering administratively useful organizational knowledge. It is not the citizen with his rights and duties, but the subject with his body and life that is the object of the new need for knowledge, which to begin with is content with knowledge about public finances and statistics on birth and death, illness and culpability, labor and commerce, the welfare and poverty of the population. Foucault already sees in this the beginnings of a biopolitics being built up gradually under the official umbrella of juristically conducted discourses related to the sovereignty of the state. There arises thereby another disciplinary power detached from the normative language game. To the degree that the human sciences become the medium of this power, and the panoptical form of supervision is permitted to penetrate into all the pores of the subjugated body and the objectified soul, it is condensed into a new, precisely modern, power complex.

Foucault treats the transfer of punishment from torture to imprisonment as an exemplary process in connection with which he wants to demonstrate the provenance of modern anthropocentric thought in modern technologies of domination. He conceives the excessive punishments and tortures to which criminals were subjected in the Classical age as a theater for the ruthlessly staged power of an avenging sovereign, which was experienced quite ambivalently by the people. In the modern age, the demonstrative inflicting of corporal torment is replaced by a loss of freedom through imprisonment that is shielded from the outside world. Foucault interprets the panoptic prison as an apparatus that not only renders the prisoners pliable, but transforms them. The all-pervasive, normalizing influence of an omnipresent disciplinary power reaches, via training the body, into everyday behavior and produces an altered moral stance; at any rate, it is supposed to promote the motivation for regulated labor and an ordered life. These penal technologies could spread rapidly at the end of the eighteenth century because the prison was only one element in a rich ensemble of bodily disciplines that were established at the same time in factories and workhouses, in barracks, schools, hospitals, and prisons. It was the human sciences that then, in a subtle manner, extended the normalizing effects of these bodily disciplines into the innermost sphere of scientifically objectified persons and populations who were simultaneously driven back into subjectivity.[7] *In their very form*, the human sciences are supposed to present an amalgam of knowledge and power; *the formation of power and the formation of knowledge compose an indissoluble unity.*

Such a strong thesis cannot, of course, be grounded just with functionalist arguments. Foucault only shows how disciplinary effects, similar to the effects of technologies of power, can be obtained through the application of knowledge from the human sciences in therapies and social technologies. In order to prove what he wants, he would have to demonstrate (for example, in the framework of a transcendental-pragmatic epistemology) that specific strategies of power are transposed into corresponding strategies for the objectification of ordinary language experiences, and consequently that they prejudice the meaning of the use of theoretical propositions about object domains constituted in this way.[8] Foucault never took up again his earlier ideas on the epistemological role of the clinical gaze, although they point in this direction. Otherwise he could scarcely have avoided noticing that in the 1970s objectifying approaches no longer dominated the field in the human sciences; they were competing instead with hermeneutical and critical approaches that were tailored in their forms of knowledge to possibilities of application *other* than manipulation of self and of others. In *The Order of Things*, Foucault traced the human sciences back to the constitutive force of a will to knowledge explained in terms of the history of metaphysics. The theory of power has to hide this connection, as has been shown. Henceforth, the place for a theory of constitution remains unoccupied. The "will to knowledge" comes up again in the title of the first volume of *The History of Sexuality* (1976), but in a shape fully altered by the theory of power. It has lost the transcendental meaning of a structurally generated will to knowing self-mastery and taken on the empirical visage of a special technology of power which, along with other technologies of power, makes possible the sciences of man.

This tangible positivizing of the will to truth and to knowledge becomes clear in a self-critique presented by Foucault in Berkeley in 1980. There he acknowledges that the analysis of technologies of domination carried out in *Discipline and Punish* results in a one-sided picture: "If one wants to analyze the genealogy of the subject in Western societies, one has to take into account not only the techniques of domination but also techniques of the self. Let's say one has to take into account the interaction between those two types of techniques, the point where the technologies of domination of individuals over one another have recourse to processes by which the individual acts upon himself."[9] These technologies that encourage individuals to test themselves conscientiously and discover the truth about themselves Foucault traces, as is well known, back to the practices of confession, to the Christian examination of conscience in general. Structurally similar practices, which penetrate all realms of education in the eighteenth century, install an armory of instruments for self-observation and self-questioning, with the perception of one's own sexual stimulation and that of others at the center of attention. Finally, psychoanalysis gives the form of scientifically established therapy to these technologies of truth, which do not open up the interior of individuals, but produce interiority for the first time by means of an ever thicker web of relations to self.[10]

Foucault's genealogy of the human sciences enters on the scene in an irritating double role. On the one hand, it plays the *empirical role* of an analysis of technologies of power that are meant to explain the functional social context of the science of man. Here power relationships are of interest as conditions for the rise of scientific knowledge and as its social effects. On the other hand, the same genealogy plays the *transcendental role* of an analysis of technologies of power that are meant to explain how scientific discourse about man is possible at all. Here the interest is in power relationships as constitutive conditions for scientific knowledge. These two epistemological roles are no longer divided into two competing approaches that are merely related to the same object, the human subject in its life-expressions. Instead, genealogical historiography is supposed to be both at once — functionalist social science and at the same time historical research into constitutive conditions.

In his basic concept of power, Foucault has forced together the idealist idea of transcendental synthesis with the presuppositions of an empiricist ontology. This approach cannot lead to a way out of the philosophy of the subject, because the concept of power that is supposed to provide a common denominator for the contrary semantic components has been taken from the repertoire of the philosophy of the subject itself. According to this philosophy, the subject can take up basically two and only two relationships toward the world of imaginable and manipulable objects: cognitive relationships regulated by the *truth* of judgments; and practical relationships regulated by the *success* of actions. Power is that by which the subject has an effect on objects in successful actions. In this connection, success in action depends upon the truth of the judgments that enter into the plan of action; via the criterion of success in action, power remains dependent on truth. Foucault abruptly reverses power's truth-dependency into the power-dependency of truth. Then foundational power no longer need be bound to the competencies of acting and judging subjects — power becomes subjectless. But no one can escape the strategic conceptual constraints of the philosophy of the subject merely by performing operations of reversal upon its basic concepts. Foucault cannot do away with all the aporias he attributes to the philosophy of the subject by means of a concept of power borrowed from the philosophy of the subject itself. So it is no wonder that the same unanswered questions come up again in a historiography (declared to be an antiscience) based on such a paradoxical basic concept. Because Foucault gives no methodological account of these incompatibilities, the reason for the one-sidedness of his empirical investigations also remains undisclosed.

With his turn toward the theory of power, Foucault expects to lead his research out of the circle in which the human sciences are hopelessly caught. Anthropocentric thought is drawn, by the dynamism of boundless self-mastery on the part of a subject become reflective, into the vortex of objectivism, that is, of the objectification of man; the genealogy of knowledge is supposed, by contrast, to rise to true objectivity of knowledge. Genealogical historiography grounded on the theory of power proposes three substitutions: In place of the hermeneutic elucidation of contexts of meaning, there is an analysis of structures that are meaningless in themselves; validity claims are of interest only as functions of power complexes; value judgments — in general, the problem of justifying criticism — are excluded in favor of value-free historical explanations. The name "antiscience" is to be understood not only by opposition to the reigning human sciences; at the same time, it signals an ambitious attempt to overcome these pseudo-sciences. Genealogical research takes their place; without imitating false models from the natural sciences, its scientific status will someday be comparable to that of the natural sciences. I think that Paul Veyne catches the real intention of his friend when he describes Foucault as the "historian in a pure state" who desires nothing else than to say stoically just how it was: "Everything is historical . . . and all 'isms' should be evacuated. In history, there are only individual or indeed unique constellations, and each is completely explicable from its own situation."[11]

Of course, Foucault's dramatic influence and his iconoclastic reputation could hardly be explained if the cool facade of radical historicism did not simply hide the passions of aesthetic modernism. Genealogy is overtaken by a fate similar to that which Foucault had seen in the human sciences: To the extent that it retreats into the reflectionless objectivity of a nonparticipatory, ascetic description of kaleidoscopically changing practices of power, genealogical historiography emerges from its cocoon as precisely the *presentistic, relativistic, cryptonormative* illusory science that it does not want to be. Whereas, according to Foucault's diagnosis, the human sciences submit to the ironic movement of scientistic self-mastery and end up in an unsalutary objectivism (or better yet — come to an end therein), a no less ironic fate overtakes genealogical historiography; it follows the movement of a radically historicist extinction of the subject and ends up in an unholy subjectivism.

III

Foucault feels like a "fortunate positivist" because he proposes three reductions that are rich in methodological implications: From the viewpoint of the ethnological observer, the understanding of meaning by interpreters participating in discourses is reduced to the explanation of discourses; validity claims are functionalistically reduced to the effects of power; the "ought" is naturalistically reduced to the "is." I am speaking of reductions because the internal aspects of *meaning*, of *truth-validity*, and of *evaluating* do not go without remainder into the externally grasped aspects of practices of power. The moments that get filtered out and suppressed return again and assert their proper rights — at first on the metatheoretical level. Foucault gets entangled in aporias as soon as he is supposed to explain what the genealogical historiographer himself does and how that performance is to be understood. That is to say, his putative objectivity of knowledge is itself put in question (1) by the involuntary *presentism* of a historiography that remains hermeneutically stuck in its starting situation; (2) by the unavoidable *relativism* of an analysis related to the present that can understand itself only as a context-dependent practical enterprise; (3) by the arbitrary *partisanship* of a criticism that cannot account for its normative foundations. Foucault is incorruptible enough to admit these incoherences — but he does not draw any consequences from them.

(1) Foucault wants to eliminate the hermeneutic problematic and thus the kind of self-relatedness that comes into play with an interpretative approach to the object domain. The geneal-

ogical historiographer should not proceed as does the practitioner of hermeneutics; he should not try to make comprehensible what actors are doing and thinking out of a context of tradition interwoven with the self-understanding of the actors. He should, rather, explain the horizon within which such utterances can appear to be meaningful at all in terms of *underlying* practices. So he will trace back the prohibition of gladiatorial fights in late Rome, for example, not to the humanizing influence of Christianity, but to the dissolution of one power formation by its successor.[12] Within the horizon of the new power complex in post-Constantinian Rome, it is, for example, entirely natural that the ruler no longer treat the people as a herd of sheep to be sheltered, but as a flock of children needing to be educated — and one must not carelessly leave children to bloodthirsty pleasure in spectacles. The speeches that justify establishing or dismantling gladiatorial fights are regarded only as objectifications of an unconscious, underlying practice of domination. As the source of all meaning, such practices are themselves meaningless; the historian has to approach them from outside in order to grasp them in their structure. For this, there is no need of any hermeneutic preunderstanding, but only of the concept of history as meaningless kaleidoscopic changes of shape in discourse totalities that have nothing in common apart from the single characteristic of being protuberances of power in general.

Against this self-understanding that holds fast to objectivity, the first glance in any one of Foucault's books teaches us that even the radical historicist can only explain the technologies of power and practices of domination by comparing them with one another — and by no means by taking any single one as a totality on its own. In doing so, one inevitably connects the viewpoints under which the comparison is proposed with his own hermeneutic point of departure. This can be seen in, among other things, the fact that Foucault cannot avoid dividing up historical epochs through implicit reference to the present. Whether he is dealing with the history of madness, of sexuality, or of punishment, the power formations of the Middle Ages, the Renaissance, and of the Classical age constantly point to the very disciplinary power, the very biopolitics, that

Foucault maintains is the fate of our present age. In the final section of *The Archeology of Knowledge*, he makes this very objection to himself, but only to avoid it: "For the moment, and as far ahead as I can see, *my* discourse, far from determining the locus in which *it* speaks, is avoiding the ground on which it could find support."[13] Foucault is aware of the aporias raised by a procedure that wants to be objectivistic but must remain diagnostic of its time — but he does not provide any answer to them.

Only in the context of his interpretation of Nietzsche does Foucault yield to the familiar melody of a *professing* irrationalism. Here the self-extinction or the "sacrifice of the knowing subject" that the radical historicist has to demand of himself only for the sake of the objectivity of purely structural analysis undergoes an ironic shift of meaning into its opposite: "In appearance, or rather, according to the mask it bears, historical consciousness is neutral, devoid of passions, and committed solely to truth. But if it examines itself and if, more generally, it interrogates the various forms of scientific consciousness in its history, it finds that all these forms and transformations are aspects of the will to knowledge: instinct, passion, the inquisitor's devotion, cruel subtlety, and malice. It discovers the violence of a position that sides against those who are happy in their ignorance. . . . The historical analysis of this rancorous will to knowledge reveals that all knowledge rests upon injustice (that there is no right, even in the act of knowing, to truth or foundation for truth)."[14]

Thus, the attempt — under the uncompromising, objectifying gaze of an analyst who comes from afar and confronts his object without any native understanding whatsoever — to explain discourse and power formations only on their own terms, turns into its opposite. The unmasking of the objectivistic illusions of *any* will to knowledge leads to agreement with a historiography that is narcissistically oriented toward the standpoint of the historian and instrumentalizes the contemplation of the past for the needs of the present: The "'wirkliche Historie' composes a genealogy of history as the vertical projection of its position."[15]

(2) Foucault's historiography can evade relativism as little as it can this acute presentism. His investigations are caught exactly in the self-referentiality that was supposed to be excluded by a naturalistic treatment of the problematic of validity. Genealogical historiography is supposed to make the practices of power, precisely in their discourse-constituting achievement, accessible to an empirical analysis. From this perspective, not only are truth claims confined to the discourses within which they arise; they exhaust their entire significance in the functional contribution they make to the self-maintenance of a given totality of discourse. That is to say, the meaning of validity claims consists in the power effects they have. On the other hand, this basic assumption of the theory of power is self-referential; if it is correct, it must destroy the foundations of the research inspired by it as well. But if the truth claims that Foucault himself raises for his genealogy of knowledge were in fact illusory and amounted to no more than the effects that this theory is capable of releasing within the circle of its adherents, then the entire undertaking of a critical unmasking of the human sciences would lose its point. Foucault pursues genealogical historiography with the serious intent of getting a science underway that is superior to the mismanaged human sciences. If, then, its superiority cannot be expressed in the fact that something more convincing enters in place of the convicted pseudo-sciences, if its superiority were only to be expressed in the effect of its suppressing the hitherto dominant scientific discourse *in fact*, Foucault's theory would exhaust itself in the politics of theory, and indeed in setting theoretical-political goals that would overburden the capacities of even so heroic a one-man enterprise. Foucault is aware of this. Consequently, he would like to single out his genealogy from all the rest of the human sciences in a manner that is reconcilable with the fundamental assumptions of his own theory. To this end, he turns genealogical historiography upon itself; the difference that can establish its preeminence above all the other human sciences is to be demonstrated in the history of its own emergence.

The genealogy of knowledge makes use of those disqualified modes of knowledge from which the established sciences set themselves apart; it provides a medium for the uprising of "subjugated knowledges." Foucault is not thinking here primarily of sedimentations of scholarship that are at once concealed and held present; he is thinking, rather, of those experiences of groups subordinated to power that have never advanced to the status of official knowledge, that have never been sufficiently articulated. It is a question of the implicit knowlege of "the people" who form the bedrock in a system of power, who are the first to experience a technology of power with their own bodies, whether as the ones suffering or as the officials manning the machinery of suffering — for example, the knowledge of those who undergo psychiatric treatment, of orderlies, of delinquents and wardens, of the inmates of concentration camps and the guards, of blacks and homosexuals, of women and of witches, of vagabonds, of children and dreamers. The genealogist directs his prospecting toward the dark ground proper to that local, marginal, and alternative knowledge "which owes its force only to the harshness with which it is opposed by everything surrounding it." These elements of knowledge are normally "disqualified as inadequate to their task or insufficiently elaborated: naive knowledges, located low down on the hierarchy, beneath the required level of cognition or scientificity."[16] There slumbers in them "a historical knowledge of struggles." Genealogy, which raises these "local memories" up to the level of "erudite knowledge," takes the side of those who resist established practices of power. From this position of counterpower, it gains a perspective that is supposed to go beyond the perspectives of the given possessors of power. From this perspective, it is supposed to be able to transcend all validity claims that are only constituted in the enchanted circle of power. This link with disqualified popular knowledge is supposed to give to the genealogist's labor of reconstruction its superiority: "Well, it seems to me that our critical discourses of the last fifteen years have in effect discovered their essential force in this association . . . [with] those disqualfied [knowledges]."[17]

This is reminiscent of an argument of the early Lukács. According to him, Marxist theory owed its freedom from ideological bias to the privileged possibilities of knowledge from a perspective of experience that had arisen with the position of the wage-laborer in the process of production. The argument was only cogent, however, within the framework of a philosophy of history that wanted to make the universal interest discernible in the class interest of the proletariat, and the self-consciousness of the species discoverable in the class consciousness of the proletariat. Foucault's concept of power does not permit such a concept of counterpower that grants cognitive privilege on the basis of a philosophy of history. Every counterpower already moves within the horizon of the power that it fights; and it is transformed, as soon as it is victorious, into a power complex that provokes a new counterpower. Even the genealogy of knowledge cannot break out of this cycle while it activates the uprising of the disqualified modes of knowledge and mobilizes this subjected knowledge "against the coercion of a theoretical, unitary, formal, and scientific discourse."[18] Those who conquer the theoretical avant-garde of today and overcome the current hierarchization of knowledge, themselves become the theoretical avant-garde of tomorrow and themselves establish a new hierarchy of knowledge. In any case, they cannot validate for their knowledge any superiority according to standards of truth claims that would transcend local agreements.

Thus, the attempt to preserve genealogical historiography from a relativist self-denial by means of its own tools falls short. In becoming aware of its own provenance from this alliance of scholarly and disqualified knowledge, genealogy only confirms that the validity claims of counterdiscourses count no more and no less than those of the discourses in power — they, too, *are* nothing else than the effects of power they unleash. Foucault sees this dilemma, but once again he evades any response. And once again he professes his allegiance to an embattled perspectivism only in the context of his reception of Nietzsche: "Historians take unusual pains to erase the elements in their work which reveal their grounding in a particular time and place, their preferences in a controversy — the unavoidable obstacles of their passion. Nietzsche's version of historical sense is explicit in its perspective and acknowledges its system of injustice. Its perspective is slanted, being a deliberate appraisal, affirmation, or negation; it reaches the lingering and poisonous traces in order to prescribe the best antidote."[19]

(3) It remains, finally, to examine whether Foucault succeeds in escaping the cryptonormativism of which the human sciences that preen themselves for their value-freeness are guilty in his own view. Genealogical historiography is supposed to reach behind discourse totalities (within which alone disputes over norms and values occur) with a strictly descriptive attitude. It brackets normative validity claims as well as claims to propositional truth and abstains from the question of whether some discourse and power formations could be more legitimate than others. Foucault resists the demand to take sides; he scoffs at the "gauchist dogma" which contends that power is what is evil, ugly, sterile, and dead and that that upon which power is exercised is "right, good, and rich."[20] For him, there is no "right side." Behind this is the conviction that the politics that has stood under the sign of revolution since 1789 has come to an end; that the theories that have thought out the relationship between theory and practice are passé.

Now *this* grounding of a second-order value-freeness is already by no means value-free. Foucault understands himself as a dissident who offers resistance to modern thought and humanistically disguised disciplinary power. Engagement marks his learned essays right down to the style and choice of words; the critical tenor dominates the theory no less than the self-definition of the entire work. Foucault thereby distinguishes himself, on the one hand, from the engaged positivism of a Max Weber, who wanted to separate a decisionistically chosen and openly declared value basis from an analysis carried out in a value-free way. Foucault's criticism is based more on the postmodern rhetoric of his presentation than on the postmodern assumptions of his theory.

On the other hand, Foucault also distinguishes himself from the ideology critique of a Marx, who unmasked the humanistic self-understanding of modernity by suing for the normative content of bourgeois ideals. It is not Foucault's intention to continue that counterdiscourse which modernity has carried on with itself from its very beginnings; he does not want to refine the language game of modern political theory (with its basic concepts of autonomy and heteronomy, morality and legality, emancipation and repression) and turn it against the pathologies of modernity — he wants to undermine modernity and its language games. His resistance is not to be justified as a mirror image of the current power: "If that were all," responds Foucault to a corresponding question from Bernard-Henri Levy, "there wouldn't be any resistance. Because resistance has to be like power: just as inventive, just as mobile, just as productive as it is. It has to be organized and stabilized like it is; like it, it has to come from below and be strategically shared."[21]

This dissidence draws its only justificaton from the fact that it sets traps for humanistic discourse without engaging in it; Foucault explains this strategic self-understanding from the properties of modern formations of power themselves. That disciplinary power whose local, constant, productive, and all-pervasive, capillarylike character he describes so repeatedly invades the bodies rather than the heads. It assumes the shape of a biopower that takes possession more of bodies than of minds and subjects these bodies to relentlessly normalizing constraint — without needing any normative foundation to do so. Disciplinary power functions without the detour through a necessarily false consciousness shaped within humanistic discourses and hence exposed to the criticism of counterdiscourses. The discourses of the human sciences merge with the practices of their application into an opaque power complex on which the critique of ideology makes no impression. Humanistic critique — which, like those of Marx and Freud, is based on obsolete contradictions between legitimate and illegitimate power, conscious and unconscious motives, and enters the field against the representatives of repression, exploitation, suppression, etc. — is in danger, rather, of merely strengthening a humanism that has been brought down from heaven to earth and has become a normalizing form of violence.

Now this argument may suffice for conceiving genealogical historiography no longer as critique, but as a tactic and a tool for waging a battle against a normatively unassailable formation of power. But if it is just a matter of mobilizing counterpower, of strategic battles and wily confrontations, why should we muster any resistance at all against this all-pervasive power circulating in the bloodstream of the body of modern society, instead of just adapting ourselves to it? Then the genealogy of knowledge as a weapon would be superfluous as well. It makes sense that a value-free analysis of the strengths and weaknesses of the opponent is of use to one who wants to take up the fight — but why fight at all? "Why is struggle preferable to submission? Why ought domination to be resisted? Only with the introduction of normative notions of some kind could Foucault begin to answer this question. Only with the introduction of normative notions could he begin to tell us what is wrong with the modern power/knowledge regime and why we ought to oppose it."[22] Once, in a lecture, Foucault addressed this question in passing and gave a vague suggestion of postmodern criteria of justification: "If one wants . . . to struggle against disciplines and disciplinary power, it is not toward the ancient right of sovereignty that one should turn, but toward the possibility of a new form of right, one which must indeed be antidisciplinarian, but at the same time liberated from the principle of sovereignty."[23]

Now it is a fact that in the wake of Kant, conceptions of morality and right have been developed which have long since ceased to serve the role of justifying the sovereignty of a state with a monopoly on violence; but Foucault remains silent on this theme. However, if one tries to glean the standards implicitly appealed to in his indictments of disciplinary power, one encounters familiar determinations from the normativistic language games that he has explicitly rejected. The asymmetric relationship between powerholders and those subject to power, as well as the reifying effect of technologies of power, which violate the moral and bodily integrity of subjects capable of speech and action, are objectionable for Foucault, too. Nancy Fraser has proposed an interpretation that, while it does not point a way out of this dilemma, does explain whence the cryptonormativism of this declaredly value-free historiography arises.[24]

Nietzsche's concept of the will to power and Bataille's concept of sovereignty more or less openly take in the normative experiential content of aesthetic modernity. By contrast, Foucault borrows his concept of power from the empiricist tradition; this has robbed it of the experiential potential of an at once terrifying and attractive fascination, from which the aesthetic avant-garde from Baudelaire to the Surrealists was nourished. Nevertheless, even in Foucault's hands, "power" preserves a literally aesthetic relation to the perception of the body, to the painful experience of the mistreated body. This moment even becomes determinative for the modern power formation, which owes the name of biopower to the fact that it penetrates deeply into the reified body and confiscates the whole organism along the subtle paths of scientific objectification and a subjectivity generated by technologies of truth. Biopower is the name for the form of sociation that does away with all forms of natural spontaneity and transforms the creaturely life as a whole into a substrate of empowerment. The asymmetry (replete with normative content) that Foucault sees embedded in power complexes does not hold primarily between powerful wills and coerced subjugation, but between processes of power and the bodies that are crushed within them. It is always the body that is maltreated in torture and made into a showpiece of sovereign revenge; that is taken hold of in drill, resolved into a field of mechanical forces and manipulated; that is objectified and monitored by the human sciences, even as it is stimulated in its desire and stripped naked. If Foucault's concept of power preserves for itself some remnant of aesthetic content, then it owes this to his vitalistic, *Lebensphilosophie* way of reading the body's experience of itself. *The History of Sexuality* closes with the unusual statement: "We have to dream that perhaps one day, in another economy of bodies and pleasures, it will no longer be rightly comprehensible how . . . it could have succeeded in subjecting us to the absolute sovereignty of sex."[25] This *other* economy of the body and of pleasures, about which in the meantime — with Bataille — we can only dream, would not be another economy of power, but a postmodern theory that would also give an account of the standards of critique already laid claim to implicitly. Until then, resistance can draw its motivation, if not its justification, only from the signals of body language, from that nonverbalizable language of the body on which pain has been inflicted, which refuses to be sublated into discourse.[26]

Foucault cannot, of course, make this interpretation his own, though it surely finds a basis in some of his more revealing gestures. Otherwise, like Bataille, he would have to confer upon the other of reason the status that he has denied it, with good reason, ever since *Madness and Civilization*. He is defending himself against a naturalistic metaphysics that adulates the counterpower of prediscursive referents: "What you call 'naturalism,'" he says in a reply to Bernard-Henri Levy in 1977, "signifies the idea that underneath power, with its acts of violence and its artifices, we should be able to rediscover the things themselves in their primordial vitality: behind asylum walls, the spontaneity of madness; in and through the penal system, the fertile unrest of delinquency; beneath sexual prohibitions, the purity of desire."[27] Because Foucault cannot accept this notion from *Lebensphilosophie*, he has likewise to refrain from responding to the question about the normative foundations of his critique.

IV

Foucault cannot adequately deal with the persistent problems that come up in connection with an interpretative approach to the object domain, a self-referential denial of universal validity claims, and a normative justification for critique. The categories of meaning, validity, and value are to be eliminated not only on the metatheoretical, but on the empirical level as well. Genealogical historiography deals with an object domain from which the theory of power has erased all traces of communicative actions entangled in lifeworld contexts. This suppression of basic concepts that could take into account the symbolic prestructuring of action systems burdens his empirical research with problems that, this time at least, Foucault does not address. I will pick out two problems with a venerable history in classical social theory: the issues of how social order is possible at all, and of how individual and society are related to one another.

When, like Foucault, one admits only the model of processes of subjugation, of confrontations mediated by the body, of contexts of more or less consciously strategic action; when one excludes any stabilizing of domains of action in terms of values, norms, and processes of mutual understanding and offers for these mechanisms of social integration none of the familiar equivalents from systems or exchange theories; then one is hardly able to explain just how persistent local struggles could get consolidated into institutionalized power. Axel Honneth has energetically worked out this problematic. Foucault presupposes in his descriptions institutionally sedimented disciplines, power practices, technologies of truth and of domination, but he cannot explain "how there can be derived from a social condition of uninterrupted struggle the aggregate state of a network of power, however momentary one conceives it as being."[28] Conceptual difficulties similar to those raised by the epochal establishment of discourse and power formations are posed by the phenomena for which Durkheim introduced the key term "institutionalized individualism."

If one admits only the model of empowerment, the socialization of succeeding generations can also be presented only in the image of wily confrontation. Then, however, the socialization of subjects capable of speech and action cannot be simultaneously conceived as individuation, but only as the progressive subsumption of bodies and of all vital substrata under technologies of power. The increasingly individualizing formative processes that penetrate ever broader social strata in societies with traditions that have become reflective and with action norms that are highly abstract, have to be artificially reinterpreted to make up for the categorial poverty of the empowerment model. Foucault, the theorist of power, encounters here the same problems as the institutionalist, Arnold Gehlen;[29] both theories lack a mechanism for social integration such as language, with its interlacing of the performative attitudes of speakers and hearers,[30] which could explain the individuating effects of socialization. Just like Gehlen, Foucault compensates for this bottleneck in his basic concepts by purifying the concept of individuation of all connotations of self-determination and self-realization, and reducing it to an *inner world* produced by external stimuli and fitted out with arbitrarily manipulable, representative contents.

This time the difficulty does not result from the lack of an equivalent for familiar constructions of the relationship between individual and society; rather, the issue is whether the model of an inflation of the psychic that is evoked by power techniques (or released by the disintegration of institutions) does not make it necessary to bring the growth in subjective freedom under descriptions that render unrecognizable the experience of an expanded scope for expressive self-manifestation and for autonomy.

Foucault could, of course, turn back objections of this kind as *petitio principii.* Do they not rest on traditional problematics that for Foucault have long since become objectless — together with the human sciences from whose horizon they come? We could only answer this question in the negative if what looks to us like a basic conceptual deficiency were also to affect the design and execution of empirical investigations and thus could be pinned down to specific readings and blindspots. I want at least to suggest a few perspectives from which an empirical critique of Foucault's history of the emergence of modern punishment and of sexuality might be carried out.

Discipline and Punish is set up as a genealogy of scientifically rationalized penal law and of scientifically humanized penal practice. Those technologies of domination in which disciplinary power is expressed today form the *common* matrix for humanizing punishment *and* for obtaining knowledge about human beings.[31] The rationalization of penal law and the humanization of penal practice were set in motion at the close of the eighteenth century under the rhetorical umbrella of a reform movement that justified itself normatively in concepts of law and morality. Foucault wants to show that beneath this was concealed a brutal change in the practices of power — the rise of the modern regime of power, "an adaptation and a refinement of the machinery that assumes responsibility for and places under surveillance their everyday behavior, their identity, their activity, their apparently unimportant gestures."[32] Foucault can illustrate this thesis with impressive cases; nevertheless, the thesis is false in its generality. It contends that the panopticism found in modern punishment is characteristic for the structure of societal modernization as a whole. Foucault can only propose this thesis in its generalized form because he is working with basic concepts of the theory of power for which the normative structures of the development of law remain elusive: Moral-practical learning processes have to present themselves to him as intensifications of processes of empowerment. This reduction is enacted in several steps.

Foucault *begins* by analyzing the normative language game of rational natural law in connection with the latent functions that the discourse on authority has in the age of Classicism for the establishment and the exercise of absolutist state power. The sovereignty of the state that has a monopoly on violence is also expressed in the demonstrative forms of punishment that Foucault depicts in connection with the procedures of torture and ordeal. From the same functionalist perspective, he *then* describes the advances made by the Classical language game during the reform era of the Enlightenment. They culminate, on the one hand, in the Kantian theory of morality and law and, on the other hand, in utilitarianism. Interestingly enough, Foucault does not go into the fact that these in turn serve the revolutionary establishment of a constitutionalized state power, which is to say, of a political order transferred ideologically from the sovereignty of the prince to the sovereignty of the people. This kind of regime is, after all, correlated with those normalizing forms of punishment that constitute the proper theme of *Discipline and Punish*.

Because Foucault filters out the internal aspects of the development of law, he can inconspicuously take a *third* and decisive step: Whereas the sovereign power of Classical formations of power is constituted in concepts of right and law, this normative language game is supposed to be inapplicable to the disciplinary power of the modern age; the latter is suited only to empirical, at least nonjuridical, concepts having to do with the factual steering and organization of the behavioral modes and the motives of a population rendered increasingly manipulable by science: "The procedures of normalization come to be ever more constantly engaged in the colonization of those of the law. I believe that all this can explain the global functioning of what I would call a society of normalization."[33] As the transition from doctrines of natural law to those of natural societies shows,[34] the complex life-context of modern societies as a whole can as a matter of fact be less and less construed in the natural-law categories of contractual relationships. However, this circumstance cannot justify the strategic decision (so full of consequences for Foucault's theory) to neglect the development of normative structures in connection with the modern formation of power. As soon as Foucault takes up the threads of the biopolitical establishment of disciplinary power, he lets drop the threads of the legal organization of the exercise of power and of the legitimation of the order of domination. Because of this, the ungrounded impression arises that the bourgeois constitutional state is a dysfunctional relic from the period of absolutism.

This uncircumspect leveling of culture and politics to immediate substrates of the application of violence explains the ostensible gaps in his presentation. That his history of modern penal justice is detached from the development of the constitutional state might be defended on methodological grounds. The theoretical narrowing down to the system of *carrying out* punishment is more questionable. As soon as he passes from the Classical to the modern age, Foucault pays no attention whatsoever to penal *law* and to the *law* governing penal process. Otherwise, he would have had to submit the unmistakable gains in liberality and legal security, and the expansion of civil-rights guarantees even in this area, to an exact interpretation in terms of the theory of power. However, his presentation is utterly distorted by the fact that he also filters out of the history of penal practices itself all aspects of legal regulation. In prisons, indeed, just as in clinics, schools, and military installations, there do exist those "special power relationships" that have by no means remained undisturbed by an energetically advancing enactment of legal rights — Foucault himself has been politically engaged for this cause.

This selectivity does not take anything away from the importance of his fascinating unmasking of the capillary effects of power. But his generalization, in terms of the theory of power, of such a selective reading hinders Foucault from perceiving the phenomenon actually in need of explanation: In the welfare-state democracies of the West, the spread of legal regulation has the structure of a dilemma, because it is the legal means for securing freedom that themselves endanger the freedom of their presumptive beneficiaries. Under the premises of his theory of power, Foucault so levels down the complexity of societal modernization that the disturbing paradoxes of this process cannot even become apparent to him.

The same tendency toward a leveling of ambiguous phenomena can be seen in Foucault's history of modern sexuality. This deals with the central area of internal nature becoming reflective, that is, of subjectivity in the early Romantic sense of an interiority capable of expressing itself. What is leveled down here is the problematic structure of a long-term process of individuation and interiorization (accompanied by techniques of disclosure and strategies of surveillance) that simultaneously creates new zones of alienation and normalization. Herbert Marcuse interpreted the contemporary phenomena of a sexual liberation that is controlled, socially regulated, and at the same time commercialized and administered, as "repressive desublimation." This analysis holds open the perspective of a liberating desublimation. Foucault starts from the quite similar phenomenon of a sexuality that has been disqualified, reduced to a medium of control, and stripped of all eroticism — but he sees in it the telos, the revealed secret of sexual liberation. Behind the illusory emancipation there is entrenched a power that develops its productivity through an insidiously induced compulsion to confession and voyeurism. For Foucault, "sexuality" is equivalent to a discourse and power formation that validates the innocent demand for truthfulness in regard to one's own stimulations, instinctive desires, and experiences, to which one has privileged access; and this discourse and power formation effects an inconspicuous stimulation of bodies, an intensification of pleasures, and a shaping of spiritual energies. Since the end of the eighteenth century, a net of truth techniques has been drawn about the masturbating child, the hysterical woman, the perverse adult, the procreating couple — all the places surrounded by leering pedagogues, doctors, psychologists, judges, family planners, etc.

One could show in detail how Foucault simplifies the highly complex process of a progressive problematization of internal nature into a linear history. In our context, however, what is primarily of interest is the peculiar filtering out of all the aspects under which the eroticization and internalization of subjective nature also meant a gain in freedom and expressive possibilities. C. Honegger warns against projecting present-day phenomena of repressive desublimation back into past history and suppressing once again the repressions of the past: "In the not too distant past there were commands of chastity for women, a production of female fridigity, a double standard for men, the stigmatizing of deviant sexual behavior, as well as all the kinds of degradation of love life about which Freud heard in his treatment room."[35] Foucault's objections against the Freudian model of the repression of drives, and emancipation through heightened awareness, have a surface plausibility; but this is due to the fact that freedom, as the principle of modernity, cannot be really grasped by means of the basic concepts of the philosophy of the subject.

In all attempts to grasp self-determination and self-realization, that is, freedom in the moral and the aesthetic senses, with the tools of the philosophy of the subject, one immediately runs up against an ironic inversion of what is actually intended. Repression of the self is the converse side of an autonomy that is pressed into subject-object relationships; the loss — and the narcissistic fear of loss — of self is the converse of an expressivity brought under these concepts. That the moral subject has to make an object of itself, that the expressive subject must surrender itself as such or, from fear of externalizing itself in objects, close in upon itself, does not correspond to the intuition of freedom and liberation; rather, it brings to light the constraints upon thought proper to the philosophy of the subject. Along with subject and object, however, Foucault also throws overboard that intuition that was to have been conceptualized in terms of "subjectivity." To be sure, as long as we only take into account subjects representing and dealing with objects, and subjects who externalize themselves in objects or can relate to themselves as objects, it is not possible to conceive of socialization as individuation and to write the history of modern sexuality *also* from the point of view that the internalization of subjective nature makes individuation possible. But along with the philosophy of the subject, Foucault also gets rid of the problems with respect to which that philosophy broke down. In place of socialization as individuating (which remains unconceptualized), he puts the concept of a fragmenting empowerment, a concept that is not up to the ambiguous phenomena of modernity. From his perspective, socialized individuals can only be perceived as exemplars, as standardized products of some discourse formation — as individual copies that are mechanically punched out. Gehlen, who thought from opposite political motives, but also from a similar theoretical perspective, made no secret of this: "A personality: that is an institution in a *single* instance."[36]

XI

An Alternative Way out of the Philosophy of the Subject: Communicative versus Subject-Centered Reason

I

The aporias of the theory of power leave their traces behind in the selective readings of genealogical historiography, whether of modern penal procedure or of sexuality in modern times. Unsettled methodological problems are reflected in empirical deficits. Foucault did indeed provide an illuminating critique of the entanglement of the human sciences in the philosophy of the subject: These sciences try to escape from the aporetic tangles of contradictory self-thematization by a subject seeking to know itself, but in doing so they become all the more deeply ensnared in the self-reifications of scientism. However, Foucault did not think through the aporias of his own approach well enough to see how his theory of power was overtaken by a fate similar to that of the human sciences rooted in the philosophy of the subject. His theory tries to rise above those pseudo-sciences to a more rigorous objectivity, and in doing so it gets caught all the more hopelessly in the trap of a presentist historiography, which sees itself compelled to a re-lativist self-denial and can give no account of the normative foundations of its own rhetoric. To the objectivism of self-mastery on the part of the human sciences there corresponds a subjectivism of self-forgetfulness on Foucault's part. Presentism, relativism, and cryptonormativism are the consequences of his attempt to preserve the transcendental moment proper to generative performances in the basic concept of power while driving from it every trace of subjectivity. This concept of power does not free the genealogist from contradictory self-thematizations.

Hence it would be a good idea to return once again to the unmasking of the human sciences through the critique of reason, but this time in full awareness of a fact that the successors of Nietzsche stubbornly ignore. They do not see that the philosophical counterdiscourse which, from the start, accompanied the philosophical discourse of modernity initiated by Kant already drew up a counterreckoning for subjectivity as the principle of modernity.[1] The basic conceptual aporias of the philosophy of consciousness, so acutely diagnosed by Foucault in the final chapter of *The Order of Things*, were already analyzed by Schiller, Fichte, Schelling, and Hegel in a similiar fashion. To be sure, the solutions they offer are quite different. But if, now, the theory of power also fails to provide a way out of this problematic situation, it behooves us to retrace the path of the philosophical discourse of modernity back to its starting point — in order to examine once again the directions once suggested at the chief crossroads. This is the intention behind these lectures. You will recall that I marked the places where the young Hegel, the young Marx, and even the Heidegger of *Being and Time* and Derrida in his discussion with Husserl stood before alternative paths they did *not* choose.

With Hegel and Marx, it would have been a matter of not swallowing the intuition concerning the ethical totality back into the horizon of the self-reference of the knowing and acting subject, but of explicating it in accord with the model of unconstrained consensus formation in a communication community standing under cooperative constraints. With Heidegger and Derrida it would have been a matter of ascribing the meaning-creating horizons of world interpretation not to a Dasein heroically projecting itself or to a background occurrence that shapes structures, but rather to communicatively structured lifeworlds that reproduce themselves via the palpable medium of action oriented to mutual agreement. At these places, I have already *suggested* that the paradigm of the knowledge of objects has to be replaced by the paradigm of mutual understanding between subjects capable of speech and action. Hegel and Marx did not achieve this paradigm-change; in their attempt to leave behind the metaphysics of subjectivity, Heidegger and Derrida likewise remain caught up in the intention of *Ursprungsphilosophie*. From the point where he gave a threefold analysis of the compulsion to an aporetic doubling on the part of the self-referential subject, Foucault veered off into a theory of power that has shown itself to be a dead end. He follows Heidegger and Derrida in the abstract negation of the self-referential subject, inasmuch as, put briefly, he declares "man" to be nonexistent. But unlike them, he no longer attempts to compensate, by way of temporalized originary powers, for the lost order of things that the metaphysically isolated and structurally overburdened subject tries in vain to renew from its own forces. In the end, the transcendental-historicist "power," the single constant in the ups and downs of overwhelming and overwhelmed discourses, proves to be only an equivalent for the "life" [*Leben*] of the hoary *Lebensphilosophie*. A more viable solution suggests itself if we drop the somewhat sentimental presupposition of metaphysical homelessness, and if we understand the hectic to and fro between transcendental and empirical modes of dealing with issues, between radical self-reflection and an incomprehensible element that cannot be reflectively retrieved, between the productivity of a self-generating species and a primordial element prior to all production — that is to say, when we understand the puzzle of all these doublings for what it is: a symptom of exhaustion. The paradigm of the philosophy of consciousness is exhausted. If this is so, the symptoms of exhaustion should dissolve with the transition to the paradigm of mutual understanding.

If we can presuppose for a moment the model of action oriented to reaching understanding that I have developed elsewhere,[2] the objectifying attitude in which the knowing subject regards itself as it would entities in the external world is no longer *privileged*. Fundamental to the paradigm of mutual understanding is, rather, the performative attitude of participants in interaction, who coordinate their plans for action by coming to an understanding about something in the world. When ego carries out a speech act and alter takes up a position with regard to it, the two parties enter into an interpersonal relationship. The latter is structured by the system of reciprocally interlocked perspectives among speakers, hearers, and non-participants who happen to be present at the time. On the level of grammar, this corresponds to the system of personal pronouns. Whoever has been trained in this system has learned how, in the performative attitude, to take up and to transform into one another the perspectives of the first, second, and third persons.

Now this attitude of participants in linguistically mediated interaction makes possible a *different* relationship of the subject to itself from the sort of objectifying attitude that an observer assumes toward entities in the external world. The transcendental-empirical doubling of the relation to self is only unavoidable so long as there is no alternative to this observer-perspective; only then does the subject have to view itself as the dominating counterpart to the world as a whole or as an entity appearing within it. No mediation is possible between the extramundane stance of the transcendental I and the intramundane stance of the empirical I. As soon as linguistically generated intersubjectivity gains primacy, this alternative no longer applies. Then ego stands within an interpersonal relationship that allows him to relate to himself as a participant in an interaction from the perspective of alter. And indeed this reflection undertaken from the perspective of the participant escapes the kind of objectification inevitable from the reflexively applied perspective of the observer. Everything gets frozen into an object under the gaze of the third person, whether directed inwardly or outwardly. The first person, who turns back upon himself in a performative attitude from the angle of vision of the second person, can *recapitulate* [*nachvollziehen*] the acts it just carried out. In place of reflectively objectified knowledge — the knowledge proper to self-consciousness — we have a recapitulating reconstruction of knowledge already employed.

What earlier was relegated to transcendental philosophy, namely the intuitive analysis of self-consciousness, now gets adapted to the circle of reconstructive sciences that try to make explicit, from the perspective of those participating in discourses and interactions, and by means of analyzing successful or distorted utterances, the pretheoretical grasp of rules on the part of competently speaking, acting, and knowing subjects. Because such reconstructive attempts are no longer aimed at a realm of the intelligible beyond that of appearances, but at the actually exercised rule-knowledge that is deposited in correctly generated utterances, the ontological separation between the transcendental and the empirical is no longer applicable. As can be shown in connection with Jean Piaget's genetic structuralism, reconstructive and empirical assumptions can be brought together in one and the same theory.[3] In this way, the spell of an unresolved back-and-forth between two aspects of self-thematization that are as inevitable as they are incompatible is broken. Consequently, we do not need hybrid theories any more to close the gap between the transcendental and the empirical.

The same holds true for the doubling of the relation to self in the dimension of making the unconscious conscious. Here, according to Foucault, the thought of subject philosophy oscillates back and forth between heroic exertions bent on reflectively transforming what is in-itself into what is for-itself, and the recognition of an opaque background that stubbornly escapes the transparency of self-consciousness. If we make the transition to the paradigm of mutual understanding, these two aspects of self-thematization are no longer incompatible. Insofar as speakers and hearers straightforwardly achieve a mutual understanding about something in the world, they move within the horizon of their common lifeworld; this remains in the background of the participants — as an intuitively known, unproblematic, and unanalyzable, holistic background. The speech situation is the segment of a lifeworld tailored to the relevant theme; it both forms a *context* and furnishes *resources* for the process of mutual understanding. The lifeworld forms a horizon and at the same time offers a store of things taken for granted in the given culture from which communicative participants draw consensual interpretative patterns in their efforts at interpretation. The solidarities of groups integrated by values and the competences of socialized individuals belong, as do culturally ingrained background assumptions, to the components of the lifeworld.

In order to be able to make these kinds of statements, we naturally have to undertake a change in perspective: We can only get insight into the lifeworld *a tergo*. From the straightforward perspective of acting subjects oriented to mutual understanding, the lifeworld that is always only "co-given" has to evade thematization. As a totality that makes possible the identities and biographical projects of groups and individuals, it is present only prereflectively. Indeed, the practically employed rule-knowledge sedimented in utterances can be reconstructed from the perspective of participants, but not the ever-receding context and the always-in-the-background resources of the lifeworld as a whole. We need a *theoretically constituted perspective* to be able to treat communicative action as the medium through which the lifeworld as a whole is reproduced. Even from this vantage point, only formal-pragmatic statements are possible, statements related to the structures of the lifeworld in general, and not to determinate lifeworlds in their concrete historical configurations. Of course, interaction participants then no longer appear as originators who master situations with the help of accountable actions, but as the *products* of the traditions in which they stand, of the solidary groups to which they belong, and of the socialization processes within which they grow up. This is to say that the lifeworld reproduces itself to the extent that these three functions, which transcend the perspectives of the actors, are fulfilled: the propagation of cultural traditions, the integration of groups by norms and values, and the socialization of succeeding generations. But what comes into view in this manner are the properties of communicatively structured lifeworlds *in general.*

Whoever wants to become reflectively aware of the individual totality of any individual biography or of a particular way of life has to recur to the perspective of the participants, give up the intention of rational reconstruction, and simply proceed historically. Narrative tools can, if necessary, be stylized into a dialogically conducted self-critique, for which the analytic conversation between doctor and patient offers a suitable model. This self-critique, which is aimed at eliminating pseudo-nature, that is, the pseudo-aprioris made up of unconsciously motivated perceptual barriers and compulsions to action, is related to the narratively recollected entirety of a course of life or way of life. The analytic dissolution of hypostatizations, of self-engendered objective illusions, is due to an experience of reflection. But its liberating force is directed toward *single* illusions: It cannot make transparent the *totality* of a course of life in the process of individuation or of a collective way of life.

The two heritages of self-reflection that get beyond the limits of the philosophy of consciousness have different aims and scopes. *Rational reconstruction* subscribes to the program of heightening consciousness, but is directed toward anonymous rule systems and does not refer to totalities. In contrast, *methodically carried out self-critique* is related to totalities, and yet in the awareness that it can never completely illuminate the implicit, the prepredicative, the not focally present background of the lifeworld.[4] As can be shown through the example of psychoanalysis, as interpreted in terms of communication theory,[5] the two procedures of reconstruction and of self-critique can still be brought together within the framework of one and the same theory. These two aspects of self-thematization on the part of the knowing subject are also not irreconcilable; in this respect, too, hybrid theories that overcome contradictions by force are superfluous.

Something similar holds true of the third doubling of the subject as an originally creative actor simultaneously alienated from its origin. If the formal-pragmatic concept of the lifeworld is going to be made fruitful for the purposes of social theory, it has to be transformed into an empirically usable concept and integrated with the concept of a self-regulating system into a two-level concept of society. Furthermore, a careful separation between problems of developmental logic and those of developmental dynamics is necessary so that social evolution and social history can be methodically discriminated from each other and related to each other. Finally, social theory has to remain aware of the context of its own emergence and of its position in the contemporary context; even basic concepts that are starkly universalist have a temporal core.[6] If, with the aid of these operations, one succeeds in steering between the Scylla of absolutism and the Charybdis of relativism,[7] we are no longer faced with the alternatives of the conception of world history as a process of self-generation (whether of the spirit or of the species), on the one hand, and, on the other hand, the conception of an impenetrable dispensation that makes the power of lost origins felt through the negativity of withdrawal and deprival.

I cannot go into these complicated interconnections here. I only wanted to suggest how a paradigm-change can render objectless those dilemmas out of which Foucault explains the perilous dynamics of a subjectivity that is bent on knowledge and falls prey to pseudo-sciences. The change of paradigm from subject-centered to communicative reason also encourages us to resume once again the counterdiscourse that accompanied modernity from the beginning. Since Nietzsche's radical critique of reason cannot be consistently carried out along the lines of a critique of metaphysics or of a theory of power, we are directed toward a *different* way out of the philosophy of the subject. Perhaps the grounds for the self-critique of a modernity in collapse can be considered under other premises such that we can do justice to the motives, virulent since Nietzsche, for a precipitous leavetaking of modernity. It must be made clear that the purism of pure reason is not resurrected again in communicative reason.

II

During the last decade, the radical critique of reason has become fashionable. A study by Hartmut and Gernot Böhme, who take up Foucault's idea of the rise of the modern form of knowledge in connection with to the work and biography of Kant, is exemplary in theme and execution. In the style of a historiography of science expanded by cultural and social history, the authors take a look, so to speak, at what goes on behind the back of the critique of pure and of practical reason. For example, they seek the real motives for the critique of reason in the debate with the spiritual clairvoyant, Swedenborg, in whom Kant is supposed to have recognized his dark twin, his repressed counterimage. They pursue these motives into the sphere of the personal, into the, as it were, abstract conduct (turned away from everything sexual, bodily, and imaginative) of a scholarly life marked by hypochondria, crotchetiness, and immobility. The authors marshal before our eyes the "costs of reason" in terms of psychohistory. They undertake this cost/ benefit accounting ingenuously with psychoanalytic arguments and document it with historical data, though without being able to specify the place at which such arguments could claim any weight — if indeed the thesis they are concerned with is supposed to make sense.

Kant had carried out his critique of reason from reason's own perspective, that is to say, in the form of a rigorously argued self-limitation of reason. If, now, the production costs of this self-confining reason (which places anything metaphysical off limits) are to be made clear, we require a horizon of reason reaching beyond this drawing of boundaries in which the transcending discourse that adds up the bill can operate. This further radicalized critique of reason would have to postulate a more far-reaching and *comprehensive* reason. But the Böhme brothers do not intend to cast out the devil by Beelzebub; instead, with Foucault, they see in the transition from an exclusive reason (in the Kantian mold) to a comprehensive reason merely "the completion of the power-technique of exclusion by the power-technique of permeation."[8] If they were to be consistent, their own investigation of the other of reason would have to occupy a position utterly heterogeneous to reason — but what does consistency count for in a place that is a priori inaccessible to rational discourse? In this text, the paradoxes repeatedly played out since Nietzsche leave behind no recognizable traces of unrest. This methodological enmity toward reason may have something to do with the type of historical innocence with which studies of this kind today move in the no-man's-land between argumentation, narration, and fiction.[9] The New Critique of Reason suppresses that almost 200-year-old counterdiscourse inherent in modernity itself which I am trying to recall in these lectures.

The latter discourse set out from Kantian philosophy as an unconscious expression of the modern age and pursued the goal of enlightening the Enlightenment about its own narrowmindedness. The New Critique of Reason denies the continuity with this counterdiscourse, within which it nevertheless still

stands: "No longer can it be a matter of completing the project
of modernity (Habermas); it has to be a matter of revising it.
Also, the Enlightenment has not remained incomplete, but
unenlightened."[10] The intention of revising the Enlightenment
with the very tools of the Enlightenment is, however, what
united the critics of Kant from the start — Schiller with Schlegel, Fichte with the Tübingen seminarians. Further on we read:
"Kant's philosophy was initiated as the enterprise of drawing
boundaries. But nothing was said about the fact that drawing
boundaries is a dynamic process, that reason retreated to firm
ground and abandoned other areas, that drawing boundaries
means self-inclusion and exclusion of others." At the start of
our lectures, we saw how Hegel, along with Schelling and
Hölderlin, saw as so many provocations the philosophy of reflection's achievements of delimitation — the opposition of
faith and knowledge, of infinite and finite, the separation of
spirit and nature, of understanding and sensibility, of duty and
inclination. We saw how they tracked the estrangement of an
overblown subjective reason from internal and external nature
right into the "positivities" of the demolished *Sittlichkeit* of
everyday political and private life. Indeed, Hegel saw the vanishing of the power of reconciliation from the life of mankind
as the source of an objective need for philosophy. At any rate,
he interpreted the boundaries drawn by subject-centered reason not as exclusions from but as dichotomies within reason,
and ascribed to philosophy an access to the totalilty *that encompasses within itself* subjective reason and its other. Our authors'
distrust is directed against this, when they continue: "Whatever
reason is, however, remains unclear as long as its other is not
thought along with it (in its irreducibility). For reason can be
deceived about itself, take itself to be the whole (Hegel), or
pretend to comprehend the totality."

   This is just the objection that the Young Hegelians once
made good against the master. They brought a suit against
absolute reason in which the other of reason, what is always
prior to it, was supposed to be rehabilitated in its own proper
right. The concept of a *situated reason* issued from this process
of desublimation; its relationship to the historicity of time, to
the facticity of external nature, to the decentered subjectivity

of internal nature, and to the material character of society was defined neither by inclusion nor by exclusion, but by a praxis of projecting and developing essential powers that takes place under conditions "not themselves chosen." Society is portrayed as practices in which reason is embodied. This praxis takes place in the dimension of historical time; it mediates the inner nature of needful individuals with an external nature objectified by labor, within the horizon of a surrounding cosmic nature. This social practice is the place where a historically situated, bodily incarnated reason, confronted by external nature, is concretely mediated with its other. Whether this mediating practice is successful depends on its internal constitution, on the degrees of bifurcation and of reconciliation in the socially institutionalized context of life. What was called the system of egoism and divided ethical totality in Schiller and Hegel is transformed by Marx into a society split into social classes. Just as in Schiller and in the young Hegel, the social bond — that is, the community-forming and solidarity-building force of unalienated cooperation and living together — ultimately decides whether reason embodied in social practices is in touch with history and nature. It is the dichotomized society itself that exacts the repression of death, the leveling of historical consciousness, and the subjugation of both internal and external nature.

Within the context of the philosophy of history, the praxis philosophy of the young Marx has the significance of disconnecting Hegel's model of diremption from an *inclusive* concept of reason that incorporated even the other of reason in its totality. The reason of praxis philosophy is understood as finite; nevertheless it remains tied to a *comprehensive* reason — in the form of a critical social theory — insofar as it realizes that it could not identify the historical limits of subject-centered reason — as embodied in bourgeois social relations — without transcending them. Whoever fastens obstinately upon the model of exclusion has to be closed to this Hegelian insight, which, as is evident in Marx, can be had without paying the price of abolutizing the spirit. From such a restricted perspective, the Hegelian defect attending the birth of post-Hegelian theory is still also effective "where reason is criticized as instrumental, repressive, narrow: in Horkheimer and Adorno. Their critique still takes place in the name of a superior reason, namely, the comprehensive reason, to which the intention of totality is conceded, though it was always disputed when it came to real reason. There is no comprehensive reason. One should have learned from Freud or even from Nietzsche that reason does not exist apart from its other and that — functionally considered — it becomes necessary in virtue of this other."[11]

With this assertion, the Böhme brothers call to mind the place where Nietzsche, having recourse to the Romantic heritage, once set a totalizing critique of reason in opposition to an intrinsically dialectical Enlightenment. The dialectic of enlightenment would indeed only have played itself out if reason were robbed of any transcendent force and, in virtual impotence, remained confined, in the madness of its autonomy, to those boundaries that Kant had defined for understanding and for any state based on understanding: "That the subject of reason wants to owe no one and nothing outside itself is its ideal and its insanity at once."[12] Only if reason shows itself to be essentially narcissistic — an identifying, only seemingly universal power, bent upon self-assertion and particular self-aggrandizement, subjugating everything around it as an object — can the other of reason be thought for its part as a spontaneous, creative power that is at the ground of Being, a power that is simultaneously vital and unperspicuous, that is no longer illuminated by any spark of reason. Only reason as reduced to the subjective faculty of understanding and purposive activity corresponds to the image of an *exclusive* reason that further uproots itself the more it strives triumphally for the heights, until, withered, it falls victim to the power of its concealed heterogeneous origin. The dynamism of self-destruction, in which the secret of the dialectic of enlightenment supposedly comes to light, can only function if reason cannot produce anything from itself except that naked power to which it actually hopes to provide an alternative, namely the unforced force of a better insight.

This move explains, moreover, the drastic leveling of Kant's architectonic of reason that results from the Nietzsche-inspired reading of Kant; it has to obliterate the connection of the critiques of pure and practical reason with the critique of judgment, so as to reduce the former to a theory of alienated, external nature and the latter to a theory of domination over internal nature.[13]

Whereas the *diremption model* of reason distinguishes solidary social practice as the locus of a historically situated reason in which the threads of outer nature, inner nature, and society converge, in the *exclusion model* of reason the space opened up by utopian thought gets completely filled in with an irreconcilable reason reduced to bare power. Here social practice only serves as the stage upon which disciplinary power finds ever new scenarios. It is haunted by a reason denied the power to gain access, without coercion, to what is prior to it. In its putative sovereignty, reason that has evaporated into subjectivity becomes the plaything of unmediated forces working upon it, as it were, mechanically — forces of the internal and external nature that have been excluded and rendered into objects.

The other of this self-inflated subjectivity is no longer the dirempted totality, which makes itself felt primarily in the avenging power of destroyed reciprocities and in the fateful causality of distorted communicative relationships, as well as through suffering from the disfigured totality of social life, from alienated inner and outer nature. In the model of exclusion, this complicated structure of a subjective reason that is socially divided and thereby torn away from nature is peculiarly de-differentiated: "The other of reason is nature, the human body, fantasy, desire, the feelings — or better: all this insofar as reason has not been able to appropriate it."[14] Thus, it is directly the vital forces of a split-off and repressed subjective nature, it is the sorts of phenomena rediscovered by Romanticism — dreams, fantasies, madness, orgiastic excitement, ecstacy — it is the aesthetic, body-centered experiences of a decentered subjectivity that function as the placeholders for the other of reason. To be sure, early Romanticism still wanted to establish art, in the form of a new mythology, as a public institution in the midst of social life; it wanted to elevate the excitement radiating from this into an equivalent for the unifying power of religion. Nietzsche was the first to transfer this potential for excitement into the beyond of modern society and of history overall. The modern origin of aesthetic experience heightened in an avant-garde fashion remains concealed.

The potential for excitement, stylized into the other of reason, becomes at once esoteric and pseudonymous; it comes up under different names — as Being, as the heterogeneous, as power. The cosmic nature of the metaphysicians and the God of the philosophers become blurred into an enchanting reminiscence, a moving remembrance on the part of the metaphysically and religiously isolated subject. The order from which this subject has emancipated himself — which is to say, internal and external nature in their unalienated form — appears now only in the past tense, as the archaic origin of metaphysics for Heidegger, as a turning pont in the archeology of the human sciences for Foucault — and also, somewhat more fashionably, as follows: "Separated from the body, whose libidinous potencies could have supplied images of happiness, separated from a maternal nature, which embraced the archaic *image* of symbiotic wholeness and nurturing protection, separated from the feminine, mingling with which belonged to the primal images of happiness — the philosophy of a reason robbed of all images generated only a grandiose consciousness of the superiority in principle of the intelligible over nature and over the lowliness of the body and the woman. . . . Philosophy attributed to reason an omnipotence, infinity, and future perfection, whereas *the lost childlike relationship to nature* did not appear."[15]

Nonetheless, these recollections of origins by the modern subject serve as points of reference for responses to the question that the more consistent among Nietzsche's followers did not try to evade. As long as we speak in narrative form of the other of reason (whatever it might be called), and as long as this factor that is heterogeneous to discursive thought comes up in portrayals of the history of philosophy and science as a name without any further qualifications, the pose of innocence cannot make up for this underselling of the critique of reason inaugurated by Kant. In Heidegger and Foucault, subjective nature as the placeholder for the other has disappeared, because it can no longer be declared the other of reason once it is brought into scientific discourse as the individual or collective unconscious in the concepts of Freud or Jung, of Lacan or Lévi-Strauss. Whether in the form of meditative thought [*Andenken*] or of genealogy, Heidegger and Foucault want to initiate a *special discourse* that claims to operate *outside* the horizon of reason without being utterly irrational. To be sure, this merely shifts the paradox.

Reason is supposed to be criticizable in its historical forms from the perspective of the other that has been excluded from it; this requires, then, an ultimate act of self-reflection that surpasses itself, and indeed an act of reason for which the place of the *genitivus subjectivus* would have to be occupied by the other of reason. Subjectivity, as the relation-to-self of the knowing and acting subject, is represented in the bipolar relationship of self-reflection. This figure is retained, and yet subjectivity is supposed to appear only in the place reserved for the object. Heidegger and Foucault elaborate this paradox in a structurally similar way, inasmuch as they *generate* what is heterogeneous to reason by way of a self-exiling of reason, a banishing of reason from its own territory. This operation is understood as an unmasking reversal of the self-idolizing that subjectivity carries on and at the same time conceals from itself. In the process, it ascribes attributes to itself that it borrows from the shattered religious and metaphysical concepts of order. Conversely, the other they seek, which is heterogeneous to reason and still related to it as its heterogeneous factor, results from a radical finitizing of the absolute for which subjectivity had falsely substituted itself. As we have seen, Heidegger chooses time as the dimension of finitizing and conceives the other of reason as an anonymous, primordial power, set aflow temporally; Foucault chooses the dimension of spatial centering in the experience of one's own body and conceives the other of reason as the anonymous source of the empowerment of interactions tied to the body.

We have seen that this elaboration of the paradox by no means amounts to its solution; the paradox is withdrawn into the special status of extraordinary discourse. Just as meditative thought pertains to a mystified Being, genealogy pertains to power. Meditative thought is supposed to open up a privileged access to metaphysically buried truth; genealogy is supposed to take the place of the apparently degenerate human sciences. Whereas Heidegger remains reticent about the kind of privilege that is his — so that one is not sure of how the genre of his late philosophy could be judged in any sense — Foucault has carried out his work unpretentiously to the very last, in the awareness of being unable to dodge his methodological aporias.

III

The spatial metaphor of inclusive and exclusive reason reveals that the supposedly radical critique of reason remains tied to the presuppositions of the philosophy of the subject from which it wanted to free itself. Only a reason to which we ascribe a "power of the keys" could either include or exclude. Hence, inside and outside are linked with domination and subjugation; and the overcoming of reason-as-powerholder is linked with breaking open the prison gates and vouchsafing release into an indeterminate freedom. Thus, the other of reason remains the mirror image of reason in power. Surrender and letting-be remain as chained to the desire for control as the rebellion of counterpower does to the oppression of power. Those who would like to leave all paradigms behind along with the paradigm of the philosophy of consciousness, and go forth into the clearing of postmodernity, will just not be able to free themselves from the concepts of subject-centered reason and its impressively illustrated topography.

Since early Romanticism, limit experiences of an aesthetic and mystical kind have always been claimed for the purpose of a rapturous transcendence of the subject. The mystic is blinded by the light of the absolute and closes his eyes; aesthetic ecstasy finds expression in the stunning and dizzying effects of (the illuminating) shock. In both cases, the source of the experience of being shaken up evades any specification. In this indeterminacy, we can make out only the silhouette of the paradigm under attack — the outline of what has been deconstructed. In this constellation, which persists from Nietzsche to Heidegger and Foucault, there arises a readiness for excitement without any proper object; in its wake, subcultures are formed which simultaneously allay and keep alive their excitement in the face of future truths (of which they have been notified in an unspecified way) by means of cultic actions without any cultic object. This scurrilous game with religiously and aesthetically toned ecstasy finds an audience especially in circles of intellectuals who are prepared to make their *sacrificium intellectus* on the altar of their needs for orientation.

But here, too, a paradigm only loses its force when it is negated in a *determinate* manner by a *different* paradigm, that is, when it is devalued in an *insightful* way; it is certainly resistant to any simple invocation of the extinction of the subject. Even the furious labor of deconstruction has identifiable consequences only when the paradigm of self-consciousness, of the relation-to-self of a subject knowing and acting in isolation, is replaced by a different one — by the paradigm of mutual understanding, that is, of the intersubjective relationship between individuals who are socialized through communication and reciprocally recognize one another. Only then does the critique of the domineering thought of subject-centered reason emerge in a *determinate* form — namely, as a critique of Western "logocentrism," which is diagnosed not as an excess but as a deficit of rationality. Instead of overtrumping modernity, it takes up again the counterdiscourse inherent in modernity and leads it away from the battle lines between Hegel and Nietzsche, from which there is no exit. This critique renounces the high-flown originality of a return to archaic origins; it unleashes the subversive force of modern thought itself against the paradigm of the philosophy of consciousness that was installed in the period from Descartes to Kant.

The critique of the Western emphasis on logos inspired by Nietzsche proceeds in a destructive manner. It demonstrates that the embodied, speaking and acting subject is not master in its own house; it draws from this the conclusion that the subject positing itself in knowledge is in fact dependent upon something prior, anonymous, and transsubjective — be it the dispensation of Being, the accident of structure-formation, or the generative power of some discourse formation. The logos of an omnipotent subject thus appears as a misadventure of misguided specialization, which is as rich in consequences as it is wrongheaded. The hope awakened by such post-Nietzschean analyses has constantly the same quality of expectant indeterminacy. Once the defenses of subject-centered reason are razed, the logos, which for so long had held together an interiority protected by power, hollow within and aggressive without, will collapse into itself. It has to be delivered over to its other, whatever that may be.

A different, less dramatic, but step-by-step testable critique of the Western emphasis on logos starts from an attack on the abstractions surrounding logos itself, as free of language, as universalist, and as disembodied. It conceives of intersubjective understanding as the·telos inscribed into communication in ordinary language, and of the logocentrism of Western thought, heightened by the philosophy of consciousness, as a systematic *foreshortening* and *distortion* of a potential always already operative in the communicative practice of everyday life, but only selectively exploited. As long as Occidental self-understanding views human beings as distinguished in their relationship to the world by their monopoly on encountering entities, knowing and dealing with objects, making true statements, and implementing plans, reason remains confined ontologically, epistemologically, or in terms of linguistic analysis to only one of its dimensions. The relationship of the human being to the world is cognitivistically reduced: Ontologically, the world is reduced to the world of entities as a whole (as the totality of objects that can be represented and of existing states of affairs); epistemologically, our relationship to that world is reduced to the capacity to know existing states of affairs or to bring them about in a purposive-rational fashion; semantically, it is reduced to fact-stating discourse in which assertoric sentences are used — and no validity claim is admitted besides propositional truth, which is available *in foro interno*.

Language philosophy — from Plato to Popper — has concentrated this logocentrism into the affirmation that the linguistic function of representing states of affairs is the sole human monopoly. Whereas human beings share the so-called appellative and expressive functions (Bühler) with animals, only the representative function is supposed to be constitutive of reason.[16] However, evidence from more recent ethology, especially experiments with the artificially induced acquisition of language by chimpanzees, teaches us that it is not the use of propositions per se, but only the *communicative use* of propositionally differentiated language that is proper to our sociocultural form of life and is constitutive for the level of a genuinely social reproduction of life. In terms of language philosophy, the equiprimordiality and equal value of the three fundamental linguistic functions come into view as soon as we abandon the analytic level of the judgment or the sentence and expand our analysis to speech acts, precisely to the communicative use of sentences. Elementary speech acts display a structure in which three components are mutually combined: the propositional component for representing (or mentioning) states of affairs; the illocutionary component for taking up interpersonal relationships; and finally, the linguistic components that bring the intention of the speaker to expression. The clarification, in terms of speech-act theory, of the complex linguistic functions of representation, the establishment of interpersonal relationships, and the expression of one's own subjective experiences has far-reaching consequences for (a) the theory of meaning, (b) the ontological presuppositions of the theory of communication, and (c) the concept of rationality itself. Here I will only point out these consequences to the extent that they are directly relevant to (d) a *new orientation* for the critique of instrumental reason.

(a) Truth-condition semantics, as it has been developed from Frege to Dummett and Davidson, proceeds — as does the Husserlian theory of meaning — from the logocentric assumption that the truth reference of the assertoric sentence (and the indirect truth reference of intentional sentences related to the implementation of plans) offers a suitable point of departure for the explication of the linguistic accomplishment of mutual understanding generally. Thus, this theory arrives at the principle that we understand a sentence when we know the conditions under which it is true. (For understanding intentional and imperative sentences it requires a corresponding knowledge of "conditions for success."[17]) The pragmatically expanded theory of meaning overcomes this fixation on the fact-mirroring function of language. Like truth-condition semantics, it affirms an internal connection between meaning and validity, but it does not reduce this to the validity proper to truth. Correlative to the three fundamental functions of language, each elementary speech act as a whole can be contested under three different aspects of validity. The hearer can reject the utterance of a speaker *in toto* by either disputing the *truth* of the proposition asserted in it (or of the existential presuppositions of its propositional content), or the *rightness* of the speech act in view of the normative context of the utterance (or the legitimacy of the presupposed context itself), or the *truthfulness* of the intention expressed by the speaker (that is, the agreement of what is meant with what is stated). Hence, the internal connection of meaning and validity holds for the *entire spectrum* of linguistic meanings — and not just for the meaning of expressions that can be expanded into assertoric sentences. It holds true not only for constative speech acts, but for any given speech act, that we understand its meaning when we know the conditions under which it can be accepted as valid.

(b) If, however, not just constative but also regulative and expressive speech acts can be connected with validity claims and accepted as valid or rejected as invalid, the basic, ontological framework of the philosophy of consciousness (which has remained normative for linguistic philosophy as well, with exceptions such as Austin) proves to be too narrow. The "world" to which subjects can relate with their representations or propositions was hitherto conceived of as the totality of objects or existing states of affairs. The objective world is considered the correlative of all true assertoric sentences. But if normative rightness and subjective truthfulness are introduced as validity claims analogous to truth, "worlds" analogous to the world of facts have to be postulated for legitimately regulated interpersonal relationships and for attributable subjective experiences — a "world" not only for what is "objective," which appears to us in the attitude of the third person, but also one for what it normative, to which we feel obliged in the attitude of addresses, as well as one for what is subjective, which we either disclose or conceal to a public in the attitude of the first person. With any speech act, the speaker takes up a relation to something in the objective world, something in a common social world, and something in his own subjective world. The legacy of logocentrism is still noticeable in the terminological difficulty of expanding the ontological concept of "world" in this way.

The phenomenological concept (elaborated by Heidegger in particular) of a referential context, a lifeworld, that forms the unquestioned context for processes of mutual understanding — behind the backs of participants in interaction, so to speak — needs a corresponding expansion. Participants draw from this *lifeworld* not just consensual patterns of interpretation (the background knowledge from which propositional contents are fed), but also normatively reliable patterns of social relations (the tacitly presupposed solidarities on which illocutionary acts are based) and the competences acquired in socialization processes (the background of the speaker's intentions).

(c) "Rationality" refers in the first instance to the disposition of speaking and acting subjects to acquire and use fallible knowledge. As long as the basic concepts of the philosophy of consciousness lead us to understand knowledge exclusively as knowledge of something in the objective world, rationality is assessed by how the isolated subject orients himself to representational and propositional contents. Subject-centered reason finds its criteria in standards of truth and success that govern the relationships of knowing and purposively acting subjects to the world of possible objects or states of affairs. By contrast, as soon as we conceive of knowledge as communicatively mediated, rationality is assessed in terms of the capacity of responsible participants in interaction to orient themselves in relation to validity claims geared to intersubjective recognition. Communicative reason finds its criteria in the argumentative procedures for directly or indirectly redeeming claims to propositional truth, normative rightness, subjective truthfulness, and aesthetic harmony.[18]

Thus, a procedural concept of rationality can be worked out in terms of the interdependence of various forms of argumentation, that is to say, with the help of a pragmatic logic of argumentation. This concept is richer than that of purposive rationality, which is tailored to the cognitive-instrumental dimension, because it integrates the moral-practical as well as the aesthetic-expressive domains; it is an explicitation of the rational potential built into the validity basis of speech. This communicative rationality recalls older ideas of logos, inasmuch as it brings along with it the connotations of a noncoercively unifying, consensus-building force of a discourse in which the participants overcome their at first subjectively biased views in favor of a rationally motivated agreement. Communicative reason is expressed in a decentered understanding of the world.

(d) From this perspective, both cognitive-instrumental mastery of an objectivated nature (and society) and narcissistically overinflated autonomy (in the sense of purposively rational self-assertion) are derivative moments that have been rendered independent from the communicative structures of the lifeworld, that is, from the intersubjectivity of relationships of mutual understanding and relationships of reciprocal recognition. Subject-centered reason is the *product of division and usurpation*, indeed of a social process in the course of which a subordinated moment assumes the place of the whole, without having the power to assimilate the structure of the whole. Horkheimer and Adorno have, like Foucault, described this process of a self-overburdening and self-reifying subjectivity as a world-historical process. But both sides missed its deeper irony, which consists in the fact that the communicative potential of reason first had to be released in the patterns of modern lifeworlds before the unfettered imperatives of the economic and administrative subsystems could react back on the vulnerable practice of everyday life and could thereby promote the cognitive-instrumental dimension to domination over the suppressed moments of practical reason. The communicative potential of reason has been simultaneously developed and distorted in the course of capitalist modernization.

The paradoxical contemporaneity and interdependence of the two processes can only be grasped if the false alternative set up by Max Weber, with his opposition between substantive and formal rationality, is overcome. Its underlying assumption is that the disenchantment of religious-metaphysical world views robs rationality, along with the contents of tradition, of all substantive connotations and thereby strips it of its power to have a structure-forming influence on the lifeworld beyond the purposive-rational organization of means. As opposed to this, I would like to insist that, despite its purely procedural character as disburdened of all religious and metaphysical mortgages, communicative reason is directly implicated in social life-processes insofar as acts of mutual understanding take on the role of a mechanism for coordinating action. The network of communicative actions is nourished by resources of the lifeworld and is at the same time the *medium* by which concrete forms of life are reproduced.

Hence, the theory of communicative action can reconstruct Hegel's concept of the ethical context of life (independently of premises of the philosophy of consciousness). It disenchants the unfathomable causality of fate, which is distinguished from the destining of Being by reason of its *inexorable immanence*. Unlike the "from-time-immemorial" character of the happening of Being or of power, the pseudo-natural dynamics of impaired communicative life-contexts retains something of the character of a destining for which one is *"at fault" oneself* — though one can speak of "fault" here only in an intersubjective sense, that is, in the sense of an involuntary product of an entanglement that, however things stand with individual accountability, communicative agents would have to ascribe to communal responsibility. It is not by chance that suicides set loose a type of shock among those close to them, which allows even the most hardhearted to discover something of the *unavoidable communality* of such a fate.

IV

In the theory of communicative action, the feedback process by which lifeworld and everyday communicative practice are intertwined takes over the mediating role that Marx and Western Marxism had reserved to social practice. In this social practice, reason as historically situated, bodily incarnated, and confronted by nature was supposed to be mediated with its other. If communicative action is now going to take over the same mediating function, the theory of communicative action is going to be suspected of representing just another version of praxis philosophy. In fact, both are supposed to take care of the same task: to conceive of rational practice as reason concretized in history, society, body, and language.

We have traced the way praxis philosophy substituted labor for self-consciousness and then got caught in the fetters of the production paradigm. The praxis philosophy renewed by phenomenology and anthropology, which has at its disposal the tools of the Husserlian analysis of the lifeworld, has learned from the critique of Marxian productivism. It relativizes the status of labor and joins in the aporetic attempts to accommodate the externalization of subjective spirit, the temporalization, socialization, and embodiment of situated reason, within *other* subject-object relationships. Inasmuch as it makes use of phenomenological-anthropological tools of thought, praxis philosophy renounces originality precisely at the point where it cannot afford to: in specifying praxis as a rationally structured process of mediation. It is once again subjected to the dichotomizing basic concepts of the philosophy of the subject: *History* is projected and made by subjects who find themselves in turn already projected and made in the historical process (Sartre); *society* appears to be an objective network of relations that is either set, as a normative order, above the heads of subjects with their transcendentally prior mutual understandings (Alfred Schütz) or is generated by them, as instrumental orders, in the battle of reciprocal objectifications (Kojève); the subject either finds itself centered in its *body* (Merleau-Ponty) or is related eccentrically to itself, regarding its body as an object (Plessner). Thought that is tied to the philosophy of the subject cannot bridge over these dichotomies but, as Foucault so acutely diagnosed, oscillates helplessly between one and the other pole.

Not even the linguistic turn of praxis philosophy leads to a paradigm change. Speaking subjects are either masters or shepherds of their linguistic systems. Either they make use of language in a way that is creative of meaning, to disclose their world innovatively, or they are always already moving around within a horizon of world-disclosure taken care of for them by language itself and constantly shifting behind their backs —

language as the medium of creative practice (Castoriadis) or as differential event (Heidegger, Derrida).

Thanks to the approach of linguistic philosophy, Cornelius Castoriadis, with his theory of the imaginary institution, can boldly advance praxis philosophy. In order to give back again to the concept of social practice its revolutionary explosiveness and normative content, he conceives of action no longer expressivistically, but poetically-demiurgically, as the originless creation of absolutely new and unique patterns, whereby each of them discloses an incomparable horizon of meaning. The guarantee of the rational content of modernity — or self-consciousness, authentic self-realization, and self-determination in solidarity — is represented as an imaginary force creative of language. This, of course, comes uncomfortably close to a Being operating without reason. In the end, there is only a rhetorical difference between voluntaristic "institution" and fatalistic "dispensation."

According to Castoriadis, society is split (like transcendental subjectivity) into the generating and the generated, the instituting and the instituted, whereby the stream of the imaginary, as originative of meaning, flows into changing linguistic world views. This ontological creation of absolutely new, constantly different and unique totalities of meaning occurs like a dispensation of Being; one cannot see how this *demiurgic setting-in-action* of historical truths could be transposed into the *revolutionary project* proper to the practice of consciously acting, autonomous, self-realizing individuals. Autonomy and heteronomy are ultimately supposed to be assessed in terms of the authenticity of the self-transparency of a society that does not hide its imaginary origin beneath extrasocietal projections and knows itself explicitly as a self-instituting society. But who is the subject of this knowledge? Castoriadis acknowledges no reason for revolutionizing reified society except the existentialist resolve: "because we will it." Thus, he has to allow himself to be asked who this "we" of the radical willing might be, if indeed the socialized individuals are merely "instituted" by the "social imaginary." Castoriadis ends where Simmel began: with *Lebensphilosophie.*[19]

This results from the concept of language Castoriadis borrows from hermeneutics as well as from structuralism. Castoriadis proceeds — as do Heidegger, Derrida, and Foucualt, in their own ways — from the notion that an ontological difference exists between language and the things spoken about, between the constitutive understanding of the world and what is constituted in the world. This difference means that language discloses the horizon of meaning within which knowing and acting subjects interpret states of affairs, that is, encounter things and people and have experiences in dealing with them. The world-disclosing function of language is conceived on analogy with the generative accomplishments of transcendental consciousness, prescinding, naturally, from the sheerly formal and supratemporal character of the latter. The linguistic world view is a concrete and historical a priori; it fixes interpretative prespectives that are substantive and variable and that cannot be gone behind. This constitutive world-understanding changes independently of what subjects experience concerning conditions in the world interpreted in the light of this preunderstanding, and independently of what they can *learn* from their practical dealings with anything in the world. No matter whether this metahistorical transformation of linguistic world views is conceived of as Being, différance, power, or imagination, and whether it is endowed with connotations of a mystical experience of salvation, of aesthetic shock, of creaturely pain, or of creative intoxication: What all these concepts have in common is the peculiar uncoupling of the horizon-constituting productivity of language from the consequences of an intramundane practice that is wholly prejudiced by the linguistic system. Any interaction between world-disclosing language and learning processes in the world is excluded.

In this respect, praxis philosophy had distinguished itself sharply from every kind of linguistic historicism. It conceived of social production as the self-generative process of the species, and the transformation of external nature achieved through labor as an impulse to a learning self-transformation of our own nature. The world of ideas, in light of which socialized producers interpret a pregiven, historically formed nature, changes in turn as a function of the learning processes connected with their transformative activity. By no means does this *innerworldly praxis* owe its *world-building effects* to a mechanical dependence of the suprastructure upon the basis, but to two simple facts: The world of ideas is what first makes possible determinate interpretations of a nature that is then cooperatively worked upon; but it is affected in turn by the learning processes set in motion by social labor. Contrary to linguistic historicism, which hypostatizes the world-disclosing force of language, historical materialism takes into account (as do, later on, pragmatism and genetic structuralism) a dialectical relationship between the world-view structures that make intramundane practice possible by means of a prior understanding of meaning, on the one hand, and, on the other, learning processes deposited in the transformation of world-view structures.

This reciprocal causality goes back to an intrinsic connection between meaning and validity, which nevertheless does not eliminate the difference between the two. Meaning could not exhaust validity. Heidegger jumped to conclusions in identifying the disclosure of meaning-horizons with the truth of meaningful utterances; it is only the *conditions* for the validity of utterances that change with the horizon of meaning — the changed understanding of meaning has to prove itself in experience and in dealing with what can come up within its horizon. And yet praxis philosophy is unable to exploit the superiority it possesses in this respect, because, as we have seen, with its paradigm of production it screens out of the validity spectrum of reason every dimension except those of truth and efficiency. Accordingly, what is learned in innerworldly practice can only accumulate in the development of the forces of production. With this productivist conceptual strategy, the normative content of modernity can no longer be grasped; it can at most be tacitly used to circle about a purposive rationality that has grown into a totality in the exercise of an accusatory negative dialectics.

This unfortunate consequence may be what moved Castoriadis to entrust the rational content of socialism (that is, of a form of life that is supposed to make autonomy and self-realization in solidarity possible) to a demiurge creative of meaning, which brushes aside the difference between meaning and validity and no longer relies upon the profane verification of its creations. A totally different perspective results when we transfer the concept of praxis from labor to communicative action. Then we recognize the interdependences between world-disclosing systems of language and intramundane learning processes along the entire spectrum of validity: Learning processes are no longer channeled only into processes of social labor (and ultimately into cognitive-instrumental dealings with an objectified nature). As soon as we drop the paradigm of production, we can affirm the internal connection between meaning and validity for the whole reservoir of meaning — not just for the segment of meaning of linguistic expressions that play a role in assertoric and intentional sentences. In communicative action, which requires taking yes/no positions on claims of rightness and truthfulness no less than reactions to claims of truth and efficiency, the background knowledge of the lifeworld is submitted to an ongoing test across its entire breadth. To this extent, the concrete a priori of world-disclosing language systems is exposed — right down to their widely ramifying ontological presuppositions — to an indirect revision in the light of our dealings with the intramundane.

This does not mean that the internal connection between meaning and validity is to be undone now from the other side. The potency to create meaning, which in our day has largely retreated into aesthetic precincts, retains the contingency of genuinely innovative forces.

V

There is a more serious question: whether the concepts of communicative action and of the transcending force of universalistic validity claims do not reestablish an idealism that is incompatible with the naturalistic insights of historical materialism. Does not a lifeworld that is supposed to be reproduced only via the medium of action oriented to mutual understanding get cut off from its material life processes? Naturally, the lifeworld is materially reproduced by way of the results and consequences of the goal-directed actions with which its members intervene in the world. But these instrumental actions are interlaced with communicative ones insofar as they represent the execution of plans that are linked to the plans of other interaction participants by way of common definitions of situations and processes of mutual understanding. Along these paths, the solutions to problems in the sphere of social labor are also plugged into the medium of action oriented by mutual understanding. The theory of communicative action takes into account the fact that the symbolic reproduction of the lifeworld and its material reproduction are internally interdependent.

It is not so simple to counter the suspicion that with the concept of action oriented to validity claims the idealism of a pure, nonsituated reason slips in again, and the dichotomies between the realms of the transcendental and the empirical are given new life in another form.

There is no pure reason that might don linguistic clothing only in the second place. Reason is by its very nature incarnated in contexts of communicative action and in structures of the lifeworld.[20] To the extent that the plans and actions of different actors are interconnected in historical time and across social space through the use of speech oriented toward mutual agreement, taking yes/no positions on criticizable validity claims, however implicitly, gains a key function in *everyday* practice. Agreement arrived at through communication, which is measured by the intersubjective recognition of validity claims, makes possible a networking of social interactions and lifeworld contexts. Of course, these validity claims have a Janus face: As claims, they transcend any local context; at the same time, they have to be raised here and now and be de facto recognized if they are going to bear the agreement of interaction participants that is needed for effective cooperation. The transcendent moment of *universal* validity bursts every provinciality asunder; the obligatory moment of accepted validity claims renders them carriers of a *context-bound* everyday practice. Inasmuch as communicative agents reciprocally raise validity claims with their speech acts, they are relying on the potential of assailable grounds. Hence, a moment of *unconditionality* is built into *factual* processes of mutual understanding — the validity laid claim to is distinguished from the social currency of a de facto established practice and yet serves it as the foundation of an existing consensus. The validity claimed for propositions and norms transcends spaces and times, "*blots out*" *space and time*; but the claim is always raised *here and now*, in specific contexts, and is either accepted or rejected with factual consequences for action. Karl-Otto Apel speaks in a suggestive way about the entwinement of the real communication community with an ideal one.[21]

The communicative practice of everyday life is, as it were, reflected in itself. This "reflection" is no longer a matter of the cognitive subject relating to itself in an objectivating manner. The stratification of discourse and action built into communicative action takes the place of this prelinguistic and isolated reflection. For factually raised validity claims point directly or indirectly to arguments by which they can be worked out and in some cases resolved. This argumentative debate about hypothetical validity claims can be described as the reflective form of communicative action: a relation-to-self that does without the compulsion to objectification found in the basic concepts of the philosophy of the subject. That is to say, the "vis-à-vis" of proponents and opponents reproduces at a reflective level that basic form of intersubjective relationship which always mediates the self-relation of the speaker through the performative relation to an addressee. The tense interconnection of the ideal and the real is also, and especially clearly, manifest in discourse itself. Once participants enter into argumentation, they cannot avoid supposing, in a reciprocal way, that the conditions for an ideal speech situation have been sufficiently met. And yet they realize that their discourse is never definitively "purified" of the motives and compulsions that have been filtered out. As little as we can do without the supposition of a purified discourse, we have equally to make do with "unpurified" discourse.

At the end of the fifth lecture, I indicated that the internal connection between contexts of justification and contexts of discovery, between validity and genesis, is never utterly severed. The task of justification, or, in other words, the critique of validity claims carried out from the perspective of a participant, cannot ultimately be separated from a genetic consideration that issues in an ideology critique — carried out from a third-person perspective — of the mixing of power claims and validity claims. Ever since Plato and Democritus, the history of philosophy has been dominated by two opposed impulses: One relentlessly elaborates the transcendent power of abstractive reason and the emancipatory unconditionality of the intelligible, whereas the other strives to unmask the imaginary purity of reason in a materialist fashion.

In contrast, dialectical thought has enlisted the subversive power of materialism to undercut these false alternatives. It does not respond to the banishment of everything empirical from the realm of ideas merely by scornfully reducing relationships of validity to the powers that triumph behind their back. Rather, the theory of communicative action regards the dialectic of knowing and not knowing as embedded within the dialectic of successful and unsuccessful mutual understanding.

Communicative reason makes itself felt in the binding force of intersubjective understanding and reciprocal recognition. At the same time, it circumscribes the universe of a common form of life. Within this universe, the irrational cannot be separated from the rational in the same way as, according to Parmenides, ignorance could be separated from the kind of knowledge that, as the absolutely affirmative, rules over the "nothing." Following Jacob Böhme and Isaac Luria, Schelling correctly insisted that mistakes, crimes, and deceptions are not simply without reason; they are forms of manifestation of the inversion of reason. The violation of claims to truth, correctness, and sincerity affects the whole permeated by the bond of reason. There is no escape and no refuge for the few who are in the truth and are supposed to take their leave of the many who stay behind in the darkness of their blindness, as the day takes leave of the night. Any violation of the structures of rational life together, to which all lay claim, affects everyone equally. This is what the young Hegel meant by the ethical totality that is disrupted by the deed of the criminal and that can only be restored by insight into the indivisibility of suffering due to alienation. The same idea motivates Klaus Heinrich in his confrontation of Parmenides with Jonah.

In the idea of the convenant made by Yahweh with the people of Israel, there is the germ of the dialectic of betrayal and avenging force: "Keeping the covenant with God is the symbol of fidelity; breaking this covenant is the model of betrayal. To keep faith with God is to keep faith with life-giving Being itself — in oneself and others. To deny it in any domain of being means breaking the covenant with God and betraying one's own foundation. . . . Thus, betrayal of another is simultaneously betrayal of oneself; and every protest against betrayal is not just protest in one's own name, but in the name of the other at the same time. . . . The idea that each being is potentially a 'covenant partner' in the fight against betrayal, including anyone who betrays himself and me, is the only counterbalance against the stoic resignation already formulated by Parmenides when he made a cut between those who know and the mass of the ignorant. The concept of 'enlightenment' familiar to us is unthinkable without the concept of a potentially universal confederation against betrayal."[22] Peirce and Mead were the first to raise this religious motif of a confederation to philosophical status in the form of a consensus theory of truth and a communication theory of society. The theory of communicative action joins itself with this pragmatist tradition; like Hegel in his early fragment on crime and punishment, it, too, lets itself be guided by an intuition that can be expressed in the concepts of the Old Testament as follows: In the restlessness of the real conditions of life, there broods an ambivalence that is due to the dialectic of betrayal and avenging force.[23]

In fact, we can by no means always, or even only often, fulfill those improbable pragmatic presuppositions from which we nevertheless set forth in day-to-day communicative practice — and, in the sense of transcendental necessity, from which we *have to* set forth. For this reason, sociocultural forms of life stand under the structural restrictions of a communicative reason *at once claimed and denied.*

The reason operating in communicative action not only stands under, so to speak, external, situational constraints; its own conditions of possibility necessitate its branching out into the dimensions of historical time, social space, and body-centered experiences. That is to say, the rational potential of speech is interwoven with the *resources* of any particular given lifeworld. To the extent that the lifeworld fulfills the resource function, it has the character of an intuitive, unshakeably certain, and holistic knowledge, which cannot be made problematic at will — and in this respect it does not represent "knowledge" in any strict sense of the word. This amalgam of background assumptions, solidarities, and skills bred through socialization constitutes a conservative counterweight against the risk of dissent inherent in processes of reaching understanding that work through validity claims.

As a resource from which interaction participants support utterances capable of reaching consensus, the lifeworld constitutes an equivalent for what the philosophy of the subject had ascribed to consciousness in general as synthetic accomplishments. Now, of course, the generative accomplishments are related not to the form but to the content of possible mutual understanding. To this extent, *concrete* forms of life replace transcendental consciousness in its function of creating unity. In culturally embodied self-understandings, intuitively present group solidarities, and the competences of socialized individuals that are brought into play as know-how, the reason expressed in communicative action is mediated with the traditions, social practices, and body-centered complexes of experience that coalesce into *particular* totalities. These particular forms of life, which only emerge in the plural, are certainly not connected with each other only through a web of family resemblances; they exhibit structures common to lifeworlds in general. But these universal structures are only stamped on particular life forms through the medium of action oriented to mutual understanding by which they have to be reproduced. This explains why the importance of these universal structures can increase in the course of historical processes of differentiation. This is also the key to the rationalization of the lifeworld and to the successive release of the rational potential contained in communicative action. This historical tendency can account for the normative content of a modernity threatened by self-destruction without drawing upon the constructions of the philosophy of history.

Excursus on Cornelius Castoriadis:
The Imaginary Institution

The fact that poststructuralism, with its wholesale rejection of modern forms of life, finds an audience is surely connected with the fact that the efforts of praxis philosophy to reformulate the project of modernity along Marxist lines has suffered a loss in credibility. The young Marcuse made the first attempt to renew praxis philosophy out of the spirit of Husserl and Heidegger. Sartre followed him in this with his *Critique of Dialectical Reason*. Castoriadis has given this tradition new life by introducing a unique linguistic turn. His work has a central place among the new departures in praxis philosophy that have evolved since the mid-1960s, especially in Eastern Europe (in Prague, Budapest, Zagreb, and Belgrade), and that for a decade enlivened the discussions at the Summer School of Korčula. It is the most original, ambitious, and reflective attempt to think through the liberating mediation of history, society, external and internal nature once again as praxis.

Castoriadis, too, starts from the "contradiction" between living and dead labor. Capitalism has simultaneously to "lay claim to human activity, in the most proper sense, on the part of subjects under its sway . . . and to dehumanize this activity."[1] The cooperation of self-governing industrial workers serves here as the model for a praxis that has not been dehumanized. But Castoriadis does not develop this activity in an emphatic sense along the lines of processing and technically producing objects. Like mere reflex action, instrumental action also constitutes a contrasting limit case from which essential characteristics of praxis as self-actuation is lacking: Action is reduced to predictable behavioral routines in both types. Castoriadis (like Aristotle) finds the characteristics of an unabridged praxis in instances of political, artistic, medical, and educational practice. They all bear their purposes within themselves and cannot be reduced to the purposive-rational organization of means. Praxis follows a project, not in the manner in which a theory precedes its application, but as an anticipation that can be corrected and enlarged in the course of practical enactment. Praxis is related to a totality of life achievements in which it is at the same time embedded; as a totality, it escapes any objectifying grasp. And finally, praxis aims at promoting autonomy, from which, at the same time, it itself issues: "What is striven for (the development of autonomy) stands in an intimate relationship with that whereby the striving occurs (the exercise of autonomy). . . . To be sure, it has to take into account the concrete network of causal relations that pervade its domain. Still, in choosing its mode of operation, praxis can never simply follow some calculus — not because this would be too complicated, but because such a means prescinds *per definitionem* from the decisive factor — autonomy" (129).

Castoriadis goes beyond the Aristotelian concept by radicalizing the specification that praxis is always directed toward others as toward autonomous beings, through adding the proviso that no one can seriously will autonomy without willing it *for all* (183). Then, too, the further specification that praxis is future-oriented and brings new things into being is owed to the modern consciousness of time. By taking initiative, the agent transcends all given determinations and makes a new beginning. Praxis is essentially creative and generates the "radically other." Above all, emancipatory praxis is creative *par excellence*, and Castoriadis would like to free it from all theoreticist misunderstandings. Such praxis is aimed at the transformation "of present society into another one established organizationally for the autonomy of everyone. And carrying out this change has to come from people's autonomous action" (134). Enlightenment through social theory is guided by this interest. The revolutionary project surely directs the analysis of historical processes. But we can always only know history within and from history: "The ultimate point of conjunction for these two projects — of understanding and of transforming — can always only be discovered in the living present of history, which would not be a historical present if it did not transcend itself toward a future that we still have to make" (281).

Thus, Castoriadis revives the Aristotelian concept of praxis with the help of a radical hermeneutic self-interpretation of modern time-consciousness, in order to work out the original meaning of an emancipatory politics against Marxist dogmatism. Yet this actionist construction of praxis would scarcely go beyond the position once aimed against the orthodoxy of the Second International by Karl Korsch if Castoriadis did not develop a political philosophy and social theory from this starting point. In doing so, he is concerned with concepts of the political and social that generalize in a certain way the specific meaning of revolutionary praxis. In a manner quite similar to Hannah Arendt,[2] Castoriadis directs his gaze toward those rare historical moments in which the mass, from which institutions are formed, is still in flux — that is, toward the productive moments of the *foundation* of new institutions: "Those moments in which society as instituting breaks into society as instituted, in which society as already institutionally set up destroys itself with the help of society as founding institutions (that is, in which it creates itself as a *different* institutional order) provide a vivid and exciting picture . . . of the social-historical 'now.' . . . Even a society that appears concerned only to conserve itself persists only through ceaselessly changing itself" (342ff.).

Castoriadis works out the normal case of the political from the limit case of the act of founding an institution; and he interprets this in turn from a horizon of aesthetic experience, as the ecstatic moment erupting from the continuum of time when something absolutely new is founded. Only in this way does he think he can lay bare the essentially productive core of the reproduction of society. Social process is the generation of radically different patterns, a demiurge setting itself to work, the continuous creation of new types embodied in ever different exemplary ways — in short, the self-positing and ontological genesis of ever new "worlds." In this conception, the late Heidegger is combined with the early Fichte in a Marxist fashion. The self-instituting society replaces the self-positing subject; what gets instituted is a creative world-interpretation, an innovative meaning, a new universe of significations. Castoriadis calls this world-disclosing meaning the central imaginary dimension — it gushes up as a magma of meanings from the volcano of historical time into the institutions of society: "Without a productive, creative, or . . . radical imaginary dimension, as revealed in the indivisible unity of social action and the simultaneous elaboration of a universe of meaning, history is neither possible nor conceivable" (251). The imaginary dimension determines the lifestyle, the *Volksgeist*, of a society or an epoch. Castoriadis talks about a "primordial occupation of world and self by a meaning that has not been dictated to a society by real factors, because, on the contrary, it is this meaning that assigns these real factors their importance and preferred place in the universe" (220).

Everything else depends, of course, on how Castoriadis correlates society as the instituting of a world with intramundane praxis. He is interested in a self-conscious, autonomous conduct of life, which is supposed to make possible authentic self-realization and freedom in solidarity. He has to solve the problem of conceiving the world-disclosing function of language in such a way that it can connect up with a concept of praxis with normative content. My thesis is that Castoriadis lacks a solution, because his concept of society in terms of fundamental ontology leaves no room for an intersubjective praxis for which socialized individuals are *accountable*. In the end, social praxis disappears in the anonymous hurly-burly of the institutionalization of ever new worlds from the imaginary dimension.

Castoriadis correctly stresses the equiprimordiality of saying and doing, speaking and making, *legein* and *teukhein*, against a productivist narrowing of the concept of praxis. In both these dimensions, human action is related to something in the world — to the at once resistant and yet workable material encountered in the world and in need of interpretation. Castoriadis has only the concept of the objective world at his disposal for this "primary stratum" upon which society has to "rely"; it is nature or the totality of entities that provides counterpressure to any given socially instituted world. Accordingly, "making" is reduced to purposive intervention in the world of existing states of affairs, and "speaking" to the logical semantics of fact-reporting speech insofar as it is constitutive for the functional circuit of instrumental action. *Legein* und *teukhein* are forms of expression of identity thinking: "Just as *legein* embodies the identifying and quantitative-logical dimension of language and of social communication, so this dimension of social action is materialized in *teukhein*" (442). Moreover, the natural substrate of what can be encountered in the world is, in a wholly conventional manner, brought under subject-object relationships and conceived as something that can be represented or produced. However, the social praxis being considered by Castoriadis transcends any embodiment of identity thinking or of purposive rationality. This is why the understanding [*Verstand*], which occurs here as the faculty governed by the logic of identity and of sets, while it is not supposed to operate in the light of reason [*Vernunft*], is supposed to be overwhelmed by the plenitude of meaning overflowing from the imaginary dimension. The world of objects conceived in terms of the philosophy of the subject is a framework that merely secures contact with the innerworldly substrate of nature in the dimensions of representing and producing. Everything encountered in these contact zones and mediated by *legein* and *teukhein*, however, is already disclosed within a prior horizon of meaning. And this is owed solely to the imaginary dimension.

Intramundane praxis can gain no independence in relation to the power of this imaginary magma of meaning, because the concept of language used by Castoriadis permits no differentiation between meaning and validity. As with Heidegger, the "truth" of semantic world-disclosure also founds the propositional truth of statements; it prejudices the validity of linguistic utterances generally. As a result, intramundane praxis cannot get learning processes going. At any rate, there is no accumulation of knowledge that could affect the previous interpretation of the world and burst a given totality of meaning — not even in the dimensions of the natural sciences and the forces of production: "Indeed, the naturally given always impinges upon society as something resistant, but also as something that can be shaped; however, *what* it is that is resistant or workable — as well as how — depends on the given social world under consideration. That hydrogen atoms can be fused is a statement that has meaning for the present society and no other" (581). Why a society institutes a specific horizon of meanings is a question Castoriadis has to reject as meaningless. One cannot ask about the provenance of what exists from time immemorial (589). The institution of any world is a creation *ex nihilo* (591).

When the relationship of the world-disclosing imaginary dimension to labor and interaction is set up in this way, however, one can no longer conceive of autonomous action as intramundane praxis; instead, Castoriadis has to assimilate it to the language-creating, world-projecting, world-devouring praxis of the social demiurge itself. But praxis thereby loses precisely the traits of human action that Castoriadis rightly emphasizes — the characteristics of a context-dependent intersubjective undertaking under finite conditions. The finitude of praxis is traceable not just to the resistance of a workable external nature, but also to the constraints of an existence that is historical, social, and embodied. A praxis that coincides with the *creatio continua* of novel interpretations of the world and with ontological genesis, itself projects the historical times and the social spaces, and itself opens up the dimensions for possible constraints. To be sure, Castoriadis uses the figures of thought familiar to us from theogony and from Fichte's *Wissenschaftslehre* to set internal limits, in the form of an institutionalized society, to the infinite actuality of a self-instituting society. As in the expressivist model of a spirit that loses itself in its own objectifications, the breaking point of self-alienation is built into the ontological model of society. If the productive flow of ontological genesis comes to a standstill, the institutionalized society becomes hardened in relation to its own origins: "The alienation or heteronomy of society is a self-alienation in which society conceals both its own being as self-institution and its essential temporality" (608).

This conception has two unfortunate consequences. By assimilating intramundane praxis to a linguistic world-disclosure hypostatized into a history of Being, Castoriadis can no longer *localize* the political struggle for an autonomous way of life —

the very emancipatory, creative-projective praxis with which Castoriadis is ultimately concerned. For he either has to call the agents back, as Heidegger does, from their intramundane, subject-crazed lostness into the sphere of the nonmanipulable, and thus into an auratic heteronomy vis-à-vis the primordial happening of a self-instituting society — and this would amount only to an ironic inversion of praxis philosophy into another variant of poststructuralism. Or he has to displace the autonomy of social praxis, which cannot be redeemed intra-mundanely, into the primordial happening itself — but then he has to support the world-disclosing productivity of language on an absolute ego and return in fact to a speculative philosophy of consciousness. This fits with the personification of society as a poetic demiurge that releases ever new world-types from itself. In this case, the theodicy problem recurs in a new form: To whom should the fall of institutionalized society from the origins of its self-instituting be attributed, if not to the language-creating demiurge?

The second, far more earthly but hardly less unfortunate consequence is the return of a problem belabored in vain by the philosophy of consciousness from Fichte to Husserl: an explanation of the intersubjectivity of social praxis that is compelled to begin from the premise of isolated consciousness. Castoriadis postulates a second stream of the imaginary dimension, namely, in the individual unconscious, which constitutes the monadic core of subjectivity in early childhood. In the process, it becomes clear that the imaginary dimension, the image-creating fantasy steered by drives, is even prior to language as the world-constituting medium of the imaginary dimension of society. From this prelinguistic fantasy-production on the part of inner nature (familiar to Castoriadis as a psychoanalyst), there issues in each case a new and unique private world that runs up against the socially institutionalized world in the course of childhood development and gets integrated in and subordinated to the latter after the resolution of the oedipal conflict. The psychic streams of the imaginary dimension have their source in the springs of each's own subjective nature. They compete with the collective stream of the imaginary dimension emanating from society in a manner similar to that in which private worlds compete with public ones. Socialized individuals do not enter into intersubjective relationships with one another in any genuine sense of the term. In the socially institutionalized world view, everyone is previously in mutual agreement with everyone else, a priori, as if there were a transcendental consciousness; as they grow up, individuals try to assert their respective private worlds, as monads, against this preestablished harmony. Castoriadis cannot provide us with a figure for the mediation between the individual and society. Society breaks down the childlike monads and transforms them. The type proper to the socially institutionalized world is impressed upon the individual. Thus, the process of socialization is depicted on the model of crafts production. The socialized individual is produced and, as in Durkheim, remains divided into monad and member of society. Castoriadis calls the oedipal separation, which "becomes for the individual a fixed, well-distinguished installation of a private and a public world" (498), a puzzle: "If one does not wish to close one's eyes to what psyche and society are, one cannot help but notice that the social individual does not grow like a plant but is created/fabricated by society. This, of course, requires a violent break with the initial state of the psyche and its demands — a break that only a social institution can effect" (524). Intrapsychic conflicts are not internally linked with social ones; instead, psyche and society stand in a kind of metaphysical opposition to one another.

If, with George Herbert Mead, we understand the process of socialization itself as one of individuation, the sought-for mediation between individual and society is less "puzzling." Then, of course, the structuralist concept of language, restricted to the logical-semantic dimension, has to be expanded; language has to be conceived of as a medium that both draws each participant in interaction into a community of communication, as one of its members, and at the same time subjects him to an unrelenting compulsion toward individuation. That is to say, the integration of the perspectives of speaker, hearer, and observer, as well as the intermeshing of this structure with a system of world perspectives that coordinates the objective world with the social and the subjective worlds, are pragmatic presuppositions of a correct use of grammatical sentences in speech acts.[3]

If, with the help of this pragmatically expanded notion of language, one reformulates the concept of praxis in the sense of communicative action, the universal characteristics of praxis are no longer confined to *legein* and *teukhein,* that is, to the conditions (requiring interpretation) for contact with a nature that is encountered in the functional circuit of instrumental action. Praxis then operates instead in the light of a communicative reason, which imposes on interaction participants an orientation toward validity claims and thereby makes possible a world-*transforming* accumulation of knowledge. To be sure, in communicative action, too, particular lifeworld contexts are due to the world-*disclosing* function of a language that is shared by the respective participants. And the linguistic system also sets the conditions for the validity of utterances generated by its means. But now the internal connection between meaning and validity is symmetrical: The meaning of an utterance does not prejudice whether conditions of validity and the correlative validity claims are satisfied within intramundane, world-appropriating praxis or not. Social praxis is linguistically constituted, but language, too, has to *prove itself* through this praxis, in terms of what is encountered within the horizon disclosed by it. However, if world-disclosure and proven praxis in the world mutually presuppose one another, then meaning-creating innovations are so intermeshed with learning processes, and both of them are so anchored in the general structures of action oriented toward reaching understanding, that the reproduction of a lifeworld always takes place *also* by virtue of the productivity of its members.

XII

The Normative Content of
Modernity

I

The radical critique of reason exacts a high price for taking
leave of modernity. In the first place, these discourses can and
want to give no account of their own position. Negative dialectics, genealogy, and deconstruction alike avoid those categories
in accord with which modern knowledge has been differentiated — by no means accidentally — and on the basis of which
we today understand texts. They cannot be unequivocally classified with either philosophy or science, with moral and legal
theory, or with literature and art. At the same time, they resist
any return to forms of religious thought, whether dogmatic or
heretical. So an incongruity arises between these "theories,"
which raise validity claims only to renounce them, and the kind
of institutionalization they undergo within the business of science. There is an asymmetry between the rhetorical gesture
with which these discourses demand understanding and the
critical treatment to which they are subjected institutionally,
for example in the framework of an academic lecture. No
matter whether Adorno paradoxically reclaims truth-validity,
or Foucault refuses to draw consequences from manifest contradictions; no matter whether Heidegger and Derrida evade
the obligation to provide grounds by fleeing into the esoteric
or by fusing the logical with the rhetorical: There always
emerges a symbiosis of incompatibles, an amalgam that resists
"normal" scientific analysis at its core. Things are only shifted

to a different place if we change the frame of reference and no longer treat the same discourse as philosophy or science, but as a piece of literature. That the self-referential critique of reason is located everywhere and nowhere, so to speak, in discourses without a place, renders it almost immune to competing interpretations. Such discourses unsettle the institutionalized standards of fallibilism; they always allow for a final word, even when the argument is already lost: that the opponent has misunderstood the meaning of the language game and has committed a category mistake in the *sorts* of responses he has been making.

The variations of a critique of reason with reckless disregard for its own foundations are related to one another in another respect as well. They are guided by normative intuitions that go beyond what they can accommodate in terms of the indirectly affirmed "other of reason." Whether modernity is described as a constellation of life that is reified and used, or as one that is technologically manipulated, or as one that is totalitarian, rife with power, homogenized, imprisoned — the denunciations are constantly inspired by a special sensitivity for complex injuries and subtle violations. Inscribed in this sensitivity is the picture of an undamaged intersubjectivity that the young Hegel first projected as an ethical totality. With the counterconcepts (injected as empty formulas) of Being, sovereignty, power, difference, and nonidentity, this critique points to the contents of aesthetic experience; but the values derived therefrom and explicitly laid claim to — the values of grace and illumination, ecstatic rapture, bodily integrity, wish-fulfillment, and caring intimacy — do not cover the moral change that these authors tacitly envision in connection with a life practice that is intact — and not only in the sense of reconciling inner nature. Between the declared normative foundations and the concealed ones there is a disparity that can be explained by the *undialectical* rejection of subjectivity. Not only the devastating consequences of an objectifying relation-to-self are condemned along with this principle of modernity, but also the *other* connotations once associated with subjectivity as an unredeemed promise: the prospect of a self-conscious practice, in which the solidary self-determination of all was to be joined with the self-realization of each. What is thrown out is precisely what a modernity reassuring itself once meant by the concepts of self-consciousness, self-determination, and self-realization.

A further defect of these discourses is explained by their totalizing repudiation of modern forms of life: Although they are interesting in regard to fundamentals, they remain undifferentiated in their results. The criteria according to which Hegel and Marx, and even Max Weber and Lukács, distinguished between emancipatory-reconciling aspects of social rationalization and repressive-alienating aspects have been blunted. In the meantime, critique has taken hold of and demolished the sorts of concepts by which those aspects could be distinguished from one another so that their paradoxical entanglement became visible. Enlightenment and manipulation, the conscious and the unconscious, forces of production and forces of destruction, expressive self-realization and repressive desublimation, effects that ensure freedom and those that remove it, truth and ideology — now all these moments flow into one another. They are not linked to one another as, say, conflicting elements in a disastrous functional context — unwilling accomplices in a contradictory process permeated by oppositional conflict. Now the differences and oppositions are so undermined and even collapsed that critique can no longer discern contrasts, shadings, and ambivalent tones within the flat and faded landscape of a totally administered, calculated, and power-laden world. To be sure, Adorno's theory of the administered world and Foucault's theory of power are more fertile, and simply more informative, than Heidegger's or Derrida's lucubrations on technology as an instrumental frame [*Gestell*] or on the totalitarian nature of the political order. But they are all insensitive to the highly *ambivalent* content of cultural and social modernity. This leveling can also be seen in the diachronic comparison of modern forms of life with premodern ones. The high price earlier exacted from the mass of the population (in the dimensions of bodily labor, material conditions, possibilities of individual choice, security of law and punishment, political participation, and schooling) is barely even noticed.

It is worthy of note that in the various approaches to the critique of reason, no systematic place is envisaged for everyday practice. Pragmatism, phenomenology, and hermeneutic philosophy have bestowed an epistemological status upon the categories of everyday action, speech, and common life. Marx even singled out everyday practice as the locus where the rational content of philosophy was supposed to flow into the life forms of an emancipated society. But Nietzsche so directed the gaze of his successors to the phenomena of the extraordinary that they contemptuously glide over the practice of everyday life as something derivative or inauthentic. As we have seen,[1] in communicative action the creative moment of the linguistic constitution of the world forms *one syndrome* with the cognitive-instrumental, moral-practical, and expressive moments of the intramundane linguistic functions of representation, interpersonal relation, and subjective expression. In the modern world, "value spheres" have been differentiated out from each of these moments — namely, on the one hand, art, literature, and a criticism specialized in questions of taste, around the axis of *world-disclosure*; and, on the other hand, problem-solving discourses specialized in questions of truth and justice, around the axis of *intramundane learning processes*. These knowledge systems of art and criticism, science and philosophy, law and morality, have become the more split off from ordinary communication the more strictly and one-sidedly they each have to do with one linguistic function and one aspect of validity. But they should not be considered on account of this abstraction per se as phenomena of decline symptomatic of subject-centered reason.

To Nietzscheanism, the differentiation of science and morality appears as the formative process of a reason that at once usurps and stifles the poetic, world-disclosing power of art. Cultural modernity seems a realm of horrors, marked by the totalitarian traits of a subject-centered reason that structurally overburdens itself. Three simple facts are filtered out of this picture: First, the fact that those aesthetic experiences in the light of which true nature is supposed to reveal itself to an exclusive reason are due to the same process of differentiation as science and morality. Then the fact that cultural modernity also owes its division into special discourses for questions of taste, truth, and justice to an increase in knowledge that is hard to dispute. And especially the fact that it is only the modalities of interchange between these knowledge systems and everyday practice that determine whether the gains from such abstraction affect the lifeworld destructively.

From the viewpoint of individual cultural spheres of value, the syndrome of the everyday world appears as "life" or as "practice" or as "ethos," over against which stands "art" or "theory" or "morality." We have already spoken about the mediating roles of criticism and philosophy in another context. For criticism, the relationship between "art" and "life" is just as problematic as the relationship between "theory" and "practice" or between "morality" and "ethos" is for philosophy. The *unmediated* transposition of specialized knowledge into the private and public spheres of the everyday world can endanger the autonomy and independent logics of the knowledge systems, on the one hand, and it can violate the integrity of lifeworld contexts, on the other. A knowledge specialized in only one validity claim, which, without sticking to its specific context, bounces across the whole spectrum of validity, unsettles the equilibrium of the lifeworld's communicative infrastructure. Insufficiently complex incursions of this sort lead to the aestheticizing, or the scienticizing, or the moralizing of particular domains of life and give rise to effects for which expressivist countercultures, technocratically carried out reforms, or fundamentalist movements can serve as drastic examples.

The profounder paradoxes of *societal* rationalization, however, are still not even touched by the complicated relationships between ordinary and expert *cultures*. They have to do with the systematically induced reification of everyday practice, to which I will return presently. However, the very first steps along the path to differentiation in the picture of the ambiguously rationalized lifeworld of modern societies already bring to our awareness the problem that will concern us in this last lecture.

De-differentiations are built into the leveling critique of reason only on the basis of descriptions that are guided in turn by normative intuitions. This normative content has to be acquired and justified from the rational potential inherent in everyday practice, if it is not to remain arbitrary. The concept of a communicative reason that transcends subject-centered reason, which I have provisionally introduced, is intended to lead away from the paradoxes and levelings of a self-referential critique of reason. On another front, it has to be upheld against the competing approach of a systems theory that utterly shoves the problematic of rationality aside, strips away *any* notion of reason as an old European drag, and then light-footedly takes over from the philosophy of the subject (as well as from the theory of power advanced by its sharpest opponents). This double battlefront makes the rehabilitation of the concept of reason a doubly risky business. It has to protect itself on both flanks from getting caught in the traps of the kind of subject-centered thinking that failed to keep the unforced force of reason free both from the *totalitarian* characteristics of an *instrumental* reason that objectifies everything around it, itself included, and from the *totalizing* characteristics of an *inclusive* reason that incorporates everything and, as a unity, ultimately triumphs over every distinction. Praxis philosophy hoped to derive the normative content of modernity from the reason embodied in the mediations of social practice. If the basic concept of communicative action replaces that of social labor, is the totality-perspective built into that concept radically altered?

II

According to Marx, social praxis extends in the dimensions of historical time and social space; within the horizon of a surrounding *nature-in-itself*, which also cosmically encompasses the history of the species, it mediates the *subjective nature* of cooperating individuals with the *nature objectivated* by our bodily interventions. The mediating process of labor is therefore related to nature under three different aspects: to the *experienced* needs and desires of subjective nature; to the objective nature *apprehended* and *elaborated through objectification*; to the nature *presupposed* by labor as its horizon and foundation. As we have seen in the third lecture, labor is thereby interpreted along the lines of an aesthetics of production and portrayed as a circular process of externalizing, objectifying, and appropriating essential forces. Accordingly, the process of the self-mediation of nature assumes into itself the *self-realization* of the acting *subjects* functioning within it. Both are processes of self-generation; they are produced out of their own products. Similarly, the society issuing from this praxis is conceived as a product of the forces and relationships of production created within it and by it. This figure of thought from praxis philosophy forces us to permit the moments of labor and nature — initially related distinctly to one another — to be absorbed into the totality of a self-referential process of reproduction. Ultimately, it is nature itself that reproduces itself through the reproduction of the subject-writ-large, society, and of the subjects active within it. Marx did not escape the totality thinking of Hegel. This changes if social praxis is no longer thought of primarily as a labor process.

The complementary concepts of communicative action and lifeworld introduce a difference that — unlike the difference between labor and nature — is not reabsorbed into a higher unity as its moments. To be sure, the reproduction of the lifeworld is nourished by the contributions of communicative action, even as the latter is dependent in turn upon the resources of the lifeworld.[2] But we should not think of this circular process on the model of self-generation, as a production out of its own products, and then associate it with self-realization. Otherwise, we would hypostatize the process of mutual understanding into an event of mediation (as happens to the labor process in praxis philosophy) and inflate the lifeworld into the totality of a higher-level subject (as happens to spirit in the philosophy of reflection). The difference between lifeworld and communicative action is not taken back in any unity; it is even *deepened* to the extent that the reproduction of the lifeworld is no longer merely routed *through* the medium of action oriented toward reaching understanding, but is saddled *on* the interpretative performances of its agents. To the degree that the yes/no decisions that sustain the communicative practice of everyday life do not derive from an ascribed normative

consensus, but emerge from the cooperative interpretative processes of the participants themselves, *concrete* forms of life and
universal structures of the lifeworld become separated. Naturally, there are family resemblances among the plurality of
totalities of life forms; they overlap and interlock, but they are
not embraced in turn by some supertotality. Multiplicity and
diffusion arise in the course of an abstraction process through
which the *contents* of particular lifeworlds are set off ever more
starkly from the universal *structures* of the lifeworld.

Considered as a *resource*, the lifeworld is divided in accord
with the "given" components of speech acts (that is, their propositional, illocutionary, and intentional components) into culture, society, and person. I call *culture*[3] the store of knowledge
from which those engaged in communicative action draw interpretations susceptible of consensus as they come to an understanding about something in the world. I call *society* (in the
narrower sense of a component of the lifeworld) the legitimate
orders from which those engaged in communicative action
gather a solidarity, based on belonging to groups, as they enter
into interpersonal relationships with one another. *Personality*
serves as a term of art for acquired competences that render a
subject capable of speech and action and hence able to participate in processes of mutual understanding in a given context
and to maintain his own identity in the shifting contexts of
interaction. This conceptual strategy breaks with the traditional
conception — also held by the philosophy of the subject and
praxis philosophy — that societies are composed of collectivities
and these in turn of individuals. Individuals and groups are
"members" of a lifeworld only in a metaphorical sense.

The symbolic reproduction of the lifeworld does take place
as a circular process. The structural nuclei of the lifeworld are
"made possible" by their correlative processes of reproduction,
and these in turn are "made possible" by contributions of communicative action. *Cultural reproduction* ensures that (in the semantic dimension) newly arising situations can be connected
up with existing conditions in the world; it secures the continuity of tradition and a coherency of knowledge sufficient
for the consensus needs of everyday practice. *Social integration*
ensures that newly arising situations (in the dimension of social

space) can be connected up with existing conditions in the world; it takes care of the coordination of action by means of legitimately regulated interpersonal relationships and lends constancy to the identity of groups. Finally, the *socialization* of members ensures that newly arising situations (in the dimension of historical time) can be connected up with existing world conditions; it secures the acquisition of generalized capacities for action for future generations and takes care of harmonizing individual life histories and collective life forms. Thus, interpretative schemata susceptible of consensus (or "valid knowledge"), legitimately ordered interpersonal relationships (or "solidarities"), and capacities for interaction (or "personal identities") are renewed in these three processes of reproduction.

If this is accepted as a theoretical description of a balanced and undistorted reproduction of the lifeworld, we can pursue the following question, first of all by means of a thought experiment: In which direction would the structures of the lifeworld have to vary if the undistorted reproduction of a concrete life form were to be less and less guaranteed by traditional, customary, time-tested, and consensual stocks of knowledge and had to be secured instead by a risky search for consensus, that is, by the cooperative achievements of those engaged in communicative action themselves?

This is certainly an idealized projection, but not an utterly arbitrary one, since actual lines of development in modern lifeworlds stand out against the background of this thought experiment: the abstraction of *universal* lifeworld structures from the particular configurations of totalities of forms of life that arise only as plural. On the cultural level, the traditional nuclei that guarantee identity separate off from the concrete contents with which they were once closely woven in mythical world views. They shrink to abstract elements such as concepts of the objective, social, and subjective worlds, presuppositions of communication, procedures of argumentation, abstract basic values, etc. On the level of society, general principles are crystallized out of the particular contexts to which they were once bound in primitive societies. In modern societies, principles of legality and morality prevail which are less and less tailored to particular life forms. On the level of personality, the cognitive structures acquired in the process of socialization are dissociated ever more emphatically from the contents of cultural knowledge with which they were initially integrated in "concrete thinking." The objects with respect to which formal competences can be exercised become ever more variable. If we single out of these trends only the degree of freedom gained by the structural components of the lifeworld, the following vanishing points result: for culture, a condition of the constant revision of traditions that have been unthawed, that is, that have become reflective; for society, a condition of the dependence of legitimate orders upon formal and ultimately discursive procedures for establishing and grounding norms; for personality, a condition of the risk-filled self-direction of a highly abstract ego-identity. There arise structural pressures toward the critical dissolution of guaranteed knowledge, the establishment of generalized values and norms, and self-directed individuation (since abstract ego-identities point toward self-realization in autonomous life projects).

This separation of form and content is a distant reminder of the traditional determination of a "rational practice": Self-consciousness returns in the form of a culture become reflexive; self-determination in the form of generalized values and norms; self-realization in that of the advanced individuation of socialized subjects. But the growth in reflexivity, in universalism, and in individuation undergone by the structural core of the lifeworld in the course of its differentiation now no longer fits the description of an intensification within the dimensions of the subject's relation-to-self. And only under this description — that is, from the perspective of the philosophy of the subject — could societal rationalization, the unfolding of the rational potential of social practice, be represented as the self-reflection of a societal macrosubject. The theory of communication can do without this figure of thought. Now the increasing reflexivity of culture, the generalization of values and norms, and the heightened individuation of socialized subjects, the enhancement of critical consciousness, autonomous will formation, and individuation — that is, the strengthening of the moments of rationality once attributed to the practice of subjects — takes place under conditions of an ever more extensive and ever more finely woven net of linguistically generated intersubjectivity. Rationalization of the lifeworld means differentiation and condensation at once — a thickening of the floating web of intersubjective threads that simultaneously holds together the ever more sharply differentiated components of culture, society, and person. The reproductive mode of the lifeworld does not change linearly in the direction indicated by the catchwords "reflexivity," "abstract universalism," and "individuation." Rather, the rationalized lifeworld secures the continuity of its contexts of meaning with the discontinuous tools of critique; it preserves the context of social integration by the risky means of an individualistically isolating universalism; and it sublimates the overwhelming power of the genealogical nexus into a fragile and vulnerable universality by means of an extremely individualized socialization. The more abstractly the differentiated structures of the lifeworld operate in the ever more particularized forms of life, the more the rational potential of action oriented toward reaching understanding evolves solely by these *means*. This can be clarified by the following thought experiment.

Continuities in the semantic field would not have to be severed even if cultural reproduction could now occur *only* by way of critique. In a structurally differentiated lifeworld, the development of the potential for negation inherent in the process of reaching agreement in language becomes a *necessary* condition for texts to connect up with one another and for traditions — which live, of course, from the power of conviction — to continue. Nor would the intersubjective net knit together in social space out of relations of reciprocal recognition have to be torn apart if social integration could now occur *only* by way of a universalism that was abstract and at the same time individualistically tailored. The procedures of discursive will formation established in the structurally differentiated lifeworld are set up to secure the social bond of all with all precisely through equal consideration of the interests of each individual. This means that as a participant in discourses, the individual, with his irreplaceable yes or no, is only fully on his own under the presupposition that he remains bound to a universal community by way of a cooperative quest for truth. Not even the substance of the universal within the historical succession of generations would have to dissolve away into nothing if processes of socialization could now advance *only* across the threshold of extreme individuation. In the structurally differentiated lifeworld, we merely acknowledge a principle that was in operation from the beginning: to wit, that socialization takes place in the same proportion as individuation, just as, inversely, individuals are constituted socially. With the system of personal pronouns, a relentless pressure toward individuation is built into the use of language oriented toward mutual understanding that is proper to socializing interaction. At the same time, the force of an intersubjectivity pressing toward socialization comes to the fore through the same linguistic medium.

Figures of thought from the theory of intersubjectivity thus render intelligible why critical testing and a fallibilist consciousness even enhance the continuity of a tradition that has stripped away its quasi-natural state of being. They make comprehensible why abstract, universalistic procedures for discursive will formation even strengthen solidarity in life contexts that are no longer legitimated by tradition. They help us to understand why an expanded scope for individuation and self-realization even condenses and stabilizes a process of socialization detached from fixed models of socialization.

If one retrieves the normative content of modernity in this manner — a content that gets away from the concepts of praxis philosophy, if not from its intentions — the three moments once assembled into the "dialectic of enlightenment" now fall apart: As the principle of modernity, subjectivity was supposed to determine its normative content as well; at the same time, subject-centered reason led to abstractions that fragmented the ethical totality; and yet only self-reflection, which emanated from subjectivity and strove to get beyond its narrow-mindedness, supposedly proved itself equal to the task of reconciliation. In its own way, praxis philosophy made this program its own. For Marx, the analysis of class antagonisms, their revolutionary overthrow, and the unleashing of the emancipatory content of stored-up forces of production were three conceptually interconnected moments. In this respect, the notion of reason derived from the structures of linguistically generated intersubjectivity and concretized in terms of rationaliation processes in the lifeworld provides no equivalent for the concept of an intrinsically rational praxis that was deployed in the philosophy of history. As soon as we give up praxis philosophy's understanding of society as a self-referential subject-writ-large, encompassing all individual subjects, the corresponding models for the diagnosis and mastery of crisis — division and revolution — are no longer applicable. Because the successive releasing of the rational potential inherent in communicative action is no longer thought of as self-reflection writ large, this specification of the normative content of modernity can prejudge neither the conceptual tools for diagnosing crises nor the way of overcoming them.

The probability of conflict-free reproduction by no means increases with the degree of rationalization of the lifeworld — it is only that the level at which conflicts can arise is shifted. With the differentiation of the structures of the lifeworld, the forms in which social pathologies appear are multiplied according to which aspects of which structural factors are insufficiently taken care of: Loss of meaning, conditions of anomie, and psychopathologies are the most obvious kinds of symptoms, but not the only ones.[4] As a result, the causes of social pathologies, which in the model of a division within a macro-subject are still *clustered* around class antagonism, now break up into widely scattered historical contingencies. The pathological characteristics of modern societies now fit into patterns only to the extent that a predominance of economic and bureaucratic rationality — of cognitive-instrumental forms of rationality generally — makes itself felt. The jagged profile of rationality potentials that *have been unevenly exploited* excludes from our explanatory approach the idea of a stagnated circular process of self-mediation in a *divided* macrosubject.[5]

It is obvious that with these considerations we have not yet touched at all on the question from which praxis philosophy started. As long as we leave the material reproduction of the lifeworld out of consideration, as we have until now, we will not even reach the level of the older problematic. Indeed, Marx selected "labor" as his basic category because he could see how the structures of bourgeois society were *ever more strongly* stamped by abstract labor, that is, by the type of gainful labor steered by the market, valorized in a capitalist fashion, and organized into businesses. In the meantime, this tendency has clearly slackened.[6] But the *type* of social pathology analyzed by Marx in terms of the real abstractions characteristic of alienated labor has not thereby disappeared.

III

The approach of communication theory seems to be able to salvage the normative content of modernity only at the cost of idealist abstractions. Once again suspicion is cast on the purism of a purely communicative reason — this time on an abstract description of rationalized lifeworlds that does not take into account the constraints of material reproduction. In order to defuse this suspicion, we have to show that the theory of communication can contribute to explaining how it is that in the modern period an economy organized in the form of markets is functionally intermeshed with a state that has a monopoly on power, how it gains autonomy as a piece of norm-free sociality over against the lifeworld, and how it opposes its own imperatives based on system maintenance to the rational imperatives of the lifeworld. Marx was the first to analyze this conflict between system imperatives and lifeworld imperatives, in the form of a dialectic of dead labor and living labor, of abstract labor and concrete labor; and he vividly illustrated it with materials from social history concerning the irruption of new modes of production into traditional lifeworlds. Meanwhile, the kind of system rationality that first became evident in the independent logic of capital self-realization has taken over other domains of action as well.

No matter how structurally differentiated lifeworlds may be, no matter whether they have developed highly specialized subsystems (and subparts of subparts of subsystems) for the functional domains of cultural reproduction, social integration, and socialization — the complexity of any lifeworld is narrowly restricted by the limits of the strain that can be placed upon the mechanism of mutual understanding. In the degree that a lifeworld is rationalized, the expenditure of understanding borne by the communicative agents themselves increases. This also increases the risk of dissent in a communication that generates a bonding effect only via the double negation of validity claims. Ordinary language is a risky mechanism for coordinating action; it is also expensive, immobile, and restricted in what it can accomplish. The meaning of the individual speech act cannot be detached from the lifeworld's complex horizon of meaning; it remains entwined with the intuitively present background knowledge of interaction participants. The plenitude of connotations, the functional richness, and the capacity for variation proper to the use of language oriented toward mutual understanding is only the reverse side of a relationship to totality that does not allow for any arbitrary expansion of the capacity to achieve understanding in everyday practice.

Because lifeworlds can afford only a restricted outlay for coordination and understanding, at a certain level of complexity ordinary language has to be disencumbered by the sorts of special languages that Talcott Parsons studied in connection with the example of money. When the medium for coordinating action no longer has to be called upon for *all* linguistic functions at once, then there is a disburdening effect. The binding of communicatively guided action to contexts of the lifeworld is also reduced by the partial replacement of ordinary language. Social processes set free in this way become "deworlded," that is, released from those relationships to the totality and those structures of intersubjectivity by which culture, society, and personality are interlaced with one another. Functions of material reproduction are especially open to this kind of disburdening because they do not per se need to be fulfilled by communicative actions. Changes in conditions in the material substrate can be traced back directly to the aggregate results and consequences of goal-directed interventions in the objective world. To be sure, these teleological actions need coordination too; they have to be socially integrated. But the integration can occur by way of an *impoverished* and *standardized* language that coordinates functionally specialized activities — for instance, the production and distribution of goods and services — without burdening social integration with the expense of risky and uneconomical processes of mutual understanding, and without connecting up with processes of cultural transmission and socialization through the medium of ordinary language. Evidently the medium of money satisfies these conditions for a specially encoded steering language. It has branched off from normal language as a special code that is tailored to special situations (of exchange); it conditions decisions for action on the basis of a built-in preference structure (of supply and demand), in a way that is effective for coordination but without having to lay claim to the resources of the lifeworld.

However, money makes possible not only specifically deworlded forms of interaction, but the formation of a functionally specialized subsystem that articulates its relationships to the environment via money. Considered historically, capitalism saw the rise of an economic system that regulates internal exchanges as well as interchanges with its noneconomic environments (private households and the state) through monetary channels. The institutionalization of wage labor on the one hand, and that of a state based on taxation on the other, was as constitutive of the new mode of production as was the organizational form of the capitalist enterprise inside the economic system. Complementary environments were formed in the measure that the productive process was shifted over to wage labor and the apparatus of government was linked to production via taxes on those employed. On the one side, the state apparatus became dependent upon a media-steered economic system; this led, among other things, to the assimilation of official and personal power to the structure of a steering medium; that is, power became assimilated to money. On the other side, traditional forms of labor and of life broke down under the grip of gainful labor organized in business enterprises. The plebeianizing of the rural population and the proletarianizing of the labor force highly concentrated in cities became the first exemplary case of a systemically induced reification of everyday practice.

With exchange processes operating through media there emerges in modern societies a third level of autonomous functional contexts — above the level of simple interactions as well as beyond the level of forms of organization still bound to the lifeworld. Contexts of interaction that have gained autonomy as subsystems and that go beyond the horizon of the lifeworld congeal into the second nature of a norm-free sociality. This decoupling of system from lifeworld is experienced within modern lifeworlds as a *reification of life forms*. Hegel reacted to this basic experience with the concept of the "positive" and the idea of a dirempted ethical totality; Marx started more specifically from alienated industrial labor and class antagonisms. Operating under premises of the philosophy of the subject, they both nevertheless underestimated the independent logic of systemically integrated domains of action that are dissociated from structures of intersubjectivity to such an extent that they no longer exhibit any structural analogies with socially integrated domains of action differentiated *within* the lifeworld. For Hegel and Marx, the system of needs or capitalist society arose from processes of abstraction that still pointed to ethical totality or rational praxis and remained subject to their structures. These abstractions constituted nonindependent moments within the self-relation and self-movement of a higher-level subject, into which they would flow once again. In Marx, this overcoming [*Aufhebung*] takes the shape of a revolutionary praxis, which breaks the systemic logic of capital's self-realization, brings the independent economic process back into the horizon of the lifeworld again, and frees the realm of freedom from the dictates of the realm of necessity. In attacking the private ownership of the means of production, the revolution simultaneously strikes at the institutional foundations of the medium through which the capitalist economy was differentiated out. The lifeworld rigidified under the law of value is to be given back its spontaneity; at that very moment, the objective illusion of capital will dissolve away into nothing.

As we have seen, this melting down of systemically reified domains of action into a spontaneous relation-to-self of spirit or of society already met with strong opposition from the Right Hegelians of the first generation. Against the de-differentiation of state and society, they insisted on the objective distinction between the societal system and the governmental subject. Their neoconservative successors gave this thesis an affirmative twist. Hans Freyer and Joachim Ritter saw in the dynamic of the reification of culture and society only the reverse side of the constitution of a realm of subjective freedom worth striving for. Arnold Gehlen criticized even the latter as an empty subjectivity released from all objective imperatives. Even those who, following Lukács, fastened upon the concept of reification came to agree more and more with their opponents in their description; they were increasingly impressed with the impotence of subjects in relation to the feedback processes of self-regulating systems, over which they could have no influence. It makes almost no difference whether the one indicts as a negative totality what the other celebrates as a crystallization; or whether the one denounces as reification what the other technocratically lays down as the law of reality. For decades, this trend in the social-theoretical diagnosis of the age has been heading toward the point that systems functionalism makes into its own point: It allows the subjects themselves to degenerate into systems. It tacitly sets a seal on "the end of the individual," which Adorno encircled with his negative dialectic and protested against as a self-inflicted fate. Niklas Luhmann simply presupposes that the structures of intersubjectivity have collapsed and that individuals have become disengaged from their lifeworlds — that personal and social systems form environments for each other.[7] The barbaric condition predicted by Marx in case revolutionary praxis failed is characterized by a complete subsumption of the lifeworld under the imperatives of a valorization process decoupled from use-values and concrete labor. Undisturbed by this, systems functionalism proceeds from the assumption that this condition has already set in — not merely at the entrance to the capitalist economy, but in the forecourts of *every* functional system. The marginalized lifeworld could survive only if it were to be transformed in turn into a media-steered subsystem and if it were to shed everyday communicative practice like a snakeskin.

On the one hand, Luhmann's version of systems functionalism takes up the heritage of the philosophy of the subject; it replaces the self-relating subject with a self-relating system. On the other hand, it radicalizes Nietzsche's critique of reason by withdrawing any kind of claim to reason along with the relationship to the totality of the lifeworld.[8]

The fact that Luhmann draws upon the reflective content of these two opposed traditions and brings motifs from Kant and Nietzsche together in a cybernetic language game indicates the level at which he establishes social systems theory. Luhmann takes the same characteristics that Foucault attributed to discourse formations with the help of a transcendental-historical concept of power and transfers them to meaning-elaborating systems that operate in a self-relating fashion.[9] Since he also relinquishes the intention of a critique of reason together with the concept of reason, he can turn all the statements that Foucault made by way of denunciation into descriptive ones. In this respect, Luhmann pushes the neoconservative affirmation of social modernity to a peak, and also to heights of reflection where everything the advocates of postmodernity could come up with has already been thought of — without any complaints and in a more differentiated manner. Moreover, systems functionalism is not open to the objection of being unable to give an account of its own status; it places itself without any hesitation within the system of science and comes forward with a claim to "disciplinary universality." Nor can it be charged with a tendency toward leveling. At most, Luhmann's theory, which is today incomparable when it comes to its power of conceptualization, its theoretical imaginativeness, and its capacity for processing information, raises doubts as to whether the price for its "gains in abstraction" is not too high. The tireless shredding machine of reconceptualization separates out the "undercomplex" lifeworld as an indigestible residue — precisely the realm of phenomena of interest to a social theory that has not burned all bridges to the prescientific experience of crisis.

In regard to the capitalist economy, Marx did not distinguish between the new level of system differentiation brought about by a media-steered economic system and the class-specific forms of its institutionalization. For him, abolishing class structures and melting down the independent systemic logic of functionally differentiated and reified domains of interaction formed a single syndrome. Luhmann commits a complementary error. Faced with the new level of the differentiation of systems, he overlooks the fact that media such as money and power, via which functional systems set themselves off from the lifeworld, have in turn to be institutionalized in the lifeworld. This is why the class-specific distributive effects of the media's being anchored in property laws and constitutional norms do not come into view at all. "Inclusion," in the sense of the equal rights of all individuals to access to all functional systems, thus appears as a systemically necessary outcome of the process of differentiation.[10] Whereas for Marx systemically autonomous functional contexts go up in smoke after a successful revolution, for Luhmann the lifeworld now has already lost all significance in the functionally differentiated societies of the modern world. What disappears from both perspectives is the mutual interpenetration and opposition of system and lifeworld imperatives, which explains the double-front character of societal modernization.

The paradoxes of societal rationalization, which I have developed elsewhere,[11] may be summarized in an oversimplified way as follows. The rationalization of the lifeworld had to reach a certain maturity before the media of money and power could be legally institutionalized in it. The two functional systems of the market economy and the administrative state, which grew beyond the horizon of the political orders of stratified class societies, destroyed the traditional life forms of old European society to begin with. The internal dynamic of these two functionally intermeshed subsystems, however, also reacts back upon the rationalized life forms of modern society that made them possible, to the extent that processes of monetarization and bureaucratization penetrate the core domains of cultural reproduction, social integration, and socialization. Forms of interaction shaped by these media cannot encroach upon realms of life that by their function are dependent on action oriented to mutual understanding without the appearance of pathological side effects. In the political systems of advanced capitalist societies, we find compromise structures that, historically considered, can be conceived of as reactions on the part of the lifeworld to the independent systemic logic and growth in complexity proper to the capitalist economic process and a state apparatus with a monopoly on force. These origins have left their traces on the options that remain open to us in a social-welfare state in crisis.[12]

The options are determined by the logic of a politics adjusted to the system imperatives of economy and state. The two media-steered subsystems, which constitute environments for one another, are supposed to be intelligently attuned to one another — and not simply to reciprocally externalize their costs so as to burden a total system incapable of self-reflection. Within the scope of such a politics, only the correctly dosed distribution of problems as between the subsystems of state and economy is in dispute. One side sees the causes of crisis in the unleashing of the dynamics proper to the economy; the other side, in the bureaucratic fetters imposed on the former. The corresponding therapies are a social subduing of capitalism or a displacement of problems from administrative planning back to the market. The one side sees the source of the systemically induced disturbances of everyday life in monetarized labor power; the other, in the bureaucratic crippling of personal initiative. But both sides agree in assigning a merely passive role to the vulnerable domains of lifeworld interaction as against the motors of societal modernization: state and economy.

Meanwhile, the legitimists of the social-welfare state are everywhere in retreat, while the neoconservatives complacently undertake to terminate the social-welfare-state compromise — or at least to redefine its conditions. In return for an energetic improvement of the valorization conditions of capital, neoconservatives accept in the bargain costs that can be shifted in the short term to the lifeworld of the underprivileged and marginalized, but also risks that rebound upon society as a whole. There arise the new class structures of a society segmented on its ever widening margins. Economic growth is kept going by innovations that for the first time are *intentionally* tied to an armaments spiral that has gone out of control. At the same time, the intrinsic normative logic of rationalized lifeworlds now finds expression, however selectively, not only in the classical demands for more distributive justice, but in the wide spectrum of so-called postmaterial values, in the interest in conserving the natural bases of human life and in preserving the internal communicative structures of highly differentiated life forms. So it is that system imperatives and lifeworld imperatives form new frictional surfaces that spark new conflicts which cannot be dealt with in the existing compromise structures. The question posed today is whether a new compromise can be arranged in accord with the old rules of system-oriented politics — or whether the crisis management attuned to crises that are systemically caused and perceived as systemic will be undermined by social movements no longer oriented to the system's steering needs, but to the *processes at the boundaries* between system and lifeworld.

IV

With this question we touch upon the other moment — the possibility of mastering crises in grand format, for which praxis philosophy once offered the means of revolutionary praxis. If society as a whole is no longer thought of as a higher-level subject that knows itself, determines itself, and realizes itself, there are no paths of relation-to-self upon which the revolutionaries could enter in order to work with, for, and on the crippled macrosubject. Without a self-relating macrosubject, anything like a self-reflective knowledge on the part of the social totality is just as *inconceivable* as society's having an influence upon itself. As soon as the higher-level intersubjectivity of public processes of opinion and consensus formation takes the place of the higher-level subject of society as a whole, relationships-to-self of this kind lose their meaning. It is questionable whether under these changed premises it still makes any sense to speak of a "society exercising influence upon itself."

For a society to influence itself in this sense it must have, on the one hand, a reflexive center, where it builds up a knowledge of itself in a process of self-understanding, and, on the other hand, an executive system that, as a part, can act for the whole and influence the whole. Can modern societies meet these conditions? Systems theory projects a picture of them as a-centric societies "without central organs."[13] On this account, the lifeworld has disintegrated without remainder into the functionally specialized subsystems such as economy, state, education, science, etc. These systemic monads, which have replaced withered intersubjective relationships with functional connections, are symmetrically related to one another, but their precarious equilibrium is not susceptible of being regulated for society as a whole. They must reciprocally balance one another, since none of the total societal functions that come to the fore with them attains a *primacy* for society as a whole. None of the subsystems could occupy the top of a hierarchy and represent the whole the way the emperor could once do for the empire in stratified societies. Modern societies no longer have at their disposal an authoritative center for self-reflection and steering.

From the viewpoint of systems theory, only the subsystems develop anything like a *self-consciousness*, and they do so only in view of their *own* function. The whole is reflected in the partial system's self-consciousness only from the perspective of that system, as its respective social *environment*: "Hence, a consensus functional for society as a whole about what is and what is valid is difficult, in fact impossible; what is used as a consensus functions in the form of a recognized provisional arrangement. In addition to this, there are the really productive syntheses of reality that are functionally specific at the levels of complexity that individual functional systems can achieve for themselves but can no longer add up to a comprehensive world view in the sense of a *congregatio corporum*, or a *universitas rerum*."[14] Luhmann elaborates on this "provisional arrangement" in a footnote as follows: "It was a peculiar decision of Husserlian philosophy, with considerable ramifications for sociological discussions, to endow this provisional arrangement with the status of an ultimately valid basis of a concrete a priori by giving it the title of 'lifeworld.'" It is sociologically untenable to postulate for the lifeworld any kind of "primacy in being."

The legacy of Husserlian apriorism may mean a burden for various versions of social phenomenology;[15] but the communications-theoretic concept of the lifeworld has been freed from the mortgages of transcendental philosophy. If one is to take the basic fact of *linguistic* socialization into account, one will be hard put to do without this notion. Participants in interaction cannot carry out speech acts that are effective for coordination unless they impute to everyone involved an intersubjectively shared lifeworld that is angled toward the situation of discourse and anchored in bodily centers. For those acting in the first person singular or plural with an orientation to mutual understanding, each lifeworld constitutes a totality of meaning relations and referential connections with a zero point in the coordinate system shaped by historical time, social space, and semantic field. Moreover, the different lifeworlds that collide with one another do not stand *next to each other* without any mutual understanding. As totalities, they follow the pull of their claims to universality and work out their differences until their horizons of understanding "fuse" with one another, as Gadamer puts it. Consequently, even modern, largely decentered societies maintain in their everyday communicative action a virtual center of self-understanding, from which even functionally specified systems of action remain within intuitive reach, as long as they do not outgrow the horizon of the lifeworld. This center is, of course, a projection, but it is an effective one. The polycentric projections of the totality — which anticipate, outdo, and incorporate one another — generate competing centers. Even collective identities dance back and forth in the flux of interpretations, and are actually more suited to the image of a fragile network than to that of a stable center of self-reflection.

Nevertheless, everyday practice affords a locus for spontaneous processes of self-understanding and identity formation, even in nonstratified societies that no longer have a knowledge of themselves available in the traditional forms of representative self-presentation. Even in modern societies, a diffuse common consciousness takes shape from the polyphonous and obscure projections of the totality. This common consciousness can be concentrated and more clearly articulated around specific themes and ordered contributions; it achieves greater clarity in the higher-level, concentrated communicative processes of a public sphere. Technologies of communication — such as book publishing and the press, first of all, and then radio and television — make utterances available for practically any context, and make possible a highly differentiated network of public spheres — local and transregional, literary, scientific, and political, within parties or associations, media-dependent or subcultural. Within these public spheres, processes of opinion and consensus formation, which depend upon diffusion and mutual interpenetration no matter how specialized they are, get institutionalized. The boundaries are porous; each public sphere is open to other public spheres. To their discursive structures they owe a universalist tendency that is hardly concealed. All partial public spheres point to a comprehensive public sphere in which society as a whole fashions a knowledge of itself. The European Enlightenment elaborated this experience and took it up into its programmatic formulas.

What Luhmann calls "the consensus functioning for the whole of society" is context-dependent and fallible — provisional in fact. But this reflexive knowledge on the part of society as a whole *exists*. Only now it is due to the higher-level intersubjectivity of public spheres and hence can no longer satisfy the sharp criteria of self-reflection by a higher-level subject. Of course, such a center of self-understanding is insufficient for a society to exercise influence over itself; for this, it would also require a central steering authority that could receive and translate into action the knowledge and the impulses from the public sphere.

According to the normative ideas of our political tradition, the democratically legitimated apparatus of state — having been shifted from the sovereignty of princes to the sovereignty of the people — is supposed to be able to put into effect the opinion and will of the citizenry as a public. The citizens themselves participate in the formation of collective consciousness, but they cannot act collectively. Can the government do so? "Collective action" would mean that the government would transpose the intersubjectively constituted self-knowledge of society organizationally into the self-determination of society. And yet, even on systems-theoretic grounds, one has to doubt this possibility. As a matter of fact, today politics has become an affair of a functionally specialized subsystem; and the latter does not dispose over the measure of autonomy relative to the other subsystems that would be required for central steering, that is, for an influence of society as a totality upon itself, an influence that comes from it and goes back to it.

In modern societies, there obviously exists an asymmetry between the (weak) capacities for intersubjective self-understanding and the (missing) capacities for the self-organization of society as a whole. Under these changed premises, there is no equivalent for the philosophy of the subject's model of self-influence in general and for the Hegelian-Marxist understanding of revolutionary action in particular.

This insight has come into broad effect, carried along by a specific experience that labor parties and unions have had, above all, in their attempts to realize the social-welfare-state project since the end of the Second World War. I am talking neither about the economic problems that cropped up as a result of successful social-welfare legislation during the period of reconstruction, nor about the limits upon the power and the ability of planning administrations to intervene, nor about problems of *steering* at all. I mean, rather, a characteristic transformation in the perception of the democratically legitimated state power that had to be brought to bear in pursuing the goal of "socially taming" the naturelike capitalist economic system, and especially the goal of neutralizing the destructive side effects of its crisis-filled expansion on the existence and life-world of dependent workers.[16] Advocates of the social-welfare state regarded it as unproblematic that an active government should intervene not only in the economic cycle but also in the life cycle of its citizens — the goal indeed was to reform the living conditions of the citizens by way of reforming the conditions of labor and employment. Underlying this was the democratic tradition's idea that society could exercise an influence over itself by the neutral means of political-administrative power. Just this expectation has been disappointed.

In the meantime, an increasingly dense network of legal norms, of governmental and paragovernmental bureaucracies, has been drawn over the everyday life of its actual and potential clients. Extensive discussions about legal regulation and bureaucratization in general, about the counterproductive effects of government welfare policies in particular, about the professionalization and scientization of social services have drawn attention to circumstances that make one thing clear: The legal-administrative means of translating social-welfare programs into action are not some passive, as it were, propertyless medium. They are connected, rather, with a praxis that involves isolation of facts, normalization, and surveillance, the reifying and subjectivating violence of which Foucault has traced right down into the most delicate capillary tributaries of everyday communication. The deformations of a lifeworld that is regulated, fragmented, monitored, and looked after are surely more subtle than the palpable forms of material exploitation and impoverishment; but internalized social conflicts that have shifted from the corporeal to the psychic are not therefore less destructive.

Today one sees the contradiction inherent in the social-welfare-state project as such. Its substantive goal was to set free life forms structured in an egalitarian way, which were supposed at the same time to open up space for individual self-realization and spontaneity; but too great a demand was placed upon the medium of power in expecting it to call forth new forms of life. Once the state has been differentiated out as one among many media-steered functional systems, it should no longer be regarded as the central steering authority in which society brings together its capabilities for organizing itself. A functional system that has grown beyond the horizon of the lifeworld and become independent, that shuts itself off from perspectives of society as a whole, and that can perceive society as a whole only from the perspective of a subsystem, stands over against processes of opinion and will formation in a general public sphere, which, however diffuse, are still directed to society as a whole.

A new, as it were stereoscopically sharpened view of "the political" emerges from the historical disillusionment with a bureaucratically coagulated social-welfare-state project. In addition to the independent systemic logic of a power medium that only seems to be usable in a purposive-rational manner, another dimension becomes visible. The public sphere as political, in which complex societies can acquire normative distance from themselves and work out experiences of crisis collectively, takes on a remoteness from the political system similar to the remoteness it previously had from the economic system. The political system has acquired a similarly problematic character, or at least one with two battlefronts. Now it is itself perceived as a source of steering problems, and not simply as a means for the solution of problems. Thus, we have become conscious of *the difference between steering problems and problems of mutual understanding.* We can see the difference between systemic disequilibria and lifeworld pathologies, between disturbances of material reproduction and deficiencies in the symbolic reproduction of the lifeworld. We come to recognize the distinction between the deficits that inflexible structures of the lifeworld can cause in the maintenance of the systems of employment and domination (via the withdrawal of motivation or legitimation), on the one hand, and manifestations of a colonization of the lifeworld by the imperatives of functional systems that externalize their costs on the other. Such phenomena demonstrate once more that the achievements of steering and those of mutual understanding are resources that cannot be freely substituted for one another. Money and power can neither buy nor compel solidarity and meaning. In brief, the result of the process of disillusionment is a new state of consciousness in which the social-welfare-state project becomes reflexive to a certain extent and aims at taming not just the capitalist economy, but the state itself.

However, if not only capitalism, but also the interventionist state itself is to be "socially tamed," the task has to be defined anew. The welfare-state project entrusted the planning capacity of public administrations with having a stimulating influence upon the self-steering mechanism of a *different* subsystem. If this "regulation," applied so very indirectly, is now supposed to extend to the organizational performances of the state, the mode of influence may not be specified again as indirect steering, for a new *steering* potential could only be furnished by *another* subsystem. Even if we could come up with a supplementary system of this sort, after a further round of disappointment and distantiation we would again face the problem that *perceptions of crises in the lifeworld* cannot be translated without remainder into *systems-related problems of steering.*

Instead, it is a question of building up restraining barriers for the exchanges between system and lifeworld and of building in sensors for the exchanges between lifeworld and system. At any rate, limit problems of this sort are posed as soon as a highly rationalized lifeworld is to be shielded against the intolerable imperatives of the occupational system or against the penetrating side effects of the administrative provision for life. The systemic spell cast by the capitalist labor market over the life histories of those able to work, by the network of responsible, regulating, and supervising public authorities over the life forms of their clients, and by the now autonomous nuclear arms race over the life expectancy of peoples, cannot be broken by systems learning to function better. Rather, impulses from the lifeworld must be able to enter into the self-steering of functional systems.[17] Of course, this would require altering the relationship between autonomous, self-organized public spheres, on the one hand, and realms of action steered by money and power, on the other, or in other words: a new division of powers within the dimension of social integration. The socially integrating power of solidarity would have to be in a position to assert itself against the systemically integrating steering media of money and power.

I call those public spheres autonomous which are neither bred nor kept by a political system for purposes of creating legitimation. Centers of concentrated communication that arise spontaneously out of microdomains of everyday practice can develop into autonomous public spheres and consolidate as self-supporting higher-level intersubjectivities only to the degree that the lifeworld potential for self-organization and for the self-organized use of the means of communication are utilized. Forms of self-organization strengthen the collective capacity for action. Grassroots organizations, however, may not cross the threshold to the formal organization of independent systems. Otherwise they will pay for the indisputable gain in complexity by having organizational goals detached from the orientations and attitudes of their members and dependent instead upon imperatives of maintaining and expanding organizational power. The lack of symmetry between capacities for self-reflection and for self-organization that we have ascribed to modern societies as a whole is repeated on the level of the self-organization of processes of opinion and will formation.

This need not be an obstacle, if one considers that the indirect influence of functionally differentiated subsystems on the individual mechanisms of self-steering means something altogether different from the goal-oriented influence of society upon itself. Their self-referential closedness renders the functional systems of politics and economics immune against attempts at intervention in the sense of *direct* interventions. Yet this same characteristic also renders systems sensitive to stimuli aimed at increasing their capacity for self-reflection, that is, their sensitivity to the reactions of the environment to their own activities. Self-organized public spheres must develop the prudent combination of power and intelligent self-restraint that is needed to sensitize the self-steering mechanisms of the state and the economy to the goal-oriented outcomes of radical democratic will formation. In place of the model of society influencing itself, we have the model of boundary conflicts — which are held in check by the lifeworld — between the lifeworld and two subsystems that are superior to it in complexity and can be influenced by it only indirectly, but on whose performances it at the same time depends.

Autonomous public spheres can draw their strength only from the resources of largely rationalized lifeworlds. This holds true especially for culture, that is to say, for science's and philosophy's potential for interpretations of self and world, for the enlightenment potential of strictly universalistic legal and moral representations, and, not last, for the radical experiential contents of aesthetic modernity. It is no accident that social movements today take on cultural-revolutionary traits. Nonetheless, a structural weakness can be noticed here that is indigenous to all modern lifeworlds. Social movements get their thrust-power from threats to well-defined collective identities. Although such identities always remain tied to the particularism of a special form of life, they have to assimilate the normative content of modernity — the fallibilism, universalism, and subjectivism that undermine the force and concrete shape of any given particularity. Until now, the democratic, constitutional nation-state that emerged from the French Revolution was the only identity formation successful on a world-historical scale that could unite these two moments of the universal and the particular without coercion. The Communist party has been unable to replace the identity of the nation-state. If not in the nation, in what other soil can universalistic value orientations today take root?[18] The Atlantic community of values crystallized around NATO is hardly more than a propaganda formula for ministers of defense. The Europe of de Gaulle and Adenauer merely furnishes the superstructure for the basis of trade relations. Quite recently, left intellectuals have been projecting a completely different design as a counter-image to the Europe of the Common Market.

The dream of such a completely different European identity, which assimilates in a decisive way the legacy of Occidental rationalism, is taking shape at a time when the United States is getting ready to fall back into the illusions of the early modern period under the banner of a "second American Revolution." In the utopias painted in the old romances about the state, rational forms of life entered into a deceptive symbiosis with the technological mastery of nature and the ruthless mobilization of social labor power. This equation of happiness and emancipation with power and production has been a source of irritation for the self-understanding of modernity from the start — and it has called forth two centuries of criticism of modernity.

But the same utopian (in the bad sense) gestures of mastery are living on now in a caricature that moves the masses. The science fiction of Star Wars is just good enough for the ideology planners to spark — with the macabre vision of a militarized space — an innovative thrust that would give the colossus of worldwide capitalism sufficient footing for its next round of technological development. Old Europe could only find its way clear to a new identity if it opposed to this short circuit of economic growth, arms race, and "traditional values" the vision of breaking out of these self-inflicted systemic constraints, if it put an end to the confused idea that the normative content of modernity that is stored in rationalized lifeworlds could be set free only by means of ever more complex systems. The idea

that the capacity to compete on an international scale —
whether in markets or in outer space — is indispensable for
our very survival is one of those everyday certitudes in which
systemic constraints are condensed. Each one justifies the expansion and intensification of its own forces by the expansion
and intensification of the forces of the others, as if it were not
the ground rules of social Darwinism that are at the bottom of
the play of forces. Modern Europe has created the spiritual
presuppositions and the material foundations for a world in
which this mentality has taken the place of reason. That is the
real heart of the critique of reason since Nietzsche. Who else
but Europe could draw from *its own* traditions the insight, the
energy, the courage of vision — everything that would be
necessary to strip from the (no longer metaphysical, but metabiological) premises of a blind compulsion to system maintenance and system expansion their power to shape our
mentality.

Excursus on Luhmann's
Appropriation of the Philosophy of the
Subject through Systems Theory

Niklas Luhmann has presented us with the "basic outline" for a general theory of society.[1] In it, he draws up an interim balance for the expansive and decades-long development of his theory, so that we can now survey the project as a whole. At least, one thinks oneself better able to comprehend what is going on before one's eyes. It is not so much the disciplinary tradition of social theory from Comte to Parsons that Luhmann tries to connect up with, as the history of problems associated with the philosophy of the subject from Kant to Husserl. His systems theory does not, say, lead sociology onto the secure path of science; rather, it presents itself as the successor to an abandoned philosophy. It seeks to inherit the basic terms and problematics of the philosophy of the subject, while at the same time surpassing it in its capacity for solving problems. It thereby effects a shift in perspective that leaves the self-critique of a modernity at odds with itself without any object. A systems theory of society applied to itself can do nothing but take up an affirmative stance toward modern society's growth in complexity. What interests me is whether, together with this distantiated reinscription of the philosophy of the subject,[2] systems theory also ends up with the kinds of problems that beset those who left us this inheritance — problems that, ever since Hegel's death, have given rise to the very doubts concerning subject-centered reason as the principle of modernity that I have discussed in these lectures.

I

If one wants to insert in place of the concept of the knowing subject that was developed from Descartes to Kant the concept of system that has been developed in connection with cybernetics and biology, and wants to do so at the same level of discussion, then the following rearrangements become necessary. The system-environment relationship takes the place of the inside-outside relationship between the knowing subject and the world as the totality of knowable objects. Knowledge of the world and of the self was the problem by reference to which the conscious accomplishments of the subject were judged. Now this problem is subordinated to that of the maintenance and expansion of systems. The system's relation to itself is modeled after that of the subject. Systems cannot relate to anything else without relating to themselves and reflexively ascertaining themselves. Nevertheless, the "self" of the system is distinguished from that of the subject because it does not consolidate into the "I" of the apperceptive "I think" that, according to Kant's formulation, has to be able to accompany all my representations. Systems theory has to remove from the "self" of the relation-to-self all connotations of an identity of self-consciousness established by synthetic performances. Self-relatedness is characteristic of individual systemic accomplishments in their mode of operation; but no center in which the system as a whole is made present to itself and knows itself in the form of self-consciousness issues from these punctual relations-to-self. In this way, the concept of reflexivity is separated from that of consciousness. But then an equivalent is needed for the conscious substrate of the self-relatedness that is distinctive of the level of sociocultural life. As an emergent attainment corresponding to consciousness, Luhmann introduces a peculiar concept of "meaning." In doing so, he draws upon phenomenological descriptions by Husserl, for whom the meaning of a symbolic expression refers to an underlying intention; "intention" is a more primitive notion than "meaning." Correspondingly, Luhmann defines "meaning" prelinguistically as a referential context of actualizable possibilities that is related to the intentionality of experience and action. Meaning-processing or meaning-using systems are substituted for subjects capable of being self-conscious.

Viewed against the background of the movement of thought from Kant through Hegel to Marx, this conceptual substitution, in which thought-figures from the philosophy of consciousness are retained in the form of structural analogies, gives rise to some revealing consequences. The *first* has to do with the empiricist turn of the transcendental-philosophical starting point. The system-environment relationship is thought out altogether in accord with the model of a world constituted by transcendental consciousness. In demarcating itself from its environment, the system *constitutes* the latter as a universal horizon of meaning for itself. But meaning-processing systems emerge only in the plural; they arise and maintain themselves under the contingent boundary conditions of a hypercomplex environment and are not previously harmonized, as are empirical subjects, in the form of unity of transcendental consciousness in general. In place of the one, transcendentally grounded world, we have many system-relative environments.[3] The systems theorist finds a multiplicity of system-environment relationships in his object domain. In this regard, the distinction between the transcendental and the empirical loses its significance.

Second, with this decision, systems theory *transcends* the limits of subjective Idealism, as Hegel did in his time. Hegel not only gained access to the temporal dimension of the history of the emergence of the transcendental subject; he also found the basic structure of self-consciousness outside the knowing subject, embodied in the realms of objective and absolute spirit. It is not only subjective spirit that is characterized by traits of subjectivity, but objective and absolute spirit as well. Like Hegel with his concept of spirit, Luhmann with his concept of a meaning-processing system gains the freedom of movement required to submit society as a social system to a study similar to that of consciousness as a psychic system. Meaning-processing systems coincide as little with systems dependent on consciousness as does spirit with subjective spirit. On the other hand, empiricist premises require a clear line of separation between events internal to the system and those in the system's environment. Hence, all systems are environments for one another, mutually amplifying the enviromental complexity each has to master. Unlike subjects, they cannot join together into aggregates of higher-level systems; nor are they embedded from the start in such a totality, as its moments. In this respect, then, systems theory does not imitate the step from subjective to objective Idealism.

Third, there is a parallel here with Marx, who replaced "self-consciousness" with "praxis" and gave to the formative process of spirit a naturalistic turn. Social labor was supposed to mediate the metabolic process between the "species" and external nature objectified into an environment. In this way, the circular process that starts with the expenditure of labor power and returns to the regeneration of labor power via the production and use of produced goods could be represented as the reproductive self-generation of the species. Systems theory treats this as a special case of autopoiesis. What Marx regarded as holding true for the material reproduction of society holds true for self-relating systems in general; every element used in the system has to be generated by this system itself and cannot be taken over from its environment "ready-made." The self-relatedness of the operations of meaning-processing systems has the primarily practical meaning of *self-generation*, not the theoretical meaning of self-presentation.

Under there premises, systems theory also shares with Marxist social theory a reflection upon the context of its own emergence and application. The cognitive accomplishments of systems theory show themselves upon reflection to be a component and function of the social processes to which it is directed as its object. Yet Marxist theory holds on to a concept of reason that allows it to establish an internal connection between self-reflection and the validity of truth, on the one hand, and emancipation from the constraints of internal and external nature, on the other.[4] Systems theory lets cognitive acts, even its own, meld into the system's achievement of mastering complexity and thus takes away from knowledge any moment of unconditionality. Systems theory understands itself as functional analysis and, owing to the reference problems that come with this method, sees itself as seamlessly woven into the functional contexts of systemic self-maintenance — with neither the power nor the intention of transcending these contexts in any way.[5]

Fourth, the philosophically reflected changeover to the systems paradigm results in a far-reaching revision of the conceptual framework of the Western tradition, which has been fixated on being, thinking, and truth. The nonontological frame of reference is unmistakable once it becomes clear that research in systems theory itself is conceived of as a subsystem (of the scientific and societal systems) with its own environment. In this environment, the system-environment relationships that we come across constitute the complexity that systems theory must register and deal with. Thus, the ontological premises of a self-sustaining world of rationally ordered entities, as well as the epistemological premises of a world of representable objects related to knowing subjects and the semantic premises of a world of existing states of affairs related to assertoric sentences, are all devalued at a stroke. Any premise thst, in metaphysics, epistemology, or linguistic theory, postulates the ultimacy of a cosmic order, a subject-object relationship, or a relation between sentences and states of affairs is set aside without discussion. Luhmann's systems theory effects a shift in thought from metaphysics to metabiology. However the expression "metaphysics" may have chanced to arise, one could attribute to it the meaning of a thinking that proceeds from the "for us" of physical appearances and asks what lies behind them. Then we can use the term "metabiological" for a thinking that starts from the "for itself" of organic life and goes behind it — the cybernetically described, basic phenomenon of the self-maintenance of self-relating systems in the face of hypercomplex environments.

The difference from the environment maintained by the system itself is treated as ultimate. Reason as specified in relation to being, thought, or proposition is replaced by the self-enhancing self-maintenance of the system. By taking this approach, Luhmann also goes beyond a critique of reason that aims at revealing the power of self-maintenance to be the latent essence of subject-centered reason. Under the title of systems rationality, reason, now liquidated as irrational, *professes* exactly this function: It *is* the ensemble of the conditions that make system maintenance possible. Functionalist reason expresses itself in the ironic self-denial of a reason shrunk down to the reduction of complexity — "shrunk down" because the meta-biological frame of reference does not go beyond the logocentric limitations of metaphysics, transcendental philosophy, and semantics (as does the theory of communication, with its concept of communicative reason developed in terms of linguistic functions and validity claims) but undermines it. Reason once again becomes a superstructure of life. In this respect, nothing is changed by promoting "life" to the organizational level of "meaning." For as we shall see, with a concept of meaning conceived in functionalist terms, the internal connection between meaning and validity dissolves. The same thing happens as with Foucault: The interest in truth (and validity in general) is restricted to the effects of holding-something-as-true.

Finally, the shift from subject to system has yet a *fifth* consequence relevant to our context. With the concept of subject, a self constituted in self-knowledge is attributed to every possible relation-to-self. The centripetal force that permits every movement of spirit to culminate and come to rest only in self-consciousness is also inherent in self-determination and self-realization. As soon as the system takes the place of the "self" in the relation-to-self, the possibility of a centering comprehension of the whole in self-knowledge disappears; the structure of self-relatedness attaches now only to the individual element. It ensures the closure of a system that is simultaneously open to the environment, not by means of a center but through connections with the periphery: "The self of self-reference is never the totality of a closed system, nor is it ever the referring itself" — the self-mediation elevated by Hegel to an absolute — "It is always a matter of those moments in the constitutive context of open systems that support its autopoiesis. . . . The justification for our speaking here of (partial or concomitant) self-reference derives from the fact that we are dealing with the conditions of the possibility of autopoietic self-production" (630).

This self-lessness of self-relating systems is reflected in the a-centric character of societies that have, on the whole, shifted over to functional differentiation: "The consequence of this is that there is no specifiable standpoint left from which the whole — whether one names it society or state — can be accurately observed" (630). The unity of modern societies always presents itself differently from the perspectives of their different subsystems. Already on analytic grounds, there can no longer be any central perspective of a self-consciousness proper to a social system as a whole. But if modern societies have no possibility whatsoever of shaping a rational identity, then we are without any point of reference for a critique of modernity. Even if one wanted to cling to this critique *without any direction*, it would have to founder on the reality of a process of societal differentiation that has long since advanced beyond the traditional European concepts of reason. And yet, precisely in Luhmann's pathos, in this sense of reality connected with institutionalized subrationalities, one encounters a quite German legacy carried down from the (eventually sceptical) Right Hegelians to Gehlen. Let us cast our gaze backwards once again.

Because the relation-to-self as conceived by the philosophy of the subject presupposes the identity of the self-knowing subject as the supreme point of reference, the movement of thought from Kant to Hegel could rely upon an inner logic; in the end, even the difference between the synthesis that establishes unity and the multiplicity encompassed by it demands a final identity that embraces both identity and non-identity. That was the theme of Hegel's *Differenzschrift*. From the same conceptual perspective, Hegel worked out the basic experience of cultural and social modernity — the overloading of the socially integrative capacity of traditional European lifeworlds by the Enlightenment critique of religion and the importunity of systemically objectified social relations in the capitalist economy and the bureaucratic state. A fundamental motif of the philosophy of reconciliation — that reason was supposed to take over religion's role of social integration — grew both out of the contemporary experience of crisis and, *at the same time*, out of this tendency ingrained in the philosophy of the subject. The diagnosis of the age owed its particular articulation of the problems to a dialectic of objectification rooted in the concept of self-consciousness proper to the philosophy of the subject and first worked out by Fichte. Because self-reflection has to make into an object something that, as the spontaneous source of all subjectivity, escapes the form of objects in general, the reason performing the reconciliation cannot be conceived on the model of the objectifying relation-to-self of the knowing subject (that is, on the model of the "philosophy of reflection"). Otherwise, a finite faculty would be posited absolutely, and the place of reason would be usurped by an idolized understanding. On this model, Hegel conceived the abstractions of mental and social life as something merely "positive." They could supposedly be overcome only by way of radicalized self-reflection — by a movement that had its telos in absolute knowledge, in the self-knowledge of the whole.

Because the "self" of the relation-to-self disappears with the changeover from subject to system, systems theory has at its disposal no figure of thought that corresponds to the injurious and oppressive act of reification. In the philosophy of the subject's concept of relation-to-self, the reification of subjectivity is structurally built in as a possibility for going wrong. A *comparable* category-mistake could reside here in a system misunderstanding itself as an environment; but this possibility is excluded by definition. The processes of demarcation connected with any formation of a system cannot be plastered with connotations of "exclusion" or "proscription." It is a completely normal process that a system, in forming itself, distantiates itself from something as its environment. Considered historically, the establishment of the status of wage-labor and the rise of an industrial proletariat, as well as the inclusion of the populace under centralized administrations, were by no means painless processes. But even if systems theory could formulate the problems connected with such processes, it would have to dispute the possibility of modern societies having a perception of crises that could not be scaled down to the perspective of a special subsystem.

If functionally differentiated societies have no identity available to them, they also cannot form a rational identity: "Societal rationality would require that the problems loosed upon the environment by society be reflected in the social system, at least to the extent that they impinge back on the society — that is to say, that they be brought into societal communication processes. Within limits, this can happen *within* the individual functional systems — as, for instance, when physicians catch sight of the illnesses they themselves have caused. More typically, however, functional systems burden other functional systems via the environment. What is especially lacking is a social subsystem for perceiving environmental interdependencies. Such a thing cannot exist with functional differentiation, for that would mean that the society itself would have to be found again in the society. The principle of differentiation makes the issue of rationality all the more urgent — and all the more unsolvable" (645). With a certain disdain, Luhmann rejects the relevant attempts at a solution within the philosophy of the subject: "Simple minds want to counter here with ethics. Hegel's state is not much better. And the Marxian hope for a revolution is no improvement" (599).

In the last lecture, I set forth the arguments that speak against the philosophy of the subject's construction of a consciousness embracing the total society. If individuals are integrated and subordinated as parts to the higher-level subject of society as a whole, there arises a zero-sum game in which modern phenomena such as the expanding scope for movement and the increasing degrees of freedom cannot be adequately accommodated. There are also difficulties with the idea of a consciousness of society as a whole, represented as the self-reflection of a subject-writ-large. In differentiated societies, the very demanding types of knowledge directed to the totality of society occur at most within specialized systems of knowledge, but not at the center of society, as a self-knowledge on the part of the whole society. On the other hand, we have come to know an alternative conceptual strategy that keeps us from having to give up altogether the notion of a self-representation of society. Public spheres can be conceived of as higher-level intersubjectivities. Identity-forming self-ascriptions can be articulated within them. And in the more highly aggregated public, a consciousness of the total society can be articulated. This no longer has to satisfy the demands for precision that the philosophy of the subject had to set for self-consciousness.

Society's knowledge of itself is concentrated neither in philosophy nor in social theory.

In virtue of this common consciousness, however diffuse and controversial it may be, the society as a whole can gain normative distance from itself and can react to perceptions of crisis, or, in other words, it can accomplish just what Luhmann denies as a meaningful possibility for it: "What it would mean for modern society to inquire about its rationality" is clear to Luhmann; with each reflective step, "the issue of rationality would become all the more urgent and all the more unsolvable." Hence, the question should not be posed at all: "The framework of the problem of rationality does not say that society would have to solve problems of this kind in order to ensure its survival. Evolution is sufficient for survival" (654).

The highly aggregated and publicly condensed processes for opinion formation and will formation, which are nevertheless close to the lifeworld, reveal the close interweaving of socialization and individuation, of ego and group identities. Luhmann, who does not have the concept of linguistically generated intersubjectivity at his disposal, can only think of these kinds of internal interconnections on the model of inclusion by the whole of the parts contained within it. He regards this figure of thought as "humanistic"[6] and keeps his distance from it. As the example of Parsons shows, it is just this conceptual proximity to the philosophy of the subject that makes it tempting simply to imitate the classical model and lay out the social system (in Parsons: the action system) as the whole that contains psychic systems as subsystems. But then the very real defects of the philosophy of the subject would pass over into systems theory. That is why Luhmann resolves upon a solution about whose strategic-theoretic significance he is altogether clear: "Once one regards people as part of the environment of society (rather than as part of society itself), this alters the premises of every traditional problematic, including the premises of classical humanism" (288). And conversely: "Whoever clings to these premises and seeks to represent a concern for humanity by means of them has therefore to emerge as an opponent of systems theory's claim to universality" (92).

As a matter of fact, this methodological antihumanism[7] is aimed not against a thought figure that is mistaken because it embraces concretistic parts within the whole, but against a "concern for humanity" that also cannot manage without this concretism of the whole and its parts; I am talking about the "concern" to conceptualize modern society in such a way that the possibility of distantiating itself from itself as a whole and of working out its perceptions of crisis within the higher-level communication processes of the public sphere is not already negatively prejudiced by the choice of basic concepts. Naturally, the construct of a public sphere that could fulfill this function has no place once communicative action and the intersubjectively shared lifeworld slip between system types that, as in the case of the psychic and the social systems, constitute environments for one another and have only external relationships to one another.

II

The flow of official documents among administrative authorities and the monadically encapsulated consciousness of a Robinson Crusoe provide the guiding images for the conceptual uncoupling of the social and psychic systems, according to which the one is supposedly based solely on communication and the other solely on consciousness.[8]

In this abstract separation of psychic and social systems, a legacy of the philosophy of the subject makes itself felt: The system-environment relationship affords just as little conceptual connection with the genuinely linguistic intersubjectivity proper to agreement and communicatively shared meaning as did the subject-object relationship. At any rate, Luhmann oscillates between constructing intersubjectivity out of the intermeshing of individual perspectives tied to individual subjects — a transformation through evolution theory of solutions advanced by the philosophy of the subject from Fichte to Husserl — and, on the other hand, treating individual consciousness and self-sustaining systems of perspectives as equiprimordial from an evolutionary point of view.[9]

This second conception also suffers from the lack of suitable basic concepts from the theory of language, just as the classical conception had. Luhmann has to introduce "meaning" as a neutral concept in relation to "communication" and "consciousness," but in such a manner that meaning can branch out into different typical modes of meaning-processing. Otherwise, the systems working on the basis of consciousness and communication could not constitute environments for one another. Although systems theory gives to the same questions responses that are structurally similar to those given by the philosophy of the subject in its day, social theory finds itself in a new situation of argument today. The suprasubjective *status of language as prior to subjects* has been worked out not only in the Humboldtian tradition of the *Geisteswissenschaften*, but also in the analytic philosophy of language, as well as in pragmatism and structuralism (which have had a considerable influence on social theory by way of George Herbert Mead and Claude Lévi-Strauss). In view of this background in the history of theory, it becomes clear what a burden is assumed by a theory that divides up linguistic structures that cover both the psychic and the social dimensions into two different systems. Now that the outline of Luhmann's theory has been sketched out more clearly, one also sees how much energy has to be expended in order to master the problems flowing from this one basic decision.

Suprasubjective linguistic structures would entwine society and individual too tightly with one another. An intersubjectivity of mutual understanding among agents that is achieved via expressions with identical meanings and criticizable validity claims would be too strong a tie between psychic and social systems as well as between different psychic systems. Systems can only contingently influence one another from outside; their interaction lacks any *internal* regulation. This is why Luhmann has first of all to cut language and communicative action down to so small a size that the internal intermeshing of cultural reproduction, social integration, and socialization disappear from view.

Linguistic expression is assigned a subordinate status as against the concept of meaning introduced in phenomenological terms. Language exists only for symbolically generalizing prior occurrences of meaning; it measures out, as it were, the stream of experience into recognizable identities (136ff.).[10] Furthermore, language remains secondary in relation to consciousness. The solitary life of the soul, including discursive thought, is not formed by language from the very outset. Structuring by language only articulates the spontaneous flow of consciousness by pauses and lends it the capacity to form episodes (367ff.). Besides this, however, language is also not constitutive for processes of mutual understanding; it operates "in the mind" even prior to any communication. To the extent that language is involved in organizing series of representations and processes of thought, it by no means functions as an internalized derivative of speech (137, 367). Every one of these theses is highly controversial; they would have to be grounded in specialized contexts of the philosophy of language. In any case, such questions cannot be dispatched by means of phenomenological pointers, even less so by definitions.

Luhmann's strategy is clear: If the achievement of linguistic symbols is exhausted by articulating, abstracting, and generalizing prelinguistic conscious processes and meaning connections, communication carried on by linguistic means cannot be explained in terms of specifically linguistic conditions of possibility. And if language can no longer be taken into account as a structure that makes possible the intrinsic connection among understanding, meaning, identity of signification, and intersubjective validity, the *path of language analysis* cannot lead to an explanation of understanding expressions with identical meaning, of consensus (or dissensus) about the validity of linguistic utterances, of the commonality of any intersubjectively shared context of meaning and reference — that is, to an explanation of communicative participation in a lifeworld that is represented in a linguistic world view. The aspects of linguistically generated intersubjectivity must be derived, rather, as self-generated artifacts from the reciprocal reactions among meaning-processing systems. Here Luhmann makes use of figures of thought familiar from empiricism.

Thus, for instance, the understanding of meaning arises, below the level of linguistic understanding, out of mutual observation on the part of psychic systems that know that each operates self-relatedly and so becomes present itself in the perceived environment of the respective others. In this way, there evolves a spiral of any number of repeated mirrorings of observations of self and other. Then an *understanding* of the differences between interpretative perspectives is formed by way of the observation of reciprocal *observings*. Thus, this social dimension of meaning does not come about through a convergence of horizons of understanding, which are brought together around identical significations and intersubjectively recognized validity claims and are fused into a consensus about what is meant or said. No common denominator can be built up among different psychic systems, unless it be an autocatalytically emergent social system, which is immediately locked again within its own systemic perspectives and draws back into its own egocentric observational standpoints: "This capacity to process information may suffice for the few aspects relevant to interaction (among mutually observing, self-referential systems). They remain separate, they do not fuse, they do not understand one another better than before; they concentrate upon what they can observe about the other as system-in-an-environment, as input and output, and they learn self-referentially, each within its own observational perspective. They can try to influence what they observe through their own action, and they can learn once again from feedback. In this way, an emergent order can arise. . . . We call this . . . the social system" (157).

Social systems process meaning in the form of communication. For this, language is used. But it does not make expressions with identical significations available; it only permits signs to be substituted for meaning. Meaning is still tailored to the difference between perspectives of comprehension. Alter and ego can of course "be strengthened in their belief that they mean the same thing through using signs with the same meaning" (220). Language is so underdetermined as a medium of communication that it is not designed to overcome the egocentrism of individual systemic perspectives through higher-level supra- or transsystemic common perspectives. Mutual understanding does not come to term in agreement in the strict sense any more than different systems have *the same* meanings at their disposal. The separation between the social dimension and the substantial dimension [*Sachdimension*] is meant to exclude precisely what one is inclined to regard as the telos of language: to ground *my* understanding of something [*Sache*] with reference to the *possibility of a consensus we* reach with one another concerning it. Further, the validity of an utterance is not supposed to be grounded upon the intersubjective recognition of criticizable validity claims, but upon a consent that exists either only for ego or only for alter. Language affords no solid basis upon which ago could *meet* with alter in a consensus about something: "My consent is a consent only in relation to your consent, but my consent is not your consent, and there are no sorts of substantive arguments or rational grounds that could in the end ensure the coincidence of the two (again, from out of the substantive dimension)" (113). The "fusion" of social and substantive dimensions, which makes it possible to think just that, is regarded by Luhmann as the "cardinal sin of humanism" (119).

The complex of problems considered up to this point is related in general to an empiricistic dissolution of the transsubjective foundations of processes of mutual understanding — that is, the use of expressions identical in meaning and the formation of consensus on the basis of validity claims — in order to undercut the structures of linguistically generated intersubjectivity with a minimalist concept of language. Individual consciousness and society acquire the autarchy proper to individual systems that can form environments for one another only when their exchanges are not regulated by internal relationships, that is, when culture, society, and person are no longer *internally* bound up with the lifeworld. A second complex of problems follows immediately upon the first as soon as the latter are worked out and the premise has been secured that psychic and social systems make contact with one another only contingently and only enter into the kind of interdependence that results from external relationships. For then what was taken apart in a first step must be put back together again, step by step. Those interweavings of individual and society, of individual life history and collective life form, of individuation and social constitution, which we have explained (under the aspects of cultural reproduction, social integration, and socialization) in terms of the cooperation of *internally intermeshed* components of the lifeworld, have now to be made plausible in terms of the intersection of *external relationships*, with the aid of additional hypotheses.

For example, one notion useful for this purpose is that of "interpenetration"; this refers to the situation in which two systems that are environments for each other spontaneously restrict the degrees of freedom within such an external relationship in order to render themselves mutually dependent upon one another in forming structures. There is social or interhuman interpenetration present when "the two systems reciprocally make each other possible by each bringing its pre-constituted internal complexity into the other" (290). Intimate relationships or moral expectations, for instance, are supposed to be explained with the help of this idea. Thus is to be explained every phenomenon that proves perplexing so long as one assumes that psychic and social systems are not basically coordinated with one another. Under this premise, for instance, the process of socialization can only be understood as an individual achievement of the psychic system: "Socialization is always self-socialization" (327). The concept of individuality offers similar difficulties. Once the internal connection between sociation and individuation is severed, the normatively substantive concept of individuality can only be used as an iterable "formula of self-description" (360ff.).

This strategy of concept formation, which I can only recall briefly here, is explained by the fact that theory becomes cumulatively entangled in the problematic outcomes of a single basic decision. By separating the psychic and social aspects, Luhmann pulls apart, as it were, the life of the species and that of its instances, in order to redistribute it into two mutually *external* systems, even though the *internal* connection between the two aspects is indeed constitutive for linguistically constituted forms of life. To be sure, these indications cannot take the place of arguments and counterarguments. But even the level at which arguments could be exchanged is not easy to determine. For, contrary to the self-understanding of its author, this systems theory is not suited to the comparatively modest format of a theory that is "universal" only in the specialized sense of being tailored to one discipline. It is not really sociology, but more like those metatheoretical projects that fill the function of world views.

I see Luhmann's theory as an ingenious continuation of a tradition that has left a strong imprint upon the self-understanding of early modernity in Europe and thereby reflected in turn the selective pattern of Occidental rationalism. The cognitive-instrumental one-sidedness of cultural and societal rationalization was also expressed in philosophical attempts to establish an objectivistic self-understanding of human beings and their world — initially in mechanistic and later in materialistic and physicalistic world views, which reduced the mental to the physical by means of more or less complicated theories. In Anglo-Saxon countries to this very day, analytical materialism keeps discussions of the mind/body relationship alive; to this very day, physicalistic or other scientistic background convictions underwrite the demand that everything intuitively known be alienated from the perspective of a natural-scientific observer — that we understand ourselves in terms of objects. For objectivistic self-understanding, what matters, naturally, is not any explanation of detail but the unique act of inverting the natural attitude to the world. The lifeworld itself is to be brought into the perspective of self-objectification in such a way that everything that is normally disclosed to us within its horizon — performatively, as it were — appears from an extramundane angle of vision as an occurrence purely and simply foreign to all meaning, extrinsic and accidental, explicable only in accord with natural-scientific models.

As long as mechanics, biochemistry, and neurophysiology have supplied the languages and models, we have not been able to get beyond general and abstract correlations and foundational discussions about mind and body. Descriptive systems stemming from the natural sciences are too remote from everyday experiences to be suitable for channeling distantiating self-descriptions into the lifeworld in a differentiated manner and along a broad front. This changes with the language of general systems theory that has developed from cybernetics and with the application of its models in various life sciences. The models derived from intelligent performances and tailored to organic life come a lot closer to the sociocultural form of life than classical mechanics. As Luhmann's astonishing job of translation demonstrates, this language can be so flexibly adapted and expanded that it yields novel, not merely objectivating but objectivistic descriptions even of subtle phenomena of the lifeworld. One has to bear in mind that innovative social theories, with their paradigms, were always anchored in society itself and never belonged exclusively to the system of the sciences. In any case, to the extent that systems theory penetrates into the lifeworld, introducing into it a metabiological perspective from which it then learns to understand itself as a system in an environment-with-other-systems-in-an-environment — as if the world process took place through nothing but system-environment differences — to that extent there is an objectifying effect.

In this way, subject-centered reason is replaced by systems rationality. As a result, the critique of reason carried out as a critique of metaphysics and a critique of power, which we have considered in these lectures, is deprived of its object. To the degree that systems theory does not merely make its specific disciplinary contribution within the system of the sciences but also penetrates the lifeworld with its claim to universality, it replaces metaphysical background convictions with metabiological ones. Hence, the conflict between the objectivists and the subjectivists loses its point. It may be that "linguistically generated intersubjectivity" and "self-referentially closed system" are now the catchwords for a controversy that will take the place of the discredited mind-body problematic.

Notes

Preface

1. Jürgen Habermas, "Modernity versus Postmodernity," *New German Critique* 22(1981):3–14.

2. Jean-François Lyotard, *The Postmodern Condition: A Report on Knowledge* (Minneapolis, 1984). On this see Axel Honneth, "Der Affekt gegen das Allgemeine," *Merkur* 430(December 1984):893ff.; Richard Rorty, "Habermas and Lyotard on Postmodernity," in Richard Bernstein, ed., *Habermas and Modernity* (Cambridge, MA, and Oxford, 1985), pp. 161–175; and my reply: "Questions and Counterquestions," ibid., pp. 192–216.

3. On this see Peter Bürger, *Zur Kritik der idealistischen Ästhetik* (Frankfurt, 1983); H. R. Jauss, "Der literarische Prozess des Modernismus von Rousseau bis Adorno," in L. von Friedeburg and J. Habermas, eds., *Adorno-Konferenz 1983* (Frankfurt, 1983), pp. 95ff.; Albrecht Wellmer, *Zur Dialektik von Moderne und Postmoderne* (Frankfurt, 1985).

4. Contained in Karl Heinz Bohrer, ed., *Mythos und Moderne* (Frankfurt, 1982), pp. 415–430. Parts of this appeared in English as "The Entwinement of Myth and Enlightenment," *New German Critique* 26(1982):13–30.

5. Jürgen Habermas, *Die Neue Unübersichtlichkeit* (Frankfurt, 1985).

Lecture I
Modernity's Consciousness of Time and Its Need for Self-Reassurance

1. Max Weber, *The Protestant Ethic and the Spirit of Capitalism* (New York, 1958), p. 25.

2. On this see Jürgen Habermas, *The Theory of Communicative Action*, volume 1 (Boston, 1983), chapter II.

3. See the article on "Modernization" by James Coleman in *The Encyclopedia of the Social Sciences*, vol. 10, at p. 397.

4. Arnold Gehlen, "Über kulturelle Kristallisation," in *Studien zur Anthropologie* (Neuwied, 1963), p. 321.

387

Notes to pages 4–10

5. H. E. Holthusen, in his essay "Heimweh nach Geschichte," *Merkur* 430(1984):1916ff., suggests that Gehlen may have borrowed the term *"posthistoire"* from his intellectual ally Hendrik de Man.

6. Reinhart Koselleck, "'Neuzeit,'" in *Futures Past: On the Semantics of Historical Time* (Cambridge, MA, 1985), pp. 231–266; here p. 241.

7. Ibid., p. 250.

8. Ibid., pp. 246ff.

9. G. W. F. Hegel, "The Preface to the *Phenomenology*," in W. Kaufmann, ed., *Texts and Commentary* (New York, 1966), p. 20.

10. G. W. F. Hegel, *The Philosophy of History* (New York, 1956), p. 442.

11. Koselleck, *Futures Past*, pp. 267ff.

12. Hans Blumenberg, *Die Legitimität der Neuzeit* (Frankfurt, 1966), p. 72. A revised edition appeared in 1974 and has been translated as *The Legitimacy of the Modern Age* (Cambridge, MA, 1983).

13. G. W. F. Hegel, "The Positivity of the Christian Religion," in *On Christianity. Early Theological Writings by Hegel* (New York, 1948), p. 159.

14. H. V. Gumbrecht, "Modern," in O. Brunner, W. Conze, and R. Koselleck, eds., *Geschichtliche Grundbegriffe*, Bd. 4, pp. 93ff.

15. H. R. Jauss, "Ursprung und Bedeutung der Fortschrittsidee in der 'Querelle des Anciens et des Modernes,'" in H. Kuhn and F. Wiedmann, eds., *Die Philosophie und die Frage nach dem Fortschritt* (Munich, 1964), pp. 51ff.

16. For what follows I am drawing upon H. R. Jauss, "Literarische Tradition und gegenwärtiges Bewusstsein der Modernität," in *Literaturgeschichte als Provokation* (Frankfurt, 1970), pp. 11ff. See also his "Der literarische Prozess des Modernismus von Rousseau bis Adorno," in L. von Friedeburg and J. Habermas, eds., *Adorno-Konferenz 1983* (Frankfurt, 1983), pp. 95ff.

17. Charles Baudelaire, "The Painter of Modern Life," in *Selected Writings on Art and Artists* (New York and Harmondsworth, 1972), pp. 390–435; here p. 403.

18. "In order that any form of modernity may be worthy of becoming antiquity, the mysterious beauty that human life unintentionally puts into it must have been extracted from it" (ibid., p. 404).

19. Ibid., p. 392.

20. Ibid., p. 435.

21. "All share the same characteristic of opposition and revolt; all are representations of what is best in human pride, of that need, which is too rare, to combat and destroy triviality" (ibid., p. 421).

22. Ibid., p. 402.

23. Walter Benjamin, "Theses on the Philosophy of History," in *Illuminations* (New York, 1969), pp. 253–264; here p. 261.

24. Ibid., p. 263.

25. Koselleck, "'Space of Experience' and 'Horizon of Expectation,'" in *Futures Past,* p. 276.

26. Ibid., p. 279.

27. "There is no document of civilization which is not at the same time a document of barbarism. And just as such a document is not free of barbarism, barbarism taints also the manner in which it was transmitted from one owner to another" (Thesis VII).

28. See Helmut Peukert, "Dimensions, Fundamental Problems, and Aporias of a Theory of Communicative Action," in *Science, Action, and Fundamental Theology: Toward a Theology of Communicative Action* (Cambridge, MA, 1984), pp. 163–210; see also my reply to H. Ottmann in "A Reply to My Critics," in J. B. Thompson and D. Held, eds., *Habermas: Critical Debates* (Cambridge, MA, and London, 1982), pp. 245ff.

29. G. W. F. Hegel, *The Difference Between the Fichtean and Schellingian Systems of Philosophy* (Reseda, CA, 1978), p. 10; henceforth cited as *The Difference.*

30. *Hegel's Philosophy of Right* (Oxford, 1952), p. 286.

31. *Hegel's Lectures on the History of Philosophy,* vol. III (New York, 1896; reprinted 1968), p. 423.

32. *Hegel's Philosophy of Right,* p. 112.

33. Ibid., p. 295.

34. *Hegel's Lectures on the History of Philosophy,* vol. I (New York, 1892; reprinted 1968), p. 423.

35. Ibid., vol. III, p. 549.

36. G. W. F. Hegel, *Lectures on the Philosophy of Religion* (London, 1968).

37. Hegel, *The Philosophy of History,* p. 440.

38. Ibid.

39. Ibid.

40. *Hegel's Philosophy of Right,* p. 75.

41. G. W. F. Hegel, *On Art, Religion, Philosophy* (New York, 1970), p. 99.

42. Ibid., p. 98.

43. Ibid.

44. See the résumé in #124 of *Hegel's Philosophy of Right:* "The right of the subject's particularity . . . is the pivot and center of the difference between antiquity and modern times. This right in its infinity is given expression in Christianity and it has become the universal effective principle of a new form of civilization. Amongst the primary shapes which this right assumes are love, romanticism, the quest for eternal salvation

of the individual, etc.; next come moral convictions and conscience; and finally, the other forms, some of which come into prominence . . . as the principle of civil society and as moments in the constitution of the state, while others appear in the course of history, particularly in the history of art, science, and philosophy" (p. 84).

45. See Immanuel Kant, *Critique of Pure Reason* (New York, 1961), p. 601, at B779.

46. Hegel, *The Difference*, p. 13.

47. G. W. F. Hegel, *The Phenomenology of Mind* (New York, 1966, 2nd ed.), pp. 509–513.

48. Hegel, *The Difference*, p. 12.

49. "If the power of unification disappears from the life of men, and if the contrasts have lost their living relationship and reciprocity and have achieved independence, the need for philosophy arises. Thus far, it is a contingency. But in the given diremption it is a necessary attempt to sublate the opposition of the solidified subjectivity and objectivity, and to conceive the 'being-as-having-become' [*das Gewordenseyn*] of the intellectual and real world as a becoming [*ein Werden*]" (Hegel, *The Difference*, p. 12).

50. Ibid., pp. 15ff.

Lecture II
Hegel's Concept of Modernity

1. G. W. F. Hegel, *Faith and Knowledge* (Albany, 1977), p. 55. [The exclamation mark is Habermas's. — tr.]

2. G. W. F. Hegel, *The Difference Between the Fichtean and Schellingian Systems of Philosophy* (Reseda, CA, 1978), p. 11.

3. Dieter Henrich, "Historische Voraussetzungen von Hegels System," in *Hegel im Kontext* (Frankfurt, 1971), p. 55.

4. G. W. F. Hegel, "The Positivity of the Christian Religion," in *On Christianity. Early Theological Writings by Hegel* (New York, 1948), p. 70. Henceforth cited as "Positivity."

5. Hegel plays on this with the observation: "The method of treating the Christian religion which is in vogue today takes reason and morality as a basis for testing it and draws on the spirit of nations and epochs for help in explaining it. By one group of our contemporaries, whose learning, clarity of reasoning, and good intentions entitle them to great respect, this method is regarded as a beneficent 'Illumination' which leads mankind toward its goal, toward truth and virtue. By another group, which is respectable on the strength of the same learning and equally well-meaning aims, and which in addition has the support of governments and the wisdom of centuries, this method is decried as downright degeneracy" (Hegel, "Positivity," p. 67). Compare Henrich, "Historische Voraussetzungen," pp. 52ff.

6. G. W. F. Hegel, "Fragmente über Volksreligion und Christentum" (1783–1794), in the recent edition of his works, G. W. F. Hegel, *Surhkamp-Werkausgabe*, Bd. 1, p. 103.

7. Ibid., p. 33.

8. Ibid., p. 10. The expressions "*Moral*" and "*Sittlichkeit*" are still used synonymously by the young Hegel.

9. Ibid., p. 33

10. Ibid., p. 77.

11. Ibid., p. 41

12. G. W. F. Hegel, "Entwürfe über Religion und Liebe," *Suhrkamp-Werkausgabe*, Bd. 1, p. 254.

13. For the political writings of the young Hegel, see *Suhrkamp-Werkausgabe*, Bd. 1: "Anmerkungen zu den 'Vertraulichen Briefen über das vormalige staatsrechtliche Verhältnis des Waadtlandes zur Stadt Bern' (von J. J. Cart)" (1798), pp. 255–267. "Dass die Magistrate von den Bürgern gewählt werden müssen (Über die neuesten inneren Verhältnisse Württemburgs)" (1798), pp. 268–273. English translation: "On The Recent Domestic Affairs of Wurtemberg, Especially on the Inadequacy of the Municipal Constitution," in *Hegel's Political Writings* (Oxford, 1964), pp. 243–245; and "Proceedings of the Estates Assembly in the Kingdom of Wurtemberg 1815–1816," ibid., pp. 246–293.
"Die Verfassung Deutschlands" (1800–1802), pp. 451–610. English translation: "The German Constitution," in *Hegel's Political Writings*, pp. 141–242.
"Fragmente historischer und politischer Studien aus der Berner und Frankfurter Zeit" (ca. 1795–1798), pp. 428–448.
In the political writings, the counterpart to the critique of the Enlightenment is still missing. As is well known, Hegel makes up for this in the section on "Absolute Freedom and Terror" in the *Phenomenology of Mind* (New York, 1966), pp. 599–610. Here, too, the critique is aimed at a philosophical party that opposes with abstract demands an old regime entrenched behind its positivity. On the other hand, the crisis experience finds a still more honest, or at least more direct, expression in the political writings than in the theological ones. Hegel practically vows to break through the need of the day, the feeling of contradiction, the need for change, the pressure, the barriers: "The picture of better and juster times has become lively in the souls of men, and a longing, a sighing for purer and freer conditions, has moved all hearts and set them at variance with the actuality (of the present)" (*Hegel's Political Writings*, p. 243).
See also my afterword to G. W. F. Hegel, *Politische Schriften* (Frankfurt, 1966), pp. 343ff.

14. *Hegel's Political Writings*, p. 146.

15. Hegel, *Suhrkamp-Werkausgabe*, Bd. 1, pp. 219 and 234–235.

16. Hegel, "The Spirit of Christianity and Its Fate," in *On Christianity*, p. 207.

17. Ibid., p. 211.

18. Ibid., pp. 228ff.

19. I am leaving to one side the Jena *Realphilosophie* in which the young Hegel's approach via a theory of intersubjectivity left its traces. See my "Labor and Interaction: Remarks on Hegel's Jena *Philosophy of Mind*," in *Theory and Practice* (Boston, 1973), pp. 142–169.

20. Rüdiger Bubner, ed., *Das älteste Systemprogramm* (Bonn, 1973). As to the origins of this manuscript, see the contributions to C. Jamme and H. Schneider, eds., *Mythologie der Vernunft* (Frankfurt, 1984).

21. G. W. F. Hegel, "Das älteste Systemprogramm des deutschen Idealismus," *Suhrkamp-Werkausgabe*, Bd. 1, p. 236.

22. "So in the end, enlightened and unenlightened must extend their hands to one another; mythology must become philosophical and the people rational; and philosophy must become mythological in order to make philosophy sensible" (*Suhrkamp-Werkausgabe*, Bd. 1, p. 236).

23. See the excursus on Schiller's "Letters on the Aesthetic Education of Man" in this volume.

24. Henrich, "Historische Voraussetzungen," pp. 61ff.

25. Hegel, *Difference*, p. 33.

26. Hegel, *Faith and Knowledge*, p. 74.

27. Hegel, *Difference*, p. 33.

28. Henrich, "Hegel und Hölderlin," in *Hegel im Kontext*, pp. 35ff.

29. H. R. Jauss, "Schlegels und Schillers Replik," in *Literaturgeschichte als Provokation* (Frankfurt, 1970), pp. 67ff.

30. G. W. F. Hegel, *On Art, Religion, Philosophy* (New York, 1970), p. 93.

31. G. W. F. Hegel, *Aesthetics. Lectures on Fine Arts* (Oxford, 1975), vol. I, p. 103.

32. Ibid., p. 596.

33. Ibid., p. 79.

34. Hegel, *On Art, Religion, Philosophy*, p. 162.

35. G. W. F. Hegel, *The Christian Religion. Lectures on the Philosophy of Religion, Part III. The Revelatory, Consummate, Absolute Religion* (Missoula, MT, 1979), p. 295.

36. Ibid., p. 297.

37. *Hegel's Philosophy of Right* (Oxford, 1952), p. 267.

38. Ibid., pp. 125, 267.

39. Ibid., p. 266.

40. Ibid., p. 125.

41. G. W. F. Hegel, *Jenaer Schriften* (*Suhrkamp-Werkausgabe*, Bd. 2), p. 482.

42. *Hegel's Philosophy of Right*, p. 161.

43. Hegel worked out the crisis structure of civil society in his Lectures on the Philosophy of Right held during the winter semester of 1819/20 even more energetically than he did in the book version. See D. Henrich, "Einleitung" to G. W. F. Hegel, *Philosophie des Rechts. Die Vorlesung von 1819/20 in einer Nachschrift* (Frankfurt, 1983), pp. 18ff.

44. See R. P. Horstmann, "Probleme der Wandlung in Hegels Jenaer Systemkonzeption," *Philosophische Rundschau* 9(1972):95ff.; and "Über die Rolle der bürgerlichen Philosophie in Hegels politischer Philosophie," *Hegel-Studien* 9(1974):209ff.

45. G. W. F. Hegel, *Jenenser Realphilosophie*, ed. Hoffmeister (Leipzig, 1931), p. 248.

46. With these words Hegel characterizes the tragedy that the absolute, eternally at play with itself, performs in the realm of the ethical. G. W. F. Hegel, "Aufsätze aus dem Kritischen Journal der Philosophie," *Suhrkamp-Werkausgabe*, Bd. 2, p. 495.

47. Henrich, "Einleitung" to *Die Vorlesung von 1819/20*, p. 31.

48. "When the gospel is no longer preached to the poor, when the salt has lost its savor and all basic feastdays are quietly removed, then the people, for whose still oppressed reason truth can only exist in representation, know that there can be no help any longer for pressures inside themselves" (Hegel, *The Christian Religion*, p. 295).

49. Hegel, *Die Vorlesung von 1819/20*, p. 51.

50. G. W. F. Hegel, *Jenaer Schriften* (*Suhrkamp-Werkausgabe*, Bd. 2), p. 175. [The exclamation mark is Habermas's. — tr.]

51. Ibid.

Excursus on Schiller's "Letters on the Aesthetic Education of Man"

1. Friedrich Schiller, *On the Aesthetic Education of Man in a Series of Letters* (New Haven, 1954), p. 25. Hereafter cited in text by page number.

2. Herbert Marcuse, "Fortschritt im Lichte der Psychoanalyse," in *Freud in der Gegenwart*, *Frankfurter Beiträge zur Soziologie*, Bd. 6 (Frankfurt, 1957), p. 438.

3. Hannah Arendt, *Lectures on Kant's Political Philosophy*, edited by R. Beiner (Chicago, 1982).

4. Herbert Marcuse, *Counterrevolution and Revolt* (Boston, 1972).

Lecture III
Three Perspectives: Left Hegelians, Right Hegelians, and Nietzsche

1. See H. Schnädelbach's brilliant presentation of the largely superseded tradition of "School Philosophy" in his *Philosophy in Germany 183–1933* (Cambridge, 1984).

2. Karl Löwith, *From Hegel to Nietzsche* (New York, 1964).

3. Karl Löwith, "Einleitung" to *Die Hegelsche Linke*, edited by K. Löwith (Stuttgart, 1962), p. 38.

4. The relation of history to reason remains constitutive for the discourse of modernity — for better or worse. Whoever participates in this discourse (and nothing about this has changed up to our own day) makes a distinct use of the expressions "reason" and "rationality." They are used neither in accord with the game rules of ontology to characterize God or being as a whole; nor in accord with the game rules of empiricists to characterize individual subjects capable of knowledge and action. Reason is valid neither as something ready-made, as an objective teleology that is manifested in nature or history, nor as a mere subjective faculty. Instead, the patterns looked for in historical events yield encoded indications of unfinished, interrupted, and misguided processes of self-formation that transcend the subjective consciousness of the individual. As

393

Notes to pages 57–62

subjects relate to internal and external nature, the social and cultural life-context in which they exist is reproduced through them. The reproduction of life forms and life histories leaves behind impressions in the soft medium of history which, under the strained gaze of those seeking clues, solidify into indicators or structures. This specifically modern gaze is guided by an interest in self-reassurance. Constantly irritated by the risk of deception and self-deception, it snatches nonetheless at configurations and structures from which it deciphers formative processes in which both learning and mislearning are entwined. So the discourse of modernity places the sphere of nonbeing and the mutable under the determinations of insight and error; it transports reason into a realm that was held to be simply meaningless and unsusceptible to theory by Greek ontology as well as by the modern philosophy of the subject. Through drawing on false theoretical models, this risky undertaking was at first derailed into the dogmatism of philosophy of history and thus called for the reaction of historicism. But those who conduct the discourse in a *serious fashion* know that it must steer between Scylla and Charybdis.

5. Michel Foucault, "Intellectuals and Power," in *Language, Counter-Memory, Practice* (Ithaca, 1977), pp. 205–217.

6. For a defense of the conservative distribution of the burden of proof, see Hermann Lübbe, *Fortschritt als Orientierungsproblem* (Freiburg, 1975).

7. "Manifesto of the Communist Party," in Robert C. Tucker, ed., *The Marx-Engels Reader* (New York and London, 1978), p. 476.

8. "Critique of Hegel's Philosophy of Right. Introduction," in Q. Hoare and Lucio Colletti, eds., *Karl Marx, Early Writings* (New York, 1975), pp. 245–246.

9. "The Communist Manifesto," p. 485.

10. Ibid., p. 483.

11. Ibid., p. 477.

12. He justifies this path with an interesting application of the theorem of the non-contemporaneity of the contemporaneous: "The German philosophy of law and of the state is the only German history which stands on an equal footing with the official modern present. . . . We are the philosophical contemporaries of the present without being its historical contemporaries" ("Critique of Hegel's Philosophy of Right. Introduction," p. 249).

13. The young Marx interprets the relation between state and society in action-theoretic terms, from the perspective of the complementary roles of "citoyen" and "bourgeois" — the citizen of the state and the private person with civil rights. The seemingly sovereign citizen leads a double life, "celestial and terrestrial. He lives in the political community, where he regards himself as a communal being, and in civil society, where he acts simply as a private individual, treats other men as means, degrades himself to the role of a mere means, and becomes the plaything of alien forces" ("The Jewish Question," in *The Marx/Engels Reader*, p. 34). In this way the idealism of the bourgeois state covers up the consummation of the materialism of civil society, the realization of its egoistic content. The meaning of the bourgeois revolution is twofold: It emancipates civil society from politics, as well as from the semblance of having a universal content; at the same time it instrumentalizes the communal being constituted in ideal independence for "the sphere of human needs, labour, private interests and civil law" (ibid. p. 46) in which the state finds its natural basis. Marx sees in the social content of the rights of man that "the sphere in which man functions as

a species-being is degraded to a level below the sphere where he functions as a partial being, and finally that it is man as bourgeois and not man as a citizen who is considered the true and authentic man" (ibid. p. 43).

14. Ibid., p. 46.

15. By "praxis philosophy" I mean not only the different versions of Western Marxism that go back to Gramsci and Lukács (such as Critical Theory and the Budapest School; the existentialism of Sartre, Merleau-Ponty, and Castoriadis; the phenomenology of Enzo Paci and the Yugoslavian *Praxis* philosophers), but also the radically democratic kinds of American Pragmatism (G. H. Mead, Dewey) and of analytic philosophy (Charles Taylor). See the instructive comparison by Richard J. Bernstein, *Praxis and Action* (Philadelphia, 1971).

16. "Critique of Hegel's Doctrine of State," in *Karl Marx. Early Writings*, pp. 187–188.

17. Charles Taylor, *Hegel* (Cambridge, 1975), chapter I, pp. 13ff.

18. See my critique of the foundations of praxis philosophy in "A Reply to My Critics," in J. Thompson and D. Held, eds., *Habermas: Critical Debates* (Cambridge, MA, and London, 1982), pp. 219–283, here pp. 223ff.

19. See the "Excursus on the Obsolescence of the Production Paradigm," below.

20. T. W. Adorno, *Negative Dialektik*, Bd. 6 of his *Werke* (Frankfurt, 1973), p. 192.

21. See lecture V, below.

22. P. Steinfels, *The Neo-Conservatives* (New York, 1979); R. Saage, "Neokonservatives Denken in der Bundesrepublik," in *Ruckkehr zum starken Staat?* (Frankfurt, 1983), pp. 228ff.; H. Dubiel, *Die Buchstabierung des Fortschritts* (Frankfurt, 1985).

23. Lorenz von Stein's three-volume *Geschichte der sozialen Bewegung in Frankreich* (Darmstadt, 1959), published first in 1849, is a continuation of his work on *Sozialismus und Communismus des heutigen Frankreich*.

24. H. F. W. Hinrichs, "Politische Vorlesungen," in H. Lübbe, ed., *Die Hegelsche Rechte* (Stuttgart, 1962), p. 89.

25. Rosenkranz's treatises on the concepts of the political party and public opinion dramatically reflect the irruption of modern time-consciousness into the sphere of Hegel's *Philosophy of Right* (see Lübbe, ed., *Die Hegelsche Recht*, pp. 59ff. and 65ff.). In the "legal proceedings" that the future institutes against the past, the historical continuum is fragmented into a succession of actual ties. A public opinion that is continually being transformed is the medium of this conflict, which not only flares up between the parties of progress and of inertia, but penetrates within the parties themselves; it pulls each party into the whirlpool of polarization between future and past and splits it into factions, wings, and cliques. Even the image of an avant-garde, which embodies the future in present-day movements, is not foreign to the liberals — in the *Communist Manifesto* it only finds its most decisive formulation.

26. Oppenheim polemicizes against "the blind domination of competition, supply and demand," against "the tyranny of capital and of the great landed properties," which, left to themselves, "would always give rise to an oligarchy of owners" (in Lübbe, ed.,

Die Hegelsche Recht, pp. 186ff.). The state is supposed to intervene in the putative "sanctuary of industrial conditions": "Unmoved, the administration . . . has looked on as the big capitalists dug a drainage ditch in which, under the deceptive covering of free competition, all national resources, all wealth, and all happiness had to flow off" (ibid., p. 193). Hinrich sees that the system of labor and of needs can redeem the promise of subjective freedom only if even "the laborer is vouchsafed enough to sustain his life and to become intelligent, to be put in a condition to acquire property" (ibid., p. 131). And Rosenkranz expects a "new, bloody revolution," if the "urgent social questions" have not been solved (ibid., p. 150).

27. H. Lübbe still defends this position today, without change, in "Aspekte der politischen Philosophie des Bürgers," in *Philosophie nach der Aufklärung* (Dusseldorf, 1980), pp. 211ff.

28. "How can one administer in common something that forms no finished whole and is daily born anew and shaped anew in an endless and endlessly manifold production?" (Oppenheim, in Lübbe, ed., *Die Hegelsche Recht,* p. 196).

29. Rosenkranz, in Lübbe, ed., *Die Hegelsche Recht,* p. 72.

30. On the pertinent writings of E. Forsthoff, E. R. Huber, K. Larenz, and others, see already H. Marcuse, "Der Kampf gegen den Liberalismus in der totalitären Staatsauffassung," *Zeitschrift für Sozialforschung* 3(1934):161ff.

31. This decomposition was initiated by the Left Hegelians. The methodological reflections on the rapidly burgeoning natural sciences and *Geisteswissenschaften* — positivism and historicism — then soon discredited everything that wanted to reach out beyond the "mere thought of the understanding" [*blosses Verstandesdenken*]. Rosenkranz had still spoken about the undying majesty of the spirit reigning in history — this kind of philosophy of history was over and done with by the close of the nineteenth century. From that time on, whoever wanted to fasten upon the idea of overcoming civil society in the state had only the nominalist concept of political power at their disposal, a concept from which Max Weber had removed all connotations of reason. The state could at most be loaded in an existentialist manner with meanings from the friend-foe relationship.

32. H. Freyer, *Weltgeschichte Europas,* 2 vols. (Wiesbaden, 1948), and *Theorie des gegenwärtigen Zeitalters* (Stuttgart, 1955); J. Ritter, *Metaphysik und Politik* (Frankfurt, 1969).

33. J. Habermas, "Neo-Conservative Culture Criticism in the United States and West Germany," *Telos* 56(1983):75–89.

34. J. Ritter, *Hegel and the French Revolution* (Cambridge, MA, 1982), p. 75.

35. Ibid., p. 61.

36. Ibid,. p. 81.

37. J. Ritter, "Subjektivität und industrielle Gesellschaft," in *Subjektivität* (Frankfurt, 1974), p. 138.

38. J. Ritter, "Die Aufgabe der Geisteswissenschaften in der modernen Gesellschaft," in *Subjektivität,* p. 131.

39. See H. Schnädelbach, *Geschichtsphilosophie nach Hegel. Die Probleme des Historismus* (Freiburg, 1974).

40. J. Ritter, "Landschaft. Zur Funktion des Ästhetischen in der modernen Gesellschaft," in *Subjektivität*, pp. 141ff.

41. See lecture XI, below.

Excursus on the Obsolescence of the Production Paradigm

1. On this see H. Brunkhorst, "Paradigmatikern und Theoriendynamik der Kritischen Theorie der Gesellschaft," *Soziale Welt* (1983), pp. 25ff.

2. J. Habermas, *The Theory of Communicative Action*, volume 1, *Reason and the Rationalization of Society* (Boston, 1984); volume 2, *Lifeworld and System: A Critique of Functionalist Reason* (Boston, 1987).

3. Georg Lukács, *Zur Ontologie des gesellschaftlichen Seins*, 3 volumes (Neuwied, 1971ff.).

4. Peter Berger and Thomas Luckmann, *The Social Construction of Reality: A Treatise in the Sociology of Knowledge* (New York, 1966), p. 34.

5. Charles Taylor, *Hegel* (Cambridge, 1975), pp. 13ff., 80ff.

6. Berger and Luckman, *Social Construction*, p. 60.

7. Ibid., p. 61.

8. Ibid., p. 89.

9. Agnes Heller, *Das Alltagsleben* (Frankfurt, 1978), and *Alltag und Geschichte* (Neuwied, 1970).

10. Heller, *Das Alltagsleben*, pp. 182ff.

11. Heller, *Alltag und Geschichte*, pp. 25ff.

12. Claus Offe, "Work, The Key Sociological Category?" *Disorganized Capitalism* (Cambridge, MA, and Oxford, 1985), pp. 129–150.

13. G. Markus, "Die Welt menschlicher Objekte," in *Arbeit, Handlung, Normativität*, edited by A. Honneth and U. Jaeggi (Frankfurt, 1980), pp. 12ff.; expanded version: *Langage et production* (Paris, 1982).

14. Ibid., p. 28.

15. Ibid., p. 36.

16. Ibid., p. 74.

17. Ibid., p. 51; italics in original.

18. Ibid., p. 50.

19. Ibid., p. 114.

Lecture IV
The Entry into Postmodernity: Nietzsche as a Turning Point

1. Friedrich Nietzsche, *On the Advantage and Disadvantage of History for Life* (Cambridge, 1980), pp. 24–25.

2. Ibid., pp. 62 and 37.

3. Ibid., p. 41.

4. Ibid., p. 21.

5. Ibid., p. 24.

6. Ibid., p. 45.

7. This is true of Horkheimer and Adorno as well; in this respect they are close to Nietzsche, Bataille, and Heidegger. See lecture V.

8. Friedrich Nietzsche, *The Birth of Tragedy and the Case of Wagner* (New York, 1967), p. 136.

9. Nietzsche, *Advantage and Disadvantage*, p. 38.

10. Ibid., pp. 32, 64.

11. Richard Wagner, *Sämtlich Schriften and Dichtungen*, Bd. 10, p. 211.

12. Ibid., p. 172.

13. Nietzsche, *The Birth of Tragedy*, p. 59.

14. Nietzsche, "Attempt at Self-Criticism," in *The Birth of Tragedy*, p. 25. See the *Nachlass*, volume 12 of Nietzsche's *Sämtliche Werke*, edited by G. Colli and M. Montinari (Berlin, 1967ff.), p. 117.

15. M. Frank, *Der kommende Gott. Vorlesungen über die neue Mythologie* (Frankfurt, 1982), pp. 180ff.

16. *Schellings Werke*, edited by M. Schröter, volume II, p. 629.

17. Friedrich Schlegel, *Kritische Ausgabe*, volume I, p. 312.

18. Hegel, *Suhrkamp-Werkausgabe*, volume 1, p. 235.

19. *Schellings Werke*, volume II, p. 628.

20. Ibid., p. 629.

21. Schlegel, *Kritische Ausgabe*, volume II, p. 317.

22. Ibid., p. 314.

23. Schlegel, "Athenaeum Fragment Nr. 252," ibid., volume II, p. 207; see also K. H. Bohrer, "Friedrich Schegels Rede über die Mythologie," in K. H. Bohrer, ed., *Mythos und Moderne* (Frankfurt, 1983), pp. 52ff.

24. Schlegel, *Kritische Ausgabe*, volume II, p. 319.

25. On this expression see W. Lange, "Tod ist bei Göttern immer ein Vorteil," in Bohrer, ed., *Mythos und Moderne*, p. 127.

26. Frank, *Der kommende Gott*, pp. 12ff.

27. M. Frank investigates the equation of Dionysius with Christ in connection with Hölderlin's elegy "Brot und Wein" in *Der kommende Gott*, pp. 257–342. See, too, P. Szondi, *Hölderlin Studien* (Frankfurt, 1970), pp. 95ff.

28. See the beginning of the song "Patmos": "Wo aber Gefahr ist, wachst das Rettende auch," in Hölderlin, *Sämtliche Werke*, volume 2, edited by V. F. Beissher, p. 173. In English: "But where danger is, grows the saving power also," in F. Hölderlin, *Poems and Fragments*, translated by Michael Hamburger (Ann Arbor, 1966), pp. 462–463.

29. In this connection Jacob Taubes makes the observation that Schelling, in view of this threshold, distinguished sharply between archaic and historical consciousness, between the philosophy of mythology and that of revelation: "The program of the late Schelling is called not 'Being and Time,' but 'Being and Times.' The time of myth and the time of revelation are qualitatively different" (J. Taubes, "Zur Konjunktur des Polytheismus," in Bohrer, ed., *Mythos und Moderne*, p. 463).

30. *Nietzsche Contra Wagner*, volume 6 of Nietzsche's *Sämtliche Werke*, pp. 431–432.

31. Nietzsche, *The Birth of Tragedy*, p. 46.

32. Ibid., p. 36.

33. He stylizes Socrates, who falls into the error of believing that thinking extends to the deepest abysses of being, into a theoretical countertype of the artist: "Whenever the truth is uncovered, the artist will always cling with rapt gaze to what still remains a covering even after such uncovering; but the theoretical man enjoys and finds satisfaction in the *discarded covering*" (ibid., p. 94). Nietzsche rails just as energetically against the moral explanation of the aesthetic from Aristotle until Schiller: "If you would explain the tragic myth, the first requirement is to seek the pleasure that is peculiar to it in the purely aesthetic sphere, without transgressing into the region of pity, fear, or the morally sublime. How can the ugly and the disharmonic, the content of the tragic myth, stimulate aesthetic pleasure?" (ibid., p. 141).

34. Nietzsche summarizes this teaching in the statement, "Every evil the sight of which edifies a god is justified." See *On the Genealogy of Morals* (New York, 1969), p. 69.

35. Nietzsche, *The Birth of Tragedy*, pp. 22ff.: "Attempt at Self-Criticism." See also, in his *Sämtliche Werke*, volume 5, p. 168; volume 12, p. 140.

36. J. Habermas, "Zu Nietzsches Erkenntnistheorie," in *Zur Logik der Sozialwissenschaften* (Frankfurt, 1982), pp. 505ff.

37. Nietzsche, *On the Genealogy of Morals*, p. 96.

38. Nietzsche, *The Birth of Tragedy*, pp. 18, 19.

39. See *On the Genealogy of Morals*, pp. 145–153.

40. Nietzsche, *Sämtliche Werke*, volume 12, pp. 159ff.

41. Friedrich Nietzsche, *Beyond Good and Evil. Prelude to a Philosophy of the Future* (New York, 1966), p. 235.

42. Between 1936 and 1946 (that is, between the *Introduction to Metaphysics*, which still shows traces of the fascist Heidegger, and the "Letter on Humanism," which introduces the postwar philosophy), Heidegger was continually occupied with Nietzsche. The idea of the history of Being was formed in an intensive dialogue with Nietzsche. Heiddeger explicitly acknowledges this in the 1961 foreword to the two volumes that document this segment of his path of thought. See Martin Heidegger, *Nietzsche* (Pfullingen, 1961), pp. 9ff.

43. This fiction has been demolished without remainder by the edition of Giorgio Colli and Mazzino Montinar; see their commentary to the late work, in Nietzsche's *Sämtliche Werke*, volume 14, pp. 383ff., and the chronology of Nietzsche's life, in volume 15, p. 1.

44. Martin Heidegger, *Nietzsche*, volume 1: *The Will to Power as Art* (New York, 1979), p. 4.

45. Ibid., p. 19.

46. Ibid., p. 131.

47. In this respect, Oskar Becker demonstrates an incomparably greater sensibility with his dualistic counterproposal to Heidegger's fundamental ontology; see Oskar Becker, "Von der Hinfälligkeit des Schönen und der Abenteuerlichkeit des Künstlers" and "Von der Abenteuerlichkeit des Künstlers und der vorsichtigen Verwegenheit des Philosophen," in *Dasein und Dawesen. Gesammelte philosophische Aufsätze* (Pfullingen, 1963), pp. 11ff. and 103ff.

48. Heidegger, *Nietzsche*, volume 1, p. 200.

49. Martin Heidegger, "Nachwort zu *Was ist metaphysik?*" in *Wegmarken* (Frankfurt, 1978), p. 309.

50. Heidegger sums up his first Nietzsche lectures with the words: "From the perspective of the essence of Being, art has to be conceived of as the basic happening of beings, as the authentically creative moment."

51. Georges Bataille, introduction to *Der heilige Eros* (Frankfurt, 1982), pp. 10ff.

52. Ibid., p. 29.

Lecture V
The Entwinement of Myth and Enlightenment: Max Horkheimer and Theodor Adorno

1. K. Heinrich, *Versuch über die Schwierigkeit Nein zu sagen* (Frankfurt, 1964).

2. Max Horkheimer and Theodor Adorno, *Dialektik der Aufklärung* (Amsterdam, 1947). English translation: *Dialectic of Enlightenment* (New York, 1972), p. xvi; cited in the text as DE. (See my introduction to the new German edition published in 1985 by Suhrkamp Verlag.)

3. K. Heinrich, *Dahlemer Vorlesungen* (Basel/Frankfurt, 1981), pp. 112ff.

4. "The discovery that symbolic communication with the deity through sacrifice is not real must be an age-old experience. The sacrificial representation that a fashionable irrationalism has so exalted cannot be separated from the deification of human sacrifice — the deceit of a priestly rationalization of death by means of an apotheosis of the predestined victim" (DE, pp. 50–51).

5. Max Weber, "Science as a Vocation," in *From Max Weber: Essays in Sociology* (New York, 1965), p. 148.

6. Jürgen Habermas, *The Theory of Communicative Action*, volume 1: *Reason and the Rationalization of Society* (Boston, 1984), chapter II.

7. Theodor W. Adorno, *Gesammelte Schriften*, volume 1 (Frankfurt, 1973) pp. 345ff.

8. Helmut Dubiel, *Theory and Politics* (Cambridge, MA, 1985), part I.

9. See especially Max Horkheimer, *Critique of Instrumental Reason* (New York, 1974).

10. He already styled himself an "antisociologist," as do his neoconservative successors; see H. Baier, "Die Gesellschaft — ein langer Schatten des toten Gottes," *Nietzsche-Studien* 10/11 (Berlin, 1982), pp. 6ff.

11. See also Peter Pütz, "Nietzsche and Critical Theory," *Telos* 50(1981–1982):103–114.

12. Friedrich Nietzsche, *On the Genealogy of Morals* (New York, 1969), p. 84.

13. Ibid.

14. Ibid., pp. 84–85.

15. J. Habermas, "Nachwort" to F. Nietzsche, *Erkenntnistheoretische Schriften* (Frankfurt, 1968), pp. 237ff.

16. Pointed out by Gilles Deleuze, *Nietzsche and Philosophy* (New York, 1983), pp. 32ff.

17. Nietzsche, *Genealogy*, p. 153.

18. Friedrich Nietzsche, *Beyond Good and Evil. Prelude to a Philosophy of the Future* (New York, 1966), p. 341.

19. Ibid., p. 199.

20. Nietzsche, *Genealogy*, pp. 103–107.

21. Ibid., p. 36.

22. The mediating function of the judgment of taste in the reduction of yes/no positions on criticizable validity claims to the "Yes" and "No" in relation to imperative expressions of will can also be seen in the manner in which Nietzsche, along with the concept of *propositional truth*, revises the concept of *world* built into our grammar: "Indeed, what forces us at all to suppose that there is an essential opposition of 'true' and 'false'? Is it not sufficient to assume degrees of apparentness and, as it were, lighter and darker shadows and shades of appearance — different 'values' to use the language of painters? Why couldn't the world *that concerns us* be a fiction? And if somebody asks: 'but to a fiction there surely belongs an author?' — couldn't one answer

simply: *why?* Doesn't this 'belongs' perhaps belong to the fiction too? By now is one not permitted to be a bit ironic about the subject no less than about the predicate and object? Shouldn't the philosopher be permitted to rise above faith in grammar?" (*Beyond Good and Evil*, p. 236).

23. Deleuze, *Nietzsche and Philosophy*, pp. 103ff.

24. Nietzsche, *Genealogy*, pp. 27–28.

25. Ibid., p. 112.

26. Here I am interested in the structure of the argument. Once he has destroyed the foundations of the critique of ideology by a self-referential use of this critique, Nietzsche saves his own position as an unmasking critic only by recourse to a figure of thought associated with the myth of origins. The ideological content of the *Genealogy of Morals* and Nietzsche's battle against modern ideas in general — in which the more cultivated among the despisers of democracy, now as ever, show a conspicuous interest — is another matter altogether. See R. Maurer, "Nietzsche und die Kritische Theorie," and G. Rohrmoser, "Nietzsches Kritik der Moral," *Nietzsche-Studien* 10/11 (Berlin, 1982), pp. 34ff. and 328ff.

27. H. Fink-Eitel, "Michel Foucaults Analytik der Macht," in F. A. Kittler, ed., *Austreibung des Geistes aus den Geisteswissenschaften* (Paderborn, 1980), pp. 38ff.; Axel Honneth and Hans Joas, *Soziales Handeln und menschliche Natur* (Frankfurt, 1980), pp. 123ff.

28. H. Schnädelbach, "Über historische Aufklärung," *Allgemeine Zeitschrift für Philosophie* (1979), pp. 17ff.

29. Besides the work referred to in note 6, see the second volume of *The Theory of Communicative Action*, subtitled *Lifeworld and System: A Critique of Functionalist Reason* (Boston, 1987).

Lecture VI
The Undermining of Western Rationalism through the Critique of Metaphysics: Martin Heidegger

1. Martin Heidegger, "Einleitung zu *Was ist Metaphysik?*" in *Wegmarken* (Frankfurt, 1978), pp. 361ff.

2. Martin Heidegger, *Nietzsche* (Pfullingen, 1961), 2 volumes; here volume 2, p. 333. [The four-volume English edition of *Nietzsche* — volumes 1, 2, and 4 of which have been issued (New York, 1979, 1984, 1982) — contains a somewhat different selection and ordering of material. For that reason, references will be given here to both the German and the English editions (with the exception of passages from the forthcoming volume 3). The German edition will be called N and the English edition NE. — tr.]

3. N, volume 2., p. 313.

4. N, volume 2, p. 61; NE, volume 4, p. 28.

5. N, volume 2, pp. 141ff. and 193ff.; NE, volume 4, pp. 96ff. and 139ff.

6. N, volume 2, pp. 145ff.; NE, volume 4, pp. 99ff.

7. N, volume 2, p. 149; NE, volume 4, p. 103.

8. N, volume 1, p. 480.

9. N, volume 1, p. 579.

10. N, volume 1, p. 656.

11. N, volume 1, p. 479.

12. N, volume 2, p. 355; NE, volume 4, p. 215.

13. N, volume 2, p. 353; NE, volume 4, p. 214.

14. Already in *Being and Time*, Heidegger talks about the "destruction of the history of ontology."

15. N, volume 2, p. 367; NE, volume 4, p. 225.

16. Martin Heidegger, "Letter on Humanism," in *Basic Writings* (London, 1978), p. 235.

17. Ibid., p. 216.

18. N, volume 1, p. 580.

19. N, volume 1, pp. 578ff.

20. N, volume 1, p. 579.

21. Heidegger, "Letter on Humanism," p. 235.

22. Ibid.

23. N, volume 1, p. 580.

24. Fritz K. Ringer, *The Decline of the German Mandarins* (Cambridge, MA, 1969). On this, see my review in *Philosophisch-politische Profile* (Frankfurt, 1981), pp. 485ff.

25. Reiner Schürmann sees the end of metaphysics in the fact that the succession of epochs in which ontological understanding was determined by the dominance of particular principles has come to a close. Postmodernity stands under the sign of the dying out of *any* form of unifying interpretation of the world guided by principles; it bears the anarchistic traits of a polycentric world that sacrifices its previous categorial differentiations. With the familiar constellation of knowing and acting, the concept of the political also changes. Schürmann characterizes the structural change through the following features: (1) abolishing the primacy of teleology in action; (2) abolishing the primacy of responsibility in the legitimation of action; (3) change into action as a protest against the administered world; (4) disinterest in the future of mankind; (5) anarchy as the essence of what is "doable." See Reiner Schürmann, "Questioning the Foundation of Practical Philosophy," *Human Studies* 1(1980):357ff.; "Political Thinking in Heidegger," *Social Research* 45(1978):191ff.; "Le principe d'anarchie," in *Heidegger et la question de l'agir* (Paris, 1982).

26. From this perspective, Walter Schulz specifies the "Philosophiegeschichtlichen Ort Martin Heideggers," *Philosophische Rundschau* (1953):65ff. and 211ff.; republished in Otto Pöggeler, ed., *Heidegger* (Cologne, 1969), pp. 95ff.

27. Georg Simmel, "Zur Philosophie der Kultur," in *Philosophische Kultur* (Berlin, 1983). See also my afterword to that work, "Simmel als Zeitdiagnostiker," pp. 243–253.

28. Martin Heidegger, *Being and Time* (New York, 1962), p. 73. Henceforth cited in text by page numbers of the English translation.

29. Schulz, "Über den philosophiegeschichtliche Ort Martin Heideggers," p. 115.

30. Martin Heidegger, *The Essence of Reasons* (Evanston, 1969), p. 93.

31. Ibid., p. 105.

32. Ibid., p. 111.

33. This can be seen in the form of the statements by means of which Ernst Tugendhat attempts a semantic reconstruction of the content of the second part of *Being and Time*; see Ernst Tugendhat, *Self-Consciousness and Self-Determination* (Cambridge, MA, 1986), the eighth to tenth lectures.

34. Ernst Tugendhat, "Heideggers Idee von Wahrheit," in Pöggeler, ed., *Heidegger*, p. 296; also *Der Wahrheitsbegriff bei Husserl und Heidegger* (Berlin, 1967).

35. See the excursus on Castoriadis following lecture XI.

36. Heidegger's written copy, dating from 1945, was first published by his son in 1983: *Das Selbstbehauptung der deutschen Universität. Das Rektorat 1933/34* (Frankfurt, 1983). [English translation: "The Self-Assertion of the German University," *Review of Metaphysics* 38(1985):467–502, here p. 486.] In connection with this publication, M. Schreiber reported in the *Frankfurter Allgemeine Zeitung* of 20 July 1984 on "New Details of a Future Heidegger Biography," which emerged from the recent research of the Freiburg historian Hugo Ott.

37. Ibid., p. 39.

38. Oskar Becker already drew my attention to this during my student days. I am grateful to Victor Farias for letting me look at his as yet unpublished study of Heidegger's national-revolutionary phase.

39. Heidegger's reaction to the readmission of a Catholic Student Association fits in here. In a letter of 2 June 1934 to the *Reichsführer* of the student body, he speaks of a "public victory of Catholicism." He warns: "One is still not familiar with Catholic tactics. Some day this will take its toll with a vengeance." This is quoted in Guido Schneeberger, *Nachlese zu Heidegger* (Bern, 1962), p. 206. On the "New Paganism," see W. Bröcker, *Dialektik, Positivismus, Mythologie* (Frankfurt, 1958), chapters 2 and 3.

40. Schneeberger, *Nachlese zu Heidegger*, pp. 145ff.

41. In section 74 of *Being and Time*, Heidegger already takes his analyses of the basic constitution of historicality to the point at which the fate of the individual is implicated with the fate of the people: "But if fateful Dasein as Being-in-the-world exists essentially in Being-with-others, its historicizing is a co-historicizing and determinative for it as destiny [*Geschick*]. This is how we designate the historicizing of the community, of a people" (p. 436). As regards the significance of the later term "destining of Being" [*Seinsgeschick*], it is certainly no mere accident that Heidegger introduces the expression "destiny" in this *völkischen* connection. However, the existentialist priority of the individual Dasein over the collective Dasein of the community — which will later be turned

into just the opposite by the national-revolutionary reinterpretation — is quite clear from the context. The structure of care is developed in connection with the Dasein that is "in each case mine." Resoluteness to one's "ownmost potentiality for Being" is a matter for the individual, who must first be resolved in order then to be able to experience "Dasein's fateful destiny in and with its 'generation'" (p. 436). The irresolute individual can "'have' no fate [*Schicksal*]."

42. Schneeberger, *Nachlese zu Heidegger*, pp. 159ff.

43. William Richardson brought to my attention the point of connection for this concept that is already to be found in Heidegger's "On the Essence of Truth" (*Basic Writings*, pp. 113–141). In the seventh section, he treats of "Untruth as Errancy." Like truth, errancy belongs to the basic constitution of Dasein: "Errancy is the open site for and ground of error. Error is not just isolated mistakes but rather the realm (the domain) of the history of those entanglements in which all kinds of erring get interwoven" (p. 136). This concept of errancy as an objective scope does not, to be sure, offer anything more than a point of connection; for truth and error are still related to one another in the same way as the disclosure and concealing of beings (p. 137). In my view, this text — first published in 1943 and based on the text of a lecture from 1930, which was "revised several times" — does not permit any clear interpretation in the sense of Heidegger's later thought.

44. Martin Heidegger, *An Introduction to Metaphysics* (New Haven, 1956), p. 199.

45. See the precise presentation by Reiner Schürmann, "Political Thinking in Heidegger," *Social Research* 45(1978):191.

Lecture VII
Beyond a Temporalized Philosophy of Origins: Jacque Derrida's Critique of Phonocentrism

1. Jacques Derrida, "The Ends of Man," in *Margins of Philosophy* (Chicago, 1982), pp. 109–136.

2. Jacques Derrida, *Of Grammatology* (Baltimore, 1974), pp. 18–26.

3. Ibid., p. 14.

4. Derrida, "The Ends of Man," p. 130.

5. Pierre Bourdieu, *Die politische Ontologie M. Heideggers* (Frankfurt, 1976), pp. 17ff.

6. Derrida, "The Ends of Man," p. 136.

7. I. J. Gelb, *A Study in Writing: The Foundations of Grammatology* (Chicago, 1952).

8. Derrida, *Of Grammatology*, p. 10.

9. Ibid.

10. Jacques Derrida, *Writing and Difference* (Chicago, 1978), p. 10.

11. Jacques Derrida, "Signature Event Context," in *Margins of Philosophy*, pp. 307–330, esp. 315, 322.

12. Derrida, *Of Grammatology*, p. 69.

13. Ibid., p. 19.

14. Jacques Derrida, *Speech and Phenomena* (Evanston, 1973), which includes the related essay "Form and Meaning: A Note on the Phenomenology of Language."

15. Edmund Husserl, *Logical Investigations*, volume I: *Expression and Meaning* (London, 1970), pp. 269–333.

16. Ibid., p. 237.

17. Ernst Tugendhat, *Vorlesungen zur Einführung in die sprachanalytische Philosophie* (Frankfurt, 1976), pp. 212ff.; Jürgen Habermas, *Theorie des kommunikativen Handelns* (Frankfurt, 1981), volume 2, pp. 15ff.

18. From this standpoint, it also becomes clear that even a semanticism enlightened by language analysis still proceeds under presuppositions of the philosophy of consciousness.

19. Husserl, *Logical Investigations* I, p. 277.

20. Ibid.

21. Ibid., pp. 279.

22. Ibid.

23. Ibid., p. 305.

24. Ibid., p. 333.

25. Ibid.

26. Ibid., p. 294.

27. Ibid., p. 321.

28. Derrida, *Speech and Phenomena*.

29. Ibid., p. 50.

30. Ibid., p. 52.

31. Husserl, *Logical Investigations* I, p. 328.

32. Derrida, *Speech and Phenomena*, p. 78.

33. Ibid.

34. Derrida, *Of Grammatology*, p. 20.

35. Derrida, *Speech and Phenomena*, p. 102.

36. J. Derrida, "Différance," in *Margins of Philosophy*, pp. 1–27, here p. 8.

37. Derrida, *Speech and Phenomena*, p. 103.

38. Derrida, *Of Grammatology*, p. 44. See also the excellent exposition by Jonathan Culler in *On Deconstruction* (Ithaca, 1982), pp. 89–110.

39. Ferdinand de Saussure, *Course in General Linguistics* (New York, 1966), p. 164.

40. Derrida, *Of Grammatology*, p. 163.

41. Ibid., p. 47.

42. Ibid., p. 49. See also "Semiology and Grammatology: Interview with Julia Kristeva," in *Positions* (Chicago, 1981), pp. 15–36.

43. About "differance" Derrida states: "It governs nothing, reigns over nothing, and nowhere exercises any authority. It is not announced by a capital letter. Not only is there no kingdom of differance, but differance instigates the subversion of every kingdom" (*Margins of Philosophy*, p. 22).

44. Derrida, *Of Grammatology*, p. 16.

45. Gershom Scholem, *On the Kabbalah and Its Symbolism* (New York, 1965), p. 30.

46. My interpretation finds support in an article by Susan Handelman, which I came to only after writing this (thanks to a tip from Jonathan Culler): "Jacques Derrida and the Heretic Hermeneutic," in M. Krapnick, ed., *Displacement, Derrida and After* (Bloomington, 1983), pp. 98ff. Handelman reminds us of an interesting citation from Levinas that Derrida appropriates in his essay on the latter: "To love the Torah more than God is protection against the madness of direct contact with the holy." She stresses Derrida's affinity with the Rabbinic tradition, especially with its cabalistic and heretical radicalizations: "The statement [of Levinas] is striking and eminently Rabbinic — the Torah, the Law, Scripture, he says, are even more important than He. We might say that Derrida and the Jewish heretic hermeneutic do precisely that: forsake God but perpetuate a Torah, Scripture, or Law in their own displaced and ambivalent way" (p. 115). Handelman also refers to the devaluation of the original transmission of the divine word in favor of the oral Torah, which in the course of the history of exile claimed a growing authority, in the end even a dominant authority: "That is, all later Rabbinic interpretation shared the same divine origin as the Torah of Moses; interpretation, in Derridean terms, was 'always already there.' Human interpretation and commentary thus become part of the Divine Revelation. The boundaries between text and commentary are fluid in a way that is difficult to imagine for a sacred text, but this fluidity is a central tenet of contemporary critical theory, especially in Derrida" (p. 101). Furthermore, Handelman throws light on Derrida's denunciation of Western logocentrism as phonocentrism by locating it in the religious-historical context of the repeated defense of the letter against the spirit. In this way, Derrida is given a place within Jewish apologetics. Pauline Christianity had discredited the interpretation history of the oral Torah as the "dead letter" in contrast to the "living spirit" (2 Corinthians 3,6) of the immediate presence of Christ. Paul sets himself against the Jews who fasten on the letter and do not want to give up the scripture in favor of the logos of the Christian revelation. "Derrida's choice of writing to oppose to Western logocentrism is a reemergence of Rabbinic hermeneutics in a displaced way. Derrida will undo Graeco-Christian theology and move us back from ontology to grammatology, from Being to Text, from Logos to Ecriture — Scripture" (p. 111). It is of great importance in this context that Derrida, unlike Heidegger, does not get the motif of a God that works through absence and withdrawal from the Romantic Dionysus reception (via Hölderlin), so as to be able to turn it — as an *archaic* motif — against monotheism. Rather, the active absence of God is a motif that he gets (via Levinas) from the Jewish tradition itself. "The absent God of the Holocaust, the God who obscures his face,

paradoxically becomes for Levinas the condition of Jewish belief. . . . Judaism is then defined as this trust in an absent God" (p. 115). Of course, this gives Derrida's critique of metaphysics a different meaning from Heidegger's. The work of deconstruction fosters an unacknowledged renewal of a discourse with God that has been broken off under *modern* conditions of an ontotheology that is no longer binding. The intention is, then, not to overcome modernity by having recourse to archaic sources, but to take specific account of the conditions of modern postmetaphysical thought, under which an ontotheologically insulated discourse with God cannot be continued.

Excursus on Leveling the Genre Distinction between Philosophy and Literature

1. H. Schnädelbach, "Dialektik als Vernunftkritik," in L. von Friedeburg and J. Habermas, eds., *Adorno-Konferenz 1983* (Frankfurt, 1983), pp. 66ff.

2. This is especially true of the Yale Critics, Paul de Man, Geoffrey Hartman, J. Hillis Miller, and Harold Bloom. See J. Arac, W. Godzich, and W. Martin, eds., *The Yale Critics: Deconstruction in America* (Minneapolis, 1983). In addition to Yale, important centers of deconstructionism are located at Johns Hopkins and Cornell universities.

3. Christopher Norris, *Deconstruction: Theory and Practice* (New York and London, 1982), pp. 93, 98.

4. Paul de Man, *Blindness and Insight*, 2d ed. (Minneapolis, 1983), p. 110.

5. Jonathan Culler, *On Deconstruction* (London, 1983), p. 150.

6. Ibid., p. 181.

7. In his essay "Signature Event Context," in *Margins of Philosophy* (Chicago, 1982), pp. 307–330, Derrida devotes the last section to a discussion of Austin's theory. Searle refers to this in "Reiterating the Differences: A Reply to Derrida," *Glyph* 1(1977):198ff. Derrida's response appeared in *Glyph* 12(1977):202ff. under the title "Limited, Inc."

8. Culler, *On Deconstruction*, p. 119.

9. John Searle, *Speech Acts* (Cambridge, 1969), and *Expression and Meaning* (Cambridge, 1979).

10. Culler, *On Deconstruction*, pp. 121ff.

11. Ibid., p. 123.

12. Ibid., p. 176.

13. Compare ibid., pp. 130ff.

14. Karl Bühler, *Semiotic Foundations of Language Theory* (New York, 1982).

15. Roman Jakobson, "Linguistics and Poetics," in Thomas A. Sebeok, editor, *Style in Language* (Cambridge, MA, 1960), pp. 350–358.

16. Ibid.

17. R. Ohmann, "Speech-Acts and the Definition of Literature," *Philosophy and Rhetoric* 4(1971):17.

18. Ibid., p. 14.

19. Ibid., p. 17.

20. Geoffrey Hartman, *Saving the Text* (Baltimore, 1981), p. xxi.

21. See also "Speech, Literature, and the Space between," *New Literary History* 5(1974):34ff.

22. William Labov, *Language in the Inner City* (Philadelphia, 1972).

23. Mary Louise Pratt, *A Speech-Act Theory of Literary Discourse* (Bloomington, 1977), p. 92; I am grateful to Jonathan Culler for his reference to this interesting book.

24. Ibid., p. 148.

25. Ibid., p. 147.

26. See Jürgen Habermas, *Theory of Communicative Action*, volume 1 (Boston, 1984), pp. 273ff.

27. Richard Rorty, "Deconstruction and Circumvention" (manuscript, 1983); and *Consequences of Pragmatism* (Minneapolis, 1982), especially the introduction and chapters 6, 7, and 9.

28. Our reflections have brought us to a point from which we can see why Heidegger, Adorno, and Derrida get into this aporia at all. They all still defend themselves as if they were living in the shadow of the "last" philosopher, as did the first generation of Hegelian disciples. They are still battling against the "strong" concepts of theory, truth, and system that have actually belonged to the past for over a century and a half. They still think they have to arouse philosophy from what Derrida calls "the dream of its heart." They believe they have to tear philosophy away from the madness of expounding a theory that has the last word. Such a comprehensive, closed, and definitive system of propositions would have to be formulated in a language that is self-explanatory, that neither needs nor permits commentary, and thus that brings to a standstill the effective history in which interpretations are heaped upon interpretations without end. In this connection, Rorty speaks about the demand for a language "which can receive no gloss, requires no interpretation, cannot be distanced, cannot be sneered at by later generations. It is the hope for a vocabulary which is intrinsically and self-evidently final, not only the most comprehensive and fruitful vocabulary we have come up with so far" (Rorty, *Consequences of Pragmatism*, pp. 93ff.).

If reason were bound, under penalty of demise, to hold on to these goals of metaphysics classically pursued from Parmenides to Hegel, if reason as such (even after Hegel) stood before the alternative of either maintaining the strong concepts of theory, truth, and system that were common in the great tradition or of throwing in the sponge, then an *adequate* critique of reason would really have to grasp the roots at such a depth that it could scarcely avoid the paradoxes of self-referentiality. Nietzsche viewed the matter in this way. And, unfortunately, Heidegger, Adorno, and Derrida all still seem to confuse the universalist *problematics still maintained* in philosophy with the long since *abandoned status claims* that philosophy once alleged its answers to have. Today, however, it is clear that the scope of universalist questions — for instance, questions of the necessary conditions for the rationality of utterances, or of the universal pragmatic presuppositions of communicative action and argumentation — does indeed have to be reflected in the grammatical form of universal propositions — but not in any unconditional validity or "ultimate foundations" claimed for themselves or their theoretical framework. The fallibilist consciousness of the sciences caught up with philosophy, too, a long time ago.

With this kind of fallibilism, we, philosophers and nonphilosophers alike, do not by any means eschew truth claims. Such claims cannot be raised in the performative attitude of the first person other than as transcending space and time — precisely as claims. But we are also aware that there is no zero-context for truth claims. They are raised here and now and are open to criticism. Hence we reckon upon the trivial *possibility* that they will be revised tomorrow or someplace else. Just as it always has, philosophy understands itself as the defender of rationality in the sense of the claim of reason endogenous to our form of life. In its work, however, it prefers a combination of strong propositions with weak status claims; so little is this totalitarian, that there is no call for a totalizing critique of reason against it. On this point, see my "Die Philosophie als Platzhalter und Interpret," in *Moralbewusstsein und kommunikatives Handeln* (Frankfurt, 1983), pp. 7ff. (English translation forthcoming).

Lecture VIII
Between Eroticism and General Economics: Georges Bataille

1. Michel Leiris, "Von dem unmöglichen Bataille zu den unmöglichen Documents" (1963), in *Das Auge des Ethnologen* (Frankfurt, 1981), p. 75.

2. Michel Foucault, "A Preface to Transgression," in *Language, Counter-Memory, Practice: Selected Essays and Interviews* (Ithaca, 1974), pp. 37–38.

3. Ibid., p. 42.

4. Ibid., p. 33.

5. Ibid., p. 30.

6. See Helmut Dubiel, *Theory and Politics: Studies in the Development of Critical Theory* (Cambridge, MA, 1985), and "Die Aktualität der Gesellschaftstheorie," in L. von Friedeburg and J. Habermas, eds., *Adorno-Konferenz 1983* (Frankfurt, 1983), pp. 293ff.

7. Georges Bataille, *Die psychologische Struktur des Faschismus. Die Souveränität* (Munich, 1978).

8. Ibid., p. 19.

9. Ibid., p. 38.

10. See Alexander Mitscherlich, "Massenpsychologie und Ich-Analyse," in volume 5 of his *Gesammelte Schriften* (Frankfurt, 1983), pp. 83ff.

11. Bataille, *Faschismus*, p. 23.

12. Ibid., p. 10.

13. Ibid., p. 18.

14. Ibid., p. 22.

15. Max Horkheimer and Theodor W. Adorno, *Dialectic of Enlightenment* (New York, 1972), pp. 168ff. As for the political-economic characterization of fascism as "state capitalism," see H. Dubiel and A. Söllner, eds., *Wirtschaft, Recht und Staat im National-sozialismus. Analysen des Instituts für Sozialforschung 1939–1942* (Frankfurt, 1981), and M. Wilson, *Das Institut für Sozialforschung und seine Faschismusanalysen* (Frankfurt, 1982).

16. Max Horkheimer, *The Eclipse of Reason* (New York, 1941), p. 121.

17. Horkheimer and Adorno, *Dialectic of Enlightenment*, p. 171.

18. Georges Bataille, *Der heilige Eros* (Frankfurt, 1982), p. 89.

19. Walter Benjamin, "Critique of Violence," in *Reflections* (New York, 1978), p. 289.

20. Walter Benjamin, "Surrealism," in *Reflections*, p. 189.

21. Bataille, *Faschismus*, p. 42.

22. Ibid., pp. 42ff. Interpolation mine.

23. First published by Bataille in *La Critique Sociale* 7 (1933) [English: "The Notion of Expenditure," in Georges Bataille, *Visions of Excess: Selected Writings, 1927–1939* (Minneapolis, 1985), pp. 116–129]; German version published in Georges Bataille, *Das theoretische Werk*, volume 1 (Munich, 1975), pp. 9ff.

24. Ibid., p. 25.

25. Ibid., p. 12.

26. Ibid., p. 23.

27. Ibid., p. 22.

28. Ibid., p. 89.

29. Ibid., p. 164.

30. Bataille, *Faschismus*, p. 57.

31. Bataille, *Das theoretische Werk*, volume 1, p. 88.

32. Ibid.

33. Ibid., pp. 87ff.

34. Georges Bataille, *Das Halleluja; Die Erotik und die Faszination des Todes; Die Wiege der Menschheit; Der belastete Planet* (Munich, 1979), p. 60.

35. Ibid., pp. 67ff.

36. Ibid., p. 68.

37. "Saint-Simons Gleichnis," in J. Dautry, ed., *Saint-Simon, Ausgewählte Texte* (Berlin, 1957), pp. 141ff.

38. Bataille, *Das theoretische Werk*, volume 1, p. 179.

39. Ibid., p. 169.

40. Ibid., p. 177.

41. Ibid., p. 171.

42. Bataille refers to the classic study by Marcel Mauss, *Essai sur le Don*, in *Année Sociologique* (1923/24), pp. 30ff.

43. Bataille, *Das theoretische Werk*, volume 1, p. 105.

44. Bataille, *Der heilige Eros*, p. 57. Interpolation mine.

45. Ibid., p. 51.

46. Ibid., p. 59. Interpolation mine.

47. Ibid., p. 35.

48. Ibid., p. 65. What Bataille calls the inner experience of the erotic, Michel Leiris described in terms of a photograph showing a naked woman with a leather mask (in Bataille's journal *Documents* in 1931). This mask followed a sketch done by W. Seabrook, who had long pursued studies on the Ivory Coast. Leiris's text shows how at that time field research in anthropology, exoticism in art, and eroticism both in personal experience and in literature enter into a kind of alliance. Leiris displays the sacrilegious joy and the satanic pleasure that the fetishist registers in viewing the body of the woman masked and thus de-individuated to a sheer instance of the species: "With full consciousness, love is reduced to a natural and bestial process — since the brain is symbolically suppressed by the mask — the fatality that forces us down is finally subdued. Thanks to the mask, in our hands this woman is in the end only nature itself, shaped by blind laws, without soul or personhood, a nature that this one time, at any rate, is completely chained to us, just as this woman is also chained. The gaze, the quintessence of human expression, is blocked out for a time — which lends the woman a still more hellish and subterranean significance. And the mouth, which can only be discerned thanks to a small split, is reduced to the animal-like role of a wound. The usual ordering of decorative elements, finally, is stood entirely on its head; the body is naked and the head masked. These are all elements that make tools out of leather pieces (a material from which boots and whips are made) which correspond wonderfully to what eroticism actually is: a means of getting out of oneself, of tearing away the bonds which morality, reason, and custom impose on us; simultaneously, a way of banishing the evil forces, of defying God and the terrestrial hounds of hell representing him, by taking over their property, the whole universe, in one of its particularly significant parts — no longer differentiated out here — and subjecting it to our control." (Michel Leiris, "Das 'caput mortuum' oder die Frau des Alchemisten," in *Das Auge des Ethnologen*, pp. 260–262.)

49. Bataille, *Das theoretische Werk*, volume 1, p. 164.

50. Ibid., p. 282.

51. Ibid., p. 106.

52. Bataille, *Der heilige Eros*, p. 269.

53. Ibid.

Lecture IX
The Critique of Reason as an Unmasking of the Human Sciences: Michel Foucault

1. Michel Foucault, *Von der Subversion des Wissens* (Munich, 1974), p. 24. [From an interview with Paolo Caruso.]

2. Michel Foucault, *Wahnsinn und Gesellschaft* (Frankfurt, 1969), p. 9. [This is a translation of *Histoire de la folie*, an abridged edition of which was translated into English as *Madness and Civilization*. The English edition does not include the passage cited.]

3. Schelling and the Romantic philosophy of nature had earlier conceived of madness as the other of reason brought about by excommunication, but of course within a perspective of reconciliation alien to Foucault. To the extent that the bond of communication between the madman (or the criminal) and the rationally constituted context of public life is severed, both parts suffer a deformation — those who are now thrown back upon the compulsive normality of a reason that is merely subjective are no less disfigured than those expelled from normality. Madness and evil negate normality by endangering it in two ways — as what disrupts normality and puts it in question; but also as something that evades normality by withdrawing from it. The insane and the criminal can develop this power of active negation only as inverted reason, which is to say, thanks to those moments split off from communicative reason.

Foucault, along with Bataille and Nietzsche, renounces this figure of thought from Idealism, which is supposed to grasp a dialectic inherent in reason itself. For him, rational forms of discourse are always rooted in strata that limit monological reason. These mute foundations of meaning at the basis of Occidental rationality are themselves meaningless; they have to be exhumed like the nonlinguistic monuments of prehistory if reason is to come to light in interchange with and in opposition to its other. In this sense, the archeologist is the model of a historian of science investigating the history of reason, having learned from Nietzsche that reason develops its structure only by way of the exclusion of heterogeneous elements and only by way of a monadic centering within itself. There was no reason before monological reason. And so madness does not appear to be the result of a process of splitting off in the course of which communicative reason first became rigidified into subject-centered reason. The formative process of madness is simultaneously that of a reason which emerges in none other than the Occidental form of self-relating subjectivity. This "reason" proper to German Idealism, which was meant to be more primordial than that embodied within European culture, appears here as just that fiction by which the Occident makes itself known in its specialness, and with which it assumes a universality that is chimerical, at the same time that it both hides and pursues its claim to global dominance.

4. Foucault, *Wahnsinn und Gesellschaft*, p. 13. [The English edition, *Madness and Civilization*, does not include the passage cited.]

5. "Since we lack the original purity, our investigation of structure has to go back to that decisive point which separates reason and madness at the same time as it joins them. It must seek to uncover the constant interchange, the opaque common root, and the original opposition that bestows a meaning on the unity as well as the opposition between sense and nonsense. Thus, the lightning decision (which seems heterogeneous from inside historical time, but inconceivable outside it) which separates the buzzing of obscure insects from the language of reason and the promises of time can come to light again." (Ibid., p. 13.)

6. Michel Foucault, *The Birth of the Clinic: An Archeology of Medical Perception* (New York, 1973), p. xvii.

7. Michel Foucault, *Madness and Civilization* (New York, 1973), chapter I, pp. 3ff. (In the discussion that follows, I was unable to take into account the second and third volumes of Foucault's *History of Sexuality*, which have just appeared.)

8. Ibid., p. 209.

9. Foucault gives an impressive description of an asylum that underwent profound changes in visage and function, under the eyes, so to speak, of the psychiatrists, in the

waning days of the eighteenth century: "This village had once signified that madmen were confined, and therefore the man of reason was protected from them; now it manifested that the [separated] madman was liberated, and that, in this liberty which put him on the level with the laws of reason, he was reconciled with the man of reason. . . . Without anything at the institutions having really changed, the meaning of exclusion and of confinement begins to alter; it slowly assumes positive values, and the neutral, empty, nocturnal space in which unreason was formerly restored to its nothingness begins to be peopled by a [medically controlled] nature to which madness, liberated, is obliged to submit [as pathology]." (Ibid., p. 195. The parenthetic additions are mine.)

10. "At the periphery, an annular building; at the centre, a tower; this tower is pierced with wide windows that open onto the inner side of the ring; the peripheric building is divided into cells, each of which extends the whole width of the building; they have two windows, one on the inside, corresponding to the windows of the tower; the other, on the outside, allows the light to cross the cell from one end to the other. All that is needed, then, is to place a supervisor in a central tower and to shut up in each cell a madman, a patient, a condemned man, a worker or a schoolboy. By the effect of backlighting, one can observe from the tower, standing out precisely against the light, the small captive shadows in the cells of the periphery. They are like so many cages, so many small theatres, in which each actor is alone, perfectly individualized and constantly visible." (Michel Foucault, *Discipline and Punish: The Birth of the Prison* [New York, 1977], p. 200.) Of the functions of the old-fashioned prison — incarceration, darkening, concealing — only the first is maintained: Restriction of space for mobility is needed to fulfill the, as it were, experimental conditions for the installation of the reifying gaze: "The panopticon is a machine for dissociating the see/being seen dyad: in the peripheric ring, one is totally seen, without ever seeing; in the central tower, one sees everything without ever being seen." (Ibid., p. 202.)

11. Foucault, *Wahnsinn und Gesellschaft*, p. 480. [The English edition, *Madness and Civilization*, does not include the passage cited.]

12. Michel Foucault, "The Discourse on Language," appendix to *The Archeology of Knowledge and the Discourse on Language* (New York, 1972), at pp. 217–218.

13. Ibid., p. 219.

14. Ibid., p. 234.

15. Michel Foucault, "Nietzsche, Genealogy, History," in *Language, Counter-Memory, Practice: Selected Essays and Interviews* (Ithaca, 1977), at pp. 145–146.

16. Foucault, *The Archeology of Knowledge*, p. 7.

17. Ibid., p. 12.

18. Ibid., p. 9.

19. C. Honegger, "M. Foucault und die serielle Geschichte," *Merkur* 36(1982):501ff.

20. Foucault, "Nietzsche, Genealogy, History," p. 152.

21. For Foucault's self-critique, see *The Archeology of Knowledge*, p. 16: "Generally speaking, *Madness and Civilization* accorded far too great a place, and an enigmatic one too, to what I called an 'experiment,' thus showing to what an extent one was still close to admitting an anonymous and general subject of history."

22. Paul Veyne, *Der Eisberg der Geschichte* (Berlin, 1981), p. 42. Veyne's metaphor reminds one of Gehlen's image of "crystallization."

23. Foucault, "Nietzsche, Genealogy, History," p. 154.

24. Axel Honneth, *Kritik der Macht* (Frankfurt, 1985), pp. 121–122 [English translation forthcoming].

25. H. Fink-Eitel, "Foucaults Analytik der Macht," in I. A. Kittler, ed., *Austreibung des Geistes aus den Geisteswissenschaften* (Paderborn, 1980), p. 55.

26. For example, in an enthusiastic review of André Glucksmann's *Master Thinkers*, Foucault writes: "In the Gulag one sees not the consequences of an unhappy mistake, but the effects of the 'truest' theory in the political order. Those who sought to save themselves by sticking Marx's true beard on the false nose of Stalin were not enthused." (Michel Foucault, "La grande colère des faits," *Le Nouvel Observateur*, 9 May 1977.) The theories of power of bourgeois pessimists from Hobbes to Nietzsche have always also served as receiving stations for disappointed apostates who, in the business of realizing their ideals politically, experienced how the humanistic content of the Enlightenment and of Marxism was perverted into its barbaric opposite. Even if the year 1968 only marks a revolt and not a revolution as in 1789 or 1917, the syndromes of reneging on the left are actually quite similar and perhaps even explain the surprising circumstance that the New Philosophers in France have dealt with *topoi* similar to those of the neoconservative disciples of an older generation of disappointed communists. On both sides of the Atlantic, one runs up against the same *topoi* of the counter-Enlightenment: criticism of the seemingly inevitable terrorist consequences of global interpretations of history; critique of the role of the general intellectual intervening in the name of human reason, and also of the transposition of theoretically pretentious human sciences into a practice contemptuous of humans, either in terms of social technique or therapeutically. The figure of thought is always the same: There is a narrow-minded will to power ingrained in the very universalism of the Enlightenment, in the humanism of emancipatory ideals, and in the rational pretension of systematic thought; as soon as the theory is ready to become practical, it throws off its mask — behind which the will to power of the philosophical master thinkers, the intellectuals, the mediators of meaning — in brief, the New Class — comes to the fore. Foucault not only seems to represent these familiar motifs with a gesture of radicality, but actually to *sharpen* them with his critique of reason and to *generalize* them with his theory of power. Behind the emancipatory self-understanding of discourse in the human sciences lurks the tactic and the technology of a sheer will to self-assertion, which the genealogist sets into relief beneath the exhumed foundations of meaning of self-deceptive discourses, just as Solzhenitsyn did to the Gulag beneath the rhetoric of a sanctimonious Soviet Marxism. See P. Rippel and H. Münkler, "Der Diskurs und die Macht. Zur Nietzsche-Rezeption des Poststrukturalismus," *Politische Vierteljahresschrift* 23(1982):115ff.

27. Michel Foucault, *The Order of Things: An Archeology of the Human Sciences* (New York, 1973), p. 311.

28. See Hubert L. Dreyfus and Paul Rabinow, *Michel Foucault: Beyond Structuralism and Hermeneutics* (Chicago, 1983), pp. 21ff.

29. Foucault constructs two different series of absences. On the one hand, the painter in the picture lacks his model, the royal couple standing outside the frame of the picture; the latter are in turn unable to see the picture of themselves that is being painted — they only see the canvas from behind; finally, the spectator is missing the center of the scene, that is, the couple standing as models, to which the gaze of the

painter and of the courtesans merely directs us. Still more revealing than the absence of the objects being represented is, on the other hand, that of the subjects doing the representing, which is to say, the triple absence of the painter, the model, and the spectator who, located in front of the picture, takes in perspectives of the two others. The painter, Velasquez, actually enters into the picture, but he is not presented exactly in the act of painting — one sees him during a pause and realizes that he will disappear behind the canvas as soon as he takes up his labors again. The faces of the two models can actually be recognized unclearly in a mirror reflection, but they are not to be observed directly during the act of their portrayal. Finally, the act of the spectator is equally unrepresented — the spectator depicted entering into the picture from the right cannot take over this function. (See Foucault, *The Order of Things*, pp. 3–16, 307–311.)

30. Ibid., pp. 308–309.

31. Dreyfus and Rabinow, *Michel Foucault*, p. 30.

32. Dieter Henrich, *Fluchtlinien* (Frankfurt, 1982), pp. 125ff.

33. This might also explain why materialism can remain so alive in analytic philosophy, particularly in relation to the mind-body problem.

34. Foucault, *The Order of Things*, pp. 333–334.

35. Ibid., p. 348.

Lecture X
Some Questions Concerning the Theory of Power: Foucault Again

1. Michel Foucault, *The Order of Things: An Archeology of the Human Sciences* (New York, 1973), pp. 342–343.

2. Ibid., p. 322.

3. M. Frank directs our attention to this preference for the model of representation, which cannot be systematically justified by Foucault, in *Was Heisst Neostrukturalismus?* (Frankfurt, 1984), lectures 9 and 10.

4. Hubert Dreyfus and Paul Rabinow, *Michel Foucault: Beyond Structuralism and Hermeneutics* (Chicago, 1983), p. 84. See also Axel Honneth, *Kritik der Macht* (Frankfurt, 1985), pp. 133ff.

5. Michel Foucault, *Power/Knowledge* (New York, 1980), p. 132.

6. Ibid., p. 131.

7. "These sciences, which have so delighted our 'humanity' for over a century, have their technical matrix in the petty malicious minutiae of the disciplines and their investigations. These investigations are perhaps to psychology, psychiatry, pedagogy, criminology, and so many other strange sciences, what the terrible power of investigation was to the calm knowledge of the animals, the plants or the earth. Another power, another knowledge. On the threshold of the Classical age, Bacon, lawyer and statesman, tried to develop a methodology of investigation for the empirical sciences. What Great Observer will produce the methodology of examination for the human sciences? Unless, of course, such a thing is not possible. For, although it is true that,

in becoming a technique for the empirical sciences, the investigation has detached itself from the inquisitorial procedure in which it was historically rooted, the examination has remained extremely close to the disciplinary power that shaped it. It has always been and still is an intrinsic element of the disciplines. Of course, it seems to have undergone a speculative purification by integrating itself with such sciences as psychology and psychiatry. And, in effect, its appearance in the form of tests, interviews, interrogations and consultations is apparently in order to rectify the mechanisms of discipline: educational psychology is supposed to correct the rigors of the school, just as the medical or psychiatric interview is supposed to rectify the effects of the discipline of work. But we must not be misled; these techniques merely refer individuals from one disciplinary authority to another, and they reproduce, in a concentrated or formalized form, the schema of power-knowledge proper to each discipline. . . . The great investigation that gave rise to the sciences of nature has become detached from its politico-juridical model; the examination, on the other hand, is still caught up in disciplinary technology." (Michel Foucault, *Discipline and Punish: The Birth of the Prison* [New York, 1977], pp. 226–227.)

This passage is interesting in two respects. First, the comparison between the natural and the human sciences is meant to instruct us that both have emerged from technologies of power, but that only the natural sciences have been able to detach themselves from the context of their emergence and develop into serious discourses that actually redeem their claims to objectivity and truth. Second, Foucault is of the opinion that the human sciences could not be dissociated from the context of their emergence at all, because in their case the practices of power are not only causally involved in the history of their rise, but play a transcendental role in the constitution of their knowledge.

8. See Jürgen Habermas, *Knowledge and Human Interests* (Boston and London, 1971); more recently, Karl-Otto Apel, *Understanding and Explanation* (Cambridge, MA, 1984).

9. Michel Foucault, "Howison Lecture on Truth and Subjectivity," October 20, 1980, University of California at Berkeley, unpublished manuscript, p. 7.

10. In *The History of Sexuality*, Foucault investigates the contexts of genesis and of application to which psychoanalysis is fitted. Once again, functionalist modes of argumentation are supposed to establish what they cannot establish — namely, that technologies of power constitute the domain of scientific objects and hence also prejudice the criteria of validity for what is considered true or false within scientific discourse.

11. Paul Veyne, *Der Eisberg der Geschichte* (Berlin, 1981), p. 52.

12. Veyne also deals with this example (ibid., pp. 6ff.).

13. Michel Foucault, *The Archeology of Knowledge and the Discourse of Language* (New York, 1972), p. 205.

14. Michel Foucault, "Nietzsche, Genealogy, History," in *Language, Counter-Memory, Practice: Selected Essays and Interviews* (Ithaca, 1977), pp. 162–163.

15. Ibid., p. 157.

16. Foucault, *Power/Knowledge*, p. 82.

17. Ibid.

18. Ibid., p. 85.

19. Foucault, "Nietzsche, Genealogy, History," pp. 156–157.

20. B.-H. Levy, "Power and Sex: An Interview with Michel Foucault," *Telos* 32(1977):152–161, here p. 158.

21. "Non au sexe roi," *Le Nouvel Observateur*, 12 March 1977. [The passage quoted does not appear in the English translation of this interview cited in note 20.]

22. Nancy Fraser, "Foucault on Modern Power: Empirical Insights and Normative Confusions," *Praxis International* 1(1981):283.

23. Foucault, *Power/Knowledge*, p. 108.

24. In an article entitled "Foucault's Body-Language: A Posthumanistic Political Rhetoric?" *Salmagundi* 61(1983):55–70.

25. Michel Foucault, *The History of Sexuality*, volume 1: *An Introduction* (New York, 1978).

26. P. Sloterdijk works out this alternative in relation to the instance of the mute, bodily-expressive forms of protest of the cynic: *Kritik der zynischen Vernunft*, 2 volumes (Frankfurt, 1982). See Jürgen Habermas, "Ein Renegat der Subjektphilosophie," *Pflasterband* 159 (1983). Foucault's own investigations went in a different direction; see his afterword to the second edition of Dreyfus and Rabinow, *Michel Foucault*, pp. 229ff.

27. Levy, "Power and Sex," p. 158.

28. Honneth, *Kritik der Macht*, p. 182.

29. Arnold Gehlen, *Die Seele im technischen Zeitalter* (Hamburg, 1957).

30. Jürgen Habermas, *Theorie des kommunikativen Handelns*, volume 2 (Frankfurt, 1981), pp. 92ff.

31. Foucault, *Discipline and Punish*, p. 23.

32. Ibid., p. 77.

33. Foucault, *Power/Knowledge*, p. 107.

34. Jürgen Habermas, "Natural Law and Revolution," in *Theory and Practice* (Boston and London, 1973), pp. 82–120.

35. C. Honegger, *Überlegungen zu Michel Foucaults Entwurf einer Geschichte der Sexualität*, unpublished manuscript, 1982, p. 10.

36. Gehlen, *Die Seele*, p. 118.

Lecture XI
An Alternative Way out of the Philosophy of the Subject: Communicative versus Subject-Centered Reason

1. See the unique lecture delivered by Foucault in 1983 on Kant's "What Is Enlightenment?," in Paul Rabinow, ed., *The Foucault Reader* (New York, 1984), pp. 32–50. I refer to this in my evocation in the *t a z* (2 July 1984).

2. Jürgen Habermas, "Remarks on the Concept of Communicative Action," in G. Seebass and R. Tuomela, eds., *Social Action* (Dordrecht, 1985), pp. 151–178.

3. Jürgen Habermas, "Interpretive Social Science and Hermeneuticism," in N. Haan, R. Bellah, P. Rabinow, and W. Sullivan, eds., *Social Science as Moral Inquiry* (New York, 1983), pp. 251–270.

4. Jürgen Habermas, "A Postscript to *Knowledge and Human Interests*," *Philosophy of Social Science* 3(1973):157–189, here pp. 161ff. Also H. Dahmer, *Libido und Gesellschaft* (Frankfurt, 1982), pp. 8ff.

5. Jürgen Habermas, "The Hermeneutic Claim to Universality," in J. Bleicher, ed., *Contemporary Hermeneutics* (London and Boston, 1980), pp. 181–211.

6. Jürgen Habermas, *Theorie des kommunikativen Handelns*, volume 2 (Frankfurt, 1981), pp. 589ff. English: *Theory of Communicative Action*, volume 2: *System and Lifeworld: A Critique of Functionalist Reason* (Boston, 1987).

7. Cf. Richard J. Bernstein, *Beyond Objectivism and Relativism* (Philadelphia, 1983).

8. H. Böhme and G. Böhme, *Das Andere der Vernunft* (Frankfurt, 1983), p. 326.

9. See the excursus following lecture VII.

10. Böhme and Böhme, *Das Andere der Vernunft*, p. 11.

11. Ibid., p. 18.

12. Ibid., p. 19.

13. Whereas Schiller and Hegel want to see the moral idea of self-legislation realized in an aesthetically reconciled society or in the totality of the context of ethical life, the Böhmes can see only the work of disciplinary power in moral autonomy: "If one wanted to envision the inner judicial process conducted in the name of the moral law with regard to maxims, one would have to recur to the Protestant examination of conscience, which displaced the model of the witch trial into the interiority of humans; or better still, go forward into the cool, hygienic interrogation rooms and the silent, elegant computer arsenals of the police gone scientific, whose ideal is the categorical imperative — the uninterrupted apprehension and control of everything particular and resistant, right into the interiority of the human being." (Böhme and Böhme, *Das Andere der Vernunft*, p. 349.)

14. Ibid., p. 13.

15. Ibid., p. 23.

16. Karl-Otto Apel, "Die Logosauszeichnung der menschlichen Sprache. Die philosophische Tragweite der Sprechakttheorie" (1984), manuscript.

17. Ernst Tugendhat, *Einführung in die sprachanalytische Philosophie* (Frankfurt, 1976).

18. Albrecht Wellmer has shown that the harmony of a work of art — aesthetic truth, as it is called — can by no means be reduced, without further ado, to authenticity or sincerity; see his "Truth, Semblance and Reconciliation," *Telos* 62(1984/85):89–115.

19. See the excursus following this lecture.

20. J. H. Hamann, "Metakritik über den Purismus der Vernunft," in J. Simon, ed., *Schriften zur Sprache* (Frankfurt, 1967), pp. 213ff.

21. Karl-Otto Apel, *Towards a Transformation of Philosophy* (London, 1980), pp. 225ff. See also my response to Mary Hesse in John Thompson and David Held, eds., *Habermas: Critical Debates* (Cambridge, MA, and London, 1982), pp. 276ff.

22. K. Heinrich, *Versuch über die Schwierigkeit nein zu sagen* (Frankfurt, 1964), p. 20; see also his *Parmenides und Jona* (Frankfurt, 1966).

23. H. Brunkhorst, "Kommunikative Vernunft und rächende Gewalt," *Sozialwissenschaftliche Literatur-Rundschau* 8/9 (1983):7–34.

Excursus on Cornelius Castoriadis: The Imaginary Institution

1. Cornelius Castoriadis, *L'Institution imaginaire de la société* (Paris, 1975). The citations are to the German translation, *Gesellschaft als imaginäre Institution. Entwurf einer politischen Philosophie* (Frankfurt 1984), here p. 31. Citations by page number within the text. An English translation is forthcoming: *The Imaginary Institution of Society* (Cambridge, MA, and Oxford, 1987).

2. See Jürgen Habermas, "Hannah Arendt: On the Concept of Power," in *Philosophical-Political Profiles* (Cambridge, MA, and London, 1983), pp. 171–187.

3. On this see the title essay in Jürgen Habermas, *Moralbewusstsein und kommunikatives Handeln* (Frankfurt, 1983), pp. 152ff.

**Lecture XII
The Normative Content of Modernity**

1. See the excursus on leveling the genre distinction between philosophy and literature, section IV.

2. See figure 23 in Jürgen Habermas, *Theorie des kommunikativen Handelns*, volume 2 (Frankfurt, 1981), p. 217.

3. I base what follows on the more complete account in ibid., p. 209.

4. See figure 22 in ibid., p. 215.

5. The ideologies that cover up repressed antagonisms can no longer be ascribed to the false consciousness of collectives; they are traced back to patterns of systematically distorted, everyday communication. It is here that the external organization of discourse exerts a pressure upon the internal organization of discourse that cannot be concealed in any other way, and twists it so as to break the internal connections between meaning and validity, meaning and intention, and meaning and action. (Compare Jürgen Habermas, "Überlegungen zur Kommunikationspathologie," in *Vorstudien und Ergänzungen zur Theorie des kommunikativen Handelns* [Frankfurt, 1984], pp. 226 ff.) And it is here, in distorted communication, that we can recognize Hegel's bifurcated ethical totality and Marx's alienated praxis as forms of damaged intersubjectivity. Foucault's analyses of discourses would also have to be retrieved on this level, by means of formal pragmatics.

6. Claus Offe, "Work: The Key Sociological Category?," in *Disorganized Capitalism* (Cambridge, MA, and Oxford, 1985), pp. 129–150.

7. See the excursus on Luhmann below.

8. One can understand better that Luhmann, like the critics of reason, stands in the Nietzschean line of discipleship, if one reenacts once again, from the perspective of the philosophy of the subject, the totalization of the simple critique of reason enacted by Nietzsche. For this purpose, Dieter Henrich's reflections on fiction and truth are helpful. His starting point is the representational context of a cognitive subject operating in a self-relating way, a context that is constituted as necessary, that is valid according to its own criteria and is consistent in itself. This context, which is rational "for it," may be revealed "for us," external observers, as a fictional world, if it "can be described not as knowledge, but merely as instrumental to some mode of effective operation," in relation to some context that is prior to it and inaccessible to it. The critic doing the unmasking can distance himself from a fictive world only by confirming it as a compellingly constituted context of meaning that is not internally criticizable and is to this extent rational, and by making his own, if not these criteria, then at least criteria of rationality in general: "The critical intent can only predominate as long as rationality is ultimately unrestricted in its own *de jure* claims. Only then can the critique of fictions count as the way leading up in the end to a rationality free of fictions. But this form of critique can also be turned against the whole battery of expectations connected with rationality as such. . . . It [then] becomes a new form of justification for the invention of fictions itself." (D. Henrich, "Versuch über Fiktion und Wahrheit," in *Poetik und Hermeneutik*, volume 10 [Munich, 1984], p. 513.)

The totalizing critic of ideology who takes this step without any reservations can no longer naively regard his understanding as oriented toward truth. He identifies his own conscious life with the productivity and freedom of an underlying, fiction-creating life force. At this point, there is a parting of the ways. Either the business of criticism is expanded to cover the entirety of a reason inimical to fiction, a reason that, with immense criminal energy, represses, excludes, and excoriates whatever could interrupt the closed circle of its self-relating subjectivity and give it some distance from itself. For this radical critique of reason, valid truths can appear only in the object domain — it gets its own credentials from the horizon of the life forces that generate fictions, that is, from the horizon of aesthetic experience. There is an alternative to this aestheticization of a critique pushed to the point of paradox (an aestheticization that is generally unacknowledged, even by its practitioners — right down to Derrida). One can continue to think on the level reached by the second stage of the critique of ideology, but in a *different* direction, if one *surrenders the intention of criticism itself.* Then our interest can be directed in detail to the question of how subjects maintain themselves in their original productivity and freedom by means of the life-serving fictions of some self-relatedly constituted world. This investigation enters frontally, as it were, into the dimension opened up by the second reflection, "the dimension of an occurrence that is itself purely factual, but has the property of needing the illusion of insight for its continuation" (ibid., p. 514). The object of investigation is no longer a reason that rejects fictions, but the *poiesis* of a life-enhancing self-preservation of subjects who live with and from their fictions — fictions that, regarded functionally, can only be affirmed.

This means at the same time a *functionalist* affirmation of the validity of truth that is constitutive for the reproduction of meaningful life in general. Precisely this validity of truth in relation to the cognitive perspective of a given subject — no more, but also no less — has to be claimed by the very theory that has specialized in such knowledge of the reproduction of meaningful life. The theory has to understand itself too as a product of the self-enhancing maintenance of a subject that reproduces itself only thanks to a fictional world valid *for it.* Perspectivism loses a portion of its horror when we do not thereby think of an arbitrary subject, but of a highly specialized knowing subject trained in self-knowledge. This corresponds, more or less, to the self-application of systems theory, by which social theory relativizes itself as the accomplishment of a subsystem of society assigned to the reduction of complexity. Luhmann takes this tack.

Luhmann uses the basic concepts of cybernetics and general systems theory, which have stood up in biology, to combine the insights of Kant and Nietzsche in an original manner. The world-constituting accomplishments of a transcendental subject that has lost its status apart from and above the world and sunk to the level of empirical subjects, are reconceptualized as the accomplishments of a system that operates in a meaningful, self-relating way and is capable of forming internal representations of its environment. The fiction-creating productivity of a life-enhancing self-maintenance by subjects, for which the difference between truth and illusion has lost its meaning, is reconceptualized as the self-maintenance of a system that makes use of meaning, a self-maintenance that masters the complexity of the environment and increases its own complexity. (See the excursus on Luhmann below.)

9. Axel Honneth, *Kritik der Macht* (Frankfurt, 1985), pp. 214ff., has drawn my attention to this.

10. Niklas Luhmann, *Politische Theorie im Wohlfahrtsstaat* (Munich, 1981), pp. 25ff.

11. Habermas, *Theorie des kommunikativen Handelns*, volume 2, chapter 8.

12. See the analyses by Claus Offe in "Some Contradictions of the Modern Welfare State," in *Contradictions of the Welfare State* (Cambridge, MA, and London, 1984), pp. 147–161.

13. Luhmann, *Politische Theorie im Wohlfahrsstaat*, p. 22.

14. Niklas Luhmann, *Gesellschaftsstruktur und Semantik*, volume 1 (Frankfurt, 1980), p. 33.

15. U. Mathiessen, *Das Dickicht der Lebenswelt* (Munich, 1984).

16. I am basing what follows on the title essay in my book *Die Neue Unübersichtlichkeit* (Frankfurt, 1985). English: "The New Obscurity," *Philosophy and Social Criticism* 11/2(Winter 1986):1–18.

17. The considerations concerning a "societal steering theory" by H. Willke, *Entzauberung des Staates* (Königstein, 1983), pp. 129ff., are interesting above all because the author is sufficiently inconsistent to analyze the reciprocal influence among autopoetic systems in accord with the model of intersubjective understanding.

18. Compare Jürgen Habermas, "Können komplexe Gesellschaften eine vernünftige Identität ausbilden?," in *Zur Rekonstruktion des Historischen Materialismus* (Frankfurt, 1976), pp. 92ff.; partially translated as "On Social Identity," *Telos* 19(1974):91–103.

Excursus on Luhmann's Appropriation of the Philosophy of the Subject through Systems Theory

1. Niklas Luhmann, *Soziale Systeme* (Frankfurt, 1984). The page numbers appearing in parentheses in the text of this excursus refer to this volume.

2. As one accustomed to the same treatment, I realize of course that one does not do justice to the richness of the theory when one single-mindedly broaches it from just one angle — but in our context, only this aspect is of interest.

3. "Each self-referential system has only that contact with the environment which it makes possible itself, and has no environment *an sich*." (Luhmann, *Soziale Systeme*, p. 146.)

4. Jürgen Habermas, *Knowledge and Human Interests* (Boston and London, 1971), pp. 43ff.

5. In this respect, Luhmann follows Nietzsche and not the philosophy of the subject. Compare above, lecture XII, note 8.

6. Luhmann stresses "that for the humanist tradition the human being stood inside the social order and not outside. He was considered a component of the social order, an element of society itself. When a human being was called an individual, it was because he was an ultimate element that could not be further divided." (Luhmann, *Soziale Systeme*, p. 286.)

7. In Luhmann, the dispositions of normative antihumanism, such as those that mark the world of Arnold Gehlen, are almost completely absent.

8. Luhmann, *Soziale Systeme*, p. 142: "Meaning can be fit into a sequence that is rooted in vital bodily feeling and then appears as consciousness. But meaning can also be fit into a sequence that involves the understanding of others and then appears as communication."

9. In a number of passages, Luhmann proceeds from the assumption that psychic systems occupy a place in the evolutionary series between organic and social systems, that is, that they are genetically "earlier" than social systems. Only psychic systems possess consciousness, and persons, as carriers of consciousness, are at the basis of social systems (244ff.). This picture comes up especially in contexts where the auto-catalytic character of social systems is under consideration. If social order (in David Lewis's sense) comes about because one of the solipsistically posited agents breaks through the precarious circle of twofold contingency by a one-sided self-determination, then we have to postulate persons or "consciousness-carriers" capable of making judgments and decisions *prior to all* participation in social systems — only then does the emerging social system set itself off from this "physical-chemical-organic-psychic reality" (170ff.). On the other hand, the two types of system cannot stand on different rungs of the evolutionary ladder if both are supposed to distinguish themselves from organic systems in like manner, via the emergent property of processing meaning. Thus, in other passages (141ff.) Luhmann speaks of a coevolution, of the equiprimordial development of meaning-processing systems that mutually presuppose each other (in their environment) and are based on consciousness, on the one hand, and communication, on the other.

10. The question of how the prelinguistic meaning can be superordinated even to the intentional structure of consciousness remains open.

Name Index

critique of, by Heidegger, 144–148,
172
influence, 137, 142, 149, 358
on production, 76–82

Jacobi, Friedrich Heinrich, 23, 30
Jakobson, Roman, 200, 201, 202
Jaspers, Karl, 164
Jauss, H. R., 34
Jesus, 24, 123
Jung, Carl, 308
Jünger, Ernst, 134

Kant, Immanuel, viii, xv, 21, 23, 28, 30,
32, 42, 47, 52, 141, 142, 152, 289,
301, 367
on absolute self-consciousness and the
principle of subjectivity, 18–19
and critique of reason, 302–326
influence on modernity, 243, 260–265,
295, 368–385
Kierkegaard, Søren, 52, 54, 150, 157
Kojève, Alexandre, 239, 317
Korsch, Karl, 13, 58, 75, 329, 330
Koselleck, Reinhart, 3, 5–6, 12

Labov, William, 202
Lacan, Jacques, 55, 97, 263, 267, 308
Lask, Emil, 19, 50
Leibniz, Gottfried Wilhelm, 258
Leiris, Michel, 211, 212, 411n48
Lessing, Gotthold Ephraim, 25
Levinas, Emanuel, 165, 182
Lévi-Strauss, Claude, 238, 263, 267, 308,
379
Levy, Bernard-Henri, 283, 286
Löwith, Karl, 52, 54–55
Luckmann, Thomas, 76–78
Luhmann, Niklas, 353–385
Lukács, Georg, 48, 66, 75, 192, 223,
263, 353
as Hegelian Marxist, 53, 280–281
parallels with Bataille, 224–239, 338
Luria, Isaac, 324
Luther, Martin, 17, 26
Lyotard, Jean-François, xix

Machiavelli, Niccolo, 106
Mallarmé, Stephane, 93, 122
Mandeville, Bernard, 106
Marcuse, Herbert, 48, 50, 66, 291
and praxis philosophy, 327
on production paradigm, 75–82
relationship to Schiller, 48–50
Markus, György, 79–82

Marx, Karl, vii, xv, 13, 46, 52, 54, 75,
114, 263, 283, 295, 370
Communist Manifesto, 60–61
on Hegel, 59, 63, 304
influence on Bataille, 222–239
on labor, xvi, 64–74, 78, 393n13
on praxis, 68, 336–368, 371
Masson, André, 211
Mead, George Herbert, 2, 137, 138,
148, 325, 334, 379
Mendel, Rabbi, 182–183
Merleau-Ponty, Maurice, 262, 317
Miller, Hillis, 192
Morris, William, 66

Nietzsche, Friedrich, vii, xi, xv, 13, 44,
52, 57, 74, 131, 184, 240
on art, 123, 306–307, 339–368
comparison with Horkheimer and
Adorno, 107–130
on cult of Dionysus, 91–105, 153–154,
162, 263
emphasis on language, ix
Heidegger's critique of, 131–160
on history, 92–105, 252, 281–282
influence on Bataille, 213–238
influence on Foucault, 241–265, 278
on modernity, 55–74, 85–88, 96, 97,
139, 392n4
on power, xiii–xiv, 96, 125, 159, 284
on reason, 191, 239, 254, 301
on Richard Wagner, 87–88, 92–105,
135
Novalis, 92

Offe, Claus, 79
Ohmann, Richard, 200, 201
Oppenheim, 69, 394n26

Parmenides, 324, 325
Parsons, Talcott, 350, 368, 377
Paz, Octavio, 93
Peirce, Charles S., 137, 148, 325
Piaget, Jean, 115, 298
Plato, xii, 130, 152, 311, 324
Plessner, H., 317
Popper, Karl, 171, 311
Pratt, Mary Louise, 194, 201–210

Reinhold, Karl Leonhard, 20
Rickert, Heinrich, 141
Ritter, Joachim, 71–74, 353
Robespierre, Maximilien de, 11
Rorty, Richard, 206–207
Rosenkranz, Karl, 69, 70, 394n25

Subject and Title Index